The Royal American Regiment

CAMPAIGNS & COMMANDERS

GREGORY J. W. URWIN, SERIES EDITOR

CAMPAIGNS AND COMMANDERS

GENERAL EDITOR

Gregory J. W. Urwin, *Temple University, Philadelphia, Pennsylvania*

ADVISORY BOARD

Lawrence E. Babits, *East Carolina University, Greenville*
James C. Bradford, *Texas A&M University, College Station*
Robert M. Epstein, *U.S. Army School of Advanced Military Studies, Fort Leavenworth, Kansas*
David M. Glantz, *Carlisle, Pennsylvania*
Jerome A. Greene, *Denver, Colorado*
Victor Davis Hanson, *California State University, Fresno*
Herman Hattaway, *University of Missouri, Kansas City*
J. A. Houlding, *Rückersdorf, Germany*
Eugenia C. Kiesling, *U.S. Military Academy, West Point, New York*
Timothy K. Nenninger, *National Archives, Washington, D.C.*
Bruce Vandervort, *Virginia Military Institute, Lexington*

The Royal American Regiment

An Atlantic Microcosm, 1755–1772

Alexander V. Campbell

University of Oklahoma Press : Norman

This book is published with the
generous assistance of The McCasland
Foundation, Duncan, Oklahoma.

Library of Congress Cataloging-in-Publication Data

Campbell, Alexander V., 1957-
The Royal American Regiment : an Atlantic microcosm,
1755-1772 / Alexander V. Campbell.
  p. cm. — (Campaigns and commanders ; v. 22)
Includes bibliographical references and index.
ISBN 978-0-8061-4102-2 (hardcover : alk. paper)
1. Great Britain. Army. Royal American Regiment, 60th. 2. United
States—History—French and Indian War, 1755-1763—Regimental
histories. 3. United States—History—French and Indian War,
1755-1763—Campaigns. I. Title.
    E199.C217 2010
  973.2'6—dc22   2009033067

*The Royal American Regiment: An Atlantic Microcosm, 1755–
1772* is Volume 22 in the Campaigns and Commanders series.

The paper in this book meets the guidelines for permanence and
durability of the Committee on Production Guidelines for Book
Longevity of the Council on Library Resources, Inc. ∞

Copyright © 2010 by the University of Oklahoma Press, Norman,
Publishing Division of the University. Manufactured in the U.S.A.

All rights reserved. No part of this publication may be reproduced,
stored in a retrieval system, or transmitted, in any form or by any
means, electronic, mechanical, photocopying, recording, or
otherwise—except as permitted under Section 107 or 108 of the
United States Copyright Act—without the prior permission of the
University of Oklahoma Press.

1 2 3 4 5 6 7 8 9 10

This book is respectfully dedicated to the memory of my parents,
Athol and Jean Campbell, who taught me
never to wait for perfect weather.

"A regiment is the sum of the attributes of its myriad human elements."

Farley Mowat

Contents

List of Illustrations	xi
List of Tables	xiii
Acknowledgments	xv
Introduction: A Royal American Remembrancer	5
1. "Much regarded by the Duke": James Prevost and the Royal American Regiment	15
2. "A medley of all characters": Recruiting the Royal American Regiment	49
3. "Canada belongs to the King": The Royal American Regiment at War	80
4. "No End to their fatigues": Life within the Ranks of the Royal American Regiment	120
5. "He seated our chiefs and warriors at his table": Royal Americans and Native Americans	155
6. "I shall settle, marry and trade here": Royal Americans in the Postwar Empire	187
Conclusion: Atlantic Microcosm	216
Appendix: A Battalion List of Senior Royal American Officers	225
List of Abbreviations Used in the Notes	227
Notes	231
Bibliography	311
Index	345

Illustrations

Figures

James Prevost	16
William Augustus, Duke of Cumberland	26
Frederick Haldimand	42
Beating Orders Signed by Colonel John Stanwix	51
Augustine Prevost	60
Enlistment Certificate of Johann Cristian Klepper, 1766	77
Attack at Montmorency, 31 July 1759	106
Major General Amherst's command descending the St. Lawrence River	113
Encampment at Lake George, New York, 1759	135
Plan of Fort Ontario	149
Henry Bouquet	160
Political cartoon deriding Royal American support for Native refugees	168
Daniel Claus	170
J. F. W. DesBarres	201
A View of Annapolis Royal, Nova Scotia	219

Maps

1. Northeastern North America during the Seven Years' War 2–3
2. The Great Lakes Basin and the Upper South during the Seven Years' War and Pontiac's Rebellion 84–85
3. Plan of the Route from Albany to Fort Edward 124

Tables

1. Pennsylvania Servants' Regimental Affiliation   57
2. Birthplaces of European Volunteers Recruited on the Continent in 1756   69
3. Ethnic Composition of the Royal American Regiment, Summer 1757   73

Acknowledgments

Historical research is much like a religious pilgrimage as one travels from place to place in search of enlightenment. The publication of this book ends one such long journey for me, and I would like to recognize the assistance and support of those who have helped me along the way.

My avocational interest in the Royal American Regiment was first transformed into an M.A. thesis at the University of Maryland (Baltimore County), where Professors Jean R. Sodlerlund and Gary L. Browne served as my advisers. Professor Ian K. Steele then welcomed me into his large circle of graduate students and directed the Ph.D. dissertation on which this book is based. The hours we spent discussing subjects of mutual interest in his splendid library will always remain fond memories of my years in London, Ontario.

The professional expertise and courtesy of the staff at a number of research institutions also made my times away from home a pleasurable experience. In particular, extended stays at the Henry E. Huntington Library, the William L. Clements Library, the British Library, the National Archives at Kew, and the National Archives of Scotland seemed more vacations than work. A research grant from the David Library of the American Revolution permitted me to spend long hours in the convivial atmosphere provided by Dr. David J. Fowler and his assistants. In a private capacity, Sir Christopher Prevost provided me with details about his distinguished family's genealogy and then graciously supplied two of the illustrations for this book.

The fellowship of kindred spirits, some merely virtual, also made my task enjoyable. David G. Anderson, Prof. Fred Anderson, Robert J. Andrews, Steven B. Baker, Mr. and Mrs. Michael Buck, Dr. Michael A. Cashion, James F. Cawley, Dr. Hans Contractor, Dr. and Mrs. Joseph H. Davis, Robert B. Fullilove, Dr. John A. Houlding, Mr. and Mrs. Bruno Hutter, Timothy N. Julien, Dr. Allan J. Lyons, Lieutenant Colonel Ian M. McCulloch, Karl C. Smith, Dr. Mark G. Spencer, and Dr. R. Scott Stephenson all deserve thanks for their contributions to this project.

I am also grateful to Tamara Gaskell, Editor of the *Pennsylvania Magazine of History and Biography*, for granting permission to reprint in Chapter 2 of this book portions of my July 2005 article about foreign Protestant military migration.

Monographs exploring the Atlantic world's military dimension have rarely seen the light of day. My dissertation would likely have remained in manuscript form had it not been positively received and promoted by Professor Gregory J. W. Urwin, the editor of this series, and Dr. Charles E. Rankin at the University of Oklahoma Press. Their commitment to publishing academic studies about early North American military history puts them at the forefront of a field that has too long been ignored by others.

Finally, I must acknowledge the cheerful support and assistance of my wife, Pearl, who has learned far more about the first British Empire than I will ever know about her work in cellular and molecular medicine. She patiently waited for me to complete my intellectual marathon before she began her own.

"Tirai"
Cornwall, Ontario
13 September 2009

The Royal American Regiment

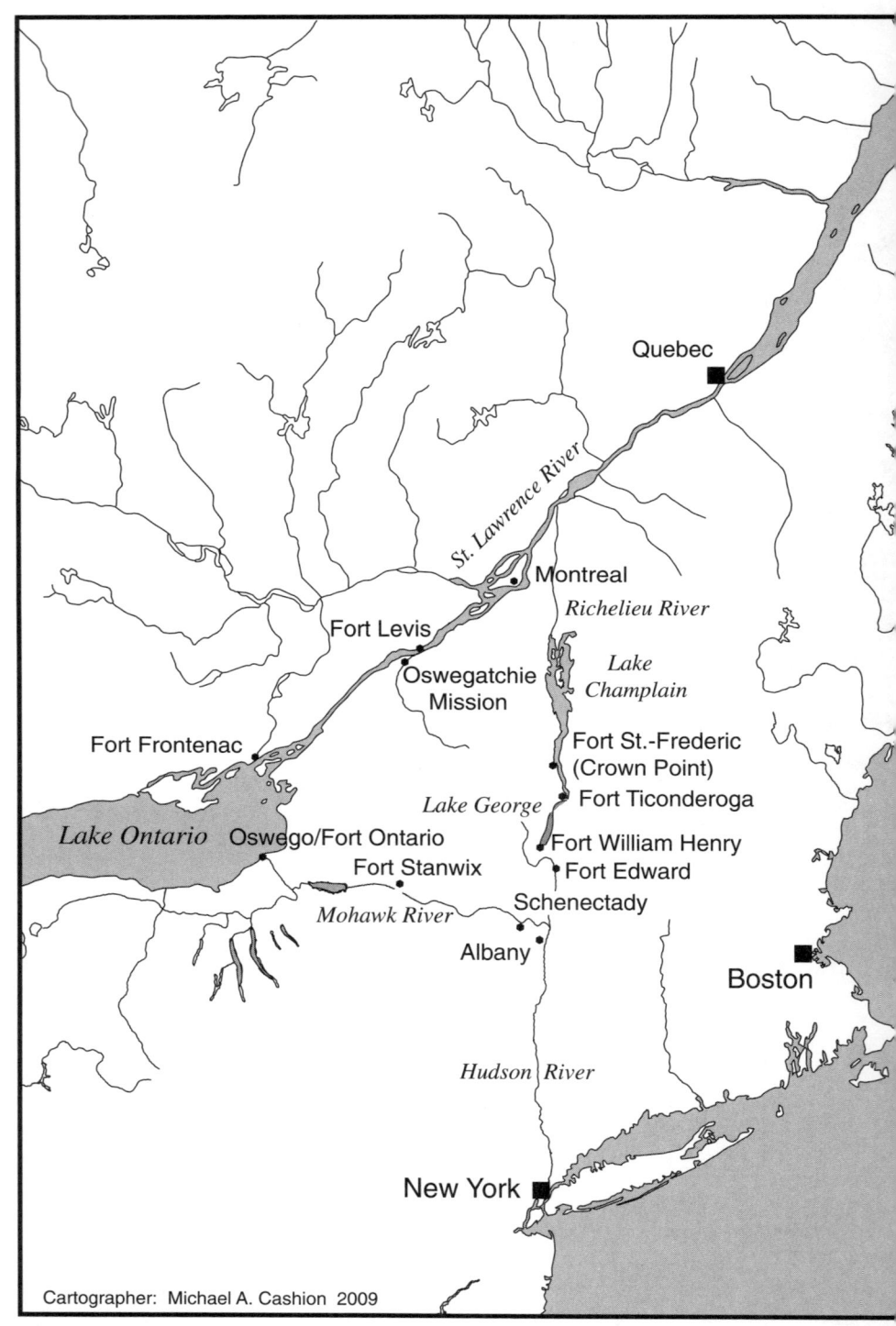

Map 1. Northeastern North America during the Seven Years' War

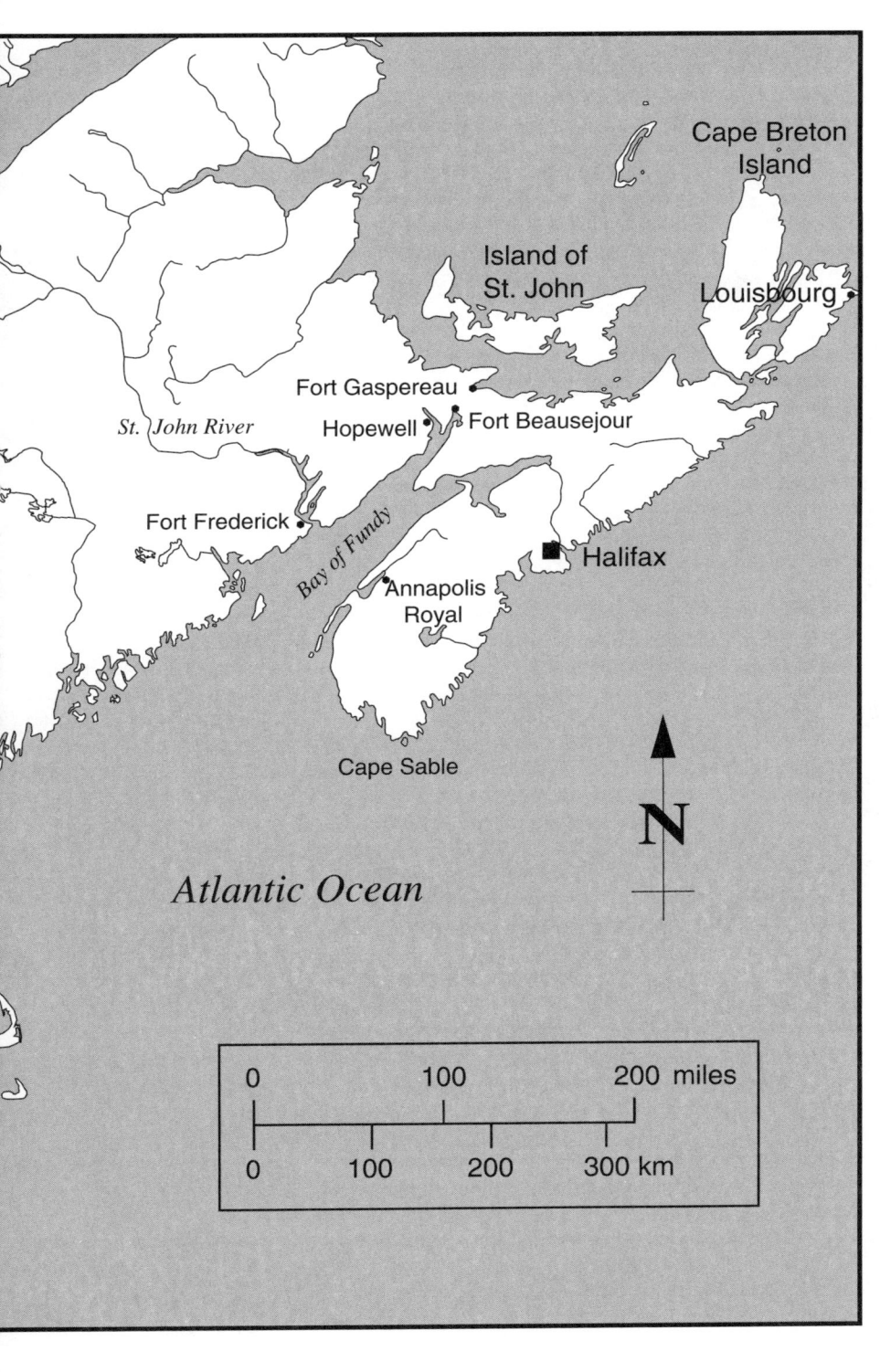

INTRODUCTION

A Royal American Remembrancer

The convoy bearing Major General James Wolfe's embalmed remains to Portsmouth, England, also repatriated some of those injured during his successful 1759 operations against Quebec. Among the convalescents was a subaltern from the 60th (Royal American) Regiment of Foot, Henry Peyton, who had been shot alongside his company commander at Montmorency Falls on 31 July 1759. Quarter for the wounded had not been granted by victorious French troops, who had robbed, beaten, and finally stabbed Captain David Ouchterlony after the battle, despite Peyton's heroic efforts to preserve his dying comrade from the scalping knife. News of these events caused a media frenzy as tales about the officers' gallantry appeared in English-language newspapers on both sides of the Atlantic. Artfully comparing them to Nisus and Euryalus, the two Trojan stalwarts lionized in the *Aeneid*, metropolitan writers rallied public support for an expensive war by projecting Virgil's saga of military brotherhood onto a New World battlefield, where Britons fought valiantly together against a ruthless foe.[1]

Although this dramatic episode from the Seven Years' War (1756–63) is now but a faint memory, public awareness about the activities of Lieutenant Peyton and his regiment continues to be shaped by others long after the Treaty of Paris ended the conflict. Two contradictory images have emerged over time. Contemporary British press accounts first popularized the notion that 60th forces were an imperial asset because of their yeoman service during the long struggle against Louis XV.[2] Such sentiment was certainly fostered inside the regimental community and enjoyed some currency among elements of the civilian population as well.[3] A century later, less flattering portrayals of these colonists in red coats were disseminated through books written by patrician New Englanders prior to the American Civil War (1860–65). Antipathy for British servicemen thus has a long intellectual pedigree and continues to flourish in some academic circles, especially within the United States.[4]

The 60th Foot's reputation and image was a natural concern for its career officers. Six weeks spent moving men and matériel across Canada's "water and wilderness" from Fort William (now Thunder Bay, Ontario) to the Red River Settlement (now Winnipeg, Manitoba) in 1870 inspired one of their number, Captain Nesbit W. Wallace, to lecture about his adventures soon after returning to England. Upon reflection, the captain realized that the physical hardships, camaraderie, desolate locales, and interaction with exotic tribal communities were all common features of military service in the Great Lakes watershed that bound successive generations of redcoats together. Publication eventually followed with the appearance in 1879 of the earliest unit history. Entitled *A Regimental Chronicle and List of Officers of the 60th, or the King's Royal Rifle Corps, Formerly the 62nd, or the Royal American Regiment of Foot*, it provides a sketch of the regiment's activities from its establishment in 1756 under King George II through the reign of his great-great-granddaughter, Queen Victoria. Continuity between past and present was an organizing theme in Wallace's study, which offered readers a detailed summary of the 60th's engagements, duty stations, and officer corps. Most important, the author explained how metropolitan officials' need to improve colonial defenses and their desire to integrate foreign Protestant settlers into the provincial mainstream prompted Whitehall to raise the largest unit ever deployed by the British army in North America.[5]

Wallace's pioneering effort reinforced views that the regiment was a consequential military force during the heyday of the first British Empire (1583–1783). Such laudatory notions resonated particularly well with residents in the mid-Atlantic states whenever they thought about their colonial past and those homegrown redcoats who had been "so very prominent in all the military movements in this country, during the war, from 1756 down to its close."[6] Significant anniversaries marking events like the founding of Pittsburgh or the battle at Bushy Run also sparked fresh interest in the 60th (Royal American) Regiment of Foot, whose service was venerated for "varied, numerous and most honorable" conduct during its formative years. Often, local historical societies or fraternal organizations placed memorial plaques at sites of interest associated with the 60th Regiment.[7]

Several more decades elapsed before Captain Lewis Butler published the first volume of *The Annals of the King's Royal Rifle Corps* in 1913. By the time he commenced this work, an impressive array of primary sources had come to light through the efforts of Sir John Fortescue, who had been originally contracted for the assignment. Butler used this material to close gaps in the historical record and provide greater detail about Royal American involvement in various campaigns than Wallace had been able to do. Yet the captain was like other Edwardians who were enthralled by frontier images thanks to the "Wild West" mania that had already swept through the British realm. This preoccupation, combined with contemporary emphasis on illustrious officers and battlefield exploits, led him to posit that regimental founders were all masters of irregular operations because they had been raised for duty along the colonial borderlands. Accordingly, Butler's study enshrined misconceptions that the 60th Foot was a special service force whose primary function was to contend with "the Red Indian in his native forest."[8]

Butler's inaugural volume was well received by a wide readership. Its influence was especially evident on a young English company commander anxious to animate the moribund regular army at the outset of the First World War, Captain John Frederick Charles Fuller. A veteran of the South African conflict (1899–1902), Fuller was a practical man who looked to the past for effective prototypes that might inspire modern combat capability. He concluded from reading Butler's tome that the Royal Americans provided an exemplary role model, worthy of emulation, because they were "the first true light infantry the British Standing Army ever had." Fuller therefore wanted to copy this unit's apparent success at developing small, mobile detachments of well-armed and motivated troops capable of dealing with an aggressive enemy.[9] Thus, one of Britain's most influential military thinkers popularized the notion that the 60th Regiment was an elite corps set apart from the rest of the army by distinctive clothing, equipment, and discipline. Fuller's imprimatur established an orthodoxy among military historians that obviated any serious reconsideration for decades.[10]

Hagiographic views promulgated by the popular camp were first challenged in the writings of George Bancroft during the mid-nineteenth century. A fervent patriot, Bancroft maintained that God had guided his country from colonial infancy to maturation at the Revolution, when ties to a depraved Old World system had been divinely severed. The Seven Years' War was key to this process since it helped to unify the population and afforded a proving ground for many of the nation's future Founding Fathers.[11] Such theo-political consciousness came naturally to one raised in a Worcester manse, where an early biography of the first American president had been written and where Washington's memory was perpetuated by a local cadet corps, the "Washington Whites," in which the author served.[12]

Republican partisans like Bancroft naturally deemed British regulars of any sort a contemptible band. Led by a tyrannical captain general, the redcoats buttressed an arbitrary regime that "regarded colonies, even when settled by men from their own land, only as sources of emolument to the mother country; colonists as an inferior caste." The author, influenced by a Whiggish preference for local militias over professional soldiers, perceived sinister forces behind the Royal Americans' creation by Westminster in 1756. Besides extending London's authoritarian tentacles over the colonies, metropolitan acceptance of foreign Protestant battalion commanders further demonstrated disdain for provincial worthies such as George Washington who were excluded from suitable leadership positions. However, had more native-born sons headed the 60th Regiment than arrogant placemen, then the line troops would have certainly achieved earlier and more consistent battlefield success.[13]

Bancroft's conviction that preemptory redcoats were more of a liability than an asset has been reprised by a new generation of scholars concerned with the pre-Revolutionary origins of American nationalism. Regular forces, an obvious symbol of the Crown's authority, provide a suitable foil against which exceptionalist historians can hypothesize growing colonial disaffection for the imperial system during the Seven Years' War. They accentuate episodes of civilian disquiet whenever 60th troops established winter quarters on reluctant hosts, impressed draught animals and wagons for logistical purposes, or welcomed indentured servants into the ranks despite their masters' protests.[14] The redcoats' conduct in operational theaters is portrayed as equally unsettling because provincial levies resented the inequitable treatment they received at the hands of foreign Protestant officers. Repeated abuse of colonial Britons by these lackeys of a corrupt political order evinced "royal" but certainly not "American" proclivities.[15]

More unflattering caricatures of Georgian servicemen appeared in Francis Parkman's numerous works. A Bostonian whose ancestors had fought for independence a century before, Parkman portrayed the king's men as inferior to the colonial auxiliaries who had marched alongside them during the last epic struggle against New France. On one hand, the redcoats, typically commanded by unimaginative aristocrats, were contemptuous, lazy, cowardly, and prone to flight before an enemy. Colonists, on the other hand, being natural backwoodsmen, always gave a good account of themselves when not fettered by European military conventions.[16] Parkman's abuse of original sources to make past events fit neatly into his grand narrative is well known, and this predilection appears in his recast of pivotal events from the Seven Years' War. In one notable flight of fancy, Parkman even imagined that Major General James Wolfe relied on "the hardy levies of the provinces" to brace his thin red lines outside Quebec's walls on 13 September 1759 even though no such colonial units were part of that storied battle order.[17]

Unlike Bancroft, Parkman displayed great interest in the history of the American republic's original inhabitants and found in their demise other examples of British army malfeasance. Writing at a time when Manifest Destiny had pushed western tribal groups to the point of extinction, the author traced the genesis of this dispossession to an earlier age when the power of the French and their American Indian allies was broken by the 1763 Treaty of Paris. The subsequent rebellion led by the Ottawa chief Pontiac was sparked in part by the behavior of "reckless and brutal" detachments of the 60th Regiment that had replaced Louis XV's garrisons throughout the Great Lakes basin. Accordingly, British forces reaped a bitter harvest as they were consistently outdone by sagacious war parties that overwhelmed all but the strongest installations. The *Conspiracy of Pontiac* encouraged readers to believe that the redcoats, whether colonial born or not, were simply ill-suited to wage war against a determined New World foe.[18]

Although scholars consider most of Parkman's works to be seriously flawed by bias and bigotry, his critique of the Royal Americans' hinterland activities are now championed by ethnohistorians who link this regiment to the ruin of tribal societies. Their indictments are more specific, condemning first battalion troops for spreading deadly pathogens among Native communities and then forcibly repatriating adopted white captives.[19] The 60th's occupation of the frontier likewise subjected helpless villagers to unbearable economic pressures when army headquarters stanched the flow of accustomed gifts, ammunition, and other manufactured items. The resulting 1763 firestorm is portrayed as an indigenous struggle for liberation against British garrisons who fared badly in most clashes with aggrieved warriors. Far from being an elite force, the Royal Americans are adjudged a hapless lot who were unable to impose Whitehall's policies on those able to resist.[20]

It is clear that popular and patrician views about the 60th Regiment's activities remain at odds because both are predicated on the false assumption that military service was essentially confined to the geopolitical sphere of human affairs. While soldiers certainly engaged in combat operations that ultimately changed international boundaries, to focus on such matters distorts the true *Sitz im Leben* (life setting) of the eighteenth century itself. An Atlantic interpretative approach, however, that underscores the synergy between the Old World and the New breaks the current hermeneutical impasse by viewing the corps within the broader social, economic, demographic, religious, and civil framework of the first British Empire. Although historians have largely ignored the military dimension of this construct to date, their interactive model of disparate faces, far-flung places, and transnational spaces applies to the Georgian land forces as well. In fact, as the ensuing study will demonstrate, army personnel were the one societal element involved in most key aspects of the Atlantic matrix during times of war and peace. One cannot claim a holistic approach to this emerging field of inquiry and overlook the important role played by the Crown's land forces, whose presence and influence grew through the Seven Years' War.[21]

A thorough investigation of the 60th (Royal American) Regiment of Foot is possible because of the information preserved in the private papers of its first three colonels-in-chief—the Earl of Loudoun; Major General James Abercromby; and Sir Jeffery Amherst, who also directed North American land operations. No other British regular unit has left behind such a rich archival legacy. Complementary material found in the papers of two Swiss mercenaries who served as field officers in the unit affords a foreign Protestant perspective of the colonial defense force. The writings of Colonels Henry Bouquet and Frederick Haldimand furnish insights about patronage networks as well as the investment schemes that some career officers undertook as part of ordinary military life. Records relating to Brigadier General John Forbes's 1758 advance against Fort Duquesne and correspondence preserved by Major General Thomas Gage complete the major documentary sources for this study. Pertinent ancillary material is drawn from government reports, period journals, notebooks, diaries, order books, maps, and the private papers of lesser figures.

This volume about the 60th Foot is divided into six principal chapters. The first recounts the improbable career of the regiment's founder, James Prevost, that "Ulysses-like wanderer," as William Pitt called him, against the backdrop of the Seven Years' War and the post–Treaty of Paris world. Through it, readers will become acquainted with the important people, places, and events associated with the regiment's formative years and the Swiss mercenary who dreamed of striking it rich in the New World through military service. Several Atlantic-world themes are also introduced. Detailed discussions about patronage, commerce, and naturalization are included so that a modern audience might understand why these issues were of tremendous importance to Prevost and his contemporaries. Although these particular subjects might not usually appear in books about the eighteenth-century British military, all three were vital to this foreign Protestant adventurer's success as he rose from the ranks of the unemployed to an armigerous lieutenant general in King George III's land forces.[22]

Transatlantic migration provides a theme linking chapters 1 and 2, with the spotlight shifting from officer elites to the rank and file, whose paths and motivations for enlistment are examined. Regular duty was not anathema to all eighteenth-century males because of special incentives offered by metropolitan authorities to encourage induction. Migration opportunities played a significant role in this equation as evinced by the presence, on the one hand, of indentured servants, redemptioners, and other voyagers to the west who took the king's shilling. Some colonial residents, on the other hand, joined the colors to have a better quality of life or to defend their backcountry farms from enemy marauders. Market pressures and other events ultimately worked against Royal American recruiters, prompting senior commanders to draft veteran troops from other regiments to complete the colonial defense force.

A discussion about the 60th's training and combat record is provided in chapter 3. Colonel Henry Bouquet's frontier exploits have certainly colored perceptions about the Royal American's contribution to the success of British arms during the Seven Years' War. Closer scrutiny of the unit's training, deployment, and operational conduct reveals, however, that it was not a revolutionary prototype in the British army's acculturation to the North American woods. Rather, Pennsylvanian detachments under Bouquet's command were the last to embrace the novel paradigms instituted by army headquarters because major tactical reformation spread from east to west in the colonies. The redcoats' lengthy training process also hindered the performance of newly gazetted corps like the Royal Americans whenever they were challenged by logistical problems, political interference, or a shortage of qualified drill instructors. From the regiment's inception, such outside forces impeded the customary training process of at least two battalions, units that acquired mandatory infantry skills much later in the war than even other regiments raised after them.

Regular troops spent little time engaged in actual combat during the three distinct seasons of their calendar year. Instead, they provided commanders with a ready workforce to maintain the logistical infrastructure of roads, fortifications, and depots needed by the army for its summer campaigns. Chapter 4 chronicles a twelve-month period in the soldiers' lives as they moved provisions toward the front, guarded supply lines along the axis of advance, and garrisoned posts built by their own hands or captured from the French. Prolonged exposure to this type of hard service, however, adversely affected the martial bearing and efficiency of those units like the first battalion that had the misfortune to occupy the Great Lakes bases following Canada's 1760 capitulation. While the notion that regulars were both laborers and fighting men remains at odds with present understanding of the redcoats' activities during the Seven Years' War, noncombat pursuits were an added burden infantrymen bore when conducting conventional operations in the New World.

The fifth chapter challenges prevailing beliefs about the dismal state of relations between the Royal Americans and American Indian communities. Since at least one of the 60th Regiment's battalions was stationed in the Great Lakes watershed between the years 1759 and 1772, officers and soldiers experienced intermittent contact with indigenous groups throughout their deployments in the *pays d'en haute* (Upper Country), as the French called all the northwestern wilderness beyond the St. Lawrence River seigneuries. This was not novel because commanders had already acquired some skills in frontier diplomacy via interaction with Cherokee and Catawba allies earlier in the war. Consequently, detachment leaders were eventually grafted into an extant sociopolitical order already evolving on the frontier between Native communities and Europeans. The British sustained such relationships through gifts of food, clothing, and ammunition even after Pontiac's Rebellion, with garrison principals also taking local wives to cement these alliances. Although conflict was not the norm between redcoats and Indians, Western military methods eventually prevailed with the appearance of Colonel Henry Bouquet and his expeditionary force in the Shawnee homeland. Royal American–American Indian interactions followed a tortuous path of trial and error before it reached a positive relational trajectory that would benefit the Crown well into the nineteenth century.

Veterans' activities in a postwar world are the focus of chapter 6. Recruits had been won to the colors with the promise of land grants in Nova Scotia or New York upon the cessation of hostilities. Unlike other pioneers, their years of duty in frontier outposts provided them with the necessary survival skills for successful settlement in various climatic zones. Interestingly, soldiers of various ethnic backgrounds requested their land grants together, suggesting that a measure of camaraderie had developed among the other ranks during their years of military service. Officers too relied on associations established during active duty to assist entrepreneurial efforts concerned chiefly with property development or natural resource extraction. Success rates for such ventures varied, but military patronage assured the viability of many efforts extending British merchant capitalism farther into the backcountry.

The interpretative approach presented in this book offers a new look at an old subject. Georgian redcoats, freed from the straitjacket of geopolitical concerns, can now be recognized as authentic cast members on the stage of Atlantic history. Not merely an infantry force of valiants, according to the popular camp, or villains, if the patrician viewpoint is to be believed, the personnel of the 60th may be appreciated for the numerous roles they played both during and after the war as administrators, advisers, artisans, authors, consumers, diplomats, explorers, family men, investors, land developers, legislators, mariners, merchants, migrants, settlers, soldiers, surveyors, and tradesmen who all contributed to the growth and vitality of the first British Empire. Their consequential presence runs through the Atlantic experience like a transversal thread on a spider's web, linking metropole and periphery.

1

"Much regarded by the Duke"

James Prevost and the Royal American Regiment

James Prevost was an unlikely paladin at the Court of St. James's until the British declaration of war against France in the spring of 1756. Thereafter, appreciation grew for his efforts to protect the kingdom's transatlantic interests through the deployment of a colonial defense corps, which would eventually become the 60th (Royal American) Regiment of Foot. Envious officials noted that key establishment figures, including William Augustus, Duke of Cumberland, the captain general of the army, supported these endeavors and thought highly of the Swiss mercenary who had providentially solved one of the imperial government's strategic problems in its hour of greatest need. Such was the strength of their burgeoning personal relationship that Prevost often attended the king's son and became a fixture in the royal entourage whenever the foreign Protestant officer was in the capital. Courtiers knew the benefits that would arise from this illustrious patronage since the newcomer, though still an alien, was "much regarded by the Duke."[1]

Colonel James Prevost's destiny was inexorably tied to the creation of the 60th (Royal American) Regiment at the outset of the Seven Years' War. While a consequential figure during the penultimate days of the first British Empire, his memory was quickly over-

A jewel-encrusted miniature believed to be of James Prevost (1725–76). Courtesy of Sir Christopher Prevost, Rochester, Kent.

shadowed by other associates who all rose to high rank in the Georgian land forces after their benefactor's premature death.[2] Obscurity's pall has been prolonged as well by scholarly indifference toward military affairs, leaving few writers to plumb the associations between eighteenth-century servicemen and the greater world around them.[3] Yet those interested in the interplay between Europe and the Americas should be intrigued by a person who transcended political and social boundaries, abetted transoceanic migration, invested widely in different commercial enterprises, contributed to the West's territorial expansion, and broadened concepts of British national identity. Because this redcoat stood among such first "Citizens of the World," a careful study of his life increases one's appreciation for the impact that one army officer could have on the English Atlantic system as he rose to great wealth and power within it.[4]

The Prewar Years, 1725–1754

James Prevost did not descend from warrior stock. Born to a Genevan jeweler on 19 December 1725, he spent formative years employed as a watchmaker's apprentice in London. Opportunities for social mobility and greater wealth that arose during the War of the Austrian Succession (1740-48) then lured the teenager to France, where he hoped to join one of the Swiss infantry corps under contract to Louis XV. An unfavorable reception by countrymen there, however, forced the aspiring officer to content himself with duty in less fashionable units posted to Piedmont-Sardinia and then the United Provinces.[5] While a company commander with the regiment *de Budé* in the Low Countries, he met and married Anna Louisa Mackay, the eldest daughter of Lieutenant Colonel Hugh Mackay of Scowrey, a Scots Brigade officer noted for long years of distinguished service to the Dutch Republic.[6]

The newlyweds were not to remain permanent residents of the United Provinces following the death of Stadtholder William IV at midcentury. Although not immediately affected by the troop reductions following his employer's shift in foreign policy, Prevost recognized that this embrace of neutrality was not a good omen for professional soldiers like himself. The major resigned from the Dutch service in due course to seek a new life elsewhere. South Carolina's liberal attitude toward foreign Protestant settlers and its flourishing economy prompted the Genevan to relocate there just as the fragile armistice established by the 1748 Treaty of Aix-la-Chapelle was being undermined by colonial expansion into the disputed Ohio Country.[7] Hostilities between rival English and French troops in these borderlands during the summer of 1754 ultimately sparked the first global war from which James Prevost was to emerge a very wealthy and influential man.[8]

Impartial observers were not surprised by Coulon de Villiers's victory over Lieutenant Colonel George Washington's at Fort Necessity on 3 July 1754, since French forces were counted among the best in the Western world. Like other early modern European monarchs, Louis XV doted on his army, which numbered approximately one hundred fifty thousand men during peacetime but mushroomed to twice that number when on campaign.[9] George II's regular infantry, by contrast, were barely sufficient to meet their normal obligations as garrison troops and adjuncts to the civil power. Fewer than forty-two thousand men served the king across his extensive dominions. Moreover, unlike Continental powerhouses, the forty-nine British line regiments were constitutionally subservient to Parliament which cut the army to skeleton strength after each major conflict. As one contemporary trenchantly observed:

> Bad success, in the beginning of a war, under such a government as subsists in England, is the necessary consequence of a war. France, from the nature of her government, constantly keeps up a great force both by land and sea; so that, no sooner has she resolved on a war with any of her neighbors than her forces are ready to march against her enemies. In England, the case is quite different: let a war be ever so necessary, a king of England can take no steps to prosecute it, before its necessity and consequences are debated in parliament; and, even when they are approved of, the forces to carry on such a war are all to be raised (a very few excepted) and disciplined.

Colonial defense was an afterthought in this equation, with perhaps four thousand overworked, ill-equipped, and inadequately prepared regulars stationed in the West Indies and North America.[10] These small numbers could be complemented by auxiliary forces in times of emergency, but local militias too were notoriously unfit, as were hastily assembled units like George Washington's, which had caused such chaos in the Ohio Valley.[11]

Metropolitan response to this New World military crisis was characteristically tempered by financial and strategic constraints. Rather than publishing an immediate declaration of war in 1754, imperial officials proceeded cautiously by resurrecting two regular New England regiments that had seen service during the North American phase of the War of the Austrian Succession—called by the colonists King George's War (1744–48). Led by their former commanders, Major General William Shirley and Sir William Pepperrell, they would ultimately brace provincial armies tasked with the seizure of key French positions guarding access to Canada, Fort St. Frédéric (Crown Point) and Fort Niagara. Another combined force consisting largely of Massachusetts Bay troops was ordered to besiege Fort Beauséjour in Nova Scotia while Major General Edward Braddock reasserted British sovereignty over the Ohio River valley by destroying Fort Duquesne. Consequently, the key French outposts of empire would fall into Anglo-colonial hands by the end of 1755, maintaining the Treaty of Aix-la-Chapelle's boundary provisions without further international incident. War Office mandarins remained unappreciative that chart room exercises formulated in London could not be conducted as easily across the forbidding North American landmass.[12]

The unexpected annihilation of redcoats along the banks of the Monongahela River was merely the first in a series of military reverses suffered during the second year of the cold war with the Bourbons. On 9 July Braddock's flying column clashed with a mixed band of French and Indian warriors who quickly outflanked the regulars and opened a withering fire. Regimental cohesion evaporated as the 1,400 soldiers tried to defend themselves from the fusillades of an unseen foe. Braddock's little army, surrounded and in an exposed position, was eventually shattered, leaving only a remnant of 583 men to emerge from the battle unscathed later that afternoon.[13] Events in the Great Lakes basin did little to restore the luster of British arms; Major General William Shirley's march against Fort Niagara and a provincial army destined for Crown Point did not even reach enemy territory.[14]

British military successes in the summer of 1755 were few and far between. Nine days after Braddock's drubbing, a small group of regulars and provincials removed a primary threat to the Halifax garrison by capturing the strategic French posts of Beauséjour and Gaspereau along the Acadian frontier.[15] This achievement was complemented three months later when William Johnson's command, guarding the northern approaches to Albany, parried a thrust by French line troops and partisans. Although victorious over one element of New Englanders, assailants under the leadership of Jean-Armand, Baron de Dieskau, who was taken prisoner during the action, had neither the numbers nor the resolve to dislodge the remaining colonists from behind their rudimentary entrenchments. Johnson's capture of Dieskau earned the victor a baronetcy from George II, a gift of £5,000 from Westminster, and the ill-deserved reputation as "the avenger of Braddock," notwithstanding that his men, with artillery support, suffered greater casualties than enemy besiegers.[16]

THE GENESIS OF THE ROYAL AMERICAN REGIMENT, 1755–1756

James Prevost and his family were oblivious to all these cataclysmic events unfolding on the other side of the Atlantic while they waited to embark for South Carolina. The Swiss household finally sailed from Spithead aboard the HMS *Blandford* on 3 August 1755 with the colony's new governor, William Henry Lyttelton. Ten days out, the perilous international situation was driven home when their small ship was intercepted by a French naval squadron and carried off to Brest. Internment was brief, however, since Louis XV did not want to detain an accredited diplomat, nor provoke George II, who he did not yet hold personally responsible for the Royal Navy's actions against his maritime fleet.[17] Accordingly, passengers and crew were repatriated to England just as the news of Major General Edward Braddock's catastrophic defeat at the Ohio Forks reached the United Kingdom. Imperial administrators were now anxious to hear from anyone with fresh ideas about how they might restore the military situation in North America.[18]

The vagaries of European power politics suddenly produced a golden moment for an unemployed soldier of fortune hoping to resettle in the New World. Potential opportunities emerged as James Prevost carefully pondered Britain's strategic problems and his own straitened circumstances. The remedy for both was the creation of a foreign Protestant defense force that the Swiss mercenary would raise in North America under governmental aegis. Prevost first discussed his scheme with key Huguenot merchant bankers, who gave it their unqualified support. The influential Guinand family then used personal contacts at the Court of St. James's to gain their protégé a hearing.[19] Henry Guinand (the elder), himself a native of Neuchâtel, took advantage of his position as deputy governor of the French Hospital to approach the charity's chief administrator, Sir John Ligonier, who was also the Lieutenant General of the Ordnance and a favorite of George II. Guinand likewise had connections to the Duke of Cumberland through his business partner, Etienne Riou, whose son, Stephen, an officer in the First Foot Guards, had dedicated the first authoritative English book on military fortification to the king's son. It was this circuitous influence network that opened palace doors for Major James Prevost, late of the Dutch service.[20]

The Genevan was not alone in the race to secure royal approval for the creation of new regiments overseas. Aside from the Duke of Argyll's proposal to employ a force of Highland Scots, a more serious challenge came from Lieutenant General James Oglethorpe, who had commanded the 42nd Foot in Georgia from its 1737 inception through demobilization twelve years later.[21] Oglethorpe enlisted the Duke of Newcastle's support in a lobbying effort to reactivate his old corps. His memorial asserted that precedence and seniority rights entitled his half-pay officers, who had already gained a great deal of experience fighting in the southern marchlands but were not presently on active duty, to full employment before others were given consideration. Their hard-won experience would benefit the realm by expediting troop deployment anywhere in the Americas. Despite such sound reasoning, however, the general's solicitations were still dismissed out of hand because of his perceived Jacobitism.[22]

Prevost's overture, by contrast, was a detailed scheme designed to meet the needs of London authorities on several levels. Cognizant that the War Office had been unable to entice many German-speaking immigrants into regular ranks, he promoted the idea that at least eighteen hundred such men would readily enlist in a separate ethnic corps led by officers fluent in their native tongue. This garrison regiment of two battalions—composed of musketeers, light infantry, grenadiers, and engineers—would strengthen colonial defenses while alleviating the need for more redcoats to be dispatched from scarce metropolitan reserves. Costs were less than hiring other professional European troops: £12,400 to raise, clothe, and equip the soldiers, with operational expenses of £2,563 per month thereafter. Traditional English fears of monarchical despotism backed by foreign bayonets was dampened by a proviso barring the legion from duty in the United Kingdom and requiring that all subsequent officers' commissions be filled by British subjects. The Swiss adventurer would engage the requisite mercenaries to command the regiment in return for the honor of being named its chief.[23]

Privy councillors, formerly at odds over New World strategy, now found that the proposed émigré battalions provided a viable compromise solution. Hawks, who had wanted a greater regular presence in the colonies, supported the foreign Protestant regiment because it would mean the loss of fewer veteran troops now needed at home to defend against a threatened French invasion. The other advisory group, which had subscribed to the Duke of Newcastle's dictum "Americans should fight Americans" continued to insist that overseas subjects bear the primary responsibility of protecting themselves. Prevost's corps received their endorsement because it tapped colonial manpower reserves exactly as prescribed.[24] Finally, both factions recognized that it was cheaper to send two hundred European staff westward than to ship entire regiments abroad. Conditional royal approval was thus granted by 22 October 1755, allowing the newly minted commander to return to the mainland in search of subordinates with a per diem of four pounds, four shillings for his salary and traveling expenses.[25]

A whirlwind tour of the United Provinces, the Holy Roman Empire, and Switzerland produced impressive results. By 1 January 1756 the colonel had been able to enroll forty-three officers and fifty noncommissioned officers (NCOs) for his corps. Their number included forty-six Swiss, thirty-one Germans, four Dutch, as well as others from Lithuania, Poland, Pomerania, and Sweden. His most valuable acquisitions were his older brother, Augustine, a captain in the regiment *de Croye*, together with Lieutenant Colonels Henry Bouquet and Frederick Haldimand, both employed by the Swiss Guards. All these veterans were drawn to the British army because prospects for field operations were far greater in George II's service than in Holland, where the Dutch government was contemplating the disbandment of even its elite foreign regiments. Perceptive soldiers could also not disregard prospects for advancement through active duty nor the rare opportunity to visit the New World.[26] A significant cash incentive helped to spur enlistment. Conscious of the axiom "Point d'argent, point de Suisse" (No money, no Swiss), Prevost was authorized to distribute gratuities on a graduated scale to all those willing to don madder livery for a period of six years: £50 to each field officer or captain; £30 to every subaltern; £20 to individual NCOs.[27]

News of the foreign Protestant unit's creation was not lauded across the land because other powerful interest groups in Britain were displeased that the pay and perks from military service had been granted to Continentals instead of themselves or their associates. The loudest howls of protest came from colonial agents who served as the London spokesmen for the various provincial legislatures.[28] Two men in particular, Robert Charles representing New York and Richard Partridge for Pennsylvania, complained that the proposed legion violated constitutional provisions against alien military employment and would cause jealousy among subjects who had already served the Crown in wartime. Further, they argued that colonial defenses would be inadvertently weakened by arming men whose fidelity to George II was unproved. To these dissenting voices were added objections from half-pay officers in want of gainful employment. The united agitation of all these people forced administrators to concede that the German-American unit could not be deployed as envisioned.[29]

Yet, despite vociferous protests, Whitehall remained committed to the idea of deploying a foreign Protestant regiment for two important reasons. First, the cabinet council reconsidered the corps' merits in light of British troop shortfalls and the Irish government's aversion to providing more North American reinforcements from the twelve thousand soldiers in its garrisons. The cupboards were practically bare in both jurisdictions, leaving little hope for the dispatch of another expeditionary force from the British Isles.[30] Second, the War Office remained convinced that German-speaking immigrants comprised a large manpower reserve that had yet to be utilized by either rival power. Although the seditious correspondence of the French sympathizer "Filius Gallicae" had not yet come to light, the politically neutral course steered by that significant community plus their low naturalization rates and continued isolation from mainstream society were deemed a potential threat to metropolitan interests. The opportunity to incorporate these people into the British camp first, through military service, became of paramount importance.[31] Privy councillors therefore remained supportive and overcame censure of the legion's distinctive ethnic character by proposing recruitment of another one thousand Anglo-Americans to dilute the alien presence, restricting the number of Continental officers to half the command positions, and ensuring that its colonel was a natural-born subject. Further complaints from provincial agents did not weaken official resolve. Ministers agreed during their 20 January 1756 meeting to seek parliamentary sanction for the colonial defense force, albeit in a further modified form.[32]

Prevost's unit underwent its final metamorphosis as administrators cast about for ways to rally political support before Lord Barrington, the secretary at war, presented his expense estimate to the House of Commons on 9 February 1756. Parliamentary oversight of the army ensured that Westminster's consent was required before the corps could be brought into existence. Precedent for colonial military recruitment had already been established during the War of Jenkins' Ear (1739–42) when four thousand provincial subjects had participated in the Cartagena expedition as members of Gooch's Regiment of Foot.[33] The prospective legion was therefore revamped according to this earlier prototype: its strength was increased by another thousand men; foreign Protestant officers were allocated fewer than half the commissions; and overall supervision was entrusted to John Campbell, the fourth Earl of Loudoun, who was appointed commander of North American operations.[34]

An able tactician, Lord Barrington broke down the controversial legislation into separate components before presenting them to legislators for approval. His first step was to gain funding for the defense force, now more than double its original size of eighteen hundred men. The secretary at war accomplished this by proposing that a comparable force to Gooch's Regiment be again raised for service to protect the nation's transatlantic interests. This deft political maneuver won the support even of William Pitt, the government's most strident defense critic who complained that such a regiment should already have been on the British Establishment. Objections were few and £81,000 was quickly appropriated to defray the costs of four redcoated battalions—now designated the Royal American Regiment of Foot—to be raised in the colonies forthwith. Having won agreement in principle to fund the new defense force, Barrington then introduced the more divisive measure empowering George II to grant commissions to foreign Protestant officers.[35]

John Bull's aversion to European mores was most evident in the pervasive notions that large standing armies posed a threat to personal liberties and were an unnecessary burden on taxpayers. Running a close second was an utter distaste for aliens whose religions, politics, and customs were antithetical to the values cherished by Englishmen of most social stripes. Understandably, the idea of giving foreign officers command of regular troops was too much for some MPs to stomach.[36] The vitriolic debates beginning on 10 February 1756 lasted for sixteen days before the bill was dispatched for review by the House of Lords. William Pitt and Charles Townshend, both recently cashiered from the administration, led the opposition. They complained that granting commissions to mercenaries violated existing constitutional provisions, that their employment would antagonize loyal subjects who had previously served in wartime, and that colonists would not enlist in battalions commanded by aliens. Horace Walpole remained unimpressed by the dissenters. He informed a friend: "We have had noting in Parliament but most tedious and long debates on a West Indian regiment, to be partly composed of Swiss and Germans settled in Pennsylvania, with some Dutch officers. The opposition neither increase in numbers or eloquence; the want of the former seems to have damped the fire of the latter." The bill to grant commissions to foreign Protestants thus received final approval of the Commons by more than a three-to-one margin. Critics did win a concession, however, by limiting the number of Continental officers to seventy: fifty mercenaries would be allowed to serve in the corps proper while twenty more could act as engineers to compensate for a lack of such specialists in the New World. A clause restricting Europeans to service in America only and another barring them from supreme regimental command complied with earlier cabinet council policy.[37]

The first contingent of Colonel Prevost's retainers was already in England when the bill granting them employment in the British service passed to the House of Lords.[38] Despite continuous objections from colonial agent William Bollan, the legislation was ratified without amendments in less than a week since peers were unwilling to block legislation that carried the Duke of Cumberland's imprimatur and that enjoyed the overwhelming support of the lower chamber. George II's assent followed on 9 March 1756, placing the 62nd (Royal American) Regiment of Foot alongside ten other temporary corps gazetted to defend Britain's interests should the conflict with France continue to escalate. The unit's establishment was backdated to 24 December 1755 so that its officers could draw their pay and determine regimental seniority from that day. James Prevost, the originator of the entire scheme, was made colonel of the force's most junior battalion.[39]

While Lord Barrington had been shepherding the necessary legislation through Westminster, the Duke of Cumberland and the new regimental commandant, the Earl of Loudoun, dealt with the minutiae of fielding four thousand colonists. Of first importance was the selection of appropriate officers, a task completed while James Prevost was still away on the mainland. Solicitations for desirable appointments inundated the War Office because military commissions were still proprietary in nature and possessed some degree of social cachet. Cumberland's protection of foreign Protestant interests was evident through his appointments of Lieutenant Colonels Henry Bouquet and Frederick Haldimand to substantive command in the two senior battalions. The duke was also instrumental in dispensing

A portrait of William Augustus, the Duke of Cumberland (1721–65), by Swiss artist David Morier. Cumberland was a keen supporter of both James Prevost and his scheme to defend the Middle Atlantic colonies with foreign Protestant manpower. Courtesy of the Council of the National Army Museum, London. (National Army Museum, Chelsea, Neg. 46193)

sixteen prized captaincies to mercenaries (40 percent of the total) and twenty-five lieutenancies, as a sign of continued royal endorsement for his Swiss favorite.[40]

Transatlantic Activities, 1756–1758

Chagrined that his role in the 62nd Regiment had been reduced to the lowliest colonelcy, Prevost had no desire to serve in North America while raw recruits were being raised, equipped, and trained for his fourth battalion. The Genevan calculated that his own financial position could be improved if he remained in Europe and left his subordinates to deal with any immediate administrative headaches. His newest profit-making venture arose from a late-February court audience during which continued anxieties about a dearth of infantrymen in the New World had been expressed because the regiments already on station remained well below established strengths.[41] Cognizant that Whitehall was then preparing legislation sanctioning the enlistment of indentured servants to shore up British defenses in the American colonies, Prevost once again utilized the Duke of Cumberland's influence to advance his own fortune.[42]

The Genevan's original quest for German-speaking officers had already proven quite lucrative; he had siphoned off at least £1,300 intended to defray the costs of some of the staff's Atlantic passage. Accounts were similarly inflated by charging London treasury officials for the pay and gratuities of phantom volunteers who never left Europe.[43] With twelve mercenary cronies still in the Netherlands and the Holy Roman Empire, Prevost prevailed on Cumberland to allow them to enlist several hundred additional ranks and NCOs for the Royal American Regiment before embarking for the New World. He assured the captain general that this new enterprise would expedite the battalions' deployment by securing a solid nucleus of veterans around which the rest of the corps could be marshaled.[44]

War Office administrators demonstrated less enthusiasm for this enterprise than did the king's son; they restricted the number of seasoned troops at first to four hundred: one hundred for each of the overseas battalions. Similarly, the quantity of prospective NCOs was reduced from one hundred to sixty, with only twenty musicians to form a regimental band.[45] The wily colonel still made a handsome profit, with the Duke of Cumberland's blessing, despite the initial

£12 limit for each enlistee conveyed across the Atlantic. By eventually squeezing £20 a head from British officials for many of the 778 recruits brought into the Royal American Regiment that summer, paying his volunteers in local currency instead of sterling, and by starting their salary only upon arrival at New York, Prevost kept the £8 difference between the estimated and final price of each transport plus all the sea pay (some £1,100) allowed by the British treasury for soldiers in transit. In addition, the Guinand brothers handled £3,240 worth of governmental subsistence contracts besides ancillary service fees relating to the recruits' march from Frankfurt am Main to their embarkation point at Stade, near Hamburg.[46]

It was the potential dividends from this £14,200 government expenditure that kept the colonel's attention riveted on Europe while his older brother, Augustine, assumed responsibility for the transport of foreign Protestant officers to the New World. The first contingent of mercenaries, precariously stowed aboard the HMS *Nottingham* and the packet ship *Harriot*, sailed westward with the troopships carrying the 35th and 42nd Regiments to America during the early spring of 1756. Arriving in New York on 14 and 15 June, the German-speaking recruiters marched immediately for Pennsylvania to begin their duties.[47] Another two months passed before the remainder of the regimental staff and equipment arrived at the Governors Island depot, where Royal American recruits were to be quartered, clothed, and trained.[48]

The newest American battalions contributed little to the 1756 campaign efforts. Following a lamentable pattern, the British military suffered a major setback with the 14 August capitulation of the Fort Oswego garrison. Both the 50th and 51st Regiments of Foot, which had been raised in the colonies the previous year, were carried off to New France in inglorious captivity. The subsequent elimination of Shirley's and Pepperrell's corps from the army establishment altered the regimental numbering system by two, transforming the Royal Americans into the 60th Regiment of Foot.[49] Reverses on the western front were compounded by the large expeditionary force of seven thousand provincials "talking much & doing little" that failed to invest Crown Point for the second straight year.[50] Their lack of aggressive spirit, in turn, allowed the victorious Marquis de Montcalm to concentrate his forces along the Lake George–Lake Champlain waterway and threaten Albany. British commanders reacted to the new strategic realities by massing all available manpower on the northern frontier. Almost fifteen hundred Royal Americans established defensive positions at Saratoga; this show of strength and the onset of winter contributed to the end of further French encroachments.[51]

Colonel James Prevost returned to the Court of St. James's from his Continental recruiting drive on the same day that French engineers began bombarding Fort Oswego into submission. He received high praise for the manner in which more than seven full companies of veteran German troops had been secured for the Royal American Regiment. As a mark of royal favor, the few remaining commissions reserved for foreign Protestants were granted to members of the Genevan's entourage despite the fact that two individuals, George Dufez and Samuel Wllyamoz, were still in the nominal employ of Louis XV.[52] Moreover, Cumberland insisted that Prevost remain in London while a final New York convoy prepared for sea before entrusting him with personal dispatches addressed to the Earl of Loudoun. The mercenary stayed in the capital for several weeks until the transports were ready to sail from Cork in late October.[53]

The Earl of Loudoun planned to end the war in 1757 by sending a British army up the St. Lawrence River to capture the enemy capital of Quebec. The Royal Americans, despite their inexperience, were expected to play an active part in the summer offensive with at least two of their battalions earmarked for the assault force. Accordingly, the entire regiment had been recruiting and training men in their winter cantonments for more than a month by the time Prevost arrived at New York on 16 January 1757.[54] Because he was still largely an unknown entity to the British officer corps, the mercenary was closely scrutinized by army staff to ensure that his formation would be ready to participate in the approaching campaign. Prevost's poor standing with the upper echelons at headquarters began when he exhibited erratic behavior during these initial months of command.[55]

The colonel's reputation as an inept soldier knowing "nothing of Duty or Service" can be partly attributed to his not having functioned as a field officer during wartime. His promotion to the rank of major with the Dutch after the War of the Austrian Succession had not qualified him to assume direction of a line regiment preparing for combat. Poor management style, most evident in the haphazard waste of men and equipment, mistreatment of soldiers, and his own imperious personality did little to endear him to British colleagues who were already suspicious of this foreign interloper.[56] Prevost also demonstrated that he was not a team player by complaining that the cream of the European recruits had been apportioned to the other three battalions, leaving his own formation bereft of their expertise. Loudoun, acting with great circumspection because of the maverick's royal connections, allowed the Swiss officer to reclaim any of the veterans he wanted, over the protests of more senior colonels who opposed the loss of bilingual soldiers.[57]

Headquarters' negative assessment of Colonel Prevost's character was not based solely on his poor performance as a battalion leader. His business affairs likewise intimated that he may not have been worthy of much trust since the Swiss officer's financial fortunes had improved while the army's situation had not. Alarmingly, both the expensive German veterans and several of the foreign Protestant officers demonstrated little capability for duty, causing skepticism to develop about their prior service records with other governments.[58] Prevost's disposal of three hundred rifled carbines acquired in Rotterdam for 100 percent profit in New York and the fact that almost half of the colonel's gentleman retainers were indebted to the colonel for a combined sum of £1,100 exemplified an unseemly preoccupation with pecuniary matters. Such discreditable financial dealings, together with his insolent attitude toward superiors, confirmed misgivings that the Genevan did not have the wherewithal to command an operational unit.[59]

Loudoun's deliberate assignment of the fourth Royal American battalion to the Halifax task force was arranged so that the peer could keep Prevost on a tight leash during the summer campaign. Amphibious operations from this advance base in Nova Scotia would then be launched against the imposing bastions of Louisbourg followed by a descent on the citadel at Quebec. When a large enemy fleet was discovered at anchor in Cape Breton waters, however, offensive actions were canceled because of the dangers associated with sailing vulnerable transports near so many French warships.[60] Troops from both the second and fourth battalions therefore spent their summer in Nova Scotia profitably engaged alongside other redcoats in military exercises, siege craft, and advanced tactical training before returning to New York with the onset of winter. Surprisingly, James Prevost was not the greatest disruptive presence on the expedition. That distinction went to Lord Charles Hay, who bitterly opposed the decision not to attack Louisbourg and publicly denounced his superior's lack of enterprise. The Swiss adventurer, however, found common cause with the mercurial nobleman and later testified on his brigade commander's behalf at a court-martial convened in London three years later.[61]

French military plans proved much more successful in 1757 with the dispatch of Major General Montcalm's army to destroy Fort William Henry. With the weight of British offensive power immobile in Nova Scotia, Louis XV's troops were able to mass along the southern shore of Lake George and cannonade isolated defenders into submission by 9 August. Before the stronghold was completely invested, however, a relief party including a detachment of two hundred men from the Royal Americans' third battalion bolstered the beleaguered garrison. Twenty-three of their number were lost during the infamous American Indian attack on the baggage train, and another forty-six comrades were carried off to Canada as prisoners.[62]

The first Royal American battalion enjoyed a much quieter year of service. Assigned to protect the southern theater of operations, they were the only redcoats guarding the extensive territory between Pennsylvania and Georgia. Numerous official requests for a regular troop presence obliged the senior corps to be separated into two equal divisions of five hundred men for these duties. Colonel John Stanwix's force remained in Pennsylvania, taking post near the frontier settlement at Carlisle where they could support either Fort Cumberland, Fort Augusta, or Philadelphia in case of enemy attack. Since no large French or Indian force threatened the backcountry that year, detachment members refined their basic infantry skills before establishing winter quarters in the town of Lancaster.[63] The five hundred men under Lieutenant Colonel Henry Bouquet's supervision constituted part of the Charles Town, South Carolina, garrison for nine months until recalled for duty in New York. This temporary independent command allowed senior mercenaries to speculate in lucrative properties there through the agency of their influential deputy.[64]

Although the war had interfered with James Prevost's initial relocation plans, he was now a much wealthier man connected to an extensive patronage network on both sides of the Atlantic Ocean. The Royal American presence in Charles Town added to the commercial appeal of this port city, where a prosperous Huguenot merchant community existed and a staple export economy promised tremendous returns.⁶⁵ In conjunction with members of the London-based Guinand family, Prevost and two of his intimates, Henry Bouquet and Frederick Haldimand, invested almost £6,000 in holdings devoted to rice and indigo cultivation. Peter Guinand, one of the patriarch's younger sons, was entrusted with management of the Beaufort County plantations.⁶⁶ Close personal ties to the Guinands also led the colonel to contribute some capital toward their modest provincial store that retailed "Negro Cloth & blankets" to the general public.⁶⁷

Prevost's desire to diversify his financial interests came at a time when he was also growing disenchanted with his position in the overseas army. Not yet wanting to retire, however, the Swiss officer implored the Duke of Cumberland to be recalled to London so that he could propose another scheme that he believed would greatly aid the British war effort. The mercenary outlined these ideas to his superior in a detailed treatise entitled *Mémoire sur la Guerre d'Amérique* enclosed in his letter of 12 May 1757. He suggested that a new colonial defense force be gazetted to range the marchlands between Nova Scotia and the Carolinas. To be constituted and paid for by the colonists themselves at a cost of £60,000, the corps would be composed of "sobres, jeunes, forts, robustes capables de suporter une très grande fatigue" (sober, strong, robust young men capable of enduring great fatigues) led by sons of the local elite. Each battalion of one thousand men—clothed, trained, and provisioned differently than other regular formations—would be capable of ravaging "Canada à tout instant feroit respecter les Anglois par les Nations Indiennes, et assuroit par la Crainte leur Amitié et le Commerce lucratif qu'on fait avec elles" (Canada at every instance to make the Indian nations respect the English and secure by fear their affection and the lucrative commerce that one does with them). Discharged veterans would be encouraged to form a colony after the war; this settlement would provide a strategic reserve of manpower should such be needed in future conflicts. Although not specifically mentioned in the report, Prevost apparently wanted the colonelcy of this unit to assure his continued station in British North America.⁶⁸

Events in Europe that summer conspired against the Genevan's plans to gain a more important employment. On 24 July 1757 British interests suffered a serious military reverse at Hastenbeck, where a large French army of one hundred thousand men overwhelmed a much smaller allied force led by the Duke of Cumberland. William Augustus, in an effort to preserve the remainder of George II's Hanoverian troops, subsequently signed a separate peace with the enemy, the Convention of Klosterzeven, which the king perceived as a disgraceful surrender; as a result, he recalled his son from the field. Cumberland returned to London but resigned all his military offices to protest this lack of faith in his tactical judgment.[69]

Turmoil within the metropolitan administration did not immediately work to James Prevost's disadvantage. Although the Swiss mercenary could no longer rely on the duke's influence to support his plans for a revamped defense force, his continued employment as colonel of the fourth battalion largely depended on the fate of his 23 May 1757 resignation letter addressed directly to the king's son instead of the secretary at war. As chance would have it, the dispatch first came across the desk of Cumberland's military secretary, Major General Robert Napier, who promptly buried it under his paperwork fearing "so many Inconveniences attending the Bustle he would make if he came back here."[70] Nor did the duke's political opponents concern themselves with a comprehensive purge of Cumberland's placemen in the overseas army. Rather, they were content with the dismissal of Loudoun as commander-in-chief before assuming greater ministerial control of the war effort. Overlooked in the upheaval among the upper echelons of the army, Prevost's request for reassignment was neglected until after he had reconsidered his position and disavowed any notions of quitting the Royal Americans.[71]

Anglo-provincial military interests began to improve appreciably during the summer of 1758. After three years of frustration, the Crown's forces demonstrated their strength and improved capabilities through the capture of Louisbourg, the portcullis to the St. Lawrence River. The second and third Royal American battalions participated in this amphibious assault against the heavily defended Cape Breton shoreline. In the face of strong fire, the redcoats drove the French troops back from their positions and into the bastioned stronghold. A seven-week siege ensued until the garrison capitulated on 27 July. Their vigorous stand, however, impeded the further advance of Major General Jeffery Amherst's army that year.[72] Second battalion troops then participated in an expedition to raze Acadian villages that still posed a threat to British settlements in Nova Scotia. These redcoats rejoined third battalion comrades in their winter quarters at Halifax after meeting little or no resistance from enemy forces along the St. John River.[73]

The capture of Fort Duquesne by Brigadier General John Forbes was the other major triumph of 1758. To eradicate this western headquarters for French and American Indian raiding parties, the Scot was given a largely provincial army braced by regular detachments drawn from the Royal Americans' first battalion and the 77th Regiment of Foot (Montgomery's Highlanders). The general executed a slow advance through the uninhabited wilderness and constructed a series of fortified depots to keep opposition forces on the defensive. Although thirty-eight Royal American casualties occurred during the Battle of Grant's Hill, this loss proved to be the only major reverse in an otherwise flawless campaign. The French garrison finally fled at news of Forbes's relentless march, destroying their installation prior to evacuation in November. British troops took possession of the charred remains and then constructed a new emplacement, Fort Pitt, nearby.[74]

The redcoats' 1758 victories at Louisbourg and Fort Duquesne were overshadowed by a tragedy that occurred when Major General James Abercromby's army of fifteen thousand men tried to drive the French away from the New York frontier. Outside the walls of Fort Carillon (Ticonderoga), which commanded the approaches to Lake Champlain, British regulars hurriedly stormed the advanced entrenchments under the false impression that large numbers of enemy reinforcements would soon bolster the garrison.[75] After several valiant but futile assaults conducted without the benefit of artillery support, Abercromby ordered his troops to retreat to their Lake George base. Elements of the first and fourth Royal American battalions suffered 281 casualties between them after this bloody action in which the British forces lost a total of nineteen hundred combatants.[76]

Major General Abercromby had little initial contact with Colonel Prevost during the planning and execution of the 1758 operations because the mercenary cloistered himself at New York sulking over the exclusion of his name from the list of those advanced to the rank of brigadier general in America. Claiming that he could not possibly lead troops with this blot on his escutcheon, Prevost refused to participate in any military maneuvers until he too received this mark of royal favor just like John Stanwix, John Forbes, Lord Viscount Howe, Edward Whitmore, and Charles Lawrence.[77] The vexed colonel therefore began a vigorous lobbying effort for promotion although constitutional experts theorized that his alien status precluded elevation to general rank.[78] With Prevost still in a state of limbo because of the confusion surrounding his resignation letter and preferment status, temporary command of the fourth battalion was given to Frederick Haldimand, who was deemed a very competent officer. Haldimand, not Prevost, thus had the unenviable task of leading the grenadier charge into the Ticonderoga abatis where so many lost their lives and he received a slight wound.[79]

Quasi retirement in New York allowed the Swiss officer ample opportunities to diversify his investment portfolio since this bustling port boasted one of the most effective privateering fleets in British North America. That summer, a twenty-gun corsair bearing the flattering appellation *Colonel Prevost* suddenly appeared on the high seas and captured several prizes with a total value of £29,260 York currency (£17,211 sterling). Although complete lists of shareholders are rare, the Royal American officer had a business relationship with Joseph Haynes, one of the vessel's principal underwriters. It is not inconceivable that Prevost also speculated in licensed piracy, especially as an investor in a ship that bore his name.[80] The colonel took to the field shortly after the Battle of Ticonderoga upon receipt of erroneous correspondence from London associates stating that his coveted promotion had been approved.[81]

The officer's arrival at the Lake George encampment could not have come at a worse time for Abercromby and his demoralized soldiers, still licking their wounds. A shortage of staff officers, however, required the commander-in-chief to give Prevost temporary rank as brigadier before banishing him to guard the rear echelon of Fort Edward with six Royal American companies from the first battalion and twelve hundred provincials.[82] From this safe vantage point, Prevost badgered his hapless superior about ways to salvage the summer campaign while boasting that enemy attacks on supply convoys had abated in his sector. There were other perks of higher office to enjoy as well since brigadiers kept a sentinel at their door, received the salutes from garrison drums, and were accompanied by a sergeant's escort when away from quarters. They were also entitled to an additional one pound, ten shillings per day in pay and had the privilege of appointing a brigade major who earned an extra ten shillings. Prevost's younger brother, James Mark, a captain in the fourth battalion, became the recipient of this plum.[83]

There can be little disagreement that during his brief tenure at Fort Edward, James Prevost acted like the eighteenth-century equivalent of the imperious Colonel Blimp, the fictitious cartoon character who preferred "the status quo ante-almost-everything." The mercenary remained out of step with the rest of the British army, which had largely shed its parade ground comportment after three years of New World warfare. Uniforms, equipment, and tactics had all undergone a visible transformation designed to meet the operational demands of the North American theater.[84] But Prevost refused to conform and was ridiculed by contemporaries for going "on one Scout in the Summer with his Horse and laced furniture, so good a Judge he is of the Nature of the Service in this Country." That was not all. The Swiss mercenary likewise antagonized civilians by trying to levy a special tax on sutlers transporting goods through his sector, and by allegedly browbeating provincial charges who did not want to work before breakfast.[85]

Lobbying and Naturalization, 1759–1762

Brigadier General James Prevost's reign of error came to an abrupt end in the fall of 1758 after the War Office denied a request for home leave and refused to confirm his field promotion. Convinced that his personal interests could not be advanced at Fort Edward, the Swiss officer traveled to New York against orders to meet with the new commander-in-chief, Major General Jeffery Amherst.[86] The erstwhile brigadier's reception at army headquarters was anything but warm, and the general stripped him of all the ceremonial trappings of higher office to which he had become accustomed. Prevost, incensed by this treatment, sailed for England on 28 February 1759 aboard the HMS *Rose* determined to sell his battalion to Lieutenant Colonel Ralph Burton of the 44th Regiment. In a final round of financial self-aggrandizement, the colonel misappropriated £1,700 from regimental coffers, leaving behind a promissory note to repay any contingency expenses not approved by metropolitan officials.[87]

It is surprising in light of Colonel James Prevost's vanity and growing wealth that he did not pay to have himself immortalized in Benjamin West's controversial painting *The Death of Wolfe*, which celebrated the triumph of British arms in 1759. The fact that he was not even in North America when the war reached its climax would have troubled him little. While not all had gone according to Whitehall's military blueprint, at least one task force had accomplished its goal by taking the war to Quebec. The 13 September battle on the Plains of Abraham achieved in a single stroke what besiegers had vainly tried to do all summer. Until that moment, however, redcoats had been unable to coax enemy forces from behind impregnable positions and onto an open battlefield where they would enjoy less of a tactical advantage.[88] Wolfe would have returned to England in disgrace had Lieutenant General Montcalm not rushed out of the capital to remove the token force of 4,260 British infantry arrayed outside the city gates. Royal American participants included second battalion detachments, entrusted with the security of the left flank, as well as troops from the third battalion who covered an evacuation route to the river.[89]

Gains were also made along the New York frontier where Major General Jeffery Amherst's army doggedly secured Fort Ticonderoga and Crown Point without any heroics, but still fell short of its ultimate objective at Montreal.[90] While Amherst labored to secure possession of Lake Champlain, a detachment of his army led by Brigadier General John Prideaux moved westward along the Mohawk River to subdue the largest remaining French garrison on the Great Lakes. Prevost's unit of the Royal American Regiment joined this expeditionary force, guarding the communications between the base at Fort Ontario and the British troops who besieged Fort Niagara. Colonel Frederick Haldimand's spirited defense of the supply lines against a superior enemy force on 5 July 1759 ensured the success of forward operations. Fort Niagara finally capitulated to the redcoats twenty days later. Fourth battalion elements remained at Oswego for the winter to assist with the reconstruction of Fort Ontario.[91]

While victorious British armies were repainting the North American map red, James Prevost spent a less triumphant year in London dealing with powerful opponents anxious to block his every move. Chief among them was the Earl of Loudoun. As titular corps commander through the spring of 1758, he was a central figure in the bureaucratic process involving the clearance of Royal American financial accounts with the War Office. The peer pointed out some irregularities in the colonel's ledgers, which caused officials to withhold payment for several years until Prevost returned £1,097 for questionable charges.[92] Plans to raise several thousand pounds from the sale of his battalion similarly came to naught because George II disapproved of anyone disposing of a royal gift for profit. Since Prevost had not purchased his colonelcy, the king would allow the Swiss adventurer to retire but not sell out of the army as he had originally intended.[93]

George II's policy against the sale of unpurchased commissions at first left Prevost with very little wiggle room. He could either resign or remain with the 60th Foot in his present capacity since Westminster's 1756 restriction on his military service meant that chances for future preferment were dim so long as this statute remained in effect. However, discussions about constitutional loopholes with the attorney general, Charles Pratt, and the solicitor general, Charles Yorke, did produce a ray of hope. Both adjudicators were developing meaningful ties to the mercenary circle: Pratt's sister would later marry Major Herbert von Munster, while Yorke's brother, Joseph, had established an amicable friendship with Colonel Prevost when the former was ambassador to The Hague.[94] These influential jurists advised the Swiss officer that foreign Protestants like himself might hold general rank in British North America if they had been colonial residents for seven years in accord with the Naturalization Act of 1740. Conceivably, even this lengthy residency requirement could be waived if Parliament passed special legislation rewarding Royal American commanders for their wartime service.[95]

The quest for expedited naturalization became James Prevost's obsession. The Swiss national realized that serious challenges lay ahead since he could not rely on the Duke of Cumberland's overt influence to change existing laws. Success would be contingent on framing the debate around national interests and not lobbying officials just for his own preferment. Downplaying personal ambitions, he informed ministers that current statutes restricting foreign Protestant officers to the Royal American Regiment inadvertently handicapped Britain's overseas war efforts in three important ways. First, it damaged morale since they could not expect to rise as high in military rank as their talents and seniority would customarily dictate.[96] Second, foreign Protestant immobility adversely affected regimental performance since British junior officers also were frozen in place with no promotion prospects within the unit itself. Their expertise was thus lost to the corps whenever they transferred out of the battalions in pursuit of higher command. Finally, aliens were sensitive to the fact that their military commissions were no longer inviolate once outside ill-defined American boundaries. Such a technicality might now destroy the internal cohesion of the army as it prepared to move beyond the territorial limits of the English dominions.[97]

There was little more the frustrated officer could accomplish in London during the spring of 1760. Mindful of the reward bestowed on those who carried dispatches of major military victories to the capital, the Swiss adventurer departed for the New World without explicit authorization from the secretary at war. Prevost hurried across the Atlantic and arrived unexpectedly at Major General Jeffery Amherst's camp only days before the British army launched an ambitious three-front offensive against Canada. The colonel tried to resume control of the fourth battalion that was to join the main expeditionary force in its descent of the St. Lawrence River from Fort Ontario to Montreal.[98] Amherst, sensing in the parvenu a liability rather than an asset, diplomatically declined his offer of service and ordered Prevost to return to New York until instructions arrived from the War Office permitting his return to the field. Frederick Haldimand remained in charge of the battalion during the triumphant campaign that culminated in the surrender of Montreal on 8 September.[99]

The colonel remained busy in New York even though he could not communicate directly with the other foreign Protestant officers who were on active duty. Instead, he relied on his two brothers, Major Augustine Prevost of the third battalion and Captain John Mark Prevost of the fourth, to circulate a petition among all their Swiss, German, and Dutch compatriots requesting that Westminster waive the seven-year residency requirement for naturalization. Support for this measure was also solicited from senior military officials in the Americas. Major General Jeffery Amherst, himself a protégé of the new captain general, Sir John Ligonier, prudently acquiesced to this subscription, promising to further the welfare of all his deserving officers.[100]

The capitulation of French troops at Montreal and their evacuation of the Upper Posts in 1760 did not bode well for the foreign Protestant officers serving in a regiment raised for duty in North America only.[101] Their fears about continued employment were compounded by anxieties about the security of their existing commercial interests or estates since aliens did not enjoy the same legal protection as British subjects. This point had been driven home when one of their number, Lieutenant John de Noyelles, who had established a successful brewing operation in the colonies after his retirement, was hindered from recovering just debts because he was deemed a stranger in the realm. Subsequent attempts to gain naturalization in New York had been undermined by opponents in that colony's assembly, foreshadowing continued provincial discrimination should Colonel Prevost not secure redress for himself and his entourage at Westminster.[102]

Impeccable timing once again favored the Swiss adventurer's arrival in London amid news of spectacular military victories and euphoria over the coronation of a new king near the end of 1760. Although the Duke of Cumberland did not resume command of the army after George III's accession, he did enjoy an equitable relationship with his royal nephew that benefited Prevost as well. Associates overseas were delighted to learn that their leader "est tres bien a la cour" (is in great favor at court).[103] The sovereign's goodwill became apparent to all on 28 October 1761 when the Genevan was promoted to the command of the first battalion over others with impeccable credentials and reliable political connections. It was from this vantage point that the alien was then able to press for a special naturalization bill. His appeal encountered little resistance from establishment figures after William Pitt's resignation from office.[104]

Charles Townshend, the new secretary at war, presented the Swiss mercenary's petition to Parliament on 10 March 1762. Citing their zeal and fidelity since 1755, Townshend reminded legislators that the foreign Protestant officers had served the Crown well by raising seventeen hundred men on both sides of the Atlantic and winning approbation for their battlefield conduct. He also made MPs aware that almost half of Prevost's retainers had been selected by headquarters for extraordinary duties without harm to British interests; in effect, wartime exigencies had already loosened Westminster's strictures against service outside the Royal American Regiment. Finally, he apprised House of Commons members that the 1740 Naturalization Act adversely affected the troops' eligibility when they were stationed beyond American territorial limits at such places as Louisbourg, Quebec, or the West Indies for more than two months at a time. According to existing statutes, the European officers and men would not be entitled to equal treatment before the law until seven years after the war's end despite the fact that they had been in the New World since 1756.[105]

This masterful presentation had its desired effect on assembled lawmakers, who prepared an ordinance naturalizing foreign Protestant servicemen after two years' duty in the 60th Regiment. A retroactive clause addressed property rights by guaranteeing the estates of those with colonial holdings acquired between the years 1756 and 1762. More important, these men were no longer prohibited from receiving overseas Crown appointments, including general rank in North America and civilian trusts ranging from justices of the peace to governor. Unlike the debates sparked by the original 1756 measure that granted regular commissions to mercenaries, no provincial agents objected to the bill, nor did opposition benches perceive it as a threat to the constitution, as Prevost's initiative began to broaden metropolitan definitions of "Briton."[106] The first to benefit were the Prevost brothers themselves: James attained the rank of lieutenant general prior to his death; Augustine was eventually promoted to major general and briefly served as commander of the British regulars in Canada during the early 1770s. Their confidants, Henry Bouquet and Frederick Haldimand, likewise entered that charmed army circle, with the latter also serving as Quebec's governor from 1777 to 1786. Even lowly subalterns rose to higher stations than earlier could have been expected. Lieutenant Joseph F. W. DesBarres was eventually appointed chief administrator of Cape Breton, eclipsing even the success of Samuel Holland, who served as Quebec's chief surveyor and a legislative councillor. Other aliens given lesser colonial offices included Daniel Claus, Michael Grass, and Conrad Gugy.[107]

Westminster's newest naturalization measures consummated foreign Protestant integration designs envisioned at the outset of the 60th Foot's establishment. The corps became a proxy for the larger expatriate community, which reveled vicariously in its achievements. It also complemented a marked Anglicization process already evident among the mercenaries who had been distributed throughout all four battalions. In a literal sense, English increasingly became the language used by European officers in official correspondence as well as among themselves.[108] Operational success also helped to incorporate the foreign Protestant element into the rest of the army as their battlefield performance earned public acclaim. Personal laurels and sacrifice reflected well on the coterie who wore the same commemorative medals as British participants "in Remembrance [of] all those Actions which have been eminently serviceable."[109]

LIEUT-GENERAL SIR FREDERICK HALDIMAND, K.B.,
GOVERNOR GENERAL OF CANADA.
Lieut.-Col. 60th Regt., 1756—72.
Col. Commdt.   ,,   1772—91.

A portrait of Sir Frederick Haldimand (1718–91), who eventually rose to the rank of lieutenant general and became the governor of Quebec after Westminster's 1762 special naturalization act. Courtesy of Library and Archives Canada. (C-018298)

The Seven Years' War had broadened during the months that James Prevost lobbied parliamentarians for accelerated naturalization. Not sated by the conquest of Canada in 1760, metropolitan officials ordered an expeditionary force commanded by Major General Robert Monckton to seize the Caribbean island of Martinique, which had already withstood an earlier invasion attempt. The 60th Regiment's third battalion, now led by Lieutenant Colonel Augustine Prevost, was one of the ten regular corps assigned to this operation.[110] After an uneventful amphibious landing, the Royal Americans garnered praise for their conduct when counterattacked by a large French force at Morne Garnier. Enemy resistance abruptly crumbled with the surrender of the island garrison to Monckton on 16 February 1762. The Martinique task force then sailed against Havana, which likewise capitulated to the redcoats after a desperate siege lasting three months.[111]

Third battalion members returned to New York from the Caribbean in the late winter of 1764 only to learn that they and fourth battalion comrades had been slated for disbandment. Army demobilization, however, allowed veterans to obtain the land grants first promised as an enlistment incentive eight years before.[112] In conformity with the Royal Proclamation of 7 October 1763, discharged servicemen received their share of "the king's reward" according to a graduated scale on any vacant Crown land in North America. Substantial numbers of former Royal Americans did petition Lieutenant Governor Cadwallader Colden for New York lands even though the majority of soldiers returned to their old civilian pursuits or found other employment in large urban centers.[113]

The Golden Years, 1763–1775

Whitehall's decision to retrench overseas forces was not good news to the foreign Protestants who had served with the two junior formations throughout the war. Nonetheless, their Genevan patron was able to use his influence at the Court of St. James's to protect the careers of his closest comrades by insisting that the bulk of extant Royal American companies be given to his associates, despite the army's customary seniority privileges.[114] The muster roll of the colonel's own reconstituted first battalion therefore contained the names of many cronies who had come to the New World in 1756: six of the nine companies were commanded by mercenary officers, three of whom transferred from the now defunct fourth battalion. Seven of the nine lieutenancies were given to men who had previously been assigned to the lowest-numbered unit. Although the second battalion contained a total of only eleven European officers, Frederick Haldimand served as its lieutenant colonel alongside two other immigrants who were also given desirable company proprietorships. Even those relegated to the half-pay list were given the right of first refusal to any regimental vacancies caused by the death or retirement of commissioned personnel.[115]

While the year 1763 finally brought spectacular triumphs to the British at the negotiating table in Europe, events did not proceed apace in the North American hinterland where Natives plotted to destroy the redcoated garrisons in their midst. These occupation troops, constituted primarily of first battalion personnel, had been in possession of the frontier forts since the capitulation of Montreal in September 1760 and were still awaiting relief from this onerous duty.[116] For years detachments in small, remote northern outposts had struggled to sustain themselves in a hostile environment. A concomitant decline in military efficiency made them easy targets for determined war parties.[117]

The attack on Detroit engineered by the Ottawa chief Pontiac came as a complete surprise to New York headquarters despite warnings from western commanders that tribal discontent could spark an insurrection. Pontiac's offensive prompted other aggrieved villagers to storm neighboring garrisons, wiping out all but Forts Detroit, Niagara, Pitt, Ligonier, and Bedford. American Indians could not have chosen a more opportune time to overthrow British suzerainty since the regular forces were only a third of their previous wartime strength and the nearest reserves remained decimated by the tropical diseases that had winnowed their ranks at Havana.[118] Lieutenant General Jeffery Amherst responded to this uprising by dispatching reinforcements from New York to Detroit via Fort Niagara. In Pennsylvania, detachments from two Highland regiments joined Colonel Henry Bouquet's expedition to support the besieged redcoats at Fort Pitt. After defeating ambushers at Bushy Run on 6 August 1763, Bouquet relieved the garrison and then later advanced into the heart of Ohio Country to make the insurgents sue for peace.[119]

Colonel Prevost's name was not listed among the 141 casualties suffered by the first battalion during the bloody hinterland uprising. Safely ensconced in London, the mercenary was given continuous leaves of absence so that he was not required to be on foreign station with his men. Further royal dispensations permitted his return home for extended periods, allowing him to purchase the family's ancestral estate of Bessingee, near Geneva, with profits made from years in the British service.[120] Metropolitan affairs, though, were never far from his mind, especially after the Duke of Cumberland came back to power in 1765 at the head of a new political administration. The king's resurgent uncle quickly acted to secure his old favorite a long-desired mark of military distinction. Instead of merely advancing him to the rank of brigadier general, George III awarded Prevost the higher honor of major general, with his elevation backdated to 3 June 1762, the day after Westminster's passage of naturalization legislation. This promotion, with its £730 annual salary, vaulted the mercenary ahead of twenty-four others already on the seniority list.[121]

The only dark cloud on the horizon was the deteriorating position of the Guinand merchant firm. Beginning in 1755, the Prevost-Guinand association had done much to further the fortunes of both families, but their ambitious investments in the Charles Town plantations foundered after the death of the resident manager, Peter Guinand. The remaining steward, Andrew Fesch, a brother of the Royal American's Captain Rudolph Fesch, then complicated financial matters by using communal assets to pay off personal debts. Such impropriety was magnified by the poor performance of another overseer, Andrew D'Ellient, who squandered his time after retiring from the 60th Regiment.[122] Failure to remove both incompetents from their positions of trust culminated in the collapse of "that unfortunate speculation in Carolina," with the partners recouping only a fraction of their initial investment. Despite this setback, the Huguenot merchants still served as the metropolitan agents for many of the mercenaries stationed in the New World.[123] Heavy speculation in Canadian bills of exchange, however, ultimately caused the London house to go bankrupt near the end of the decade, jeopardizing the prospects of those officers who had left money in its care.[124]

Life was good at court before Cumberland's premature demise on 31 October 1765 and the Guinands' financial collapse four years later.

It was during this period that Prevost secured the lieutenant colonelcy of his own first battalion for his elder brother, Augustine, who had been reduced to half pay the year before. This was a significant accomplishment because the other candidate for preferment, Sir John St. Clair, was senior in rank, British by birth, and had the support of Jeffery Amherst, who still served as the regiment's colonel-in-chief. The major general also took advantage of the continuing need for regular troops in North America by orchestrating another Continental manpower drive in the mid-1760s. This operation secured 191 foreign Protestant recruits who accompanied Augustine when he returned to supervise the family's military franchise at Quebec. The latest consignment of German soldiers, though, were not enlisted for life as they should have been and were presumably recruited on terms beneficial to the Prevosts' fortunes, just like those ten years before.[125]

The Swiss mercenary maintained good standing at St. James's and was promoted to the rank of lieutenant general on 25 March 1772. He played the role of courtier well, whether socializing with influential members of the British nobility when they were in Geneva or guiding them to Ferney, where they might visit with the freethinker Voltaire. Prevost even attended one of the king's brothers during an extended tour of the Continent in 1773.[126] He met Henry Frederick's entourage at Calais and accompanied the royal party all the way to Milan, where the newest Duke of Cumberland was to spend the winter. Although the duke and his wife were to travel incognito, the general took it upon himself to arrange all the proper military escorts that numbered as many as fifteen hundred cavalry at one time.[127] Perhaps because of this service, Prevost received one final honor from the Crown: a royal license to assume the dignities of his deceased father-in-law, Lieutenant General Hugh Mackay. Accordingly, on 27 September 1775 the mercenary registered the appropriate armorial bearings with the College of Arms in London under the name James Prevost Mackay of Scowrey.[128]

There would be precious little time for Prevost to enjoy this new distinction. He followed his namesake to the grave at Breda early in January 1776, leaving a wife and two daughters to survive him. Anna Louisa Mackay was sole beneficiary according to the plain will read on the eighth of that month by the notary public at the local mortuary house. Unfortunately, the document contained no estate description. James's older child, Constantia Anna Honor Augusta, became the wife of Count Francois Daniel Vincent Cornabee, an officer in a Walloon regiment. Isabelle Louise, the younger daughter, apparently never married and, together with her widowed mother, spent the rest of her days in Scotland.[129]

Lieutenant General James Prevost Mackay of Scowrey was a colorful figure by any standard. Although of modest origins, he achieved respectability and financial independence as a military entrepreneur who capitalized on metropolitan strategic need for his own gain. Prevost's genius was to recognize the value of a colonial defense force which would utilize foreign Protestant officers and men. Their deployment, in turn, even within the greatly expanded 60th (Royal American) Regiment of Foot, strengthened the mercenary's claims for equitable treatment in political, legal, social, and economic matters because his men had fought for Britain's national advantage.

It is clear that the Genevan adventurer was a man of influence "much regarded by the Duke" whose reach extended from Europe to the Great Lakes watershed via the Court of St. James's. This royal connection was certainly paramount with the favorable parliamentary dispensations for employment and expedited naturalization supplementary in importance. Although the Swiss officer made powerful enemies, he kept more powerful friends by being of service to those in higher station. Close family members and associates were the first to benefit. But the mercenary also worked to protect and promote the interests of those within his circle, regardless of their rank. Thus, he could call on the friendship or dutiful subordination of people from all walks of life in different parts of Europe and North America. Such wide name recognition was essential for the successful management of his complex personal and financial affairs during the ascent from jeweler's son to membership in the British elite.

Prevost's rags-to-riches story suggests that the Atlantic world was a place of opportunity where considerable fortunes could be amassed, even during wartime. The Swiss officer made his initial stake by combining recruiting experience with knowledge of migration networks and operations. He then parlayed dividends made from his battalion colonelcy and the acquisition of men for George II's land forces into a wide variety of commercial pursuits. Some, like shares in New York privateers, were profitable, while others based on the export of colonial staples were not. Despite these financial reverses, the Swiss adventurer was able to purchase his old family estate and live a comfortable life thanks to an annual income from his British military offices that potentially exceeded £2,000 by the time of his death.

Finally, it is important to bear in mind that the Genevan mercenary was not an unusual figure in the eighteenth century. He chose a respectable vocation as a young man and then improved his career prospects by honing his sales and marketing skills. His success was ultimately predicated on the ability to fire interest in his particular military ventures—especially the Royal Americans—from which he derived immense profit and prestige. What other men of lesser means found attractive about military life and why they chose to enlist with the 60th Regiment of Foot provides the subject matter for the next chapter.

2

"A MEDLEY OF ALL CHARACTERS"

Recruiting the Royal American Regiment

Dr. Robert Hamilton published his reflections on the Georgian-era British army after years of distinguished service as a military surgeon. Based on his extensive knowledge of regimental routine and institutional values, the writer's prescient observations about life in the ranks constituted more than a mere apothecary's textbook. Hamilton, a progressive who believed in a hands-on approach to medicine, suggested that colleagues become familiar with the character of those under their care—redcoats who came from many walks of life—through frequent interaction. Such associations would allow the practitioners to recognize links between disease and the psychological or social dislocation experienced by some of their patients. Hamilton cautioned, however, that building this individual rapport became more difficult during mobilization and wartime because the Crown's land forces actually became "a medley of all characters" as the army's muster rolls swelled in response to national emergencies.[1]

Hamilton's remarks about the variety of people that he had encountered in uniform would have resonated with Royal American personnel who knew that their own striking diversity was a consequence of the army's expansive search for volunteers. Britain's regiments, unlike those of its European rivals that were free from parliamentary control, could not raise troops through coercion but had to scour the Atlantic labor market for any potential recruits and secure their services through incentives at a time when domestic economies were buoyed by international strife. An analysis of this challenging task reveals how the regulated enlistment process was conducted, who joined the 60th Foot, why volunteers chose military duty over other forms of ready employment, and how the metropolitan government attempted to maintain effective strengths over time. Evidently, a limited engagement with the colors represented for many a way up or out of intolerable circumstances as well as a chance for socioeconomic advancement in the New World.

First Volunteers: The United Kingdom, 1756

Georgian infantry units conducted manpower drives with the aid and consent of civil authorities. The cooperation of both arms of the government was essential for success. Officers assigned to this detail were normally dispatched from their regimental headquarters accompanied by a select number of noncommissioned officers and drummers. They carried signed beating orders issued by superiors that authorized their activities and specified acceptable standards for all volunteers. These credentials, in turn, were presented to local magistrates who regulated the activity in their jurisdictions. Healthy male Protestants between the ages of sixteen and thirty-five, at least five feet, five inches in height, were deemed most suitable for duty. To ensure compliance, recruiting officers had to pay the return travel expenses for all those rejected by battalion commanders upon arrival at the unit depot.[2]

Community centers such as taverns, courthouses, or county fairs provided ideal settings for recruiters to entertain candidates and negotiate enlistment terms, which were more generous in wartime. A small portion of the volunteers' bounty money, also known as proclamation or levy money, was spent to drink the king's health and to outfit themselves himself with "necessaries"—typically a shirt, shoes, and stockings—for their march to the regiment. A grace period of up to four days allowed time for men to reconsider their decision, and they were not held liable for military service if they restored the bounty money and paid a fine of twenty shillings to compensate the

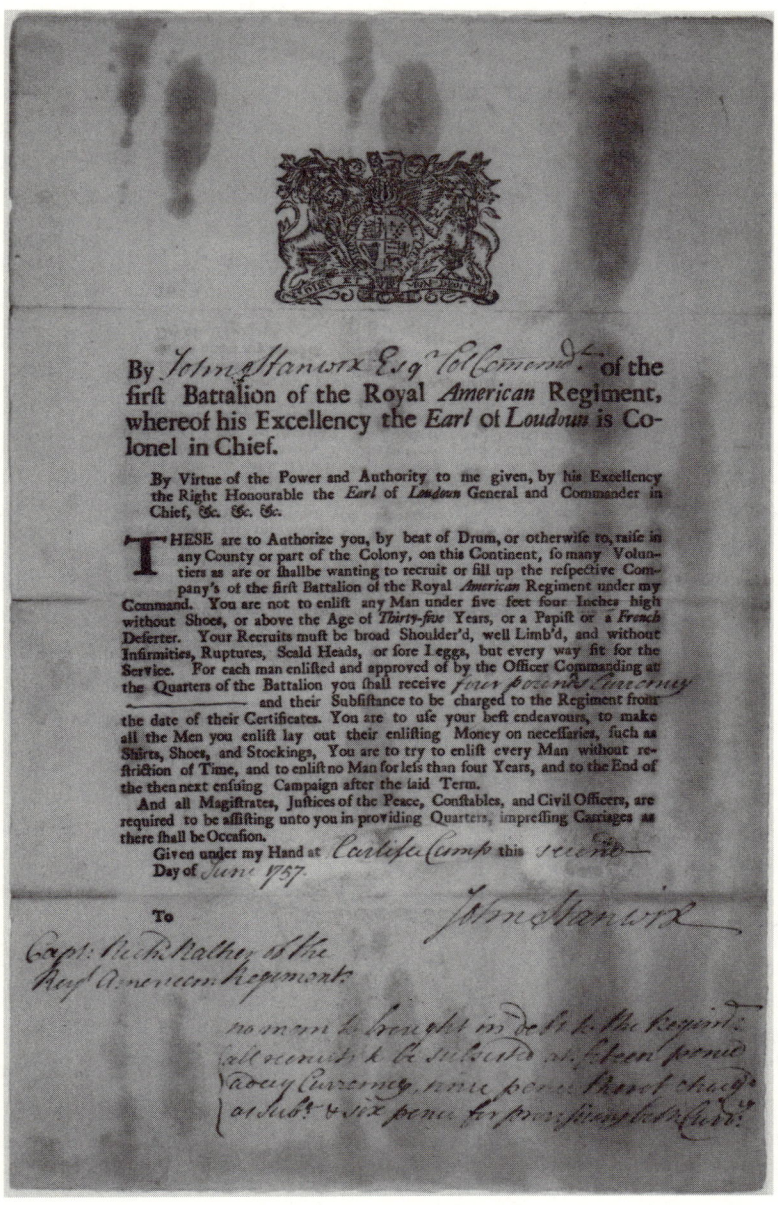

A beating order issued to Captain Richard Mather by Colonel John Stanwix at Carlisle Camp on 2 June 1757. Reproduced by permission of The Huntington Library, San Marino, Calif. (LO 3626)

officer for his efforts. Assenters then appeared before a local justice of the peace who administered the Oath of Fidelity after reading aloud the pertinent sections of the Articles of War about mutiny and desertion. The enlistment process was complete after the attending magistrate presented each volunteer with a signed copy of his attestation papers enumerating the length and conditions of service agreed upon by both parties.[3]

The 60th Regiment's distinguishing blend of ethnic groups became recognizable within weeks of the unit's March 1756 establishment. Even as the first contingents of officers and mercenaries embarked for the New World from Plymouth and Glasgow, 260 enlistees born in Scotland, Ireland, England, and Germany were ready to sail with them.[4] The Highland volunteers had been secured through the influence of the formation's Scottish colonel-in-chief, John Campbell, the fourth Earl of Loudoun, while other countrymen were being engaged to augment the strength of the 35th and 42nd Regiments already bound for North America.[5] In a similar fashion, subalterns commissioned from units on the Irish Establishment were encouraged to secure suitable enlistees before they departed for New York. Officers awaiting transit in London took advantage of recruiting opportunities in the capital even as German-speaking soldiers in the elite guard regiments were being transferred to the four new battalions.[6]

The Admiralty Office was the next unexpected source of foreign Protestant manpower. Although the Courts of St. James's and St. Germain did not officially declare war on one another until 17 May 1756, their respective naval forces had been harrying shipping lanes for months, with the Royal Navy maintaining custody of any troops found aboard French vessels. Louis XV's practice of stocking his colonial garrisons with Swiss or German soldiers worked to the benefit of the Royal Americans, who were the best prepared to utilize these reinforcements.[7] With a growing number of enemy combatants in detention, the Duke of Cumberland ordered Lieutenant Colonel Frederick Haldimand and Lieutenant Simon Fraser to entertain any Protestant prisoners willing to enter George II's service for no more than four years. Eager volunteers, preferring a redcoat to close confinement, had only to stow their possessions aboard adjacent transports that were preparing to carry the remainder of the regiment's officers, stores, and baggage to the New World.[8]

Recruiting in the Middle Colonies

Metropolitan authorities did everything in their power to aid the colonial mobilization effort by selecting their emissaries with great care. For diplomatic reasons, Majors John Rutherfurd and Augustine Prevost were appointed to lead the first wave of officers to the New World. Rutherfurd, considered to be "a man of sense & extremely well acquainted with American affairs," was chosen for this important assignment because he was the highest-ranking corps member known to the provincial elites in the Middle Colonies, where volunteers were to be sought first. In addition to the major's younger brother, Walter, who had also been made a company commander in the regiment, both the Duke of Cumberland and the Earl of Loudoun ensured that other influential Anglo-Americans, those with relatives in the colonies, or officers with prior New World service received commissions in the defense force.[9] Numbered among the earliest cadre were Abraham Bosomworth, Thomas Pinckney, Isaac Motte, and Johann Gasser from South Carolina; Daniel Claus, Donald Campbell, and John Ogilvy from New York; Francis Gordon from Virginia; and veteran British officers Sir John St. Clair, Charles Grame, Henry Gordon, Francis Pringle, and George Turnbull. Later additions with impeccable provincial connections included Henry Babcock, John Bradstreet, James DeLancey, Michael Schlatter, Rensselaer Schuyler, and Robert Stewart.[10]

Whitehall's scheme to deploy the Royal American Regiment quickly also depended on the cooperation of provincial governments where no regular units had yet been formally raised. Metropolitan authorities envisioned that each of these jurisdictions would provide troop levies for the corps as they had a decade before when Gooch's American Foot joined the 1740 Cartagena expedition.[11] If a shortfall remained, then parties from the four battalions would canvass the country between New York and Virginia, extending their activities through New England, the Carolinas, and Georgia as circumstances permitted.[12] Two additional measures were also adopted by London strategists to facilitate mobilization: Pennsylvania was declared off-limits to recruiters from other line regiments while the Royal Americans were being formed; and Parliament finally dampened a contentious legal issue by sanctioning the enlistment of indentured servants.[13]

Majors John Rutherfurd and Augustine Prevost landed at New York in the middle of June only to discover that no preparations had been made for their reception nor were there any colonial levies awaiting induction into the regiment. Royal American advance parties faced other problems as well. First, recruiters had to win men to the colors from among a general populace that knew about the high casualty rates sustained by regular forces at Cartagena and the Monongahela River—a hard sell indeed.[14] Second, the manpower drive was compromised by the balkanized state of the provincial war effort, where local interests often prevailed over any common cause. Finally, regular emissaries had to drum up volunteers in an atmosphere of "fury and confusion" occasioned by the enlistment of indentured servants. This litigious issue dogged regimental procurement efforts until word of Parliament's 6 May 1756 action reached the mainland later that summer.[15]

The indentured servant controversy immediately plunged Royal American agents into hot water even though the problem was not of their own making. The dispute's origins can be traced back to the time of the War of the Spanish Succession (1701–14) when indentured servants from Pennsylvania sidestepped their contractual obligations through enlistment in regiments deployed by neighboring colonies. A generation later, bound laborers again used this same tactic to emancipate themselves when regular troops were raised in the colonies during the War of Jenkins' Ear and King George's War.[16] Despite the common law's tenor upholding proprietarial rights, the legal status of such volunteers remained undefined through the military administrations of Major General Edward Braddock and Governor William Shirley because apprentices in Great Britain were allowed to enlist in the armed forces during national emergencies.[17] Deployment in 1754 of the two New England battalions, the 50th and 51st Foot, as well as augmentations in 1755 to the 40th, 44th, 45th, 47th, and 48th regiments already on duty in North America, placed an enormous burden on recruiters obliged to enroll a total of 5,000 new men. As before, commanders could not afford to turn away servants despite the vehement protests of owners still aggrieved by the lack of adequate compensation.[18]

Indentured servitude is a broad term used to define a mutually beneficial association between two parties based on the consensual exchange of labor in return for certain monetary considerations. In the arrangement, an immigrant agreed to serve a sponsor for a fixed period of time in exchange for paid passage to the New World. While most affluent residents in the Lower South preferred to own slaves, European servants remained attractive as an alternative workforce for colonists throughout the Middle Atlantic and Chesapeake regions. The economics were simple: an indentured servant was one-third the price of a slave and did not require a permanent commitment for personal maintenance when agriculture or commerce were at a low ebb.[19] It is important to bear in mind, however, that not all Britons willingly left their homeland for the Americas. The servant population included convicts banished into overseas captivity as well as a number of "Barbadozed" youths sold to willing buyers along the Atlantic coast by unscrupulous sea captains. Ready and reluctant immigrants alike thus constituted one caste expected to complete their times of service before being set free.[20]

Scholars generally agree that life in North America was difficult for most white menials who were forced to labor in fields, mines, and forges. They were the keenest to exchange their fetters for a redcoat so long as such privation existed.[21] Although a soldier's gross annual pay of £12 was meager by civilian standards, it was considerably more than that earned by a bondman who could expect no remuneration. Besides, regulated military discipline appeared less draconian than continued existence under an overseer's caprice, and the opportunity to see other parts of the continent proved inviting to those whose liberty of movement was curtailed by legal sanction.[22] The additional wartime incentive of two-hundred-acre land grants offered by army recruiters at the outset of the Seven Years' War were freedom dues few could expect to receive by the mid-eighteenth century. Life in the ranks clearly appeared attractive to many indentured servants fed up with their lot in colonial society.[23]

Other circumstances likewise contributed to this fabulous manpower bonanza. Special mention must be made of a subcategory of servant-enlistees who used military service as a way to escape a state of unjust enslavement. As noted earlier, the ranks of the servant caste included young males carried away by crimps to North America. An orderly attached to Major General Edward Braddock's army recorded that among recent volunteers were "several Indented Servants that had been kidnapped in England and brought over hear and sold to the Planters." For these unfortunates, the appearance of a recruiting party provided a means to ameliorate their situation since enlistment was the surest way to avoid the long arm of their masters and local judges who might penalize fugitives by adding extra time to their indentures. The prospect of free passage back to familiar English haunts after the triumph of British arms was viewed as a godsend to some detained in the New World against their will.[24]

Servant owners were the wild card in the recruitment equation. Those who felt cheated by the loss of their workers, and who believed the bounty money portion given to them by former employees was insufficient, obstructed the enlistment process by incarcerating either their laborers or recruiting officers for debt. This was the last resort for proprietors who had not yet received full recompense from any quarter despite appeals to their colonial governments.[25] When word of this impediment to the war effort finally reached London, Westminster politicians approved an act in May 1756 clarifying the responsibilities of all parties involved. While recruiting officers were given the right to accept servants into the ranks, magistrates were authorized to award owners a prorated settlement from funds provided by their provincial assembly.[26] Discontent remained palpable in some locales, however, because only politicians in Williamsburg and Annapolis halfheartedly acquiesced to the new law. Old Dominion legislators limited their financial liability by diverting a portion of an existing military appropriation bill for the reimbursement of Virginians' property rights; Maryland too restricted awards to those whose servants had entered the army during the first eighteen months of the war.[27] In Pennsylvania, the most prolific source of servant-volunteers, assemblymen refused to compensate masters directly and attempted to pass this debt of £2,272 along to the imperial government.[28]

Royal American success during the months of July and August 1756 was astonishing in light of this fractious atmosphere. Yet more than seven hundred men were inducted into the ranks as recruiting parties first began limited operations in Philadelphia's environs before additional detachments were sent north and west of the city where the majority of foreign Protestant colonists resided.[29] Even the German Town press run by nonconformist Christopher Saur did not disparage their mission, reporting that the redcoats appeared to be "tapfere, verständige, bescheiden, ehrbar und im Krieg erfahren"

Table 1. Pennsylvania Servants' Regimental Affiliation

Regiment	Number of Servant-Volunteers	Percentage
62nd	214	51.57
51st	24	5.78
50th	35	8.43
48th	19	4.58
47th	45	10.84
45th	3	0.72
44th	13	3.15
40th	4	0.96
Independent companies	5	1.20
Artillery	1	0.24
Provincials	1	0.24
"Halifax"	7	1.69
Unknown	44	10.60
TOTAL	415	100.00

Source: "Pennsylvania Servants," n.d., LO 3415, HEH.

(courageous, understanding, reasonable, and honorable men with experience in battle). Such a chary endorsement of the corps' operations indicates the tonic effect that the presence of the Royal American Regiment had on local residents. Prior to its arrival, the public had been reluctant to see bound laborers enlist in regiments garrisoned in distant Nova Scotia or along the marchlands of New York where they would provide little immediate protection. However, in view of the pervasive belief that the four battalions were being raised to range the backcountry of Pennsylvania, Maryland, and Virginia, masters were less disgruntled when their workers joined this new formation. As the data in table 1 suggest, this regiment captured the lion's share of the servants despite being the last to begin recruiting.[30]

If internal security measures had improved with the force's appearance, so too did the financial condition of servant owners, who soon benefited from the increased demand for volunteers. Fired by the bidding war between emissaries from eight of the ten regular regiments now on station, the proclamation money paid directly to enlistees, or to their masters, reached the staggering height of £10 local currency (£6 sterling) by September 1756. Although recruiters from the 40th, 45th, and 47th Regiments were not supposed to encroach on Royal American territory while the corps were being formed, orders for their retirement to Nova Scotia were not issued by the Earl of Loudoun until late that year.³¹ Meanwhile these veteran formations, with greater financial resources drawn from their noneffective funds and the additional levy money granted by Westminster at the beginning of the war, were able to outspend the 60th's recruiters, whose own regimental coffers were severely drained by Colonel James Prevost's contingent of European reinforcements still making their way across the Atlantic.³²

Philadelphia's station as the primary western terminus for foreign Protestant wayfarers also provided another rich source of volunteers, the redemptioners. These German-speaking expatriates, overwhelmingly married men with dependents, had contracted with Rotterdam merchants to work for an unspecified American master in exchange for their family's passage to the New World. Sold into servitude after their arrival in Pennsylvania by representatives of their European consignors, such new arrivals frequently joined the rural labor force in communities along the advancing frontier.³³ By 1755, however, demand for redemptioners in Cumberland, York, Northampton, and Berks counties evaporated as homesteads were evacuated following the defeat of Major General Edward Braddock's expeditionary force and the retaliatory American Indian onslaught. Even colonists in more established centers not exposed to immediate attack had grown hesitant to buy the services of a redemptioner because the maintenance of an adult with wards no longer proved cost-effective. Unredeemed passengers, trying to sustain a household in the squalid accommodations provided for them in the capital, joined the Royal Americans because no better employment could be found.³⁴

Backcountry settlers who recognized that the Royal Americans were the best means to preserve their way of life from further French incursions provided another important wellspring of Pennsylvanian recruits. Furious that the Quaker-dominated assembly had been unwilling to come to their aid after the borderlands had erupted in flames, militant Scotch-Irish and German frontiersmen banded together in "associator" companies to protect their communities in 1755. These defensive forces, in some cases outfitted only with pitchforks and axes, were soon replaced by a quasi militia sanctioned by Philadelphia legislators who also voted funds to pay for the construction of several fortifications along the colony's periphery. Still, by the early summer of 1756, these installations had not stymied American Indian war parties nor was the infant Pennsylvania Provincial Regiment yet on a sound footing.[35] With the colony's defenses in such a state of disarray and its political leadership divided over declaring war on overtly hostile tribesmen, the decisive imperial option presented by agents of the 60th attracted young men anxious to drive "the Indians from our frontiers so that our Parents and We may Cultivate our Lands again." Others who had already suffered at the hands of marauders enlisted to avenge the destruction of their homesteads.[36]

Royal American parties received practical support from Thomas Penn's local allies who sent endorsement letters to influential justices of the peace. Lieutenant John Schlosser, a native of the Rhenish Palatinate, discharged his duties in Northampton County under the aegis of two prominent residents, Timothy Horsfield and William Parsons.[37] Following the counsel of these two men, Schlosser had bilingual advertisements stating the regimental conditions of service posted throughout the county. In exchange for four years' service, both English- and German-speaking volunteers were guaranteed bounty money, a salary of fifteen Pennsylvania pence per day with provisions, as well as thorough training in the use of arms and accoutrements provided by the king.[38] The promise of a two-hundred-acre land grant for themselves or their heirs was of special interest to rural residents who had witnessed property values escalate in some regions east of the Susquehanna River during the preceding decades because of increased immigration.[39] Not mentioned in the proclamation, but later asserted by men tried for desertion, was a promise to Pennsylvanian enlistees that they would not be required to march more than one hundred miles beyond their own borders. The combined efforts of magistrates and recruiters had their desired effect: Schlosser was personally credited with garnering fifty-eight men during his stopovers at Easton and Bethlehem. Foreign Protestant officers as a group raised a total of 1,126 colonial recruits during their first two years of operations.[40]

Major John Rutherfurd had not been idle in Philadelphia while volunteers were being sought in the countryside. Assisted by confidants in the capital city, he sensed an opportunity to incorporate en masse all 1,500 troops in the frontier garrisons that were a great drain on the provincial treasury.[41] Through intermediaries, Rutherfurd offered Major James Burd a regular lieutenancy in exchange for permission to enlist the troops under his immediate command. The colonial officer, at first flattered by this overture and the assurance that his

A portrait of Augustine Prevost (1723–86). The Swiss mercenary officer supervised the inaugural recruiting effort among foreign Protestant colonists in 1756. Prevost remained in the British service for the next thirty years, rising to the rank of major general. Courtesy of Sir Christopher Prevost, Rochester, Kent.

men would not be redeployed, apparently would not permit Royal American emissaries into his camp until he received a regular commission signed by the Earl of Loudoun.[42] The commander-in-chief's hectic New York schedule, however, did not permit this affair to be settled to everyone's satisfaction before the French offensive against Oswego in August 1756 ended the brief honeymoon between 60th recruiters and Pennsylvanians.[43]

Oswego's loss immediately derailed efforts to complete the regiment because army headquarters had to concentrate all available regular forces in New York. Seven hundred Royal American recruits were hurriedly marched northward from their Philadelphia concentration point to help forestall the advance of a French army believed to number 10,000 men. This action reminded many civilians of the previous year's episode when the remains of Colonel Thomas Dunbar's redcoats had also decamped for New York, leaving the Middle Atlantic borders "exposed to the fury of the Indians, who have since his flight cut off many hundred people, and are daily perpetrating the most horrid cruelties."[44] New legislative measures, considered sensible now that battalions of the 60th would be deployed at the commander-in-chief's discretion and not remain permanently in the Middle Colonies, were taken to ensure that the Pennsylvanian troops stayed at their posts. The Duke of Cumberland only later insisted that a Royal American detachment remain permanently in the region as a goodwill gesture.[45]

Recruiting Efforts in the South

Montcalm's lightning strike at Oswego further reduced British offensive capacity by devastating the 50th and 51st Regiments of Foot, which had been raised in New England under the commands of Major General William Shirley and Sir William Pepperrell. Just 280 soldiers tending Mohawk River supply routes avoided the fate of being carried into captivity. Now in greater need of regulars to compensate for the loss of these formations, Loudoun solicited governments as far away as Georgia for levies to reinforce the Royal Americans.[46] His pleas for aid to restore the balance of power in the northern operational theater, however, were greeted with indifference by most administrations south of New York. Middle Atlantic assemblymen begged off, claiming that their governments had already provided enough redcoat recruits even as legislators in the Lower South looked to their own defenses.[47] Politicians in Maryland and Virginia were the only ones roused to action; they agreed to provide three hundred and five hundred men, respectively, for the corps.[48]

Lord Baltimore's deputy, Horatio Sharpe, had never been an avid supporter of the metropolitan initiative to place large numbers of colonists under the supervision of foreign Protestant mercenaries.

Already a field officer with aspirations of higher rank, he believed that the 60th's creation had precluded him from a proprietary command similar to that enjoyed by William Shirley of Massachusetts Bay.[49] Piqued by the loss of this consequential military appointment, he initially offered only token assistance to the regiment's first lone recruiting party: a proclamation urging all officials to cooperate in the discharge of their duties. The French victory in northwestern New York, however, spurred Sharpe to greater efforts. The governor immediately announced that he would pay £10, the going rate for local enlistees, to any Marylander willing to enter the Royal Americans.[50] This personal initiative was financed through Loudoun's contingency funds with the expectations that the bounty money would eventually be repaid by the various colonies. Nevertheless, by the end of September, only eighty men had been engaged, leaving the governor to contemplate militia conscription should the shortfall continue.[51]

Precedent was on Lieutenant Governor Horatio Sharpe's side when he sought assembly support for the imperial war effort. Annapolis legislators, who had previously sent three hundred troops to the Canadian expeditionary force raised during King George's War, again proved willing to dispatch the same number of reinforcements to New York. Accordingly, a bill appropriating £5,000 (£3,030 sterling) to pay for the recruitment of three hundred Royal Americans was passed during the fall 1756 session. This political coup, though, did not translate as easily into the Maryland countryside where fewer than 150 men had by then volunteered for service. Many prospective soldiers proved to be opportunists, taking their £10 enlistment bounty and then promptly deserting. Another eighteen months would pass before the provincial levy was fully completed.[52]

Virginia also complied with the official request for recruits. However, unlike Maryland's leaders, who had been dragged into the conflict because of the colony's territorial proximity to Fort Duquesne, members of the Old Dominion's ruling elite had spearheaded the advance into the Ohio Country and providentially raised a provincial corps for Virginia's defense in 1754. It was from this source that some of the Royal Americans' earliest Virginian volunteers were drawn as deserters made their way to enroll with line officers in Pennsylvania because of better pay and provisions. This trickle of provincial troops steadily increased through the summer, fattening the 60th's muster rolls at the Virginia Regiment's expense.[53]

Lieutenant Governor Robert Dinwiddie's prompt response to Loudoun's appeal can be seen as self-serving since the earl was the Crown's most recent appointee to the governorship of Virginia. This opportunity allowed Loudoun's deputy to demonstrate his own bona fides by personally offering a £3 (£2.6s. sterling) reward for every man who would sign a two-year engagement with the Royal Americans even before the Williamsburg assembly had a chance to deliberate about the best course of action. Assurances were also given that all recruits would be clothed and provisioned at provincial expense until they were taken into the regular forces.[54] When the House of Burgesses finally met on 20 September 1756, Dinwiddie sought their backing to finance the recruitment of 60th volunteers, provide a compensation package for servant owners, and empower him to conscript if enlistments were inadequate.[55]

Two of the three elements contained in this ambitious legislation received the assembly's assent. The burgesses voted £8,000 (£6,228 sterling) to raise five hundred men for the colonial defense force and indemnify the proprietors of servants who joined the colors of Loudoun's regiment. With public funds now in place to pay for the volunteers, Dinwiddie expeditiously assembled eighty men sent him by agents working in various parts of the colony.[56] The one cohort attracted by the province's modest financial remuneration and offer of clothing were newly arrived convicts awaiting sale. They apparently chose military service to avoid the full force of their sentences, since voluntary enlistment was an accepted form of recompense for past transgressions. Unfortunately for the Royal American Regiment, without the immediate oversight of regular officers to guide the selection process, many of the 220 volunteers entertained by provincial recruiters did not meet the army's minimum physical standards; fifty-five members of this band had to be rejected as unfit for combat operations when they arrived in New York in early 1757.[57]

The Old Dominion was never able to provide its full troop levy after delivering its initial complement of recruits to New York. By then, the Royal American's Captain Joseph Prince had arrived in Virginia to oversee the enlistment campaign, relieving the lieutenant governor of this responsibility. The company commander was able to drum up only sixty more volunteers, however, as the number of inhabitants willing to enlist steadily declined over the next few months. Moreover, since the Virginia Regiment itself was 400 troops below its established level, Dinwiddie could not persuade legislators to draft the remaining 220 men for the regulars because earlier conscription measures had sparked riots in the colony. The last 60th party left Williamsburg at the end of April without any additional enlistees to show for its efforts.[58]

The failure of Chesapeake administrators to provide timely reinforcements foreshadowed similar disappointments in North Carolina, South Carolina, and Georgia. Even though none of these Lower South legislatures were willing to comply with headquarters' request for troops, the Earl of Loudoun remained optimistic that several hundred volunteers would appear prior to the campaigning season of 1757. The source of these sanguine reports was Reverend Johann Gasser, formerly a Swiss military chaplain, who had sought pastoral employment in North America after the War of the Austrian Succession. In January 1756, on a European fund-raising drive to aid the parishioners of his congregations on the Upper and Lower Santee Forks, Gasser had been expelled from Interlaken, Switzerland, because of unauthorized attempts to secure colonists for his South Carolina charge. The fugitive cleric was then introduced to James Prevost while the colonel was engaging staff for his foreign Protestant corps in the Low Countries. A bargain was quickly struck: Gasser promised to raise six hundred troops from among his nine-thousand-member flock in return for a battalion chaplaincy and free passage back to America.[59]

Gasser disembarked from the *Harriot* packet at New York along with the first wave of foreign Protestant officers in the spring of 1756 but did not begin his recruiting effort until October. Despite great expectations, the clergyman eventually reached Charles Town with little money left and no men to show for his troubles. Further forays into the backcountry produced a total of only four volunteers because few indentured servants inhabited the region and the wage disparity in favor of free labor made regular military service attractive only to those in the most straitened circumstances.[60] As Lieutenant Colonel Henry Bouquet later observed: "There are men enough Scattered in the back Part of the two Carolinas, but they find Such encouragement and high Wages for their labour, that they despise our Pay, and those who inlist, being the worst sort, desert very Soon." The Reformed pastor's limited influence over the masses was also countervailed by local justices, who attempted to dissuade recruits at their attestations from participating in the struggle against New France. Magistrates, anxious about the reliability of their Cherokee allies and with vivid memories of the Stono Rebellion still fresh in their minds, did not want to lose the services of white male inhabitants whose presence served as a bulwark against invasion or insurrection. Gasser's persuasive powers were of little effect in communities where just one in eight eligible white males ever bore arms in this conflict. The cleric's failure to deliver the promised six hundred soldiers resulted in his removal from the battalion chaplaincy, and in this appointment being given to Michael Schlatter instead.[61]

Southern aversion to regular military service was also evident among the 155 North Carolina independents on duty with the British army in New York. This detachment, commanded by Major Edward Brice Dobbs, the governor's son, was expected to form the nucleus of Wilmington's levy for the Royal American Regiment after Oswego's fall since legislators refused to pay for their expeditionary force's return trip after its 10 November 1756 disbandment.[62] Despite Governor Dobbs's authorization to draft all his troops into the 60th Foot, British authorities were reluctant to conscript those who refused to enlist since "that measure would look Violent, and deter all Provincial Troops from Joining the Regular Troops." Rather, the Earl of Loudoun decided to return any who wanted to go home at metropolitan expense with the expectation that they might eventually take the king's shilling as some of their comrades had already done upon demobilization.[63]

Foreign Protestant Reinforcements from Europe

The last significant number of Royal American volunteers began arriving at New York in the late summer of 1756 thanks to the efforts of Colonel James Prevost, who had retained the services of 778 men during an extended recruiting campaign in the Holy Roman Empire. Aware that the War Office was in dire need of trained personnel to strengthen Britain's overseas defenses, he had suggested to metropolitan officials that the 60th Regiment be formed around a resolute core of European soldiers. Such veterans would expedite the corps' deployment by providing an immediate source of proficient instructors for the raw recruits and would furnish a ready force of trained men qualified to face enemy regulars if need be. No one opposed the idea of procuring between four hundred and five hundred mercenaries from Rotterdam at £3 per man because the United Kingdom's home defenses had just been bolstered by thousands of Hessian and Hanoverian troops to counter any French invasion. Parliament's agreement to pay a £285,000 subsidy for these German auxiliaries made the colonel's modest initial demands on the treasury for £1,500 pale in comparison. The aversion of the Dutch to the presence of British agents in their territories, however, stymied this initial drive for veterans from the United Provinces.[64]

Audaciously, Prevost hatched a more ambitious procurement scheme encompassing Switzerland and the western Hapsburg domains where a great "nursery for soldiers to the whole world" had flourished for generations. Relying on the presence of some foreign Protestant colleagues who had still not joined him in England, the colonel notified them to collect surreptitiously as many candidates for American service as they could secure while he finalized all the necessary plans with the War Office.[65] The Genevan, not wanting any financial profits jeopardized by explicit instructions, requested authorization to enlist as many suitable men as he could engage excepting those who had served in the French army or were under the age of eighteen. He likewise counseled that the normal height and age requirements for British recruits be waived for the one hundred NCOs necessary to command the men as well as the unspecified number of musicians who would form the regimental band. Finally, the mercenary advised that the proposed price of £12 per man to pay for the costs of enlisting and transporting the desired veterans from as far away as the upper reaches of the *Hochrhein* excluded consideration for any number of women and children whom he would "be indispensably Obliged to take for the Success of this affair and the acquisition of proper men."[66]

Lord Barrington, the secretary at war, was not about to give this Swiss entrepreneur free rein in Europe at British taxpayers' expense. After careful deliberation with the Earl of Loudoun and Major General Robert Napier, the Duke of Cumberland's military secretary, an amended contract limiting the scope of the enterprise was signed on 23 April 1756. While agreeing to the price of £12 per man, which was to be deducted from the Royal American Regiment's recruiting account and not charged to the public purse as an extra expense, Barrington stipulated that only four hundred men be taken into service with allowances made for another sixty NCOs to shepherd them across the ocean. Prevost was also required to have his musters certified by local magistrates at the embarkation port of Stade, and all volunteers were to be attested before New York justices as a preventive measure against fraudulent accounts or substandard recruits.[67]

Foreign Protestant agents had already begun their covert duties in Hapsburg territories while London negotiations dragged on through April 1756. Although the Holy Roman Empire's regional federations retained modest defensive establishments for their own use, unlicensed recruiting legations from abroad could face rigorous legal sanctions, such as forfeiture of their enlistees to the accredited representatives of other armed forces, heavy fines, imprisonment, and even death.[68] Royal American officers labored in the shadows for more than a month before James Prevost finalized his contract with the War Office and set this affair on a proper footing. Until that time, the colonel's men had avoided charges of *plagiat* (man-stealing) by invoking the name of the Hanoverian ruler, George Augustus (George II), who, as one of the Holy Roman Empire's nine electors, had a right to solicit troops in any jurisdiction, and only incidentally wore the British crown.[69]

Prevost's associates divided the Rhine basin into three large operational zones. Already masters of their craft, Baron Herbert von Munster took up station in what is now the modern state of Nordrhein-Westfalen, Captain Rudolph Fesch established his headquarters in Frankfurt am Main, and Captain John Rudolph Fesch made his way northward out of Basel. The only surviving disembarkation return of 164 recruits suggests just how tolerant Reich officials were of the canvassers' activities. Seventy-three men (44.5 percent of the total) were enlisted prior to 23 April 1756 when the War Office finally endorsed Colonel Prevost's proposal and dispatched the proper requisitional letters to respective capitals.[70] Despite the official protection now afforded them, the city of Frankfurt am Main provided volunteers with the securest way station before they began their long overland march to Hamburg. Britain's ambassador at The Hague, Sir Joseph Yorke, also suggested a helpful ruse should any of the recruiting parties run afoul of unsympathetic authorities. Since the sight of New World migrants was common along the principal waterways, he proposed that all soldiers and their families travel in the guise of planters heading for Pennsylvania, with certificates signed by Thomas Penn to legitimate the charade.[71]

Regional diversity distinguished this military migration from prior civilian outflows that had emanated principally from five modern regions adjacent to the Rhine River: Alsace, Baden-Württemberg, Hessen, Rheinland-Pfalz, and Switzerland. War Office returns indicate that only 54 percent sprang from these seedbeds of the earlier German diaspora. The remainder came from Austria, Bayern, Brandenburg, Niedersachsen, Nordrhein-Westfalen, Sachsen, and Thüringen as well as points beyond.[72]

Uprooted from their natal communities by previous army service, these unemployed veterans or deserters lived a transient existence in larger cities that recruiters made priority ports of call. British enlistment terms appeared most generous to this societal element. A redcoat's salary of fifteen kreuzer a day far exceeded that offered by Austrian, Prussian, or Danish competitors; substantial food allowances were provided gratis by the royal commissary; and a maximum seven-year commitment to the colors was less onerous than indefinite or life service demanded by other European monarchs. Metropolitan administrators soon relaxed their initial quota and assented to the engagement of 778 Royal American reinforcements because the spectacular success of this campaign secured more enlistees than expected.[73]

Not all of the volunteers proved to be trained infantrymen. Hunger and hard times also favored the Continental recruiting effort. Among those who enrolled in the British forces were a number of men from the Oberharz region of Niedersachsen left destitute by the closure of Clausthal's silver mines. Enlistment was the means to a better life in North America, where steady employment would be supplemented by provincial land grants after the war.[74] Rhineland detachments too roused the interest of other civilians displaced by demographic pressures and partible inheritance practices. The added benefit of free, provisioned transportation to the New World extended opportunities for family reunification to those whose relatives had already relocated to the colonies. Palatinate agents credited their success to the fact that they encountered numerous people who had "un nombre de leurs Compatriotes en Amerique, et font tres

Table 2. Birthplaces of European Volunteers Recruited on the Continent in 1756

	Number of Soldiers	Percentage
Alsace*	3	1.83
Austria	4	2.44
Baden-Württemberg*	11	6.71
Bayern	13	7.93
Brandenburg	2	1.22
Hessen (North)	28	17.07
Hessen (South)*	24	14.61
Niedersachsen	19	11.59
Nordrhein-Westfalen	4	2.44
Poland	1	0.61
Rheinland-Pfalz (North)	4	2.44
Rheinland-Pfalz (South)*	8	4.88
Sachsen	11	6.71
Scotland	2	1.22
Switzerland*	10	6.10
Thüringen	1	0.61
Unknown	19	11.59
TOTAL	164	100.00

Source: Munster's List, 27 August 1756, LO 1607, HEH.
*One of five regions that together constituted the German-speaking territories south of the Rhine-Main axis.

disposés à les y aller joindre" (a number of their fellow countrymen in America and are very disposed to join them there).[75]

Colonel Prevost realized from the outset of his mission that the exclusion of volunteers with families would jeopardize its success. While the soldiers' marital status is not recorded on the surviving disembarkation return, contemporary evidence suggests that wives and children were certainly present aboard the troopships.[76] Juvenile dependents could be transported either through exploiting a contract loophole that sanctioned the acquisition of twenty bandsmen or by employing infantrymen's sons in other military capacities. The ferment in New York created by the arrival of "some little creaturs for drumrs" suggests that this was the contrivance used by European recruiting officers to move some noncombatants across the Atlantic at government expense.[77]

Enemy privateering represented a signal threat to the safe passage of troops during wartime. The initial leg of the voyage from Stade to the Orkneys, where all four transports cleared customs in compliance with the Navigation Acts, proved uneventful for three of the vessels as did their remaining cruise to the New World. The ill-starred passengers aboard a snow called the *Industry*, however, began a very circuitous journey across the Atlantic that required a full eighteen months to complete.[78] Once clear of the port of Stromness, the ship's captain bore away from the rest of the flotilla with plans to secure some prizes. The hunter instead became the hunted and promptly fell prey to French warships on 28 August 1756. Resisting overtures to join Louis XV's army, these captured servicemen received subsistence from the Guinand merchant house during a lengthy internment until a cartel agreement was signed allowing their return to England. The well-traveled Continental volunteers finally joined the third and fourth battalions soon after their belated 11 December 1757 arrival in New York.[79]

The unforgiving maritime weather also played havoc with the last wartime contingent of foreign Protestant officers and eighty recruits who sailed in a convoy from Cork in early November 1756. A heavy storm dispersed the fleet mid passage, severely damaging one transport, the *Europa*, which subsequently struck its colors when approached by a French corsair.[80] Five mercenaries and more than fifty other redcoats surrendered themselves into enemy custody rather than remain with the listing merchantman. Abandoning their comrades to an unknown fate, Prevost's retainers spent several months in Poitiers before being exchanged. Captain George Adam Gmelin, a more resolute soul, commanded the remaining British regulars who braved the high seas for another month before reaching the safety of the Delaware River.[81]

Troop losses of this sort were offset by the recruitment of select prisoners taken from the enemy in increasing numbers during the latter half of the Seven Years' War.[82] Following the policy established in May 1756, when German-speaking recruits were solicited from detainees held by the Admiralty at Portsmouth, the 60th Foot again began accepting volunteers from the French camp after Louisbourg's capture in the summer of 1758. Second and third battalion officers made successful overtures to members of the Volontaires Etranger (Foreign Volunteers) who had formed part of that garrison. More than a hundred malnourished and ill-treated soldiers joined the ranks on condition that they be discharged after three years of service.[83] These individuals had much in common with their countrymen in uniform for they too had been recruited in Hapsburg lands during the summer of 1756 by a Swiss mercenary by the name of Fischer, and chose military service as their ticket to the New World. Enlistment with the Royal Americans allowed these newcomers to evade repatriation to Europe with the rest of the vanquished.[84]

Irish Drafts and New England Volunteers, 1757

The final major source of Royal American manpower came to the regiment via a military convention known as drafting, whereby troops stationed outside a major operational theater were used to bolster weaker combat units. Traditionally, source regiments were supposed to parade their men in files when a number would be randomly chosen for transfer, with recipient corps paying a £5 reimbursement fee for each infantryman taken.[85] Theory and practice, however, never quite meshed as Irish Establishment officers used this opportunity to dispose of all their undesirable personnel. Six hundred of these castoffs described as "Viellards, d'Infirmes, d'Yvrognes et de Voleurs" (elderly, infirm, drunkards, and thieves) sailed from Cork in the late fall of 1756 for distribution within the 60th's four battalions during the spring of 1757.[86] Simultaneously, another dubious legacy appeared from the disbanded New England battalions formerly commanded by Governor William Shirley and Sir William Pepperrell. Since the Royal Americans remained in dire need of NCOs, nineteen sergeants, twenty-four corporals, and nine drummers from the reduced corps were turned over to them at Boston; custody of 140 incarcerated New England deserters was likewise transferred at this time. All consented to serve with the 60th Foot only until 1758 when their original three-year engagements expired.[87]

This single New England trawl complemented Royal American enlistments already begun some months before. In contrast to the Carolinas, however, where there was little enthusiasm for the war against New France, 60th recruiters worked among a supportive populace that had already sent many of their sons to the front.[88] Still, Captain Harry Charteris wisely followed the advice of local officials in his hunt for volunteers primarily sought among the non-Puritan stock, such as transient West Countrymen from the Newfoundland fisheries, itinerant laborers, or former English servants. A total of 179 new names were thereby added to muster rolls before the launch of summer operations.[89]

The inclusion of Royal American battalions with the 1757 Halifax expeditionary force terminated the regiment's full press for men even though the corps remained almost seven hundred troops short of its established strength. Why had canvassers been unable to attract a full complement to the colors? One major problem was institutional since the 60th Foot simply did not have enough capable NCOs to attend the large number of recruiting parties and train hundreds of inexperienced volunteers at the same time.[90] A second issue was the army's quieting of civilian concerns about servant enlistments by instructing officers to entertain only those whose contracts were about to expire and which magistrates appraised at £3 or less. This policy limited intakes because prior enlistees typically had at least two years of outstanding service with a restitution value higher than the cap.[91] Finally, market forces disadvantaged the king's men who were financially unable to compete with local governments determined to raise their own levies for home service. New Jersey, for example, gave its volunteers a £12 enlistment bonus (£7.4s. sterling) plus a free uniform worth £8 (£5 sterling) for each yearly campaign. By contrast, the regulars' maximum offer of three pistoles (£2.11s. sterling) for a three-year engagement appeared niggardly as did their much lower wages, which often amounted to only half that given provincial soldiers.[92]

Sustaining Manpower Levels, 1757 and Beyond

Colonel John Stanwix accepted responsibility for rectifying the troop deficit when he remained behind at Carlisle, Pennsylvania, to show the flag "in the best Recruiting Quarters" that the colonies had to offer. Posted on the exposed frontier, he adopted a sagacious approach to win popular support for his regiment, and thereby increase admissions. Recognizing the importance of local connections, Stanwix accepted the sons of prominent backcountry families as gentlemen volunteers, a type of officer cadet who carried arms while awaiting promotion to ensign, before employing them on the recruiting service during the summer. Two of these men, William Clapham and John Philip Dehass, later held commissions in the Pennsylvania Regiment and remained important liaisons.[93] Next, the field officer paid

Table 3. Ethnic Composition of the Royal American Regiment Summer, 1757

Nationality	Effective Rank and File	Percentage[a] of Force	Percentage of Pennsylvania's Population, 1790
English	699	24.35	25.8
Scottish	168	5.85	7.6
Irish (including Scotch-Irish)	680	23.69	23
American	279	9.72	NA
Foreign Protestant	1,045[b]	36.40	38
TOTAL	2,871	100.00	

Sources: LO 6639, HEH; LO 1345, HEH; LO 6616, HEH; LO 4068, HEH; Thomas L. Purvis, "The European Ancestry of the United States Population, 1790," *WMQ* 3d ser., 41 (1984): 98.
[a] Based on the returns of 35 out of 40 companies.
[b] Not included among the effectives are 200 Foreign Protestants held captive in France.

influential provincial officers to procure men for the Royal Americans. Ambitious men like Captain Christian Busse also desired a regular commission and discharged their duties in hopes of military advancement. Such collaborative efforts involving community leaders resulted in the acquisition of 159 new charges before year's end.[94]

Although Whitehall's goal of raising 4,000 troops for overseas defense had not yet been completely realized, a 1757 partial enumeration of battalion personnel indicates how successful regimental recruiters had been in attracting men from both sides of the Atlantic. Two important features stand out. First, since a soldier's birthplace may not be the same as his induction point, the preponderance of European-born men is indicative of the high immigrant tide that the Middle Colonies had seen prior to the war. Indeed, the evidence suggests that the largest single British unit in the New World closely mirrored Pennsylvania's own distinctive ethnic mélange and was as "Atlantic" in character as the colony itself.

Second, notwithstanding the absence of information about the expanding complement of Germans serving in Colonel John Stanwix's detachment, this element already composed a significant portion of the regiment's strength. When the European veterans are factored into this equation, these aliens constituted more than a complete battalion of active-duty personnel, vindicating the imperial government's decision to employ Continental officers. Foreign Protestant names are almost negligible on the muster rolls of other line regiments serving in the New World.[95]

The 60th Foot reached its peak strength of 3,828 soldiers just prior to the campaigns against Louisbourg and Ticonderoga in 1758. In addition to continuous troop drafts, a growing number of trained men came to the battalions from the provincial forces raised by various colonial legislatures. This trend was of vital importance during the latter half of the war as New England and Virginia enlistees began demanding their discharges upon the completion of short engagements with the Royal Americans.[96] The earliest significant complement of provincials fell to the corps when Maryland politicians refused to continue funding the colony's independent companies in the late fall of 1757. Colonel Stanwix's battalion subsequently inherited the remains when recruiters appeared in their midst and promised the men more equitable treatment than they had received from provincial authorities at Annapolis.[97]

Representatives of the 60th operated effectively among decommissioned forces from the Middle Colonies because strong alliances had already been established with key provincial leaders. The Earl of Loudoun, with a great deal of foresight, had granted Royal American sinecures to influential colonial officers as a reward for past service, and to ensure their support in future endeavors. Two men in particular, Colonel Beamsley Glazier from New York and Colonel John Parker of the Jersey Blues, both of whom held dual commissions in regular and provincial corps alike, acted as key intermediaries. Granted continuous leaves of absence to continue managing colonial units, they remained sympathetic to their regular regiment's needs.[98] Benefactors in the Pennsylvania Regiment came from a different source: German-speaking sergeants and gentlemen volunteers attached to James Prevost's entourage who had entered the pay of the Philadelphia government rather than await a regular commission.[99] Strong patronage ties still existed within this mercenary fraternity that benefited the 60th when some colonial units were disbanded at the close of summer campaigns. Their influence was sought by battalion canvassers at demobilization points, which were considered "the most Advantagious posts for catching the Provincials when their money is gone."[100] It was probably through this means that most Africans joined the ranks. Contemporaries noted a marked black presence among auxiliary forces that funneled men like Henry Wedge, described as a "Negro" on one Royal American company return, into the line regiments.[101]

Montreal's 1760 surrender was timely for metropolitan authorities who were strained to keep their transatlantic forces at established strengths. Royal American numbers were consequently pared down from 4,000 to 2,800 men, roughly coinciding with its complement of active-duty personnel.[102] The fall of New France, however, precipitated another manpower crisis because many of those who had enlisted in 1756 had agreed to serve for four years or the duration of the conflict. Naturally, large numbers began seeking their discharges despite the war's shift into the Caribbean and the need for strong garrisons to show the flag throughout what had been New France. Headquarters, presaging modern "stop-loss" initiatives, refused to countenance many releases at this time since the army could not afford to lose the services of able-bodied veterans. Extended tours of duty were made more acceptable by financial bonuses of £3.10s. while others who reenlisted for life were each given £5.[103] Commanders placated those who had never been given home leave by assigning them to recruiting details stationed near family and friends. With a substantial number of redcoats returned to the fold, all four battalions were able to field a combined total of 2,647 soldiers in the spring of 1761.[104]

Obtaining a legal discharge from the Royal Americans in the waning days of the war was also complicated by the fact that all original regimental records, vouchers, and supporting paperwork were being vetted at New York before shipment to London for final clearance by the War Office.[105] If soldiers had not kept personal copies of attestation papers with their enlistment terms, then immediate superiors were probably unaware of the specifics because neither regimental ledgers nor induction officers were readily available for consultation.[106] Metropolitan officials did not finally approve of all the accounts until late 1762, freeing up the original documents for return to their proper custodians. Failure to discharge men in a timely manner was not just the fault of arbitrary commanders but also the consequence of eighteenth-century bureaucracy working against those who could not furnish proper credentials.[107]

Lieutenant General Jeffery Amherst realized that it was impractical to keep legions of infantrymen in the ranks despite Spain's impending entry into the conflict.[108] Without the possibility of more British troop transfusions to keep the New World garrisons strong, the commander-in-chief asked colonial administrations to solicit regular volunteers while they filled local muster rolls in the spring of 1762. Money and short service were the incentives for those willing to volunteer for the duration of the war; enlistees received an additional £5 York currency (£2.12s.) when they transferred from provincial corps into the line.[109] Only Pennsylvania and Maryland refused to support this bilateral project which eventually garnered an additional 523 redcoats. Of these soldiers, 185 were eventually absorbed by occupation forces in New France, where half of the Royal American battalions were then stationed.[110]

These final wartime recruits had little time to perfect martial skills after an armistice was signed on 10 February 1763, permitting their return home. The two senior corps, however, were not disbanded, but became part of the new fifteen-battalion-strong American Establishment.[111] Major General James Murray's detachment at Quebec found it relatively easy to secure its peacetime complement of 423 men from among careerists already in the ranks or those who did not want to be repatriated to the United Kingdom with their regiments.[112] The first battalion had a much more difficult time maintaining its strength because of long deployment throughout the Great Lakes watershed, severe losses experienced during Pontiac's revolt, and the pandemic desertion of men whose releases were long past due.[113]

Metropolitan authorities had learned by war's end that few colonists were willing to serve the colors a lifetime as most redcoats were required to do. Officials therefore decided that regiments overseas should fill their muster rolls in the British Isles.[114] Royal American recruiting efforts in the United Kingdom, however, produced mixed results between 1765 and 1766. Enlistment in the 60th was never popular in Britain because the corps had borne the brunt of the recent Native insurrection and young men were averse to long exile along the colonial frontier. Most recruits favored duty in regiments stationed elsewhere, preferring to be "hanged in England than scalped in America" as some expressed their dislike of military service in the New World.[115]

The Holy Roman Empire again provided the largest single complement of volunteers for the Royal Americans after recruiting efforts

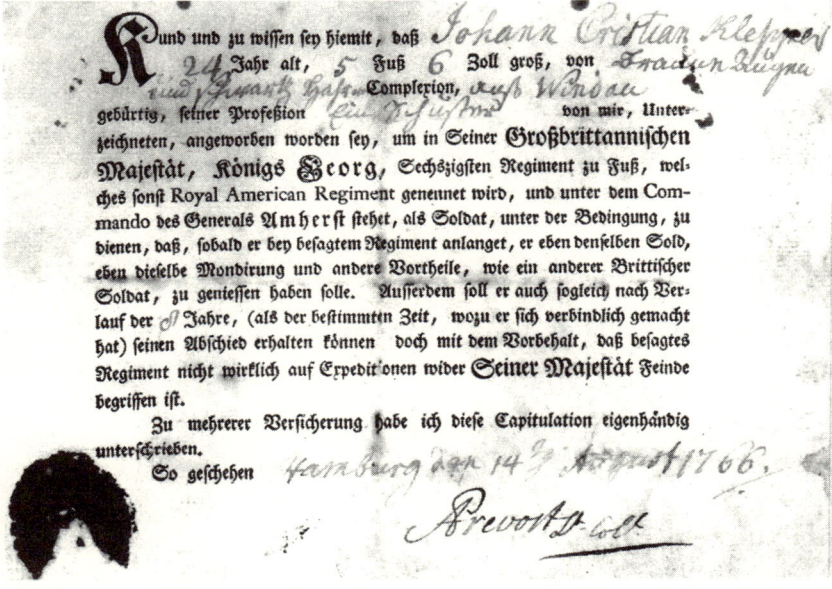

An enlistment certificate printed in German and issued to Johann Cristian Klepper at Hamburg on 14 August 1766. The document is signed by Lieutenant Colonel Augustine Prevost, who organized the recruitment of 191 Royal American volunteers on the Continent in 1766. Courtesy of the Fort Pitt Museum, Pennsylvania Historical and Museum Commission, 2008. (FP2003.6.1)

faltered in Britain during the 1760s. Nevertheless, the spectacular results of an earlier decade could not be replicated because the dynamics of foreign Protestant migration had changed after the Seven Years' War with fewer families still ready to chance an ocean passage.[116] Lieutenant Colonel Augustine Prevost's task was also complicated by the fact that enlistment terms were far less generous in peacetime than they had been in 1756 when the United Kingdom was preparing for war. Instead of short indentures of no more than seven years, free provisions, and a land grant, recruits were required to serve up to fourteen years and pay for some of their rations; nor were they offered any property upon discharge. Moreover, a final proviso stated that volunteers could not expect a release if their enlistments expired while "aus Expeditionen wider Seiner Majestat Feinde" (on expeditions against His Majesty's enemies). Even these onerous demands did not deter 191 men from embarking aboard the lone troopship carrying reinforcements from Hamburg to New York in the late fall of

1766. They were the last Europeans to join the regiment before its redeployment to the West Indies six years later.[117]

The story of Whitehall's transatlantic quest for 60th volunteers confirms the eighteenth-century maxim that armies were "a medley of all characters." Recruits from a broad range of ethnic and social backgrounds—frontiersmen, indentured servants, redemptioners, European mercenaries, and prisoners of war—readily signed short-service pacts with regimental agents. While infantrymen's wages were not always comparable to those paid civilians, government remuneration did proffer socioeconomic advantage in some respects: bound laborers and seasonal workers received a steady income; would-be emigrants obtained free passage to the New World; homesteaders acquired rights to vacant Crown land; soldiers of fortune drew rations at no cost to themselves; and enemy captives obtained liberty to remain in North America. Enlistment could even provide psychological solace that assuaged the guilt of transported felons, offered hope to those who wanted to protect their family interests from enemy attack, or a catharsis for traumatized settlers who desired revenge. For many, military duty offered amelioration from adverse circumstances.

The acquisition of 2,871 soldiers during the first year of operations, though, could not hide systemic problems plaguing initial recruiting efforts. Royal American canvassers did not always have the financial resources to compete against other regular or colonial units in an open labor market. Senior regiments had deep enough pockets to meet escalating bounty rates while local forces might offer more levy money and higher wages, but for only a single campaign. Lack of qualified NCOs also compromised early manpower drives because such vital personnel could not recruit and train soldiers at the same time. Chesapeake levies along with drafts from the Irish Establishment helped offset shortfalls temporarily and boosted numbers to a high of 3,828 troops by 1758. Thereafter, disbanded provincial units provided a steady pool of veterans until combat operations ended on the mainland. Recruiting efforts consequently shifted to Europe with mixed success for Britons disliked the idea of spending their lives in overseas battalions and only a limited number of Continental volunteers proved willing to take the king's shilling.

Britain's resolve to deploy the Royal American Regiment in its colonies proved to be a qualified success for, as we shall see in the next chapter, the battalions performed soundly during the latter half of the Seven Years' War. Although the corps never reached its authorized strength, its presence was of great strategic value with men from many regions, especially the Middle Colonies, serving under its colors. Inclusion of foreign Protestant officers and men certainly proved advantageous to recruiting efforts among key immigrant groups, allowing the 60th Foot to mirror the ethnic diversity of Pennsylvania's own heterogeneous population. The "Royal American" designation was thus no misnomer, for its ranks contained a broad cross-section of those who had relocated to the New World.

3

"CANADA BELONGS TO THE KING"

The Royal American Regiment at War

The convergence of three separate British armies at Montreal on 8 September 1760 brought an impressive end to a colonial war that had begun badly for the redcoats. French forces finally surrendered once their commanders realized that all escape routes were blocked by the 16,000 men led by Major General Jeffery Amherst. Royal American detachments from all save the first battalion participated in this checkmate operation, which was capped by the occupation of the fallen city and the recovery of some tattered regimental colors taken after the 1756 siege of Oswego. Honor had finally been restored to British arms since casualties were light, no reprisals were taken against the vanquished enemy, and Louis XV's regulars agreed not to serve again until after a peace treaty had been signed in Europe. Best of all for the Crown's interests, though, as Amherst confided to a friend, his summer crusade had secured a valuable bargaining chip for future diplomatic negotiations now that "Canada belongs to the King."[1]

Less than a decade after these momentous events, perceptions about the Royal American Regiment's contribution to British victory were shaped by the publication of Reverend William Smith's book *An Historical Account of Bouquet's Expedition against the*

Ohio Indians in 1764. This multi-edition work, containing in part an essay about Colonel Henry Bouquet's use of light troops against Indian braves, inexorably linked the 60th Foot's achievements to the guerrilla-style warfare of the frontiers.[2] Regrettably this narrow focus obscured the truth about the regiment's checkered combat record and how its performance in numerous conventional operations was compromised by political interference, erratic training schedules, unfavorable service conditions, a dearth of qualified instructors, and high casualty rates. Far from being an elite force in the vanguard of army reform, 60th battalions were often on the wrong side of the military learning curve as Georgian land forces gradually adapted to the demands of New World warfare.[3]

LEARNING THE ART OF WAR, 1756–1757

The gunpowder revolution that swept through Europe between the sixteenth and eighteenth centuries fundamentally changed the nature of Western warfare as the systematic fire of troops equipped with bayonet-tipped flintlocks came to dominate the battlefield. Britain's participation in the War of the Spanish Succession and the War of the Austrian Succession wedded her redcoats to the firelock, which required infantrymen to develop the same instant reflexes needed to load, fire, and advance or retire according to the words of command.[4] Such disciplined performance, acquired after more than two years of training, allowed smaller armies to compete against more powerful opponents either upon the field of Mars or in complex siege operations around imposing city defenses. Bastioned walls soon even ringed strategic New World locales and were a component of the Columbian Exchange process which, in part, transplanted European civilization in other parts of the globe. By the Age of Reason, then, war in the Americas, replete with regular troops, was not an amateur pursuit so long as the military-fiscal states were able to absorb the high costs of maintaining permanent forces and installations overseas.[5]

Although there was no standardized training syllabus shared by Continental armies, all regular troops followed the same general regimen, which first required progressive mastery of the manual exercise, the evolutions, and the platoon exercise. Volunteers, with firelock in hand, initially weathered "the most disagreeable days of a soldier" as they slowly assimilated the manual exercise: a drill enabling them to move their 12.4-pound "Brown Bess" muskets from the ground to their shoulders and then about their person with or without bayonets attached.[6] Next, recruits learned to perform elementary actions in concert with others. Proficiency in these simple evolutions allowed a body of troops to turn in any direction at the halt and open or close ranks when ordered. Finally, novices were taught how to load and fire their weapons through the twenty-four-motion platoon exercise. Constant practice etched these fundamental infantry skills into a soldier's psyche during the rest of his service career.[7]

Instruction about responsibilities within the grand-division, a regiment's essential tactical unit, was the focal point of the second level in the training pyramid. Unlike prior exercises, where only an NCO, or veteran, and a few recruits were required, this middle tier obliged the concentration of about a hundred men so that they could practice deploying together as on the battlefield. Such precise maneuvers were viewed as "the most important point in all the military art" because each of a battalion's four grand-divisions comprised a potential pawn on their commanding officer's chessboard. Troops, therefore, had to know their place in various configurations so that exploitable gaps did not appear in their lines or columns during combat.[8]

More personnel were needed to constitute the battalion's different fire units, which enabled the redcoats to direct sustained volleys at their enemies. Building on individual musketry skills mastered through the basic platoon exercise, teams of infantrymen in their third stage of development were taught how to load, present, and discharge their weapons in a sequential manner. These massed fusillades produced a hail of controlled fire that was lethal up to a distance of two hundred yards. Realistic drill sessions could occur, however, only when sufficient officers were present to direct the troops in the execution of their duties. Lesser detachments could practice the manual exercise, evolutions, and the platoon exercise under the guidance of a subaltern or an NCO, but several companies had to parade together for these more choreographed efforts.[9]

George II's army—unlike its Austrian, French, or Prussian counterparts—did not benefit from annual training camps where regulars participated in realistic war games.[10] Only with the outbreak of hostilities did British soldiers assemble in significant quantities for such advanced training to take place. Live shooting with powder and ball, deployment of the two battalion guns, forming squares to repel cavalry, brigade exercises—maneuvers of at least three full regiments under a general's command—mock battles, and siege craft then filled redcoats' waking hours.[11] Practical knowledge about the latter activity was essential because European campaigns inevitably involved the attack or defense of fortified places. Servicemen did not merely excavate the elaborate Vauban-style trenches that encircled their objective, but also learned how to make the wooden fascines, gabions, and mantlets necessary for protection from enemy shot. Besieged forces, by contrast, needed to perfect sally techniques, acquire rudimentary knowledge of field fortification to repair their defenses weakened by enemy bombardment, and learn how to conduct effective parapet fire. British troops received this enhanced training at irregular intervals, if at all, suggesting that two years was not overmuch time for recruits to master all the infantryman's skills.[12]

Affairs in England first conspired against War Office plans to train and deploy the 60th Foot as quickly as possible. While Lord Barrington successfully tended to legislative matters at Westminster, the Duke of Cumberland and the Earl of Loudoun wrestled with logistical problems associated with equipping four new colonial battalions from the mother country's largesse. The contract for uniforms was let to the prominent London draper Galfridus Mann, whose experience supplying other military units would expedite the production of simplified Royal American uniforms shorn of regimental lace. Leather accoutrements, halberds, swords, colors, camp equipage, and 3,741 refurbished King's Long Land Pattern muskets formed a considerable portion of the stores that had to be conveyed across the Atlantic.[13] Although all of this ordnance was to be shipped without delay, most of the regiment's two hundred tons of baggage did not reach New York until the middle of August because naval officials had difficulty crewing the twelve ships laden with these essential supplies. Another two weeks passed before all the stores were delivered to Governors Island, where a regimental depot had been established to house, clothe, and train recruits. The crucial logistical infrastructure needed to sustain the force was thus not in place until the 1756 campaigning season began to wind down in the fall of that same year.[14]

Colonial events also interfered with the goal of expeditiously transforming regimental volunteers into "fighting men" during the corps' first year of existence. As explained in the preceding chapter, officers and NCOs had to devote their initial endeavors to recruiting

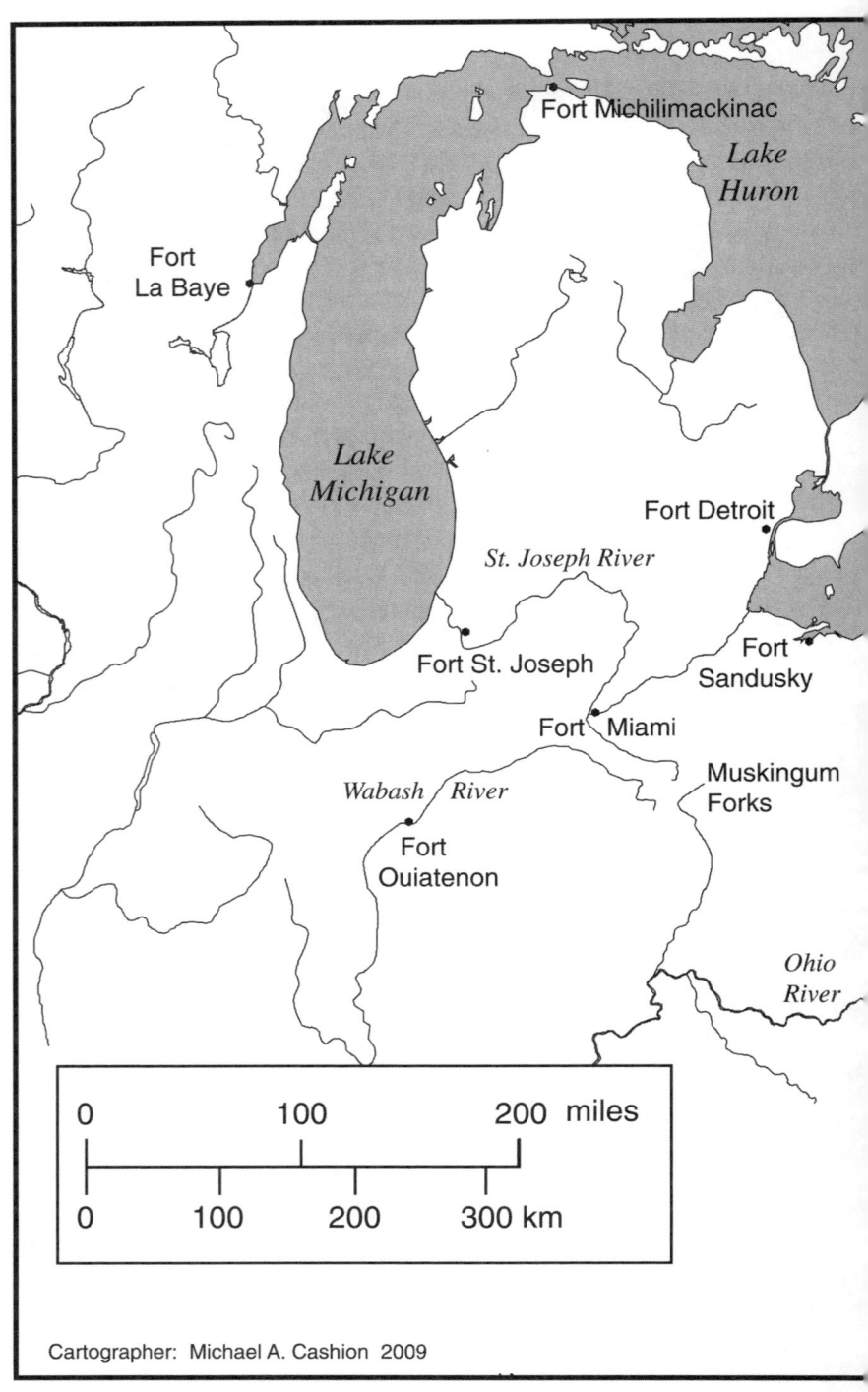

Map 2. The Great Lakes Basin and the Upper South during the Seven Years' War and Pontiac's Rebellion

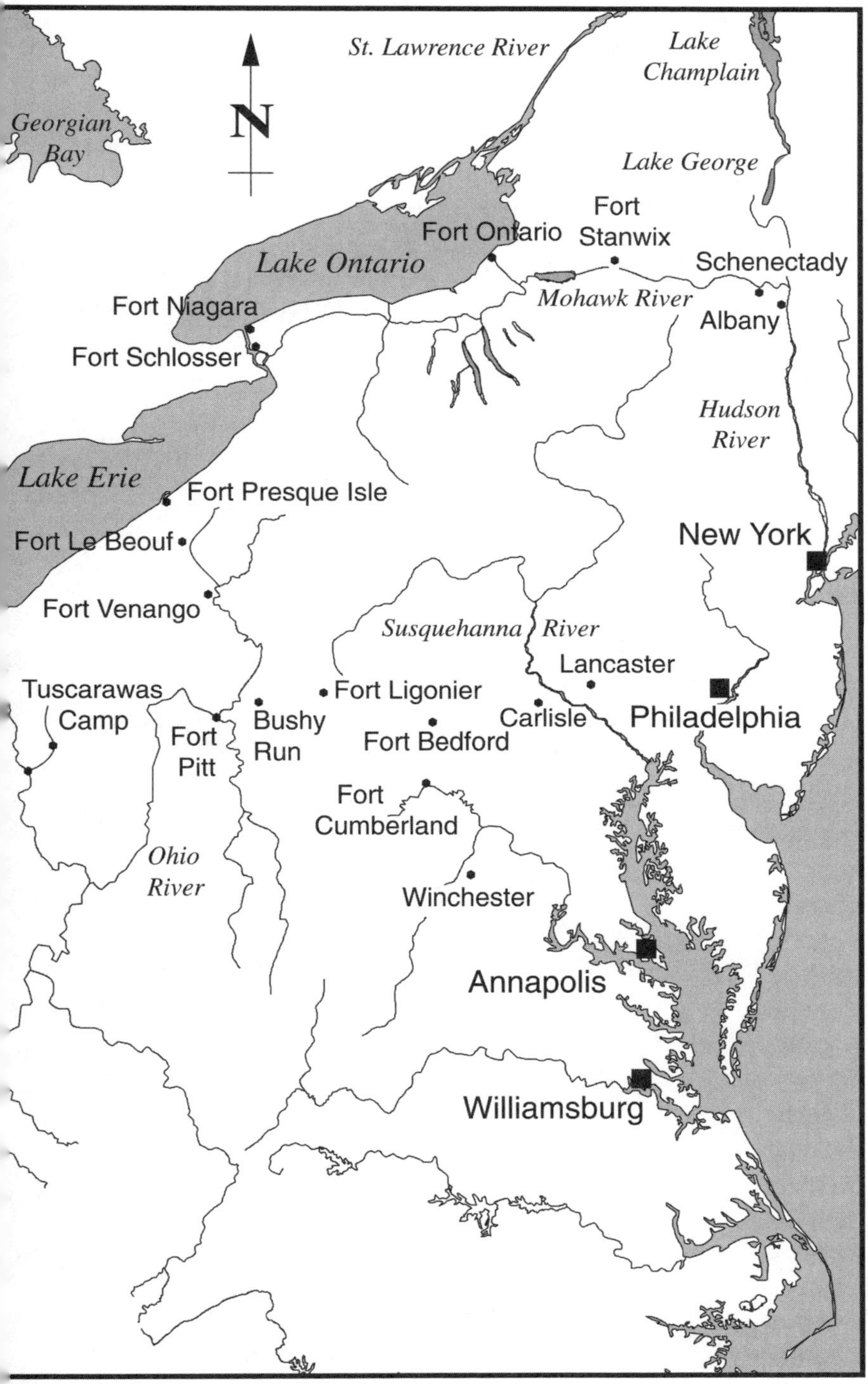

N
St. Lawrence River
Lake Champlain
Georgian Bay
Lake George
Fort Ontario
Fort Stanwix
Lake Ontario
Schenectady
Mohawk River
Fort Niagara
Albany
Fort Schlosser
Hudson River
Lake Erie
Fort Presque Isle
Fort Le Beouf
New York
Fort Venango
Susquehanna River
Lancaster
Tuscarawas Camp
Fort Ligonier
Bushy Run
Carlisle
Philadelphia
Fort Pitt
Fort Bedford
Fort Cumberland
Ohio River
Winchester
Annapolis
Williamsburg

since none of the colonial assemblies had raised the anticipated troop levies for the regulars. Even though seven hundred volunteers were enlisted by mid-August, Montcalm's Oswego offensive further retarded the Royal Americans' training efforts because their presence was needed immediately to forestall further French advances. Hastily dispatched by the Earl of Loudoun from Philadelphia to Albany, the recruits were eventually stationed at Saratoga, where they were required to escort supply convoys, keep transportation arteries in good repair, and strengthen defensive positions. Such responsibilities afforded little opportunity for any formal training during the autumn months.[15]

Dispersal to winter cantonments did not immediately improve the situation either. After dividing their 1,484 men into four skeleton battalions at New York on 27 November 1756, the first division (Colonel John Stanwix/Lieutenant Colonel Henry Bouquet) took up quarters in Philadelphia, the second (Colonel Joseph Dusseaux/Lieutenant Colonel Frederick Haldimand) remained in New York, the third (Colonel Charles Jefferyes/Lieutenant Colonel Russell Chapman) sojourned along the Chesapeake Bay, and the fourth (Colonel James Prevost/Lieutenant Colonel Sir John St. Clair) lodged in the Jerseys. Through mid-February, training remained a secondary consideration as most staff were continually obliged to drum up volunteers.[16] A dearth of qualified instructors and veterans, who could teach by example, also slowed the maturation of recruits since many of the Continental mercenaries thought to be experienced were "Raw men" still in the process of learning British drills themselves. In the interim, the Royal Americans performed a simplified version of the manual exercise; the Earl of Loudoun's dreams about providing the corps with specialized training "to qualify them for Service of the Woods" was simply not feasible with the time or personnel available.[17]

Without adequate barracks' space, the winter of 1756–57 was memorable primarily for the unrest sparked in communities where colonists were obliged to shelter regular soldiers during the inclement months. Local legislatures only grudgingly provided quarters for the king's men in taverns, private homes, or public buildings.[18] Overshadowed by popular accounts of the rows between army headquarters and various assemblies, however, is any consideration of the negative impact that these squabbles had on troop training. The cases of the first battalion quartered at Philadelphia and the third battalion encamped in company-sized units as far away as Maryland's Eastern Shore are well documented. Lack of centralized accommodations hindered the recruits' early acclimatization to army life since consistent military discipline could not be enforced by superiors when soldiers returned to inns or other dispersed lodgings for the night. Both units' poor state of readiness, "being not yet very fit for great operations," no doubt contributed to the Earl of Loudoun's decision to employ them solely in defensive capacities for the 1757 summer campaign. This move would allow those still not fit for service more time for remedial infantry instruction.[19]

The even-numbered battalions, which had enjoyed greater consolidation at New York and in the Jerseys, and made more headway in the training process than confreres stationed farther south, demonstrated "tolerable progress in their Marching, Exercise, and firings." Proficiency in these duties permitted their inclusion with the 1757 British expeditionary force designed to secure Louisbourg and then Quebec City.[20] Even though the presence of a superior French fleet at Cape Breton thwarted offensive operations that summer, time spent in Halifax proved profitable for the redcoats under the Earl of Loudoun's personal command. There, fifteen regular regiments were concentrated at one place in the North American operational theater for the first time in the war, allowing inexperienced troops to improve basic skills as well as participate in realistic war games.[21]

Although the summer encampment lasted less than five full weeks, soldiers drilled regularly and gained some acquaintance with advanced tactical maneuvers.[22] John Knox, a subaltern in the 43rd Regiment, recorded in his journal some of the activities that occurred during these field days. In addition to the company and battalion exercises all men performed, he noted:

> This morning the picquets of the line, with a working party from the army, marched to the left of the camp, where the intrenchments were thrown up; they were formed into distinct bodies; one half carried on approaches, while the other defended; frequently sallying out to obstruct the workmen, when the covering parties attacked, repulsed, and pursued them, making many prisoners: which afforded much mirth to a numerous crowd of spectators. This is in order to make the

troops acquainted with the nature of the service they are going upon; also to render the smell of powder more familiar to the young soldiers.

The "young soldiers" Knox mentioned certainly included both Royal American battalions, whose combined muster rolls from the summer of 1757 indicate that 961 of their men (60 percent) had served only twelve months or less in the ranks. Just 322 veterans (20 percent) could claim thirty-six or more months of active duty.[23] Even the martial capabilities of these troops were suspect, however, because most had been drafted from either the disbanded New England battalions or the Irish additional companies shepherded to New York by Colonel James Prevost earlier in the new year. The Boston regiments, which had endured privation along the Mohawk River–Oswego corridor for most of 1755 and 1756, were deemed "much the worst Corps on this Continent," while the Irish drafts were not of sterling quality either. Despite contemporary criticism about the stillborn invasion of New France, Loudoun's sojourn in Halifax had permitted his troops opportunity to gain more combat proficiency with the lessons learned there bearing fruit in future endeavors.[24]

The benefits of advanced training enjoyed by the Royal Americans at Halifax were not shared by their comrades relegated to garrison duties elsewhere. The star-crossed first battalion, already disadvantaged by Philadelphia legislators with respect to winter quarters, now fell victim to metropolitan political pressure when Thomas Penn and influential commercial interests entreated that regular troops protect their constituencies from French attack. Colonel John Stanwix's unit, divided into equal detachments of five companies each, had the misfortune to be selected to defend the entire landmass between Pennsylvania and South Carolina with little other assistance. Although such arrangements ensured a professional presence in strategically important areas, the practice of splitting a regiment retarded its natural evolution because there would not be enough troops present to practice firings or maneuvers in any meaningful manner. Stanwix accepted this assignment reluctantly, warning superiors that "this division must hurt us," and requested that his command be reassembled as soon as possible.[25]

Lieutenant Colonel Henry Bouquet's task force arrived in Charles Town on 15 June 1757 with expectations that the local government would have appropriate lodgings ready for their reception. Serviceable facilities, however, were never given to the 60th Foot during its nine months of detached duty in the southern garrison. Instead, first battalion members were miserably used by colonial authorities who consigned the redcoats to tents erected on the local race course before heavy summer rains turned that encampment into a quagmire. All the men were then relocated to a few derelict houses and left to fend for themselves for another two months before 160 of their number received billets in local taverns. The majority of the soldiers, however, remained in hovels with little aid granted them by legislators for fuel and other essentials. As in Philadelphia earlier that year, disease and desertion soon plagued the corps because of their poor living conditions. Barely three hundred men remained available for active duty.[26] Those able to parade spent most of their waking hours improving inadequate town defenses instead of perfecting the manual and platoon exercises. This busy schedule left even less time for advanced training with elements of the Virginia Regiment and the newly formed Montgomery's Highlanders also stationed in Charles Town.[27]

The physical exertions of the Royal Americans in South Carolina were matched by those assigned to secure the Pennsylvania frontier. Stationed at Carlisle, Colonel John Stanwix's force built a large entrenched camp capable of accommodating 1,500 troops. This stronghold, measuring 630 feet by 375 feet was erected to deter further enemy depredations west of the Susquehanna River as well as give the regulars some knowledge in field fortification work.[28] Practical experience with the pick and spade proved to be the best use of the detachment's time because its five isolated companies were continually required to send some personnel on patrols through the inhabited parts of Cumberland County. Consequential defensive sweeps certainly contributed to the reduction of Indian raids during the summer of 1757, but it came at the expense of the soldiers' progress as the demanding schedule of guard duty, combat pickets, and construction work left little opportunity for focused exercise. The adverse effect these service conditions had on this Royal American battalion's battlefield skills prompted its leader to notify headquarters that "they have never been once together since they were first formed, [I] shall take it as a great favour to be brought together this Winter, as I am Convinced they will never be a good Battalion till they are join'd."[29]

Stanwix's concern about the martial capabilities of his men was also shared by the third battalion's new proprietary colonel, Brigadier General Charles Lawrence, who assumed this dignity in September 1757. Since none of the unit's superior officers had spent any time with the force in North America, Major Augustine Prevost had proven unable to discipline the ten companies while he had been its de facto commander. Upon first meeting, Lawrence ruefully informed superiors that his corps was still not a potent combat unit.[30] In fact, the battalion was in a downward spiral following the Earl of Loudoun's decision to use them to cover Albany's northern approaches; the troops subsequently became involved in the futile defense of Fort William Henry, an event that further decreased their efficiency.[31]

The Anglo-provincial debacle at the head of Lake George was as much the responsibility of the London bureaucrats as it was the fault of the British commander-in-chief. According to the Earl of Loudoun's initial design, the upper Hudson Valley would be relegated to the operational backwaters because his proposed seaborne attack on Quebec would have kept the majority of French forces on the defensive in Canada. Contemporary wisdom, borne out by the successful defense of Fort William Henry on 19–20 March 1757, likewise suggested that a small number of regulars could withstand any modest enemy assault until relief forces raised the siege.[32] William Pitt's desire to seize Louisbourg first, before the redcoats proceeded against New France, however, relinquished the offensive initiative to the Marquis de Montcalm, who, in turn, was able to muster 8,019 regulars, militia, and Indian braves along the Lake Champlain–Lake George corridor.[33]

Like both divisions of the first battalion protecting the southern theater of operations, the Royal Americans stationed along the New York frontier spent more time laboring with spades and axes than at exercise. Assigned to garrison Fort Edward and its dependencies, the soldiers were required to assist in the completion of these fortifications, participate in fatigue parties, or escort supply trains.[34] This tedious routine was suddenly interrupted in late July when word reached Major General Daniel Webb that a large enemy force was preparing for an ascent of Lake George. The general hastened to Fort William Henry and ordered the third battalion's elite grenadier company to march with him. A 27 July 1757 war council held there determined that the garrison's defenses should be improved and that a large entrenched camp capable of holding at least a thousand reinforcements be constructed southeast of the fort. A composite company of the most experienced Royal American troops led by Lieutenant Colonel John Young participated in this forlorn effort, reaching the stronghold only hours ahead of the enemy's advance guard.[35]

The detachment's first combat operation—the regiment's debut as well—was a conventional affair with little chance of success. Montcalm's army exploited its numerical advantage in troops and artillery to isolate the British garrison before beginning a sustained bombardment of the fort soon after their trenches opened on 3 August 1757. Following a spirited weeklong resistance, defenders were forced to surrender because their ammunition was dwindling, they had lost their heaviest cannons, and more important, no relief column appeared from Fort Edward to drive the French away.[36] Contemporary accounts place Lieutenant Colonel Young in the entrenched camp for the duration of the battle; his gallant conduct there won widespread admiration. Presumably, his select men remained in the camp since the fort proper contained no more than four hundred troops at any one time. Although only twenty-three Royal Americans became casualties during the battle or as a result of the warriors' attack on the prisoners of war, all of its veteran participants save Young had to withdraw from the operational theater for the next ten months until Major General James Abercromby repudiated the capitulation signed on 9 August 1757. Their removal from the active-duty list stripped Lawrence's battalion of its most experienced cadre, which stymied the pace of further martial development.[37]

The Years of Trial and Error, 1757–1758

British defeats in ordinary engagements were magnified by continued reverses in small actions even three years into the conflict. Although individual army officers had begun to modify company training regimens to make troops more effective in a wilderness environment, regular forces had still proven inept at dealing with insurgents who continually skulked around key installations. Local auxiliaries too had not demonstrated complete mastery of *la petite guerre* (small-scale operations), and their inability to gather adequate intelligence about French designs contributed to the loss of the Lake George garrison.³⁸ To reverse this trend, the Earl of Loudoun seconded gentlemen volunteers from the various line regiments to Major Robert Rogers in hopes that they would become vectors for the spread of partisan methods throughout the army. Fifteen Royal Americans participated in this short-lived experiment, which failed largely because the famed scout was too ill with scurvy in the fall of 1757 to attend his new disciples.³⁹

A more promising design for the rapid deployment of British special servicemen was submitted to headquarters by Lieutenant Colonel Thomas Gage of the 44th Regiment. A veteran of the 1755 Braddock expedition who had been wounded leading the advance guard, he wagered his own hard-earned seniority that a light infantry force would be maintained in North America following the war. Using the proceeds from the sale of his own commission as collateral, Gage offered to raise at personal expense a five-hundred-man unit in exchange for its command. This initiative received official backing because it furnished the army with essential skirmishers at less cost and headache than those unruly rangers in the service of Major Rogers. Loudoun loaned Gage some of the start-up funds to speed the unit's readiness for the 1758 campaign and allowed his officers to select ninety-six of the best marksmen from all the line regiments as a solid nucleus of veteran NCOs and soldiers.⁴⁰

The creation of Thomas Gage's 80th (Light Infantry) Regiment of Foot solved this specialist shortage only in New York. To counteract a growing Acadian-Mi'kmaq threat to the army stationed at Halifax, headquarters turned to Captain George Scott, who had already acquired a great deal of knowledge about guerrilla warfare. Scott was accordingly given direction of a temporary light infantry detachment of 550 men drawn from the 1758 Louisbourg expeditionary force. Like Gage, the New Englander had already tried to curry official favor by providing army headquarters with uniform and equipment prototypes more serviceable than those issued to the regulars.⁴¹

The Earl of Loudoun did not remain in the New World long enough to enjoy the rewards of his visionary projects. Recalled to London in December 1757 by an ascendant William Pitt, the peer's more efficient logistical system and seasoned army were bequeathed to others destined to win immortality as the conquerors of New France.⁴² Pitt's antipathy for Loudoun, however, did not preclude him from following the same basic offensive scheme in 1758 that the former chief had proposed. British forces numbering almost 50,000 men would simultaneously move against Louisbourg, New France, and Fort Duquesne in a bid to reverse the effects of the preceding year's "inactive and unhappy Campaign." All four elements of the Royal American Regiment would finally be called on to participate in offensive operations, with the garrison force still in South Carolina returned to New York for final assignment.[43]

Brigadier General John Stanwix's continued misgivings about his battalion's suitability for combat were ignored by army staff who parceled it out unevenly among two separate commands. Six companies were assigned to the northern forces led by Major General James Abercromby, which were supposed to seize the major enemy forts along Lake Champlain and then invade Canada. The remaining four companies, with many of their number still recovering from illnesses contracted in Charles Town "by lying 8 months without Quarters and furnitures," were transferred to the largely colonial enterprise determined to eliminate the French and Indian menace at the Ohio Forks. Although Stanwix's men were proficient in just the basic exercises, this was not a weakness so long as they fought in small skirmishes or acted in a defensive capacity. In conventional tactical environments opposing other European regulars, however, their inability to function with larger formations would jeopardize the thrust into New France.[44]

Fifteen companies drawn from the first and fourth Royal American battalions formed an integral part of the largest army ever assembled at the head of Lake George. Major General James Abercromby and his troops were optimistic that their strike against Montreal would succeed as their fifteen-thousand-strong juggernaut brushed aside any resistance.[45] Plagued by the tardy arrival of provincial forces and supplies, however, the huge armada of bateaux and whaleboats did not embark until 5 July 1758. Once on the water, the troops rowed the greater part of a day and night before sighting the first enemy positions. Their unopposed landing on the morning of the sixth and the annihilation of a small French force discovered near the beachhead boded well for the success of the entire venture. Even the loss of Lord Viscount Howe, the expedition's popular second-in-command, who had been killed in a brief afternoon skirmish, did not dampen the redcoats' ardor.[46]

The Marquis de Montcalm had not been idle while Abercromby's forces executed their ponderous advance. Believing that his thirty-five hundred defenders were outnumbered by at least a five-to-one margin, the French nobleman denied his opponents the opportunity to bring their full strength against the Fort Ticonderoga garrison in a siege. To thwart this eventuality, a strong barrier fronted by an abatis—a wooden entanglement of felled trees—was hastily centered on the strategic high ground where the British would want to deploy their cannons. A reconnaissance party observed this newly constructed bulwark but failed to discern the true design of the loopholed entrenchment, characterizing it merely as "a Slight Brest worke of Logs, easy of Access on the Eveness of the Ground and so weekley bound together that it would be easy to push them down." This miscalculation, in addition to faulty intelligence suggesting that a relief force of 3,000 additional enemy troops would soon make an appearance, compelled the British commander to storm the barricade without the immediate benefit of artillery support.[47]

Major General James Abercromby's decision to overrun the suspect breastwork by a *coup de mousqueterie* was not unorthodox. In a tactical situation requiring speed, this maneuver obliged disciplined troops to march forward to the enemy position before they discharged their weapons and broke through the palisade. Contemporary wisdom dictated that the unified advance and deadly broadside of such an assault would either cause defenders to flee or die behind their parapets.[48] Following established protocols, the British commander first established an advance screen of fifty men from each regiment, known as a picket, to protect the remainder of his army while it deployed for battle. They, in turn, were supported by seven grenadier companies that preceded the main regular force, which was divided into three brigades. The companies from the first Royal American battalion were positioned on the extreme right flank of the battle line. Their sister corps and the 27th Foot, both beneficiaries of the previous year's Halifax summer camp, composed the remainder of the army's right wing.[49]

The mammoth British tidal wave of regulars did not roll across the French entrenchment as Abercromby had envisioned. Instead of overwhelming the defenders by a combined frontal assault, the redcoats' orderly advance was impeded by a massive obstacle course of pointed trees, underbrush, and stumps, which Montcalm had thrown up in front of his position. As one veteran of the 42nd Regiment remembered:

> The attack began a little past one in the afternoon, and about two the fire became general on both sides; which was exceedingly heavy, and without intermission; insomuch that the oldest soldiers present never saw so furious and so incessant a fire. The affair of Fontenoy was nothing to it: I saw both. We laboured under unsurmountable difficulties: the enemy's breastwork was about nine or ten feet high, upon the top of which they had plenty of wall-pieces fixed, and well lined on the inside with small arms. But the difficult access to their lines was what gave them a fatal advantage over us: they took care to cut down monstrous large fir and oak trees, &c. which covered all the ground from the foot of their breastwork, about the distance of a cannon-shot every way in their front. This not only broke our ranks, and made it impossible to keep our order, but put it entirely out of our power to advance briskly; which gave the enemy abundance of time to mow us down like a field of corn, with their wall-pieces and small arms, before we fired one single shot.

Confusion reigned on the battlefield as some units were pinned down by enemy fire while other battalions withdrew. Only with great difficulty were British officers able to bring their bewildered men to order before returning to the assault.[50]

Both Royal American detachments suffered from the heavy fire directed at them by French regulars. The grenadiers went to ground in an effort to survive and awaited support from the troops who marched behind them. Their relief, however, was halted by the same galling musketry before they reached the enemy's position. At British headquarters, Major General Abercromby received conflicting reports about the success of his endeavor, and only after repeated advances were stopped did he order the exhausted men to retire just before nightfall.[51] Of the first battalion's officer corps, five company commanders and eight subalterns (65 percent) were listed among the dead and wounded; 103 of the 504 redcoats (20 percent) they commanded shared a similar fate. By contrast, only nine of twenty-nine officers (31 percent) who led the fourth battalion were injured during the action with their men sustaining a 22 percent casualty rate: 25 killed and 120 wounded.[52]

While some have censured the British commander's decision not to reduce the French breastwork by field artillery before the infantry struck, participants who survived the debacle were not unanimous in their explanation for the defeat.[53] Certainly the wooden abatis received its due for disrupting the impetus of the assault, but blame was also laid on elements of the army's right wing for advancing "not in the most regular manner" before all the regulars had assembled for action. The critical first attack thus became an uncoordinated affair with the enemy engaged in piecemeal fashion. Since French defenders were not deluged by onrushing redcoats as intended, they were able to concentrate their fire as each troop column appeared and then reinforce vulnerable parts of their entrenchment at Montcalm's direction.[54]

It is no coincidence that an eyewitness singled out the right wing's misstep as a cause for the British repulse because this was where the most inexperienced unit had been posted. Aside from never having learned how to attack a fortified position, first battalion companies had not yet mastered the advanced evolutions permitting them to move forward across a battlefield with any steadiness. The previous year's separation plus an earlier abortive attempt at winter training in Philadelphia also had hindered their integration into a brigade. Their actions thus contributed to the grand assault's collapse even before it could be executed. The qualms Colonel John Stanwix felt about his men's combat skills had been justified because they were still unprepared to meet the challenges of a set-piece battle and could not act in conjunction with others.

Abercromby's dispirited regulars retired from the battlefield behind a screen of provincial troops before embarking the next morning for their base camp at the southern edge of Lake George. There, close to the site where Fort William Henry once stood, the troops prepared for another confrontation with the enemy. In anticipation of receiving reinforcements from Major General Jeffery Amherst's victorious army in Nova Scotia, the British forces rehearsed attacking an entrenched position by a coup de mousqueterie like they would certainly encounter again at Ticonderoga.[55] Only one significant change was made for the prospective assault upon the French defenses. Commanders replaced the Royal Americans' woeful first battalion in the right brigade with the veteran 17th Regiment of Foot. The former corps was then reassigned to garrison Fort Edward, well away from any future offensive operations that the New York army might undertake. To add insult to injury, the command of this rear echelon guard was entrusted to Colonel James Prevost of the fourth battalion. Since Abercromby and the Swiss mercenary had never been on cordial terms, the general may have been ridding his command of two liabilities at once.[56]

Canada's reprieve from invasion was ominous news for Brigadier General John Forbes as his army moved through the Appalachian Mountains toward Fort Duquesne. With four companies of the Royal American Regiment's first battalion in its vanguard, the expeditionary force feared that greater numbers of French-led war parties could now be loosed against them since Montreal was no longer threatened by Abercromby's advance.[57] Forbes, a cautious and prudent man, had designed his campaign in compliance with the principles of partisan warfare outlined by Turpin de Crisse in his *Essai sur l'art de la guerre*. Accordingly, the Scots officer executed a methodical march through the wilderness, provisioning his troops from fortified caches maintained by heavily guarded convoys. Unlike in the northern theater of operations, where the enemy battle order was overwhelmingly composed of French regulars and Canadian militia, Forbes's opposition in the Appalachians consisted primarily of American Indians who continually harried his lengthening supply lines. Close combat in such a woodland environment might be fought by first battalion members who had at least attained proficiency in their platoon exercises and were capable of firing their muskets in successive teams of twenty men.[58]

The record of Forbes's extraordinary campaign was marred by one significant military reverse. After enduring a summer of constant sniping by Native warriors, the expedition's second-in-command, Colonel Henry Bouquet, decided to destroy the enemy beehive that sustained the Delaware and Shawnee threat. In a preemptive strike, a force of 750 regular and colonial troops was detached from the army's advance guard to attack the Indians bivouacked outside the walls of Fort Duquesne. The soldiers, led by Major James Grant of Montgomery's Highland Battalion, were ordered to approach their objective surreptitiously, probe the auxiliaries' camp at night, and then bayonet any sleeping braves. Whether this blow succeeded or not, the main force was to establish an ambush for enemy patrols dispatched against the western army, then retire to safety with any prisoners they had taken. Despite all these carefully laid plans, British military intelligence proved faulty since the combined Franco-Indian presence at Fort Duquesne was much greater than had been believed. Instead of an easy skirmish with odds greatly in Grant's favor, the battle of 14 September 1758 proved to be another Braddockesque fiasco, which commanders had strived assiduously to avoid.[59]

Six officers and 108 select men from the first Royal American battalion joined Major James Grant's strong reconnaissance party when it left Fort Ligonier on 9 September. After a secretive five-day march, they participated in a nighttime strike team that failed to reach the Native encampment after becoming lost in the dark. Nevertheless, the ambitious Highland field officer, instead of returning to the main army with no tangible results to show for his mission, chanced a daylight encounter with the enemy. Major Grant detached an engineering party to survey Fort Duquesne and another file of troops to burn some outbuildings adjacent to the garrison. Neither party completed its assignment after alert sentries roused defenders to engage the redcoats. Caught out of a good defensive position by the their dispersal, Major Grant's forces were annihilated one detachment at a time.[60]

The fury and weight of the French onslaught caught the British completely by surprise. The columns closest to the enemy stronghold were quickly surrounded and cut to pieces by eight hundred assailants. Two full companies of Montgomery's battalion were also lost while trying to support their doomed comrades. The Royal Americans, a composite force of their best men in the western theater, were not initially involved in the action because they had been ordered to protect the baggage train after the previous evening's aborted raid. Stationed almost two miles away in a reserve position alongside 150 men from the Virginia Regiment, they were lured by the sound of gunfire toward the battlefield without express orders to engage. This unauthorized advance coincided with Major Grant's decision to fall back on their position for support, thus lessening the chances of either British force providing a cohesive defense. The relief party was quickly outflanked by the enemy as it reached the battlefield and was forced to withdraw shortly after coming under heavy fire. The Royal Americans lost four officers (66 percent) and thirty-eight men (35 percent) of their team during the engagement, a casualty rate nearly double that sustained by Stanwix's rank and file at Ticonderoga.[61]

Despite this September rout, "that nest of thieves and murderers" was subsequently abandoned by Louis XV's troops, who were unable to sustain key alliances with local tribesmen in the face of Forbes's resolute advance. A new and larger citadel, christened Fort Pitt, was begun by the British near the site of the desolate French bastions within a year of their arrival in the Ohio Valley.[62] Such strategic advantages gained by the British during the 1758 campaign, however, came at great cost to the entire first battalion. The officer corps, with 57 percent of its number rendered hors de combat, paid the highest price, leaving the mantle of active command to the few remaining gentlemen capable of performing their duties. Similarly, the cream of the rank and file was listed among the 141 casualties (17 percent) since these elite troops—the pickets and grenadiers at Ticonderoga or the composite company at Grant's Hill—had been engaged most often. Losses of this magnitude further handicapped the unit's martial development, and the battalion was relegated to garrison duty for the remainder of the war after Brigadier General John Stanwix assumed command of the western operational theater in the spring of 1759. Another year would pass before officers could report to headquarters that their men now appeared "passably good under arms."[63]

British operations against Louisbourg were more successful than those launched at Fort Ticonderoga and Grant's Hill. Built at great expense between 1719 and 1743 to protect Bourbon interests in the Gulf of St. Lawrence, the fortified town had already fallen to a small New England army in 1745. After being returned to the French court following the War of the Austrian Succession, it was preserved against another British attack in 1757 by a large naval presence.[64] The following year, however, London officials organized a larger task force to capture the "Dunkirk of No. America." The expedition against Cape Breton, under the joint command of Major General Jeffery Amherst and Admiral Edward Boscawen, faced greater difficulties than its provincial counterpart had encountered thirteen years before since the 6,000 French defenders had strengthened their forward positions along the beaches and enjoyed additional support from the fire of several vessels that had anchored in the harbor shortly before British sails appeared.[65]

Surviving accounts of the amphibious landing at Gabarus Bay on 8 June 1758 may have easily flowed from the pens of war correspondents describing the Allied descent on the Normandy beaches two centuries later. At first light, Brigadier General James Wolfe led his invasion force of grenadiers, light infantry, and Highlanders toward the shore of Kennington Cove accompanied by the broadsides from hovering frigates. Ordered not to discharge their muskets from the longboats, soldiers were expected to hazard a disputed landing, fix bayonets, and, in a test of wills like that which Abercromby's troops faced at Fort Ticonderoga, seize the French coastal entrenchments by a coup de mousqueterie. Two more regular flotillas were ordered to make feints on other vulnerable beaches, drawing attention away from the main assault. Accordingly, the Royal American's third battalion rowed toward Flat Point while second battalion troops were assigned to the right diversionary force headed for White Point.[66]

Artillery and small arms fusillades greeted the leading elements of Wolfe's force as their craft neared the shore. All but three boats escaped this blistering reception and were fortunate enough to disgorge their light troops safely at a small blind spot in the defenses. From this tiny beachhead, grenadiers formed for battle and struck the heavily fortified barricades on unprotected flanks, driving the French from their positions. Detachments from the center force then rowed from White Point to the now undefended Kennington Cove with the remainder of the army following suit. The attack, described as "desperate and presumptuous" by a French prisoner taken during the engagement, cost the infantry 103 casualties: many of these redcoats drowned after their boats sank in the heavy surf that pounded the rocky coastline.[67]

The excitement of the landing was followed by two months of tedious exertion. Major General Jeffery Amherst first ordered the construction of a three-mile-long pallisaded camp to shield his army from enemy irregulars before beginning the slow process of unloading the necessary military stores from the transports. Troops not employed in these duties were put to work on a covered artillery road needed to move the heavy guns from the beaches to Green Hill, the place selected by the engineers to begin their long-range bombardment of Louisbourg. Unlike a typical European siege, however, Cape Breton's coastal terrain would not permit excavation of a protective subterranean warren to preserve the redcoats from the heavy fire directed against them from the city's battlements. Rather, the main British force had to leapfrog toward the town by a series of fortified redoubts and breastworks built during the nighttime. It took five weeks of such exacting work to dig the rudimentary trench system from these vantage points. Only then were the emplacements ready to entertain troops or the artillery batteries that were finally unmasked on 22 July 1758.[68]

Life within the British lines was strictly regulated according to the Duke of Cumberland's 1755 standing orders and by four distinctive drum ruffles: the reveille at sunrise; the 8:00 A.M. troop for companies to assemble for daily inspection and work details; the retreat before sunset where roll call was taken and the next day's orders read; and the final tattoo when lights were extinguished for sleep. In the interim, soldiers filled their waking hours with myriad guard duties, fatigue parties, and other assignments. Much of an infantryman's time was occupied by sentry duty, either with the quarter guard, charged with policing the tent lines; or with the pickets, which furnished men for the advance alarm posts, supplied covering parties for laborers, and were always prepared to repel an enemy strike on the encampment. Quarter-guard troops were posted at 8:00 A.M. for a twenty-four-hour shift with smaller details attending senior officers, the artillery train, and the provost-marshal's prisoners. The picket guard, conversely, took their positions at the beating of retreat and remained on duty until the next cycle of sentinels relieved them the following evening.[69]

With approximately one-quarter of the army's manpower engaged in security duties, the remainder provided the brute strength needed for the siege itself. The first levies began unloading the provisions, armament, and equipment from 144 supply vessels anchored adjacent to Flat Point. These crucial military stores were then transported overland, via a newly constructed road, to be housed within the camp lines, munitions dumps, or specially prepared magazines capable of holding three weeks' rations. The logistics of furnishing powder and ammunition to each artillery piece was a Herculean task because individual guns would fire a minimum of five hundred shot during a typical siege. While supply depots grew, each regiment's more skillful artificers began supplementing the number of prefabricated gabions, open-ended wattle baskets designed to protect sappers from enemy fire when filled with earth. Other laborers were ordered to make fascines, bundles of branches used to screen the trench tops or to fill in marshy areas before the town.[70]

The bustle of the British camp abated somewhat after sunset as activities shifted to offensive operations ideally conducted under the cover of darkness. Pioneers, guarded by a screen of troops drawn from the pickets, began construction of siege lines within days after landing. Working under the direction of military engineers, they first constructed pallisaded redoubts, blockhouses, and a high earthen embankment, known as an epaulment, to shield their activities from the enfilading fire of any French naval vessels trapped in the harbor.[71] These fortified outposts, in turn, served as springboards for the troops to secure more advantageous terrain closer to the city walls where the primary artillery batteries could finally be entrenched. From the evening of 15 July, infantrymen, who were paid extra for working at night, began preparing suitable positions for the heavy ordnance despite the shot and scrap metal that rained down from the ramparts. Behind a double row of gabions, gun emplacements three feet deep were sunk to accommodate the wooden platforms needed to support the weapons and attending crews. A mortar cauldron for seven high-trajectory weapons was also readied for action.[72]

The intensive bombardment of this combined armament had the desired effect. Garrison guns protecting the Queen's bastion were quickly dismounted, and increasing numbers of deserters reported about deteriorating conditions within the city. The siege's final act was signaled on 25 July when the redcoats were issued scaling ladders to storm breaches made in the fortifications. This perilous assignment would have fallen in part to the Royal Americans' third battalion, scheduled for trench duty on 26 July, had not Louisbourg's commander decided to surrender.[73] The Chevalier de Drucour had little choice. With only twelve serviceable wall pieces left to counter the intensifying artillery barrages, 1,790 fewer defenders fit to repel the attack that would soon crash against him, and no European relief force on the horizon, a capitulation was the only reasonable means to preserve what was left of France's key overseas citadel.[74]

Major General Jeffery Amherst's successful operation against Louisbourg was more than just a tactical tour de force; it also allowed for the martial maturation of the redcoats under his command. As expected, the fourteen grenadier companies and the 550 light troops had performed well. The infantry too had mastered their role in amphibious operations, learned the intricacies of the besieger's craft, and acquired the necessary survival skills to persevere through an entire campaign. Morale was high among the Nova Scotian forces because they, unlike their compatriots serving in other New World theaters, had won a tremendous victory with very few fatalities. Even the hapless third battalion, which incurred the expedition's highest casualty rate, lost only sixty soldiers (6 percent) to death and wounds. Merely twenty-one men (2 percent) from the second battalion, now Brigadier General Robert Monckton's corps, died during the siege. The nucleus of this seasoned strike force would form the spearhead against Quebec the following year.[75]

The dispatch of Louisbourg's garrison to England as prisoners of war did not terminate an enemy presence in Nova Scotia. At least two hundred roving Mi'kmaqs had harried the British camp during the course of the siege, and French sympathizers within the remaining Acadian population were still perceived as a danger to the infant British settlements at Halifax and Lunenburg.[76] To counteract this threat, Brigadier General Monckton's amalgamated force of regulars and rangers, including his own Royal American battalion, were ordered to destroy any French villages they saw while ascending the St. John River. Modest garrisons were also to occupy strategic sites along the Bay of Fundy, thereby securing the countryside and denying potential intruders overland access to the British towns. A smaller detachment of light troops disembarked at Cape Sable to eliminate any hamlets that might support infiltrators on Nova Scotia's southwestern coast.[77]

Monckton's interdiction mission through November 1758 was somewhat effective after his troops occupied and refurbished a small fort at the mouth of the St. John. With this entry point secure, 1,200 servicemen then sailed in pursuit of two privateers and a large force of seven hundred combatants believed to be stationed somewhere farther north. However, the vessels, heavily laden with infantry and provisions, were unable to negotiate the river beyond the bottom third of its course, permitting few opportunities for the redcoats to engage with the enemy. For its part, the light infantry sent to Cape Sable—comprising irregulars from the 35th Regiment, the Royal Americans, and some rangers from Captain Joseph Gorham's companies—accomplished more by apprehending scores of Acadian families for eventual deportation to France. Yet, all 981 members of the second battalion, tried but yet relatively unscathed by combat, profited from this brief exposure to petite guerre operations and now formed the 60th Regiment's most experienced element.[78]

The split decision orchestrated by Major General James Abercromby did not please his political masters. Abercromby was recalled to London in September 1758, and management of colonial military operations was entrusted to Jeffery Amherst, who had won plaudits for his handling of the Louisbourg campaign. The War Office instructed the Royal Americans' new commander-in-chief to clear the enemy from New York's frontiers with his army while another force, under the direction of James Wolfe, finally attacked Quebec City. The fourth battalion remained attached to Amherst's central command, and the two other junior corps, still at Halifax, joined the fleet bound for the St. Lawrence River. Metropolitan strategists believed that Bourbon forces would have to sue for peace if British troops finally penetrated New France's home defenses and their far-flung interior garrisons were captured by the first battalion advancing from Fort Pitt.[79]

Colonel Henry Bouquet's division was still stationed in western Pennsylvania during the winter of 1758–59 when instructions arrived from New York headquarters instituting further changes in British military dress, deployment, and tactics to make the regulars more attuned to North American service conditions. First, the redcoats' uniforms were overhauled in accordance with some of Captain George Scott's earlier suggestions: soldiers were issued Indian leggings to protect their limbs as they traveled through the woods and their traverse was eased by the reduction of bulky equipment.[80] Second, the high command's satisfaction with the performance of the Nova Scotian light infantry resulted in the conversion of one company from each battalion into skirmishers. Management issues were also reconsidered at this time. Capitalizing on their mobility and discipline, light troops were allowed to precede even the elite grenadier companies on the march, and they were also authorized to feign retreats so that aggressive pursuers might be drawn into the sights of the regulars—a maneuver favored by Frederick the Great.[81] Finally, a radical change was made at the tactical level when British soldiers began deploying for battle in two ranks instead of three, which speeded the transition from column to line as circumstances warranted. Unlike Major General Edward Braddock, who lost the initiative upon the precipitous retreat of his vanguard, commanders could now promptly draw up their main body with the advance party while subjecting enemy forces to a withering fusillade as each company fired in succession. This precursor to William H. Russell's memorable "thin red streak tipped with a line of steel" would have its debut on 13 September 1759.[82]

The Years of Triumph, 1759–1762

Major General James Wolfe's place in the British military pantheon had not been secured by the early autumn of 1759 as his operations along the St. Lawrence River drew to a close. Thwarted at every turn by a circumspect adversary that denied the redcoats a landing on the strategic Beauport shore east of Quebec City, the British force of 8,300 infantry had remained virtually paralyzed around Orleans Island since their arrival on 27 June. Artillery batteries playing upon the capital's Lower Town from Point Levis, moreover, had not damaged Montcalm's forces "entrenched up to the chin," nor had the invader's detached camp to the east of the major French defensive belt provided a sally port. Wolfe desperately probed for weaknesses around Quebec's perimeter throughout the summer months, but his troop strength was seriously depleted through a series of impulsive amphibious landings. The Royal American contingent of 1,115 men from the second and third battalions suffered their greatest casualties in these rash ventures.[83]

British commanders by the middle of July had glimpsed just one potential weak point in the enemy lines that extended for six miles opposite their main encampment. An isolated redoubt adjacent to the confluence of the Montmorency and St. Lawrence rivers promised access to the French position if Wolfe's troops could capture the bulwark and then entice opponents to contest possession. Accordingly, on 31 July, thirteen grenadier companies, supplemented by two hundred soldiers from Monckton's battalion, were ordered to attack the vulnerable outpost, thereby drawing the defenders into a general engagement.[84] Before support troops could march to their aid from the other side of Montmorency Falls, however, the grenadiers landed and charged toward their objective. They succeeded in their first mission after capturing the redoubt and spiking the guns in two supporting artillery batteries but were driven back from the target by grapeshot

Capt. Hervey Smyth, Major General James Wolfe's aide-de-camp, drew this sketch of the British attack at Montmorency Falls. British grenadiers succeeded in the initial assault but were eventually driven back from the French lines. Detachments from the second and third Royal American battalions participated in this engagement. Courtesy of Library and Archives Canada. (C-000782)

and musketry directed at them by those higher up on the embankment. Only a sudden rain shower dampened the French fire, allowing the severely mauled troops to withdraw from the beach unmolested. The lion's share of the second battalion's 110 summer casualties (21 percent) occurred during this poorly managed action.[85]

If a cenotaph was raised at Montmorency for Monckton's men, then another memorial would be located at Pointe aux Trembles in tribute to the fallen servicemen of the third battalion. Employed like marines during the British army's ceaseless reconnaissance-in-force operations, corps members conducted three strikes above Quebec at the cost of one dead and twenty-five wounded. The first attack occurred on 21 July when a Royal American detachment, bolstered by two additional grenadier companies, seized a lightly defended magazine. The habitant militia and their Native auxiliaries broke in the face of the regulars, whose few casualties included Major Augustine Prevost, struck in the head by a musket ball.[86] The 8 August engagement was not as bloodless. In this return match, the French hotly contested an attempt to capture three floating artillery batteries used to disrupt British shipping. The Royal Americans and the 15th Regiment lost 140 redcoats during a futile attempt to land in an ebb tide against a larger mixed force of regulars, Canadians, and home guard braves who enjoyed the full advantages of wooded terrain. The sting of this reverse was somewhat alleviated eleven days later by the destruction of a large enemy supply depot at Deschambault. The expensive baggage of several French battalions disappeared in the flames that also consumed the chattel of many prominent civilians.[87]

The invader's extended line of communications and large number of detached posts provided ideal targets for enemy guerrillas. Frequent skirmishes occurred in areas not firmly under British control despite the olive branch that the redcoats extended to French civilians after landing. More shocking to the high command was the opposition's penchant for scalping defenseless prisoners of war. The discovery of six mutilated redcoats during the first week of July prompted Wolfe to warn Montcalm about the penalty anyone caught in war paint would face if this brutal practice continued.[88] Personnel on duty at the isolated encampment east of Montmorency Falls were the most vulnerable. Their close proximity to the main Beauport lines allowed French insurgents to maintain initiative and surprise throughout the summer. As one veteran recollected:

> Although the Duty of the Line in the general, was both hard and difficult, as well as dangerous, still it was generally reckoned by all, that the Duty of Montmorenci far exceeded all the rest, both for difficulty and danger:—there was scarcely a day passed without our Working parties being surprised, and very often Routed by the Skulking parties of Canadians and Indians, they often being three or four times our Numbers; and would sometimes pursue them to the very Skirts of our Camp; and very often sharp Skirmishes would happen between them, which would sometimes be attended with considerable loss, both of killed and wounded.

Fourteen Royal Americans were killed by enemy insurgents before effective countermeasures were put into place. Redcoats retaliated by razing those parishes thought to be sheltering aggressive Canadian or American Indian raiders. This scorched-earth policy was a strategic maneuver designed to replenish the shrinking English larder with plundered foodstuffs while denying a harvest that might sustain continued French resistance.[89]

Fire and sword, though, could not produce a victory by themselves against "the uncommon strength of the Country" in 1759. Wolfe's relative freedom of movement along the St. Lawrence River provided the general with a last chance for redemption; he played this card in the early morning hours of 13 September. Irregulars from the second battalion were among those who landed at an assailable inlet two miles above the capital, ascended the steep hillside, and then drove the French pickets away from a river path. By 9:00 A.M. 4,260 redcoats had followed that route to the Plains of Abraham, where they were arrayed to present as wide a front as possible. The third battalion's surviving 474-man contingent was not placed in the line of battle; rather, it covered access to the river should the infantry have to retire. Second battalion companies were posted on the army's left flank and were the sole Royal American participants in this pivotal engagement.[90]

The fierce action fought by these men in collaboration with the 15th Regiment has been largely neglected in standard accounts of the autumn battle. Stationed there to prevent a lateral attack by the Canadians and Indians who had infiltrated a wood along the Sainte-Foy road, both detachments engaged their adversaries in a running firefight that continued even after Montcalm's regulars had fled the field. Casualty rates were high during this fierce exchange despite the fact that some British grenadiers and light infantry were disbursed in three farmhouses quickly converted to fortified strong points. Later, they were again called on to assist the 78th Foot in dislodging a large enemy force that had rallied at the General Hospital. Five of the unit's 266 troops who participated in both encounters were killed, and another 80 (32 percent) were wounded, contributing to the grand total of 191 rank and file (37 percent) lost in the Quebec theater that summer.[91]

Montcalm's decision to engage Wolfe's troops on an open field instead of conserving his forces behind inviolate defenses has resulted in unwarranted condemnation. As others after him realized, the citadel's defenders could not automatically cede the strategic ground dominating the ramparts only eight hundred yards away. Brigadier General James Murray wrote the following spring, "Every One knows the Place is not tenable against an Army in possession of the Heights." The victorious redcoats spent four busy days after the battle entrenching their camp and marking out batteries for the nineteen guns that would pound the Ursuline and St. John's bastions. Such activity prompted war-weary citizens, who had already survived the Lower Town's cannonading, to spare further property damage by capitulation.[92] On 18 September a new garrison of 7,000 men assumed control of the city and unfurled the British colors over its battlements. A month later, this occupation force was left to its own devices until warm weather again permitted the Royal Navy to return with reinforcements. Although French strategists had lost round one in the critical battle for Canada, they consoled themselves throughout the winter with the thought that "the English hold only the walls" while they still controlled most of the surrounding countryside.[93]

Although Colonel de Bougainville's opinion was certainly true respecting the landmass between Montreal and the capital, British operations elsewhere had also dispossessed Louis XV of critical territory to the south and west of the St. Lawrence River. There, Anglocolonial forces commanded by Major General Jeffery Amherst had finally overrun Forts Ticonderoga and Crown Point. Rowing down Lake George as it had the year before, a combined British force invested the first barrier on 24 July 1759 and occupied it three days later following the precipitous retreat of its garrison. The French also abandoned the larger emplacement even before the Anglo-American army had an opportunity to move against it. Amherst consolidated his gains by constructing a huge fortification on the strategic vista that dominated Lake Champlain. Legions would labor for three long years on the battlements designed to protect Crown Point's approaches.[94]

Bourbon influence throughout the Great Lakes basin had also been crippled by the surrender of Fort Niagara that same summer. The fourth battalion's grenadier and light infantry were the only Royal Americans to participate in the mission that captured Niagara since the eight other companies had remained behind at Oswego to assist in the reconstruction of Fort Ontario.[95] Brigadier General John Prideaux's mixed force of regulars, colonists, and Iroquois warriors began the army's sole textbook siege of the war by investing the strong fortress on 6 July. Following Vauban's precepts, British troops first established a trench line 640 yards away from the wall and then advanced under cover of a lengthening sap. Only the 24 July appearance of a 1,300-strong French relief column from Venango threatened the besiegers when they clashed near a religious shrine not far from Niagara's main gates. Colonel James Prevost's light infantrymen joined a hastily assembled scratch party whose measured volleys routed the larger enemy force, causing Niagara's distressed garrison to ground arms the next day.[96]

The Great Lakes front also witnessed another failed attempt to bolster sagging French fortunes in the region. On 5 July 1759 the Chevalier de la Corne attacked the British rear guard at Oswego in an unsuccessful bid to cut British supply lines and trap the besiegers between two hostile forces. Fort Ontario's bastions, still only an engineer's tracing of supply barrels, were defended by Colonel Frederick Haldimand, who ordered his men to entrench themselves as quickly as possible upon word of the enemy's approach. Three well-handled artillery pieces kept the 1,191 assailants from the mission village of Oswegatchie at bay until the engagement was temporarily suspended by nightfall.[97] The struggle resumed at seven o'clock the next day and lasted throughout the morning hours. As one Royal American officer recalled:

> Colonel Haldimand during all the Attacks, was very active; the Enemy, finding all their Schemes abortive, attempted to burn our Battoes, and set them adrift, in which they might have succeeded, but a party of our Regiment sallying out of the Entrenchment at that time, beat them off, and saved 7 or 8 Battoes, that they had cut the Painters of, and set on Fire, but they were soon made fast, and the Fire extinguished. The French Indians seeing our brave Defense, and the Cowardice of the Canadians, who could never be prevailed on to run upon us, took to their Battoes. . . . It must be told, to the Honour of our Men, that they behaved uncommonly well, and never fired but when they saw an Enemy, and took very good Aim.

Nine battalion members, two dead and seven wounded, were counted among the twelve British casualties. Satisfaction over such minor losses, however, was not to last since scurvy later killed 135 more men at the new Oswego outpost before the start of the next campaign.[98]

Disease and freezing temperatures also stalked Brigadier General

James Murray's army, which held Quebec City during the winter of 1759–60. With almost half his troops felled by "fevers, dysenteries, and most obstinate scorbutic disorders," the garrison was hardpressed to cut the requisite 16,000 cords of firewood for fuel plus counter the strong enemy patrols that they met continually in the countryside. Relying heavily on the skills of their light infantrymen, who were now required to become expert in their use of snowshoes, the redcoats were able to deal with local partisans who assailed them at every turn. The British commander, cognizant that the spring thaw would herald a return to regular engagements, drove the remainder of his men to improve the citadel's defenses and resolved to fortify the high point of land rising over his new works as soon as the frost would permit excavation.[99]

Time ran out for Murray on 28 April 1760 when Francois de Levis appeared before Quebec with a force of 7,000 men determined to retake their capital. Since the occupation troops could not afford to relinquish the still defenseless Heights of Abraham to an adversary supplied with artillery, the garrison commander decided to strike first before the enemy could take possession of this strategic site dominating the city walls.[100] Despite their poor physical condition, the 3,476 redcoats performed admirably during a brisk action lasting two hours. Their light infantry seized the initiative, attacked the French vanguard, and captured an advance redoubt in due course. The Royal Americans' second battalion constituted part of the right brigade whose progress was stopped by an unexpected clash with an enemy column that appeared suddenly on their flank. Murray's scanty reserves were quickly exhausted by attempting to sustain his right wing and by the third battalion's dispatch to deal with another threat on his left. Unable to stand a battle of attrition against a superior force that had already inflicted 917 casualties on the British rank and file, the redcoats had to retreat or face complete envelopment.[101]

The battle along the Sainte-Foy Road was not the decisive victory that Levis had envisioned. Although Monckton's corps lost the services of ten men and the third battalion listed forty-one killed or wounded, the majority of combatants were able to reenter the city and stand by its defenses. Bloody but not bowed, the redcoats kept besiegers at bay for nineteen more days until the French withdrew upon sight of Royal Navy vessels in the St. Lawrence. A composite pursuit force of 2,451 troops was quickly formed from the Quebec battalions and dispatched upriver to support the activities of two other British armies converging on Montreal: one, a column composed primarily of New England provincials moving north from Crown Point, and Jeffery Amherst's task force of 11,000 men sailing down the St. Lawrence from Oswego.[102]

By 1760 Fort Levis was the sole survivor of *Festung* Quebec, a chain of outposts that had defended French sovereignty from Cape Breton Island to the Ohio River. Situated on a small island 110 miles west of Montreal, the natural strengths of this St. Lawrence River stronghold were its commanding sweep of the waterway and inaccessibility to enemy infantry. Because of critical manpower shortages, however, the western approaches were left guarded by a force of fewer than five hundred men during the last summer of the war. This weakness was readily exploited by the British expeditionary force, whose large flotilla of bateaux, whaleboats, row galleys, and small brigs reached Isle Royale (Chimney Island) on 18 August after a week's voyage from Oswego. Encampments for the Anglo-American army, which included the Royal American's fourth battalion, were constructed on all the adjacent islands as well as on both banks of the river to surround the garrison.[103]

The redcoats spent the next five days of the campaign excavating protective earthworks for themselves and their gun positions, which were unmasked on 23 August in support of an amphibious assault carried out by the massed grenadiers. After an intensive morning-long bombardment, the army's best marksmen embarked aboard Amherst's small provincial marine to rake the defenders with gunfire while the elite troops rowed for the island. Navigation proved difficult for the three principal warships, however, and all were severely damaged by French cannons, which forced the grand assault's postponement. Forty-eight hours of further heavy artillery barrages finally encouraged the garrison to submit in the late afternoon of 25 August. The fourth battalion suffered only two soldiers killed and three wounded during the battle. Presumably, these Royal Americans were all injured aboard the ships *Mohawk*, *Onondaga*, or *Williamson* during the abortive attempt to storm the island since their south-shore entrenchments were impervious to enemy fire.[104]

Captain Pierre Pouchot's delaying action was the last engagement fought by 60th troops on the North American mainland prior to the Treaty of Paris. Amherst's strong force continued down the St.

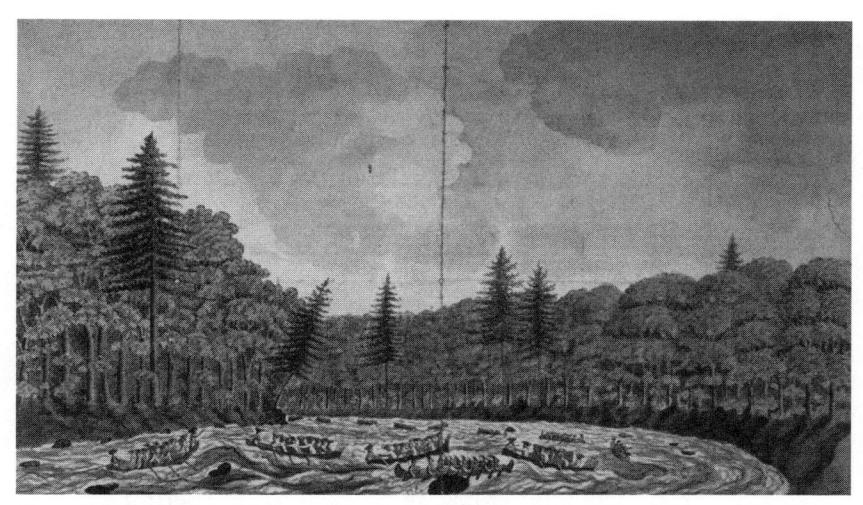

Captain Lieutenant Thomas Davies, of the Royal Artillery, drew this sketch of Major General Jeffery Amherst's large army shooting a series of rapids on the St. Lawrence River. The Royal American's fourth battalion participated in this operation that concluded with the surrender of Montreal on 8 September 1760. Courtesy of Library and Archives Canada. (C-000577)

Lawrence, shot the dangerous Long Sault Rapids, and joined with two other British armies to complete the envelopment of Montreal.

Only the third battalion, now commanded by William Haviland, would participate in the escalating Caribbean phase of the Seven Years' War, while sister detachments remained on station at Quebec City, Montreal, or languished along the western frontiers. Martinique, a notorious privateering base and rival to Jamaica's dominance of the West Indian sugar trade, became the next target for metropolitan administrators even though it had withstood an earlier British foray.[105] The army's first brigade included 703 Royal Americans; they joined 9,000 other redcoats who sailed from New York Harbor in November 1761. Before embarkation, the regulars were inspected by the commander-in-chief, who presided over a series of reviews to evaluate their martial proficiency. Lieutenant General Jeffery Amherst noted that the Royal Americans appearing before him "performed pretty well, . . . and fired very well, passed and forced a bridge, retreated over it &c." Such martial skills would still be needed in the last operations of the war.[106]

The serried defensive works surrounding Martinique's population centers were ideally married to the mountainous terrain. British officers believed that a bloodbath would occur if they hastily stormed an imposing system of entrenchments barring advance toward the capital at Fort Royal. Consequently, after landing on 17 January 1762, the redcoats spent a week establishing artillery batteries needed to support their frontal assault against the primary lines on Morne Tartenson. Brigadier General Haviland's grenadiers joined other elite elements in their relentless 24 January storm of the enemy positions. As one participant wrote:

> When the Grenadiers began to enter the Gully, the French directly perceived us, and began a brisk Fire upon us, which we were obliged to suffer for above twenty Minutes, as the Gully took us that Time to pass it, however we pushed on, and as soon as we got on the other Side we forced them from this Intrenchment, and they retired to the other; from whence as soon as we shewed our Heads above the Side of the Hill they began a most furious Fire of Small-Arms and Artillery, loaded with Grape-shot, which killed and wounded many Officers and Men, but not a Man of our Grenadiers attempted to give Way; nay on the contrary, charged the Enemy with the more Fury and carry'd this their chief Intrenchment with both the Redouts in a very few Minutes.

Troop losses were relatively light considering the dangerous nature of this operation: sixty-one fatalities with another 254 wounded. Royal American casualties included six soldiers killed and ten injured.[107]

Another battle of attrition was forecast by Major General Robert Monckton, the expedition's commander, as he surveyed the citadel from his hard-won vantage point. While enemy forces had been driven back from their first strongholds, the general recognized that they were still in possession of other redoubts that could be softened only if British guns played upon the opposing Garnier heights. His subsequent artillery fire was so accurate that it forced several thousand of the island's defenders to sally out of their emplacements abruptly during the late afternoon of 27 January. The weight of this massive onslaught fell on third battalion troops who were almost overrun but eventually routed assailants with the help of the 42nd

Regiment posted nearby. A Highland officer recalled that his men "gave the Indian Halloo, part of our Backwoods aquirments, and the brave fellows of the 60th instantly stood, as if riveted to the spot and advanced with us." A light infantry detachment acted quickly to seize the enemy's main position in the confusion following the French repulse. William Haviland quickly supported these irregulars with his own men, and, by daylight the British had turned newly captured guns against the town.[108] This initiative, which hastened Fort Royal's capitulation on 4 February, cost the battalion six men dead and five times that number wounded. Disease proved to be the redcoats' greatest enemy during the Martinique campaign, after which Royal American active strength had dwindled to 484 effectives. A full company had died from illness, and another seventy-nine troops were recuperating in the hospital.[109]

Malaria and yellow fever continued to be greater threats to the regulars than musket balls as their tropical sojourn lengthened. Instead of returning immediately to New York, Monckton's forces were required to join a grand armada preparing to sail against Havana following the 4 January 1762 declaration of war by His Britannic Majesty against Charles III, king of Spain. Nature favored Spanish colonial defenses in three ways. First, weather patterns allowed invasion fleets access to the right sea-lanes only between the months of December and August when hurricanes posed no threat to shipping. Second, Cuba's thin soil cover abetted capital's defenders because parallels could not be properly excavated. Most important, biological auxiliaries in the form of *Aedes aegypti* and anopheline mosquitoes, whose destructive powers were far greater than the eight-thousand-strong garrison, were an additional bulwark for an immune local populace. Given time, Havana's man-made fortifications, particularly the unassailable El Moro castle, would wear down an adversary's resolve as he succumbed in rapid succession to gunfire and then insect-borne microbes. No foreign invaders had yet been able to overcome these defenses.[110]

The Royal Americans faced these tremendous challenges as part of the army's first brigade, which landed east of the Cuban capital on 7 June 1762. The exotic nature of their surroundings was intensified by the appearance of cavalry that bore down on a light infantry detachment the following day. Such élan was atypical of the Havana garrison, whose horsemen were easily repulsed by the well-trained redcoats. Besiegers then spent the next seven weeks scratching out gun batteries from the meager tillage that surrounded El Moro's defenses. The local geology exacerbated the army's distress because no fresh water coursed through the "mere Rock barely covered with 2 or 3 Inches [of] soil" requiring the troops, as Sir Charles Knowles recalled, "to bring what Earth we wanted for our Batteries from a very great distance." Nevertheless, the British achieved fire superiority on 13 July and then established positions on the glacis within another week. The Spanish response was swift: 2,500 defenders attacked the advance posts on the morning of 22 July in an attempt to destroy the newest artillery positions. The third battalion, which immediately marched to support the guns, was instrumental in pushing the enemy back and inflicting heavy losses. The El Moro defensive complex was finally seized by storm on 30 July.[111]

Don Juan de Prado, Havana's governor, surrendered the city within a fortnight. His submission could not have come at a more opportune time for the British, whose camps were now decimated by malaria and yellow fever. Disease prostrated almost three times the seventy-two Royal American casualties sustained in battle. The most stricken brigades were quickly repatriated to northern climes for the recovery of their health.[112] Haviland's corps, however, remained on the island for another eleven months until Charles III's courtiers exchanged Florida for the Cuban capital. The third battalion's last posting became Pensacola, where it stayed until ordered to New York for disbandment in the spring of 1764. Two hundred and fifty-one messmates were left behind in shallow graves as a reminder of the high price paid by those dispatched on Britain's Caribbean operations.[113]

The Royal American Regiment was the largest army unit deployed by the British government during the Seven Years' War. As such, its role was not limited primarily to frontier duty since the troops participated in every major campaign on the mainland from 1758 until the capture of Havana in 1762. Their experiences indicate that eighteenth-century soldiers were not stamped from a press, but slowly acquired their infantry skills over the course of several years. Redcoats followed a progressive training program based on the manual exercise, simple parade movements, and practice in how to load and shoot quickly. The second level, which stressed movement across a battlefield, required the presence of five companies with officers and staff to direct these more complicated maneuvers. Team cohesion was refined in the third stage as troops learned to fight and fire as one body. Advanced training occurred only in wartime when the king's men became familiar with the use of battalion artillery pieces, the construction and defense of siege lines, and drills on the assault of fortified places. Mastery of all these particulars became necessary before the rank and file were truly ready to go into action.

The 60th Foot's mixed combat record indicates how military efficiency matured at different rates according to service conditions. Certainly, the corps' second battalion had the most successful battlefield performance record because political interference and adverse circumstances had minimal effect on its training regimen. Despite an initial dearth of qualified NCOs, which was a problem all 60th detachments shared, Dusseaux's and Monckton's men spent their initial winter together at New York, where they could acquire all the basic infanteering skills. Inclusion in the abortive 1757 Louisbourg expeditionary force, moreover, permitted soldiers to participate in advanced training schemes held at the Halifax encampment that same summer. There, redcoats learned about the attack and defense of fortified places. All of this practical training was put to good use during the 1758 descent on Louisbourg, where the unit gained valuable practical experience in siege work and participated in petite guerre operations along the St. John River. Second battalion detachments performed well in the 1759 Quebec campaign protecting the army's left flank during the critical engagement on the Plains of Abraham, and the unit was only humbled during the Battle of Sainte-Foy when attacked on its flanks by a stronger enemy force. Surviving elements assisted in the citadel's defense until British forces returned to the advance and forced Canada's capitulation in September 1760. Second battalion companies performed well in action provided they were placed in tactical situations for which they were prepared.

Fourth battalion troops followed much the same path as their colleagues with one exception. Heavy losses sustained at the 1758 Ticonderoga affair handicapped the maturation process because quality replacements for trained veterans became harder to find as the war progressed. Members of the corps, however, could still function in a defensive capacity as they demonstrated by fighting off enemy assailants at Fort Ontario a year later. Disciplined coordinated fire with support from artillery pieces proved more than French and Indian irregulars were willing to face. The light company too contributed to success at the shrine of *La Belle Famille* after being detached from the grenadiers laboring at the siege of Fort Niagara. Lessons learned from the 1757 Halifax encampment and the 1759 campaign against Niagara once again came into play during the siege of Fort Levis, where few casualties were taken partly because the troops had plenty of practical experience in conducting such operations. Most of the Royal Americans who set sail with Major General Jeffery Amherst from Fort Ontario in 1760 lived to witness Montreal's surrender.

Third battalion personnel began their careers under a cloud, but redeemed themselves as the war progressed. Dispersed in small packets across Pennsylvania's Lower Counties and Maryland's Eastern Shore for its first winter, recruits lost critical training time being unable to muster together in large enough numbers for exercise beyond the first level of the skills pyramid. Service conditions and combat attrition then intervened to slow the normal course of maturation. A summer spent supporting Fort Edward combined with the loss of their best elements at the Fort William Henry debacle afforded little opportunity for these volunteers to become competent infantrymen. Matters slowly improved through trials by fire at Louisbourg and Quebec. Yet, during the pivotal battle of 13 September 1759, these troops were still relegated to a tertiary role. Only five years after initial deployment did the rank and file reveal their true mettle at the capture of Martinique and the successful siege of Havana.

Colonel John Stanwix's first battalion was beset by a myriad of problems from its inception and should not be regarded as the innovative element that led the British army's adaptation to New World warfare. Political affairs at Philadelphia first derailed effective training and then contributed to the corps' division for separate duties in the Middle Atlantic and the Lower South. The campaigns of 1758 revealed how these assignments had disadvantaged first battalion members whose inexperience contributed to the failure of Major General James Abercromby's coup de mousqueterie outside Fort Ticonderoga. High casualties suffered there and at the equally critical reverse at Grant's Hill meant that there were fewer capable men available for active duty or to train replacements. Prospects brightened somewhat when all the troops were mustered together at Fort Pitt after Stanwix assumed command of the western operational theater in 1759. Ironically, after achieving combat readiness that one summer, their internal cohesion was broken the following year when they occupied former French garrisons across the Great Lakes basin. Since everything that could go wrong had gone wrong for the hapless first battalion, they were never in a state to lead the army's tactical reformations and were in fact the last to embrace them.

Redcoats learned throughout their North American deployment that military success was contingent on more than just combat performance. Support operations were equally as critical since the king's men were required to work throughout their distinctive calendar year. Regular troops thus expended immense amounts of time and energy with axes or shovels in hand before they ever came to grips with the enemy. Such physical exertions thus complemented the soldiers' battlefield accomplishments and, as we shall see in the next chapter, sped the day when Britons could rejoice at the news that "Canada belongs to the King."

4

"No End to their fatigues"

Life within the Ranks of the Royal American Regiment

Hard work was a defining feature of military service in the New World during the Seven Years' War. This reality was driven home to the redcoats as they were increasingly called on to build, supply, maintain, and preserve a far-flung defensive infrastructure that guarded the colonial boundaries. Nature and topography added to this ordeal by obliging the troops to conduct their duties in difficult terrain while exposed to North America's dramatic temperature extremes. Such onerous service conditions eventually took their toll on British regular forces, including the Royal Americans, who finally wilted under the constant grind of exhausting labor and the struggle to survive in an inhospitable climate. Quite rightly, after four years of hardship along the western frontiers, Colonel Henry Bouquet despaired for the welfare of his battalion, and noted that its morale and fitness for service was plummeting because the men could see "no End to their fatigues."[1]

The Swiss officer's lament about the strenuous nature of North American duty remains unappreciated. Common assumptions that the king's men were primarily combat troops, who left the heavy lifting to others, overlook contemporary descriptions of ordinary life in the ranks during the three seasons of a military calendar.[2] These period sources indicate that the waking hours of all regular servicemen were filled by grueling marches, continual rounds of guard duty, and demanding work regimens, the frequency of which increased during the spring and winter months when fewer personnel were available to perform essential tasks. Line regiments stationed in the colonies thus endured greater physical hardship than those posted elsewhere because of a combination of the unique wilderness environment, the logistics required to project military power against New France, and fluctuating manpower supplies available to theater commanders. Accounts of soldiers wielding axes and spades may be more prosaic than glamorous, but it is important to recognize the mundane aspects of army life that facilitated the redcoats' battlefield endeavors.[3]

The Spring Advance (April–June)

Preparations for the spring advance began weeks before the troops actually began their long march to summer encampments. In the late winter months, regimental members proficient with a needle and thread were excused from the daily routine of training, work details, and sentry duty to customize the fit of bulk-lot uniforms supplied to their unit. Annual contracts between proprietary colonels and London merchants stipulated that each soldier's outfit was to consist of a long woolen lined coat, one pair of breeches, stockings, and shoes. A shirt, cravat, and a tricorn hat were the other items provided by this agreement.[4] Newly gazetted units like the Royal Americans also received waistcoats with their initial clothing consignment; thereafter, army tailors converted old coats into vests by simply removing their sleeves. Extra shirts, linen, hose, and footwear, easily abraded by hard wear, were purchased on the local market by corps or company commanders who garnisheed a portion of their men's wages as recompense. Regardless of the supply source, a great deal of effort was expended transforming the amorphous red livery into the distinctive garments that set a "gentleman soldier" apart from the common sort.[5]

Other tradesmen from within the ranks also complemented efforts to improve their battalion's appearance, which was considered a tangible sign of fitness for service. Leather dressers restored shabby accoutrements like slings, shoulder belts, and cartridge boxes, while armorers mended the antiquated Long Land Pattern muskets originally issued to the 60th Foot.[6] The artisans' attention shifted with the annual arrival of new summer camp equipment comprising individual items such as canteens and knapsacks plus the communal property of each six-man squad: a tent, poles, stakes, kettle, and hatchet. Additional supplies, such as watch coats, pioneer capes, bells of arms, drum covers, and powder bags, all designed to protect men and material from the weather, also had to be unpacked and assessed before being issued to the troops prior to their departure from winter quarters.[7]

Regular soldiers served as the high command's primary workforce during the three critical months before the commencement of a new campaign. Since all the provincial levies did not make a strong appearance until the middle of June, the task of forwarding armaments, provisions, and supplies to the operational theater fell to the redcoats while they converged on major assembly areas at Philadelphia, New York, or Boston.[8] These demands weighed heavily on the rank and file, who were already encumbered by sixty-three pounds of personal kit before extra gear like tent poles, pegs, and cooking utensils were distributed for cartage. Although supplementary conveyance appeared in the form of company "bat" horses or civilian carts pressed into service, hapless infantrymen had to carry superfluous items not accorded space in the wagon train.[9]

The redcoats' labor responsibilities increased during each phase of their march toward the combat zone, especially after they reached major coastal centers. In important staging areas like the city of New York, transient soldiers became stevedores, ferrying military cargo to and from the quayside as well as between vessels chartered for expeditionary purposes. This was heavy work since the barrels of various caliber iron guns ranged between one and three tons each. Although lighter brass cannons were considerably easier to manipulate, they too used substantial quantities of ammunition, which had to pass through the troops' hands before being used in battle.[10] Royal Artillery gunners, for instance, expended 1,493 barrels of powder and 17,962 shot during the 1758 operations against Cape Breton. Some of this material reached Louisbourg via the agency of Royal American personnel, who exhausted themselves transshipping vital stores during April and May. About 150 men from the fourth battalion were rendered unfit for active duty by accident or injury "on account of the hard Work and Labour they were put to at New York and elsewhere" that spring.¹¹

Outbound regiments on amphibious operations enjoyed some respite during the sea voyage since participation in one of the three daily sentry cycles became their primary responsibility. Each eight-hour time block was subdivided into equal four-hour watches requiring half the roster to be on deck. The remainder formed a reserve that could be activated should enemy privateers make an appearance. Soldiers not with the security detail were expected to assist the sailors in working the vessels, manning the pumps, or raising the heavy anchors, when required. Only troops scheduled for the night watches were permitted in cramped berths during the daytime for the ships had been apportioned at a maximum rate of just two tons per man.¹²

The artillery train and ammunition were not the only basic supplies needed to sustain an army in the field. Unlike European forces that could live off the land, British units fighting on the empire's periphery had to have reliable food stocks because they usually campaigned well away from civilian sources. Whitehall solved this thorny problem by paying metropolitan contractors to provide rations for each redcoat on campaign, which were then shipped to the New World and stored in magazines near the combat zone. This was an enormous undertaking since some of the daily provender used to feed a fifteen-thousand-man force came from overseas. In New York, for instance, sloops first shuttled troops and their supplies northward to Albany, chosen as the primary distribution center because of its proximity to the confluence of the Mohawk and Hudson rivers. It then became the commissariat's responsibility to dispose of the victuals beyond that point. Although a small wagon train had been established by the Earl of Loudoun to move foodstuffs forward from the inland warehouses, the king's men were once again required to assist with the conveyance of these goods during the final leg of their journey toward Lake Ontario or Lake George.¹³

The most onerous time of the regulars' year began just north of Albany where the advent of wilderness terrain complicated efforts to finish the advance. No longer responsible for just their personal equipment or battalion baggage, the troops were harnessed to convey other essential military stores to the front. The Hudson River proved to be both a blessing and a curse in this regard since it flowed at

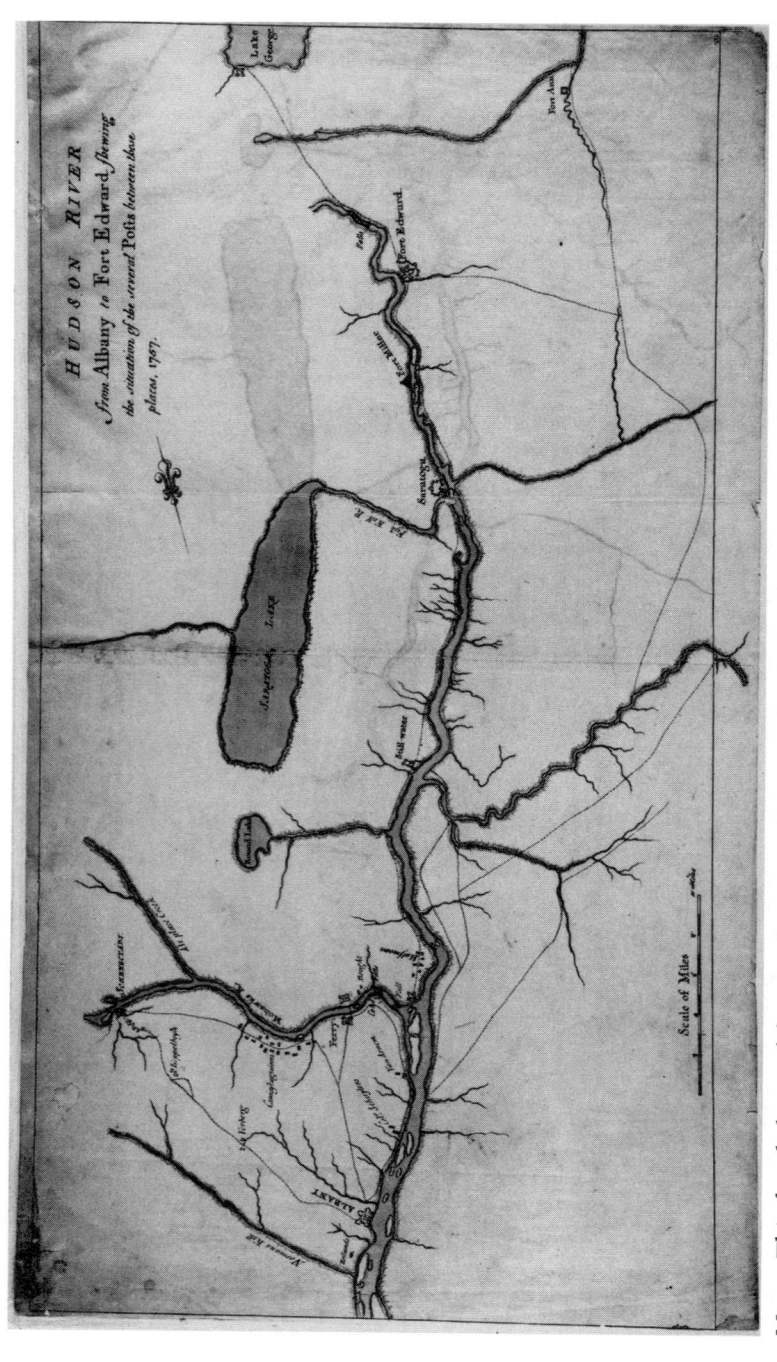

Map 3. This detailed map of the route between Albany and Fort Edward shows the British posts guarding the communication lines in the New York operational theater in 1757. Royal American detachments were active in this region throughout the war. Reproduced by permission of The Huntington Library, San Marino, Calif. (HM 15409)

varying levels through much of the operational theater. Four different types of vessels were employed to forward supplies. Large scows and gondolas proved to be the workhorses of the fleet with whaleboats used primarily as personnel carriers.[14] Shallow-draft bateaux, constructed out of local white pine, also became a familiar sight to many Royal Americans, who could be called on to help propel its ton-and-a-half payload ahead.[15]

Soldiers not immediately assigned to crew provision boats marched out of Albany in the early morning hours and traveled twelve miles north to Half Moon. From there, progress became much slower as they assisted in a series of *décharge* freight operations that circumvented three series of rapids hampering passage up the Hudson. One contemporary noted that "the fatigue is great in rowing, setting, and dragging the boats, with baggage, provisions, artillery, ammunition, tools and other necessaries on board. Much time and labour are spent in forwarding the whole over the portages." The first barrier above Stillwater required all the cargo to be unloaded and transported by wagons between three and six miles overland before being stowed aboard vessels once again. The empty boats were poled or dragged through this turbulent stretch by reinforced crews until they reached calmer water. The second obstruction, beyond Saratoga, was just a mile long and could be navigated with lighter than normal loads.[16] A complete portage was necessary only around the six-hundred-yard length of the Great Falls located eight miles away from the northern terminus of the water route at Fort Edward. At this point, all the stores were placed aboard wagons for the final fourteen-mile crossing to the shores of Lake George. Redcoats not participating directly in this "very heavy wet work" assisted the others by repairing roads and bridges along the entire supply route. During May 1758 alone, the soldiers forwarded 13,000 provision barrels, each weighing approximately 250 pounds, in this fashion. A year later, seventy tons of gunpowder and ammunition were transported in this fashion to Lake George for Amherst's drive toward Crown Point.[17]

Troops assigned duties around the Lake Ontario front endured an equally arduous journey of about three hundred miles. They first began a 142-mile ascent of the Mohawk River at the small town of Schenectady, where the bateaux had been packed to the gunwales with ammunition, food, engineering equipment, and other army stores. Fully loaded craft carried eighteen redcoats, camp equipment for three tents, and twelve barrels of provisions. Westward progress against the current was slow because of numerous rapids encountered along the route. In recalling the heavy labor required to surmount these obstacles, one veteran noted how each crew substituted oars for

> strong scutting poles, with iron at the ends, to prevent their being too soon destroyed by the stones in the river ... which abounded with many, and large ones, and in some places was so shallow, that the men were forced to wade and drag their batteaux after them. Which, together with some cataracts, or great falls of water, rendered this duty very hard and fatiguing, not being able to travel more than seven or eight English miles a day.

Each regimental flotilla was covered by at least a company of soldiers while the remaining forces marched through the countryside. All hands were pressed into service at the Little Falls and the Great Carrying Place, where both boats and gear had to be removed from the water for conveyance overland.[18]

A noticeable transition from the Hudson River drainage basin to the Lake Ontario watershed occurred during the eight-mile haul across the Great Carrying Place to navigable portions of Wood Creek. Here the second stage of the journey began as vessels and stores were launched into the prevailing current. Despite the advantageous flow, the majority of troops marched through difficult terrain because the forty-mile watercourse was obstructed by windfalls and remained too shallow to permit their embarkation. Those working the boats experienced great hardship on this stretch with "Men and Officers all Day almost in the Water dragging the Batteaus with Provision over the Shoals and Rifts." All the forces reembarked upon reaching the eastern end of Oneida Lake after a march of up to eight days. The remaining 110-mile passage was relatively easy as the vessels were rowed in orderly brigades toward their destination. One hundred yards of white water on the Oswego River alone blocked smooth progress. At this impediment, the transports were not emptied but lifted out of the river, propelled forward on log rollers past Onondaga Falls, and then refloated. Skilled pilots guided their craft another mile downstream before the soldiers took ship once again for the final descent to Fort Ontario. A one-way trip from Schenectady to the shores of the Great Lakes took approximately three full weeks to complete.[19]

British supply lines lengthened considerably following the 1759 capture of Fort Niagara and the evacuation of the French inland garrisons east of the Mississippi River twelve months later. Niagara, initially dependent on provisions from Albany magazines, became the pivotal distribution center for the region. Four companies of the Royal American's first battalion occupied this strategic post on 25 July 1760, and then began forwarding supplies to detachments at Detroit later that year.[20] Their task was hampered by the Niagara escarpment's distinctive topography. Government stores from eastern magazines traveled by water as far as the lower landing, where the vessels were emptied. Heavy wooden supply barrels should then have been conveyed by draught animals over the nine-mile route to the forward cache at Fort Schlosser, but a critical shortage of horses obliged the troops to do this job by themselves. Consequently, each 250-pound cask was carried, suspended on a pole, by a team of four redcoats over the entire distance. Such efforts, deemed "very troublesome and attended with great Labour," were just the beginning of travails.[21]

Before the schooner *Huron* and the sloop *Michigan* appeared upon the Great Lakes in mid-1762, 60th troops served as the army's western voyageurs. Until then, each supply convoy began the harrowing journey to Detroit at Fort Schlosser, where freight was loaded aboard their bateaux. Crews then had to work the craft up against the Niagara River for eighteen miles until reaching the entrance to Lake Erie. Two more weeks of intensive rowing across hazardous waters ensued before flotillas reached their destination.[22] The journey could be miserable. Soldiers packed vessels each morning with sixteen supply casks and then spent the next twelve hours at their oars before establishing shoreline camps. Foul weather impeded progress, wreaked havoc with essential baggage, and caused flimsy vessels to founder in high swells. Once the shore was gained, each bateau was completely unloaded before being dragged clear of the pounding surf by its ten-man crew. Several boats were lost on this circuit, requiring survivors to make their way as best they could back to British posts through unfamiliar terrain. Participants remembered legitimate fears at "Crossing the lakes in a justling multitude of such brittle vehicles" constantly exposed "to rains, winds, waves, dark nights, and all the perils of the mariner." Other Royal American teams then assumed responsibility for carrying matériel from Detroit to remoter garrisons.[23]

Presque Isle, situated 120 miles west of Fort Niagara, was the first way station along the lake, marking the intersection of separate operational theaters. This blockhouse constructed by Colonel Henry Bouquet served as the terminus of the Pennsylvania supply line that began at far-off Carlisle. Royal American companies in this sector, however, unlike those serving in New York who enjoyed access to water carriage, had been required to march the entire 348 miles from the eastern slopes of the Appalachian Mountains. Their heavy stores were conveyed either by civilian wagon trains or pack teams that moved up and down the line cut through the wilderness during Brigadier General John Forbes's 1758 advance against Fort Duquesne. Redcoats could cover an average of sixteen miles a day on this road if they were on the move by sunrise.[24] The French retreat from the Ohio Forks then opened the strategic Venango Trail to the victorious British army. This important link between Pittsburgh and Lake Erie was secured by elements of the 60th Regiment in July 1760 when they completed the 142-mile march from Fort Pitt in just ten days.[25]

Royal American detachments drove government livestock overland behind the army as far west as Detroit since cattle, oxen, sheep, swine, and horses could not be conveyed by open vessel. The wearisome journey from Pittsburgh took over a month to complete. Preservation of the herd was key, with the troops covering no more than fifteen miles a day as the animals stopped to graze wherever sufficient grass could be found. The lakeside trail they followed was primitive at best, "almost impassable in many places by the number of horses which have gone over it. Half of the road is nothing but dense brush, where one must use both hands and feet to get through; another quarter is nothing but swamp." Pack animals conveyed only flour for the men or salt for the livestock; redcoats shouldered their own equipment all the way to the narrows between Lakes Huron and Erie before returning to the Pennsylvania frontier on foot.[26]

Summer Encampments (July–November)

The nightmare of the spring advance ended once troops reached the army's primary base camps where they established more permanent facilities for the summer months. Since local British fortifications were too small to accommodate the thousands of troops who converged on major concentration points, large canvas cities were erected outside their walls. Each theater's quartermaster general directed this operation on ground that frequently required intensive grading by the regulars before the tent lines could be established.[27] Soldiers first meticulously cut any trees or brush that lay within their battalion's assigned perimeter. Then teams of men dug around each trunk, cut the auxiliary roots, and removed the leftover stump with block and tackle before smoothing out the entire area. Other preparative chores included the digging of suitable drains around each tent, the construction of fire pits to heat the mess kettles, and the excavation of deep latrine banks located well away from the living areas.[28]

Although sylvan, these military encampments transformed the wilderness temporarily into some of the most densely populated areas of British North America. Each regiment of 1,000 men inhabited a rectangular piece of ground measuring 170 yards wide by 320 yards deep. The rank and file pitched their small tents in ten double rows fronting the common drill square, leaving narrow intervals between each company's neighborhood. These gaps provided access to the officers, kitchens, markets, and privies located aft of the infantrymen's cramped shelters. Next, a broad boulevard twenty yards wide divided the battalion staff from the noncommissioned elements. However, here too social distinction was reinforced as the bunks of thirty or more subalterns were distributed between twenty tents. The quarters of company commanders, who were the first to enjoy private accommodations, were set off by another large passage. One more parallel distanced the captains from the abodes of their immediate superiors: the major and lieutenant colonel. The apex of the regimental social chain was reached at the intersection of the fourth avenue and the grand street running up from the parade ground.[29] This was the location of the colonel's imposing tent and marquee, containing a curtained bedstead, tables, chairs, dining service, and ample pantry; up to six wagon teams were required to carry such heavy baggage into the field. Servants' quarters, hearths, and sutlers' tents were marshaled in distinct tiers behind the commanders' lodgings.[30]

Troops labored for several weeks to construct at least one defensive line around the site to protect it against enemy attack. The simplest works were wattle fences, reinforced by earth, which could be hastily thrown up by each regiment.[31] More substantive barriers of palisades interspersed with log bastions were built as time and circumstances permitted. For these screens, soldiers first had to cut down tall trees, remove the branches, and then sharpen the tops of the stakes before their butt ends were placed in a deep trench. At points vulnerable to enemy cannons, two parallel walls of squared timber were laid twelve feet apart with the gap filled by packed earth. Stouter diamond-shaped bastions mounting defensive artillery were constructed along similar lines. A large ditch, at least seven feet deep and eighteen feet wide, hid another sturdy palisade belt, and clear fields of fire complemented the breastworks. The entire system made it extremely difficult for adversaries to storm the entrenchment without incurring heavy losses.[32]

Military life inside the pale followed a strict routine. A typical day started at first light with the men in each tent awakened by drums beating reveille. The drudge from every mess was soon at the company kitchen preparing breakfast for those not assigned to the morning fatigue parties, who paraded soon after sunrise and took their meals into the field with them. Each orderly's schedule remained the lightest, provided extraordinary duties were not assigned during one of the daily roll calls.[33] His main custodial services included cleaning the living area, airing out the tent, and changing the straw or evergreen boughs on the floor of each canvas abode. More important, this attendant also received the entire food ration for his mess, bought supplementary items from the sutlers, and delivered meals to those precluded by duty from preparing victuals for themselves.[34]

The cook's task was not an enviable one as he tried to transform an individual weekly ration of seven pounds of bread or flour, an equal amount of beef or four pounds of pork, half a pound of rice, three pints of peas, and one pound of cheese or six ounces of butter into palatable fare. The staple meal was "a soop made of the King's pease, with a piece of pork in it" since the salt meat and legumes could be easily boiled in the camp kettle; the flour measure, however, would be especially troublesome if ovens were not readily available to bake it into bread. Sea biscuit, or hardtack, was the alternative. A dietary analysis reveals that between 2,200 and 3,000 calories a day were derived from consumption of these foodstuffs, within the range of what modern adult males need to sustain energy levels. While high in protein, carbohydrates, and fat, government victuals lacked the essential nutrients derived from fresh fruit and vegetables.[35] Such deficiencies could be remedied from seasonal produce harvested from extensive garrison gardens, purchased from civilians, or gathered in the adjacent countryside at the appropriate time. Plunder taken during successful military actions also yielded extra calories. Five tons of fish captured aboard French vessels near Louisbourg, for instance, were eaten by the besiegers, as was the wide variety of livestock purloined during the 1759 expedition against Quebec.[36]

Water served as the enlisted man's chief potable throughout the year. Troops added a ginger-sugar mixture to improve the taste of brackish water taken from sources alongside their line of march.[37] Army-produced spruce beer, made by mixing thirty-one gallons of water with crushed spruce needles and five quarts of molasses, was also consumed by the other ranks at a minimum rate of two quarts per day. Although this home brew was the cheapest refreshment available, sutlers attached to each regiment stocked more palatable ales and ciders for those able to afford them. Peddlers who followed the infantry also sold tea and coffee, suggesting that soldiers, like other period consumers, opted for caffeinated drinks when supplies and their financial resources allowed.[38]

The second soldier out of the tent struggled to don his uniform before joining a small group on the parade square. Since a one-thousand-man regiment and its staff consumed over ten tons of provisions per week, the British high command had to use some available manpower to ensure the safe passage of government stores to the army. While the troops themselves were not usually a primary engine of the supply train, as they had been between May and June, elements from each corps would be detached to support the military's logistical tail. Accordingly, some infantrymen spent the day away from camp mending the roads or marching alongside the convoy as armed escorts. In either case, they would have received orders the previous evening and would now be expected to appear at the assembly point with enough equipment to sustain themselves until the detail returned. After inspection by the officers in charge of the squad, each man would be allowed to have breakfast before leaving camp.[39]

Road repair became a familiar task for Royal American troops, who were first assigned such work at Saratoga in the autumn of 1756. Although not as elaborate as Lieutenant General George Wade's highways that traversed the Scottish highlands, the sixty-five-mile route linking Albany with the northern frontier was certainly one of the busiest thoroughfares in the colonies. Uniformed laborers worked under the supervision of engineers who first surveyed the area to determine the artery's best course. Soldiers then used shovels, picks, and wheelbarrows to make the road as level as possible.[40] Lesser-traveled lanes were simply maintained by having stumps removed and the ruts covered. Utilizing axes and handbills, troops then cleared away the forest bordering the approaches. The fourteen-mile corridor between Fort Edward and Lake George received special attention because it was the area most frequented by enemy raiding parties. Here the vegetation was removed for thirty yards on both sides of the route to deny adversaries cover for ambuscades. Underbrush was also cut down for two parallel paths made at one hundred yards' distance from the road to facilitate the movement of flanking parties.[41]

Escort duty was a dangerous assignment along the northern frontier where the French and their Indian allies from Fort Ticonderoga launched repeated strikes against Albany provision trains. Native warriors clearly enjoyed the initiative in these contests since they attacked only when the odds were in their favor. British defenses were based on a relay system and a belief that strength in numbers would deter aggression; heavily defended wagon processions were rarely attacked.[42] Ideally, redcoats who protected the convoys were divided into four principal detachments: a vanguard, center guard, and rear guard, supported by flanking screens of light infantry. Those on the road aided the drivers only if the wagons became mired. Otherwise, if attacked, they remained in formation until adversaries closed on them to the point where volleys from the Brown Bess would prove their most destructive. The irregulars' assignment proved the most tiresome "of that severe Duty" because they were required to range the woods constantly to ferret out potential threats near the convoy.[43]

First battalion personnel became adept at securing military supply lines during their stays in New York and Pennsylvania. In the latter colony, Forbes's Road, which was three times longer than that connecting Albany and Lake George, provided an optimum environment for enemy infiltration. As Colonel Henry Bouquet explained to a friend, "We hardly send a Convoy without being obliged to fight for it."[44] The difficult mountainous terrain in this theater hampered supply of the forward garrisons, which relied on livestock driven over the Appalachians for some of their sustenance. A herd's slow pace, however, reduced escorts to a crawl, allowing ambushers to strike at will.

A fifty-man detachment commanded by Captain Thomas Jocelyn was attacked on Forbes's Road, near Laurel Hill, on 2 August 1759 in the worst patrol encounter of the war. Jocelyn's party killed ten of the enemy before he and three other soldiers received mortal wounds in the skirmish. Although regular casualties were usually light, constant operations of this nature took an enormous physical and psychological toll on the men, who could never be certain what danger lurked around the next defile.[45]

Three more men from each mess formed the regimental work detail. One would be assigned to the woodcutters while the other two would be marched off at 6:30 A.M. to labor on a variety of military installations, collectively known as "the king's works." Although defensive lines had already been established around the camp's periphery, they required constant reinforcement or enlargement as did the major fortifications adjacent to the compound. Brawn was the chief currency to fell trees, level ground, excavate earth for ditches or casemates, and haul stones for masonry projects.[46] It was in this capacity that Royal Americans contributed to the building of Forts Edward, Ligonier, Ontario, Pitt, Presque Isle, and Sandusky during the course of the Seven Years' War.[47] If no offensive operations were pending, redcoats exerted themselves until shortly before nightfall when the firing of a lone signal gun ended their labors. Shorter shifts lasting approximately four hours in duration allowed relays of troops to both work and train during the daylight hours. Regardless of assignment all those comprising the fatigue parties were expected to perform "a good day's work"; such was an infantryman's lot in the New World.[48]

Soldiers with specialized skills were in high demand since competent craftsmen were needed to assist the engineers with various projects. Headquarters thus obliged each regiment to specify the number and qualifications of all tradesmen within its ranks.[49] Soldiers with construction knowledge headed the list of desirables. While brute strength was a prerequisite to fell trees in the forest, float rafts to the landing place, draw timber to the building site, and then square it with an adze, greater ability was needed to supervise mills that processed logs into lumber faster than manual sawyers could. The finished products were then turned over to framers, who erected post-and-beam skeletons for the storehouses, barracks, and administration buildings that formed the center of every major installation. Roofing and siding was provided by workmen who covered roofs with locally produced shingles and by carpenters who faced exterior walls with clapboards while others built staircases and floors. Berths were then added to the interiors of living quarters, which were finally ready for occupancy after painters trimmed them with whitewash.[50]

The talents of those used to working with earth and stone were also essential for the construction of army posts. Soldiers with mining experience applied their skills to cutting through bedrock, excavating deep wells for the garrison, or fashioning artillery-proof powder magazines. Commodious storehouses were likewise dug under the curtain walls so that perishables could be preserved in the cooler subterranean air of warrens or unused casemates.[51] Other craftsmen, such as stonecutters, brick makers, and masons, complemented efforts to construct essential fort components. Durable footings for the buildings had to be set, lodgings faced with brick or stone finished, and fireplaces with chimneys erected. Artificers either performed these tasks themselves or supervised those who were less proficient. Consequently, soldiers who initially possessed few such skills became "very expert and handy" in the construction trades, acquiring valuable practical experience as they helped to build military installations.[52]

Not all of this toil was anathema to the men who received extra remuneration for some of these fatigues. Income was a real concern for regular troops whose daily wage amounted to less than six pence sterling after stoppages for uniforms, necessaries, and other company off-reckonings were withheld by the paymaster.[53] Such a mean subsistence was occasionally augmented by theater commanders, who would distribute one or two gills of rum per day whenever soldiers performed road construction or labored on the king's works in abysmal weather. These disbursements were typically made in two allowances, half in the morning and the remainder at nightfall, or the whole issue apportioned at the end of the day. Whiskey was the common substitute when rum was not readily available.[54] Supplementary pay accrued whenever labor was required on permanent military facilities, such as barracks and storehouses, or anytime men worked exclusively in the bateaux service. Watermen's earnings increased the most dramatically during the war: from fifteen additional New York pence (10d. sterling) daily in 1758 to three shillings (2s. sterling) by the end of the war. While not as spectacular, the wages of tradesmen, such as stonemasons, rose as did the compensation for general

The 1759 British encampment at Lake George, New York, is the subject of this painting by Lieutenant Thomas Davies, in which the orderly tent lines are clearly evident. Courtesy of the Fort Ticonderoga Museum.

laborers, which grew from nine to nineteen New York pence (6–12d. sterling) between 1756 and 1760.[55]

The final soldier from every tent prepared to join one of the three details providing the base's security needs. The quarter and rear guards mounted every morning for a twenty-four-hour period, whereas the pickets were posted by nightfall. A flurry of activity followed breakfast as the sentinel-designates worked on their kit since they were expected to appear in clean and neatly accoutered uniforms.[56] The quarter guards, who were stationed on the opposite side of the parade ground from their battalion, consisted of up to thirty privates under the command of a captain, two subalterns, two sergeants, and a drummer. They ensured that peace and order were maintained within the tent lines. Men caught gambling, stealing, or carousing would be detained until their fate was decided by superior authorities. After dark, a small detachment from the quarter guard reinforced the six-strong rear guard, placed at the back of the camp with the sutlers, to ensure that boisterous behavior ceased after fires were extinguished at sunset. General officers insisted that all off-duty personnel be abed shortly after the beating of tattoo so that nothing from within the camp would distract the exterior ring of sentinels.[57]

Sentries from the picket guard formed the first line of defense in case of enemy attack. Every battalion provided a captain, two subalterns, two sergeants, two drummers and fifty men for this important detail. Their responsibilities included manning the advance alarm posts as well as providing covering parties for laborers and others working beyond the range of the camp's guns. Attentiveness was essential whenever the pickets were deployed because adversaries often skulked nearby, aiming to take prisoners for intelligence purposes. Because sentinels at the most isolated posts were especially vulnerable to a quick stroke, they were not allowed to malinger, smoke, or lay down their arms during each hour-long vigil.[58] Anyone approaching their position was to be challenged three times for the proper parole at bayonet point before being shot if the correct password was not disclosed. These out guards, who were stationed around the entire camp, also had to be cognizant of anyone trying to leave the British lines surreptitiously, and sentries were empowered to fire on potential marauders or those intending to desert.[59]

Dissatisfaction with pay, clothing allowances, and rations was the primary cause for soldiers to absent themselves without permission. Commanders closely regulated their men's activities through mandatory roll calls when a company officer paraded his charges to confirm their presence in camp. Unexcused absence from any of these three or four daily reviews was equated with desertion, and delinquents were instantly confined upon first sight.[60] Opportunities for flight were also constrained by standing orders requiring redcoats and sutlers to secure valid passes, signed by at least a captain, before they were allowed to travel beyond camp lines. Sentries were ordered to arrest anyone traversing their watch zones without bona fide permits.[61] Finally, a strict dress code was maintained among the regulars since some deserters invariably tried to change their appearance by donning civilian garb before sneaking off. Daily orders stipulated when troops were allowed to work in other than full military livery.[62]

Desertion was a serious offense under the Articles of War. All recruits had Sections 2 (mutiny) and 6 (desertion) read to them when they appeared before a justice of the peace during the attestation process. No regular could plead ignorance of the indenture agreement made between himself and the king. In exchange for food, raiment, and pay, an enlistee consented to serve Georgian rulers faithfully for a stipulated amount of time. Truancy from the battalion, like evasion from a civilian master, was a breach of contract often magnified by property crime if individuals fled with their uniforms, arms, and accoutrements. All weapons with ammunition belonged to the Board of Ordnance; uniforms remained the colonel's assets until he had been completely reimbursed from wage garnishments; belts, slings, and ancillary equipment were company possessions whose loss was borne on a captain's contingency account.[63] More important, soldiers who decamped toward the enemy might provide adversaries with important details about the strength, morale, defenses, and operational plans of British forces. Deserters could also be utilized by the opposition to draw off more corps members, decreasing the size and effectiveness of redcoat units. Capital punishment was therefore quickly meted out to fugitive servicemen captured in a French uniform.[64]

Regimental courts-martial, the lowest level of the British military's two-tiered justice system, dealt with misdemeanors committed within each battalion. Rowdiness, intoxication, petty theft, or neglect of duty invariably led to incarceration by the quarter guard until a hearing could be held. Those taken into custody appeared before a review board consisting of a captain and four subalterns generally within twenty-four hours of confinement. This panel based its deliberations on the merits of the written charge, balancing eyewitness testimony with the prisoner's character and service record. Considerable weight was given to the "Custom of the Army" in these proceedings, with fines or reduction in rank ordered to reform mildly aberrant behavior.[65] Soldiers found guilty of threatening camp safety by neglect or not being present for duty, imperiling food supplies, or illegally disposing of personal rum rations drew punishments ranging from public humiliation to a sharp flogging with a cat-o'-nine-tails.[66]

General courts-martial adjudicated all capital crimes: grand larceny, rape, desertion, and mutiny. Prisoners awaiting their appearance before a solemn council of twelve company commanders and presiding field officer were treated far more severely by the provost than those confined by the quarter guard. Detainees were shackled in the most secure area of the lines, given only bread and water for nourishment, and required to wear their regimental coat inside out as a mark of shame. Hearings were held in the center of camp at a special marquee set aside for that purpose so that off-duty personnel could attend.[67] As with lower court proceedings, charges were read, testimony was evaluated, and defendants were given an opportunity to explain their actions before jury members, who then would decide their fate by a plurality of votes. German soldiers serving in the Royal Americans were provided with a translator to interpret proceedings since English was the language of command even in the 60th Foot. Very few soldiers, however, were acquitted of their crimes. Pending review of the verdict by the senior theater commander, or recommendations of clemency by the court, sentences were severe and carried out within hours of the verdict.[68]

Military authorities could not implement the wide variety of penalties assigned by the civilian judiciary for serious offenses. Transportation or long imprisonment terms were simply not feasible in temporary army encampments. By default, public flogging was the principal method used to render punishment and deter others from criminal behavior. Sentences of up to a thousand lashes were administered on the regimental parade ground.[69] Just after fatigue parties returned from their labors in the evening, prisoners were escorted to the front of the tent lines and then secured to a triangle formed by three halberds. The punishment was supervised by a drum major who assured that each of his subordinates inflicted twenty-five strokes before relinquishing the whip to a fresher arm. After each unfortunate was scourged two hundred times, they could be paraded before other regiments where the process was repeated until an attending surgeon ended the ordeal or justice was satisfied.[70]

Executions, reserved for only the most hardened offenders, were typically conducted in the morning hours after the beating of reveille. The condemned, who had previously received a chaplain's ministrations, were marched slowly past their assembled comrades or the battalion pickets wearing a noose around their neck and a placard of their crimes.[71] Pardons were sometimes granted at the gibbet because the sight of a hangman was believed to be sufficient to bring prisoners back to a proper sense of their duty. A reprieve, however, could be conditional upon acceptance of some unpleasant assignment like acting as the army's executioner for the remainder of the campaign.

Since trained men were in short supply, only those with a long history of larceny or desertion were actually hung from the gallows until sundown or dispatched by a firing squad.[72]

Exceptionalist historians, who believe that the colonies were a unique place relatively free from corrupt Old World mores, suggest that different attitudes toward discipline and military justice became wedge issues between the redcoats and some of their provincial counterparts. These scholars argue that sporadic mention of metropolitan cruelty, arrogance, godlessness, and discrimination in the diaries of Massachusetts Bay servicemen indicated that a great deal of rancor and factionalism permeated the summer camps. Therefore, in this environment, where people from different parts of the British Empire were thrown together for lengthy periods of time, colonial elements developed a greater sense of self-awareness, a proto-American identity, which spread among the citizenry after their troops' return from the front. Joint maneuvers thus actually weaken ties among Englishmen on both sides of the Atlantic, despite their being allied in a bloody war.[73]

Scenarios tracing early fissures in the first British Empire to military encampments are based on the premise that colonists and redcoats were already diverging as two separate peoples since troops from the United Kingdom were perceived "as strangers who came from a distant land" by the locals brigaded alongside them. Such assertions, however, disregard a preponderance of scholarly evidence describing the social, political, religious, economic, and cultural ties that bound George II's expansive dominions together.[74] Moreover, British regulars and their provincial counterparts shared a common ancestry with at least one-third of the king's men actually recruited in North America. The remainder originated from all parts of the United Kingdom, or from Protestant Europe, just like the majority of settlers or their near forebears. Quantitative analysis reveals that 30 percent of infantrymen in line regiments were born in England; Scots from both sides of the Highland line and Irishmen each provided almost 28 percent of enlistees; foreign Protestant names comprised 10 percent of names appearing on War Office muster rolls; and American-born personnel made up the rest. Despite heavy ethnic clustering in some units, imperial forces were not alien to the heterogeneous colonial population, whose own variegated folkways persisted for several generations.[75]

Claims about metropolitan versus colonial antipathy must be weighed in light of the persistent factionalism already extant throughout British North American society. As regular field officers knew, they would have to become mediators any time squabbles broke out among the different provincial corps. This was especially true in the northern theater where political wrangling between New England, New York, and the Jerseys over boundary lines, Indian affairs, and mutual military obligations inevitably weakened the army's cohesion whenever these auxiliary forces mustered together. Parochialism was so widespread that Brigadier General John Stanwix had to censure his largely provincial army that secured access to the Mohawk River in 1758, warning "all the Soldiers of the severall Corps not to Cast any reflection or utter any Language that is affrontg or abusive to each other, on pain of being punisht."[76]

As in other areas of colonial American history, care must be taken not to normalize the New England experience by broadly applying it to other regions. The citizen-soldiers of Massachusetts Bay were not always highly regarded by the redcoats because of their inexperience and penchant for leaving operational areas despite the strategic situation.[77] Regular officers did understand contractual obligations—their own men had signed indentures with the Crown stipulating the precise obligations of all parties involved as part of the recruitment process—but northeastern troops continually ran off in defiance of Sections 2 (mutiny) and 6 (desertion) of the Articles of War, which were read to them on parade just before operations commenced.[78] It is not surprising, then, that commanders utilized their manpower resources to best effect by relegating inconstant units to secondary roles rather than deploying them near the enemy. This was not a calculated insult to colonial martial pretensions. In an age when it took a soldier at least two years of continuous training to learn his craft, colonial regiments raised only for one campaign were less useful on the battlefield than those that remained in uniform for more than nine months at a time. Other corps, however, like the Virginia Regiment, some New York and New Jersey battalions, as well as seasoned Pennsylvanian formations, garnered praise from European veterans on account of their professionalism and steady service.[79]

Party spirit was less evident in Brigadier General John Forbes's western army, which was half the size of those operating in New York and needed the cooperation of all echelons to conquer Fort Duquesne.

Redcoats and auxiliaries marched together, endured the same physical privations, worked side by side on fortress construction, and fought in tandem whenever the enemy made an appearance. Moreover, unlike in the Lake George–Lake Champlain command, there was little bickering over duty assignments or accusations of preferential treatment because all had to pull their weight to achieve victory.[80] Dissension was also minimized because of the close personal bonds that developed between officers of both services. Aside from the numerous foreign Protestants commissioned in the Pennsylvania Regiment after stints with the Royal Americans, men like Robert Stewart, James Gorrell, and Edward Hubbard received appointments to Colonel John Stanwix's first battalion after meritorious duty with the Virginia and Maryland forces.[81]

Despite petty resentment between army elements "newly raised and collected from all parts of the Globe, from the Highlands of Scotland, Germany, &ca to South Carolina," as Brigadier General John Forbes expressed it, this association of metropolitan troops and provincial levies did possess an often overlooked commonality. Historians have isolated three principal elements in this nascent communal self-awareness: Protestantism, allegiance to the Hanoverian dynasty, and intense antipathy toward the Bourbon monarchs.[82] Granted, such a supranationality was still inchoate and was embraced by various levels of society at different times. Yet military service against Louis XV's forces did provide an ideal matrix for the evolution of a greater *British* consciousness that drew soldiers from different regions together.[83] This was especially true in the New World where Enlightenment strictures against the annihilation of one's opponents had been abandoned in the petite guerre operations conducted by a ruthless enemy. Consequently, during the desperate campaigns of the Seven Years' War, "British" or "French" were not abstract national labels but stark designations replete with meaning.[84]

Anglo-provincial armies contrived a positive group image as Britons by measuring themselves against a merciless foe. Their antagonists, usually a mixed force of French *troupes de la marine*, Canadian militia, and American Indian warriors, personified the evils of the Bourbon court through their ignoble treatment of noncombatants, prisoners, and the dead.[85] Such wanton behavior contrasted unfavorably with the chivalrous conduct of His Britannic Majesty's troops, who were deemed brave, resolute, and humane by English-speaking correspondents.[86] Notwithstanding endless provocations throughout the conflict, their superior character was most evident when Major General Jeffery Amherst's three armies converged on Montreal in 1760 but did not seek retribution for the "cruel and barbarous war" waged against them. Final triumph over a despised enemy was key to the sense of solidarity fostered among George II's subjects on both sides of the Atlantic Ocean.[87]

It is unfortunate that Puritan sensibilities have colored perceptions about the redcoats' piety since Protestantism was a collective bond unifying the entire British army.[88] Despite censure for gambling and profanity from those at least three generations removed from the Half-Way Covenant (1662), which radically diluted terms for membership in New England's Congregational churches, George II's land forces were among society's most religiously observant groups. Sunday church attendance was mandatory for off-duty personnel, who listened to sermons of spiritual and temporal merit delivered by battalion clerics or their deputies. In their absence, laymen from all ranks led proceedings. Failure to attend these obligatory functions resulted in heavy fines or other disciplinary action.[89] Primary sources also indicate that religious exercises could be held on Wednesday and Friday with additional prayers read each evening before the beating of retreat or in the morning just after sunrise.[90] The Royal Americans were fortunate to have two prominent colonists among their pastors: Reverend John Ogilvie, an Anglican priest, and Reverend Michael Schlatter, a Swiss émigré who served the German Reformed congregations in Pennsylvania. Both these men began their itinerant duties between various battalions shortly after their appointments in 1757. Schlatter's fluency in German was especially beneficial for the unit's foreign Protestant personnel, whom he instructed at least once a week in their native tongue. Ogilvie's spiritual labors among the redcoats also drew favorable comment from appreciative superiors.[91]

A third vital strand binding Britons together was fealty to the Crown. This was especially true for the redcoats, who had each sworn at induction "to be true to our Sovereign Lord King GEORGE, and to serve Him honestly and faithfully, in Defense of his Person, Crown, and Dignity, against all His Enemies or Opposers whatsoever." This close relationship between the king and his troops was reinforced in a wide variety of ways. Both George II and George III, in a tangible expression of concern for their men's welfare, insisted that all regular personnel receive new clothing allotments on the anniversary of their respective birthdays or coronations.[92] Army detachments, wherever they were stationed, reciprocated by staging regimental reviews, balls, and other festivities to commemorate such important dynastic occasions. As one Royal American officer reported: "Yesterday we celebrated the Anniversary of His Majesty's birth Day, in our little Way. We could not make the Noise & Figure that undoubtedly you did: but three tolerable Volleys at noon; a Bone Fire & 6 hand Grenades at Night, with loyal Healths & loud Huzzas, were the whole of our humble & hearty rejoicings." Other symbolic means were utilized throughout the year to remind the rank and file about their duty to king and country. For instance, the daily parole announced by commanders to their assembled men often contained references to the Crown. Such passwords as "St. James's," "King George," "King George and Queen Charlotte," or "Prince of Wales" had to be given by garrison members when they were challenged by a sentry to distinguish friend from foe. These audible reminders about shared allegiance helped sustain communal bonds among active-duty personnel.[93]

Extant orderly books reveal that royal references were most numerous on days after recent battlefield triumphs over enemy forces in the New World, Europe, or India. Right from the first victories of the war, soldiers throughout North America increasingly commemorated their comrades' valor as Britain's string of conquests at Lake George, Louisbourg, Fort Frontenac, Quebec, Montreal, Pondicherry, and Havana grew. On such occasions, military festivities provided a public forum to reinforce British homogeneity as well as raise morale through both religious and secular rites. Protestant faith was first on parade when all soldiers save the sentries were assembled in front of their tent lines for a service of prayer and thanksgiving. Theater commanders then used gunpowder for a massive pyrotechnics display to end the day on a victorious note.[94]

The *feu de joie* (rejoicing fire) was choreographed according to strict army protocol. Observance began in the early evening after divine services, with all the battalions arrayed in long ranks around the camp according to regimental seniority. The festivities were orchestrated by the senior officer and his staff, who took post on the most prominent spot to see and be seen by the troops. A twenty-one-gun royal salute by the heaviest artillery pieces began the celebration.

Even before the smoke could clear, soldiers from the most senior foot regiment then answered the cannons' roar with a barrage of musketry that was sustained by sequential battalions as their small arms' fire swept around the base perimeter like falling dominoes in a spree lasting up to fifteen minutes. By the time the most junior provincial corps had discharged its weapons, the regulars had reloaded and two additional fusillades encircled the camp before the general's three cheers were drowned out by the huzzahs of the masses and shouts of "God save the king." Afterward, normal strictures against lights in camp were relaxed and large bonfires were lit to prolong the merriment.[95] By word and deed servicemen from across the empire celebrated their joint victories over an oppressive foe in ceremonies designed to create solidarity among the rank and file.

The staccato of small arms was also heard in salutes on one other occasion: to honor comrades who died as a result of illness or enemy action. Although luminaries such as Brigadier General John Forbes, Lord Viscount Howe, or Lieutenant Colonel Roger Townshend might be buried in the consecrated grounds of colonial churchyards, most troops were interred in a common graveyard adjacent to the nearest encampment.[96] The committal service on these somber occasions was brief. Six soldiers of equal rank to the departed carried his pall to the cemetery, attended by battalion representatives from each company. A short eulogy was delivered by the chaplain before the blanket-draped body was finally lowered into the ground. The size and composition of firing parties varied according to the deceased's status, but even the fidelity of lowly privates was recognized by three musket volleys from a sergeant's party of at least twelve infantrymen.[97] Personal belongings were auctioned off at a later date, enabling the company paymaster or designated executor to satisfy outstanding debts before remitting the balance to rightful heirs.[98]

A comprehensive roster of fatigues, convoy escorts, sentry duty, parades, and exercises, all conducted within the company or battalion setting, left troops with little time for themselves; soldiers spent much of their spare time simply trying to keep body and uniform clean. Limited recreational pursuits, which might lead to incidental contact with personnel from other units, included wrestling, swimming, and fishing.[99] Socializing was primarily restricted to the evening hours before the beating of tattoo, when the quarter guard began the nightly rounds to detain those outside their tents. Repeated bans on gambling and rum sales suggest that illicit activities were perennial camp problems in the twilight hours. Such activities were discouraged because the cash-strapped troops often pawned articles of clothing and equipment to pay their debts or buy more alcohol. This inevitably led to theft of other accoutrements before the next inspection, contributing to altercations between the men.[100] Occasional diversions were offered by Indian allies who lodged adjacent to the main lines. Despite the presence of guards posted to discourage intercourse between the two communities, some soldiers willingly risked arrest to be entertained by the theatrics of a Native war dance.[101]

Autumn's first frosts did not immediately signal the end of forward operations since British troops continued to labor on construction projects until provincial forces returned home in late November.[102] Extra measures were taken at this time to protect soldiers from the plunging temperatures. Commanders procured heavier clothing like capes, mittens, flannel waistcoats, and thick stockings for their men. Living quarters, likewise, were transformed into more durable abodes by two important modifications: first, a wooden framework designed to support thatch was built around the canopies; and second, a small fireplace, with a chimney that rose above the height of the new outer shell, was installed in the rear of each tent. Such alterations, made by the troops themselves, significantly weatherproofed their canvas shelters and extended the infantry's stay along the northern frontier.[103]

Winter Cantonments and Garrisons (December–March)

The onset of frigid weather was a sign for British commanders to disband their armies after the campaigning season drew to a close. Withdrawal to winter quarters, however, did not obviate the harsh physical demands of military service since the regulars could be required to haul heavy artillery pieces for a portion of the trek. Moreover, a drop in water levels along the Hudson River corridor obliged the redcoats to carry all their personal gear sixty-one miles down the communication link from Lake George until they could be deposited in bateaux for the short run from Half Moon to Albany. At least five nightly bivouacs were required during this egress as regiments moved at staggered intervals along narrow roads that could not accommodate the whole army at one time. Troops simply lay on top of spruce boughs surrounded by large fires at night if opportunity did not permit the fabrication of adequate shelter.[104]

The town of Albany served as a temporary transit center for the battalions not assigned to secure local defenses through the winter months. While some provincial levies disbanded there, the majority turned eastward a few miles below the town at Green Bush and followed the main thoroughfares back into New England. In their footsteps trod a number of regular units assigned winter cantonments in either Massachusetts, Connecticut, or Rhode Island.[105] Corps headed for warmer climes stowed equipment aboard river sloops for the swift trip to New York City, which took less than a week. Those fortunate to be staying in the capital's environs had little farther to go; others destined for Pennsylvania or Maryland had at least another march of seventy-nine miles to Philadelphia before reaching billets there.[106] The king's men could then be required to retire overland an additional 144 miles to Annapolis if they were not embarked on vessels plying northern portions of the Chesapeake Bay. Troops moving at the accustomed rate of fourteen miles per day traveled westward toward the Susquehanna River for at least another week before they reached their final destination at Lancaster.[107]

European regulars normally used the winter months to recuperate, refit, and train for the next summer's operations. Royal American troops from the first battalion, however, were not so fortunate when they established quarters at Philadelphia in early December 1756. Without adequate barracks space for accommodations, they became pawns in a bitter revenue dispute waged between elements of the local assembly and Lieutenant Governor William Denny. Legislators, rankled that the Penn family's deputy was able to supplement his income from tavern license fees, restricted military billets to public houses knowing that the additional costs of providing soldiers with provisions, bedding, and fuel would drive modest innkeepers out of business. Almost 500 battalion members, therefore, were crowded into cramped lodgings by Christmas with 167 of their comrades still not provided for through the holiday season.[108] By then, the troops' misery was compounded by exposure to smallpox, which had begun to spread among the rank and file. Satisfactory facilities for all the redcoats were not provided until the middle of January, five weeks after the Royal Americans had marched into Philadelphia. They even had to do without a fully furnished hospital, despite the growing number of soldiers afflicted by the high fever, nausea, and muscle aches caused by the distemper. It was only following the Earl of Loudoun's threat to station an additional complement of regulars in the capital that the troops' needs were met.[109] This delay had proven costly since quartering troops in dispersed taverns without adequate supervision invariably led to drunkenness or desertion and did not prove conducive to the assimilation of new recruits.[110]

Living conditions were only marginally better for those assigned quarters in smaller rural Pennsylvania communities like Lancaster, Reading, and York, or in hamlets along Maryland's Eastern Shore. The lack of barracks and taverns in remoter locales meant that the soldiers were frequently required to transform derelict buildings into satisfactory accommodations first before they finally struck their tents for the season.[111] Once in these temporary asylums, troops then had to forage for their own fuel if politicians refused to reimburse local residents for supplying this necessity to the king's men. Only after the third winter of the conflict had colonial authorities begun to provide enough satisfactory accommodations for the redcoats to enjoy decent housing away from the front.[112]

Sixteen companies of the Royal Americans drawn from the first and fourth battalions were the first detachments not to retreat to warmer quarters when they assumed responsibility for the Lake George–Albany communications link during the winter of 1758–59, as more senior units had done earlier in the war. Their experiences in a northern stronghold presaged the difficulties other detachments would endure through 1772 when the entire force was finally transferred to the West Indies.[113] Despite marked temperature differences, both postings actually shared a great deal in common. Disease, a deleterious climate, and isolation all took their toll on the soldiers who found themselves "scattered among the Savages, & in the remotest parts of our New Frontiers." These burdens fell inordinately on Brigadier General John Stanwix's corps, which found itself stranded in the Great Lakes watershed for six consecutive years (1758–1764) at the same time muster rolls were reduced by casualties, discharges, and sickness. Accordingly, there were fewer able-bodied men available to complete essential tasks just when full complements were needed for garrison maintenance and security.[114]

Conventional wisdom maintained that fresh air, hard work, and exercise were the best preventive measures against the bane of all snowbound detachments, scurvy.[115] Notwithstanding these prescriptions, troops initially stationed around the Great Lakes watershed were decimated by this malady. The Royal Americans' fourth battalion was especially hard-hit at Fort Ontario during the winter of 1759–60. One post commander informed superiors that his force was so stricken that he would shortly have no men left "to fetch wood for the sick nor hands enough to man the Ferryboat, or to keep a Centry at this Post; when that time comes, which must be soon, we shall have no resource left, than to shut the Gates & wait our Doom." Captain Lewis Steiner's fears were justified since 135 men (18 percent) from his corps died from scurvy and another 416 soldiers (55 percent) survived bouts of the disease. Only 202 infantrymen (27 percent) were left fit for duty by the time that spring temperatures warmed the Great Lakes. Scurvy proved to be a greater nemesis than French muskets: the battalion suffered almost three times the casualty rate in winter garrisons than they had endured during the bloody repulse at Fort Ticonderoga.[116]

Fortunately, this scourge, which also incapacitated occupation forces at Niagara and Quebec that same winter, proved to be the last significant outbreak of the war. Shipments of antiscourbutics like lime juice and cider failed to arrive in time to save all those manifesting "the spungy fetid Gums of a livid Colour, with livid Blotches, and Ulcers of the Legs" that were the disease's classic symptoms.[117] Disturbed by reports of high troop mortality rates in the New World, metropolitan officials insisted that lemons, in addition to locally grown root vegetables and fruit, be included in the soldier's rations. Thereafter, eighteenth-century-style victory gardens planted with potatoes, turnips, cabbages, melons, and apples became an integral part of British compounds. Daily work details, supervised by a capable NCO, assumed responsibility for these agricultural projects situated in large fenced plots just outside the garrisons.[118]

Scurvy's threat was reduced to such an extent that the disease is not mentioned by Mrs. Anne Grant of Laggan, the daughter of Ensign Duncan McVicar, in her halcyon reminiscences about life at Fort Ontario during the early 1760s. Her eye had been captivated by the commander's residence, where he maintained an ample library and regularly entertained regimental staff. Younger subalterns, like her father, flourished in such a convivial environment through close

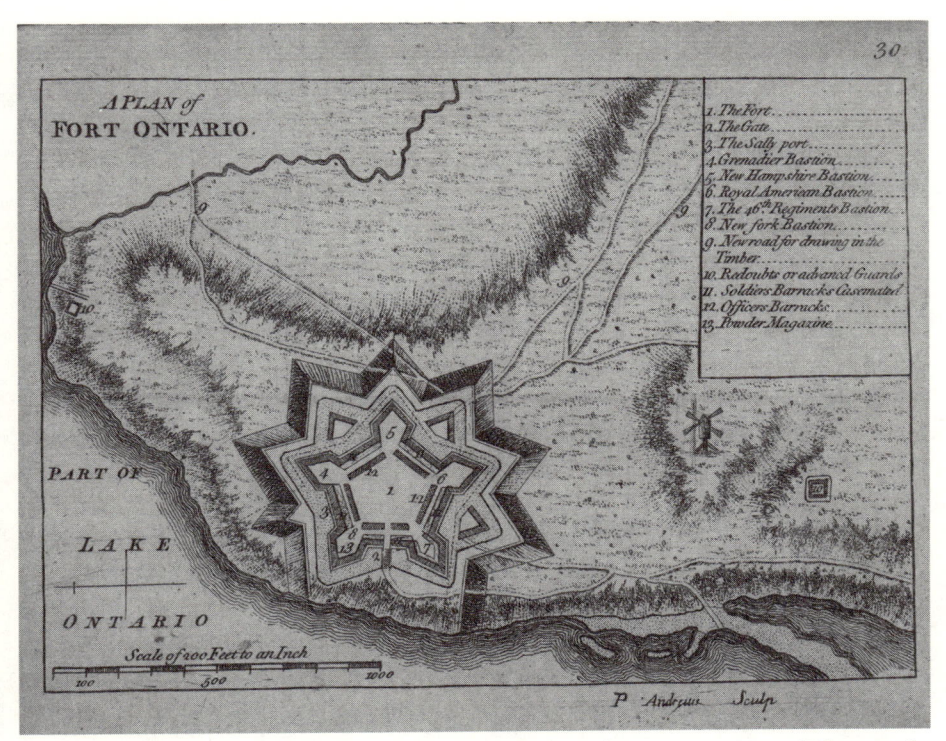

This contemporary plan of Fort Ontario appeared in John Rocque's *Set of Plans and Forts in America*, published in London in 1765. Fourth battalion personnel labored on this mammoth log-and-earth fortification between 1759 and 1760. Reproduced by permission of The Huntington Library, San Marino, Calif.

interaction with more experienced officers as well as from access to classical works on history and literature. When not employed, army gentry whiled away the hours playing chess or musical instruments and enjoyed outdoor pursuits such as hunting, fishing, and gardening.[119] Other pleasant diversions appeared when dignitaries arrived for brief visits. In one notable instance, first battalion members provided hospitality for John Bartram, who was canvassing Britain's colonies for new plants or other curiosities. Sent to the Ohio Country in 1761 by Lieutenant Colonel Sir John St. Clair, himself a diligent improver and a supporter of the Royal Society's efforts, the botanist spent several weeks exploring the region in the company of knowledgeable redcoats. Fort Pitt's commandant, Colonel Henry Bouquet, even provided armed escorts and guides for the civilian, whose work was enhanced by these likeminded soldiers interested in the natural world.[120]

Elite recollections tend to be idyllic for they seldom contain explicit references to internecine garrison disputes or mention the spartan living conditions and Herculean tasks undertaken by enlisted personnel. Certainly, a dearth of European women on the frontier was a fundamental cause for quarrels between those living in the remote posts. During wartime, military authorities had tolerated a limited number of army wives, since their ministrations as nurses, laundresses, and cooks released soldiers for more pressing tasks.[121] Quotas were fixed according to regimental establishment. Although a maximum of six females per company were allowed to join their husbands in the field, usually only four per company were accredited for one-thousand-man battalions with three approved for units mustering seven hundred rank and file. Those who refused to serve in menial capacities, however, lost their rations' privileges and were banished from camp. More dependents certainly traveled with the redcoats than were carried on battalion strengths, but such indulgence became less common as communication lines lengthened and greater fiscal restraints were placed on the overseas army after the Treaty of Paris. Sometimes even a large garrison like Niagara was home to only one white woman for months at a time.[122]

Austere lodgings, characterized by one resident as "cold and comfortless," also contributed to the ennui apparent at more remote stations. Typically, two infantry squads totaling twelve men would share a small room equipped with a fireplace, cooking implements, benches, candlestick, table, bunks, and bedding. Major emplacements like Fort Edward or Fort Pitt contained substantial housing blocks constructed and furnished by the troops who had been present during the summer months.[123] Other posts, however, like Niagara, Presque Isle, Michilimackinac, and Edward Augustus, afforded much more primitive facilities, occasionally leaving the garrison bereft of even the most basic necessities. Officers reported that their men were at times required to lay on ground floors; lodge without benefit of beds, blankets, or kitchen utensils; and endure freezing temperatures in buildings fitted solely with bark-covered roofs. Although better dwellings were built on the few Upper Country bases retained after Pontiac's Rebellion, some 60th detachments made do with inadequate shelter for much of their stay in the North American hinterland.[124]

The rank and file did not spend much time in the barracks, however, because half of their working week now passed in the guardhouse as part of the sentry detail. Garrison members habitually enjoyed only a day's respite between watch rotations because troop establishments had been reduced from one hundred to forty-five company effectives by 1763.[125] Preparations for these duties, which were designed to prevent the loss of men and equipment to desertion, theft, or fire, commenced well before breakfast when a new squad cleaned their clothing and arms prior to inspection. After their morning meal, they attended the adjutant on the parade ground where the guard was put through a rigorous drill session to keep them adept at the manual exercise and basic evolutions. The beating of assembly signaled the start of their tour when all regulars paraded between 8:00 and 10:00 A.M. to answer roll call, receive daily orders, and learn the current parole. The relief detachment was then inspected by a captain, before being marched off to the main guardroom, or any number of outlying facilities where they intermittently stood post in two-hour vigils until discharged the following day.[126]

Redcoats not involved with security duties at the frontier posts spent most of their waking hours at work. The months of December through April were particularly hazardous for the men who were felled by fever or frostbite after prolonged exposure to the elements during weekly forays into the surrounding countryside for fuel.[127] An immense amount of effort was expended harvesting timber and then drawing the heavy logs to the fort before they were cut into serviceable firewood. Bateaux were utilized as transport before the winter freeze, but this operation required troops to become immersed in cold water for long periods. When ice blocked navigation, the profound shortage of draught animals meant that infantrymen had to shuttle back and forth through the snow pulling hand sleighs piled high with wood.[128]

Men not sent to the woodlots devoted their laboring hours to the endless task of fortification upkeep and repair. These responsibilities fell into three broad categories. First, soldiers completed fabrication of any aboveground installations like blockhouses, barracks, and provisions magazines designed to preserve themselves and military stores from the weather. Next, snow had to be cleared from roofs as well as bastions, parade ground, ditches, and primary access routes so that the garrison could quickly respond to any enemy threat. Rampart interiors of principal garrisons like Fort Pitt could be two acres in size; soldiers had to cart all the snow outside the walls in wheelbarrows. Finally, fatigue parties were sent into the countryside to quarry stones and create palisade caches for use in the spring. One Royal American detachment commander at Niagara observed that such unremitting toil adversely impacted the rank and file, whose "constitutions are wore out and in a great measure they are rendered unfit for the common duty of soldiers."[129]

Although the men found the increased task load disagreeable, it became necessary for financial solvency shortly after the Seven Years' War drew to a close. Frontier service, which quickly ruined uniforms, and the abolition of free government rations conspired to squeeze the pockets of enlisted personnel. Certainly the redcoats, like other European troops, were allowed to supplement their incomes by working for civilian employers at the advance posts.[130] But any profits they made could be lost to the frequent clothing refits since shoes, shirts, and stockings were much more expensive to buy than in colonial cities or in the United Kingdom. While commanders regretted putting their men under heavy wage stoppages for clothing, this had to be done to preserve a regular appearance still regarded as a bellwether of military efficiency.[131]

The loss of free food allowances was an entirely different matter. Throughout the war, North American forces had received their government provisions at no charge in recognition of the harder work they had to perform and to ameliorate higher living expenses. With the suspension of arms, though, soldiers based in the New World found themselves placed on the same footing as other British regulars who were all required to pay four pence for their daily sustenance. Widespread dissension, however, caused successive commanders-in-chief, Lieutenant General Sir Jeffery Amherst and Major General Thomas Gage, to reduce ration prices as well as broaden the range of chores for which the troops were compensated. Whereas construction of defensive works and roads had previously earned only a gill of rum in wet weather, the redcoats now received ten New York pence (6d. sterling) when required to engage in such pursuits. Employment in the woodlots also resulted in extra income. Fellers received three New York shillings (2s. sterling) for every cord harvested, with those transporting the fuel to the forts given two shillings (1s. 4d. sterling). Headquarters' compromises allowed the men to maintain at least a meager standard of living in a period of governmental fiscal retrenchment until free ration distribution resumed again in 1771.[132]

"No End to their fatigues" was an apt contemporary assessment of daily life in Royal American ranks. Military records indicate that the redcoats' taxing schedule began during the spring advance (April–June) when they first trekked to the nearest seaport, ferried equipment to awaiting transports, and then sailed for army concentration points. Troops destined for Lake George or Lake Ontario next became porters or laborers at Albany, assisting the supply train with the movement of massive amounts of provisions and stores needed to sustain a large army in the field. At least a month would be spent in this key logistics role until enough provincial levies appeared to assume a share of this important responsibility. Troops not assigned to bateaux crews supported the advance by repairing the transportation infrastructure or carted both freight and boats around numerous river obstacles. Royal American garrisons stationed at Fort Niagara faced greater hardships than the rest because they bore the responsibility of forwarding goods all the way to Detroit. This task first required four men to carry heavy containers across the long overland trail before the supplies began a treacherous row across the waters of Lake Erie.

Summer camps (July–November) have been portrayed as sites where soldiers drawn from all corners of the Atlantic world developed negative perceptions of one another. New England levies, in particular, felt slighted by regulars who left all the menial jobs to them. Yet a thorough analysis of the redcoats' activities suggests that potential friction between various brigades was minimized because troops, who were constantly employed between dawn and dusk, had little time for fraternization with those outside their own regiment. Members of every six-man squad had a task to perform: one acted as a custodian and cook; one participated in convoy support; two labored on the king's works; one attended the woodcutters; and one stood sentry. Time for fraternization was limited to the fleeting moments between sunset and the beating of tattoo when the quarter guard began securing those not already under canvas. The few occasions for group interaction occurred primarily when forces assembled for services commemorating mutual bonds of religion, loyalty, and military victories over the despised Bourbon foe.

Before 1758, all four battalions of the 60th Foot participated in the annual withdrawal from the frontiers to warmer quarters to the south. This was hardly a holiday for the troops. Winter cantonments (December–March) were established in New England or the Middle Colonies only after heavily laden infantrymen completed difficult marches over long distances. In areas with no barracks or few public houses, redcoats had to refurbish abandoned buildings and continually forage for fuel during their occupancy. Most normal routines followed the sun except for sentry duty, which required every soldier to participate in frequent guard details for a twenty-four-hour period throughout the week. Skilled personnel were occasionally excluded from this rotation so they might complement efforts to improve the battalion's appearance, which was deemed a mark of fitness for service.

Royal American detachments began winter garrison duties by the middle of the war and remained at the advance posts until 1772. Initially, troop mortality rates climbed, but work regimens could not be decreased. Soldiers able to stand sentry were short-shifted for the safety of the entire post, while those still available for other duties continued with fort construction, gathered fuel, shoveled snow, and stockpiled building materials for later use. Troubled commanders, however, could do little to shield their men from the corrosive effects of hard labor, which was a hallmark of the American military experience. Redcoat interaction with different Native communities was the other distinctive of service life in the New World. The complex story of the 60th Regiment's engagement with a wide variety of American Indian groups provides the focus for the next chapter.

5

"He seated our chiefs and warriors at his table"

Royal Americans and Native Americans

Ho-Chunk leaders remembered the last half of the eighteenth century as a golden age. When a Royal American detachment occupied the old French post at La Baye (now Green Bay, Wisconsin) in 1761, elders quickly established strong bonds with the newcomers since the army did little to interfere with the normal course of life. Winnebagos' appreciation for the redcoats certainly grew over time because soldiers ensured delivery of beneficial European goods, treated the villagers with dignity, sought their support as valued military allies, and defended tribal interests in the metropole. Goodwill, as Hoowaunookaw (the Little Elk) fondly recalled, was maintained between both parties through successive generations and was customarily affirmed by the commander at any British garrison whenever "he seated our chiefs and warriors at his table."[1]

Little Elk's regard for the king's men stands in marked contrast to widespread belief that Royal American mistreatment of Native people contributed to the eclipse of tribal societies after the fall of New France.[2] While relations briefly deteriorated during Pontiac's Rebellion, emphasis on this anomalous period distorts the true nature of the vibrant association forged between redcoats and the First Nations they encountered between 1756 and 1772. As diplomats, neighbors, and adversaries, the regular troops were eventually grafted onto an extant sociopolitical order already evolving between Europeans and Eastern Woodland peoples. A careful study of this tripartite relationship indicates that 60th personnel, despite some missteps along the way, ultimately established sound alliances with American Indian communities that benefited the Crown for decades to come.

Diplomats

Military service and diplomacy became complementary responsibilities along the colonial marchlands, where various governments and civilian groups steered their own course in Indian affairs.[3] Royal American detachments first encountered tribesmen at a hastily arranged conference held near Easton, Pennsylvania, in November 1756. The soldiers' purely ceremonial role on this occasion was designed to impress an influential Delaware leader, Teedyuscung, with the martial appearance of an imposing army escort. Lieutenant Governor William Denny thus appeared at meetings guarded "by a party of the Royal Americans in the Front and on the Flanks, and a Detachment of Colonel Weiser's Provincials in Subdivisions in the Rear, with Colours Flying, Drums beating, and Musick playing."[4] Attendant Delaware, Mohican, Shawnee, and Six Nation representatives were oblivious to the fact that the redcoats on parade were mere recruits hurriedly supplied with uniforms for this debut. Frequent processions of regular and colonial forces in lockstep, however, prompted tribal avowals of goodwill despite their continued grievances about land matters. This opening demonstration of military might before varied American Indian legations foreshadowed other instances when regimental personnel would be required to present either the velvet glove or the iron fist according to circumstances.[5]

First battalion members had some time during the ensuing winter to refine their infantry skills before Major Herbert von Munster's "well dress'd and well disciplin'd" grenadiers were called on to serve as the lieutenant governor's bodyguard at Lancaster, Pennsylvania, where Natives again gathered to treat in the spring of 1757. Although Teedyuscung did not make a personal appearance, nor were outstanding Delaware land issues resolved, Iroquois delegates agreed to prevent the transit of raiding parties through their territory.[6] The Indians' subsequent acquiescence on this point was prompted in part by the appearance of four more Carlisle-bound regular companies that sent a clear message of metropolitan resolve to the assembled warriors. Thereafter, a strengthened Royal American presence along the frontiers contributed to a decline of enemy activities that year.[7]

John Stanwix, first elected to Westminster in 1741, was already an accomplished parliamentarian by the time he attended the Lancaster gathering with his men. While treaty negotiations were not a field officer's normal responsibility, he and his subordinates learned meaningful lessons during their inaugural exposure to backcountry diplomacy. Foremost was an appreciation for the important role played by gifts in cementing alliances between First Nations and their European partners. Such formalities were especially consequential during wartime when presents of clothing, ammunition, and trade goods sustained braves on campaign or consoled the relatives of those slain in battle.[8] The colonel's acumen became evident within days of leaving Lancaster when he placated disgruntled Cherokee scouts who were already ranging the frontiers to keep enemy raiders in check. Irritated by both the quality and quantity of items distributed by local legislators, the Cherokees would have returned to the Carolinas had not Stanwix augmented the bequest greatly and then personally received four tribal ambassadors at the head of his troops. Troubled allies were reconciled in a mixture of Old and New World protocols when mutual health was toasted, words of friendship expressed, and wampum strings changed hands. All evidence suggests that the British MP had made remarkable progress in his appreciation for borderland sensibilities within a short period of time.[9]

The remainder of the first battalion experienced a similar acculturation process after members of this force arrived in South Carolina to secure the colony that same spring. Soon after disembarkation from the transports, Lieutenant Colonel Henry Bouquet became involved in efforts to counter Bourbon influence over key Indian leaders.[10] His Royal American detachment was soon called on to parade before visiting chiefs who had gathered at Charles Town. Unlike Easton's previous fall cavalcade, this occasion was not a sham display meant to hide amateurism beneath the trappings of a resplendent military procession. The soldiers were now more proficient in their basic exercises and would have performed live-fire demonstrations for the benefit of onlookers, like the Creek chief Handsome Fellow. Such an inspection was designed to show tribesmen that regular troops, with their murderous firepower, were now deployed in the Lower South to protect British interests.[11]

As noted in Chapter 2, some Royal American officers had already served in the New World and acquired a great deal of frontier experience before the war began. The second battalion's Captain Abraham Bosomworth, a brother-in-law to the formidable Creek matriarch Mary Musgrove, was one such man whose blood ties and previous appearances around council fires made him a practical choice to strengthen military alliances with Carolina warriors. It was for this reason that the Earl of Loudoun sent Bosomworth south in early 1758 to engage a large party of tribal auxiliaries for the advance against Fort Duquesne.[12] Bosomworth was precluded by illness from attending the important Keowee conference in person, so other envoys were responsible for recruiting 652 irregulars on this occasion. The captain's health improved in time to take the field with some of these braves.[13]

Indian diplomacy continued to be a vital skill honed by Royal American officers serving in the expedition to the Ohio Forks since relations with some Native allies were strained from the start. Initially, the lack of readiness on the part of Anglo-provincial forces vexed Cherokee and Catawba headmen, who were also troubled by the fact that their warriors had not received sufficient gifts after a long journey to the rendezvous at Winchester, Virginia. Each brave expected new clothing outfits, worth about £10 apiece, plus a knife, tomahawk, powder horn, ammunition, and wampum. Favored ancillary items included guns, new locks for unserviceable firearms, blankets, pipes, ornamental silver, camp kettles, and vermilion. To these particulars would be added other "encouragements to be occasionally given for their good behaviour taking Scalps and Prisoners and some Presents on their return home for their Wives and Children."[14] Fortunately for the British, all the Natives did not decamp immediately because Bosomworth steadied tribal leaders with assurances of support and, in a fiery speech, reminded them of the threat from a common French enemy bent on enslaving them. The officer's oratory had the desired effect. After two days of deliberation, some scouts agreed to proceed against Fort Duquesne, while the rest awaited the arrival of presents from Philadelphia. The pact was sealed by a pipe shared between the captain and Kellelusstekey, the Indians' deputized spokesman who also offered wampum to his elder English brother.[15]

Bosomworth remained active through the 1758 advance by keeping a cadre of irregulars attached to the army's vanguard. Cognizant of their tendency to take the presents and then return home without performing any service whatsoever, the captain cached a substantial clothing allowance for distribution to his warriors after the expedition was over.[16] Such judicious moves kept most of this band constant through midsummer as scouts, hunters, and even laborers.[17] Their menacing appearance and aggressive patrols finally induced Ohio Indians to attend the 1758 Easton peace conference, which undermined regional support for the French alliance. As Brigadier General John Forbes appreciatively noted, "All the Northern Indians mostly our Enemies were kept in awe" by the loyal partisans managed by Captain Abraham Bosomworth.[18]

A smaller but equally capable detachment of Catawbas also accompanied the British forces. This complement of twenty-six men was an impressive delegation from a nation whose sun had already begun to set.[19] Commanded by the mixed-blood Johnny Bullen, their allegiance was sustained by Colonel Henry Bouquet's apparent adoption of the war captain according to Native customs. Such rites, culminating in a distribution of presents from the superior's largesse, brought honor to the initiate, whose social standing now reflected that of his new kinsman.[20] Although Bullen was killed in a surprise clash in late August, his warriors fought on until the end of the campaign.[21]

Henry Bouquet's growing expertise in frontier diplomacy helped secure Delaware neutrality after the enemy's abandonment of Fort Duquesne. The proceedings at the first British conference held at the Ohio Forks were choreographed to achieve this end. Chiefs arriving at the 4 December 1758 forum, like other American Indians who were "extremaly fond of show and Parade," were first saluted by musketry and artillery barrages, which they appropriately deemed a compliment. Refreshments appeared soon afterward at their lodgings, situated on the other side of the Monongahela River, so that they could cheer themselves at a safe distance from the Anglo-colonial camp. One Indian representative was then graciously entertained by the British before an invitation was extended for others to participate in the deliberations. Their sense of importance was heightened by Bou-

A contemporary portrait of Colonel Henry Bouquet (1719?–65). The first-battalion officer spent much of his North American career stationed along the colonial frontiers. An able diplomat, Bouquet combined military force and statesmanship to maintain a semblance of order in the Pennsylvania backcountry. Courtesy of the Historical Society of Pennsylvania Collection, Atwater Kent Museum, Philadelphia.

quet's reception of the delegates before a large regular escort, an entourage of officers, and numerous headmen who had already come to terms.[22]

Although extant accounts differ about the precise nature of discussions, the colonel gained concession for a British fort at this strategic site by linking trade to a continued military presence there.[23] In a diplomatic ceremony replete with familiar metaphors and symbolism, he first assured envoys that the redcoats were brothers who wanted to improve the lives of the Delaware people. Next, he quieted concerns about Native sovereignty by stating that the army had come not as conquerors but as allies who would let the ultimate fate of Louis XV's remaining garrisons be decided by tribesmen. Finally, he encouraged all who had taken up the hatchet against His Britannic Majesty to attend a formal conference in Philadelphia where their views would be sought about a pricing schedule for trade goods. The conciliatory nature of this message was underscored at its finale by the delivery of eight large wampum belts as well as calumets and commemorative medals. Two of the belts attested to British-Indian solidarity, while the silver pieces illustrated a white man clasping a brave's hand. Hunters then received gifts of gunpowder and lead so that they could provide for their families during the approaching winter.[24]

More distant groups ratified the Pittsburgh armistice in successive ceremonies through 1759. Since only a few chieftains were able to meet with Major General Jeffery Amherst at Philadelphia that April, oversight of these affairs fell to Brigadier General John Stanwix after he reassumed command of the western operational theater that spring.[25] Acquisition of Indian goods became a top priority for Stanwix, who had already learned the lesson about the importance of gift distribution. Despite chaotic supply lines, clothing and provisions for more than a thousand villagers were promptly sent to Fort Pitt.[26] The general's judicious foresight became evident when hordes of destitute Ohio Indians converged on the garrison to meet the redcoats after the collapse of French hegemony that year. Although these wares were "Scarce in the Country and so Expensive and Difficult to Transport," the British issued them as proof of their power and goodwill toward their newest allies.[27]

Peace finally settled over most of the northwestern frontier after five years of conflict. Stanwix, accompanied by his entire first battalion, gained vital exposure to the subtleties of backcountry diplomacy since many Royal American officers were fresh from New York and still "had no acquaintance with the Indians." While on duty, service personnel observed hundreds of Native families visit the fort and participated in consequential parleys that transpired throughout the summer of 1759. Tribal legations appeared most contrite at these councils, blaming hostilities either on wayward French sympathizers in their midst or on Quebec's governor, who had conspired against King George II.[28] The Royal American colonel prudently accepted these explanations for the bloodshed but insisted that further aggression cease in accordance with conventions already arranged at Easton and Fort Pitt. Commissioned personnel then smoked ceremonial pipes with chiefs who agreed to abandon the warpath in turn for being rewarded with medals, drink, and clothing. Such interaction familiarized detachment leaders with some Native behavior before they began occupying French bases in 1760.[29]

Neighbors

The first battalion's move into the Great Lakes watershed began a new phase in its relationship with Indian communities as mere diplomatic encounters gave way to firmer socioeconomic ties. Three major emplacements under their care provided regional command centers after small 60th detachments supplanted enemy garrisons throughout the hinterland. Fort Niagara, with a complement of four infantry companies, retained its role as the preeminent western trading station while occasionally seconding additional forces to Presque Isle and Detroit. Five companies based at Pittsburgh headquarters were stretched to the limit defending that new citadel plus the satellite posts dotting Forbes's Road from the Juniata River to Fort Pitt and onward to the upper reaches of Lake Erie: Bedford, Ligonier, Venango, LeBoeuf, Presque Isle, and Sandusky. The one makeshift unit ordinarily assigned duty at Detroit was most pressed for manpower to secure the strategic passage between Lakes Huron and Erie as well as ancillary bases at Michilimackinac, Sault St. Marie, La Baye, Miami, St. Joseph, and Ouiatenon. Such modest subalterns' parties of fewer than twenty men left a negligible British footprint on the vast landscape of the pays d'en haut.[30]

American Indian demand for manufactured products quickly became apparent to the redcoats after they replaced French forces as the source for these items.[31] Although headquarters cautioned against improvidence, Royal American commandants were given latitude to dispense clothing, food, wampum, and ammunition from army stores as local circumstances warranted. Even houses with substantial outbuildings were built for prominent chiefs who welcomed the king's men.[32] When demand outpaced supply, however, officers had to rely on their own wits and personal resources to make good the deficit. This imperative to purchase security with presents was so great that one subaltern lamented

> that being thus station'd in the heart of Indian Country with a handfull of men and in a manner at their mercy he was under the disagreeable necessity of cultivating a good understanding with these savages by presents of tobacco, Rum &c which he was obliged to purchase of some traders there at an exorbitant rate, most of which he is still indebted for . . . between sixty and seventy pounds NY currency [£34–40 sterling] laid out in articles for the gratification of the Indians.

Obligations of this kind may have been perceived as an unwelcome legacy from the French regime, but they were the lifeblood of reciprocal American Indian–European relationships into which the redcoats were being grafted. Prescient administrators, like Captain Donald Campbell at Detroit, recognized that the safety of his new garrison was contingent on annual gift outlays worth about £1,000.[33]

It is important to realize that New York headquarters never actually banned present distribution despite the Herculean task of transporting these expensive wares to the western posts. What the British commander-in-chief insisted on was an end to the prodigality that fostered Native dependence on the metropolitan government. Lieutenant General Jeffery Amherst had learned from correspondents that furs were being exchanged for rum instead of the life essentials required by Aboriginal families. Being indigent until more pelts could be accumulated, Natives entreated the Crown's representatives for presents to support themselves for the rest of the year. Army detachment leaders unwittingly facilitated this dysfunctional relationship by supplying villagers with ammunition, clothing, and other merchandise from government stocks when petitioned for relief.[34] To break this pernicious cycle of reliance, 60th officers were instructed to provide aid only in the face of true need, treating charitable cases with the same compassion as England's own deserving poor. Captain Simeon Ecuyer summarized his response to incessant applications for support at Fort Pitt by explaining, "Sometimes I refuse, at other times I give a little, and at other times I do not know on which foot to dance." It was not until 1770 that discretionary spending for annual Indian presents was finally limited to £300 per post.[35]

Military bases, somewhat like contemporary sectarian missions, were contact points where redcoats and Indians coexisted in a setting of "intercultural living." Aside from a gathering place for councils and attendant activities, garrisons became economic hubs, where officers purchased supplies from the local populace. Although the regulars could catch fish and were expected to grow vegetables in their post gardens, time constraints afforded little opportunity for the pursuit of large game. Native stalkers were therefore hired to supplement army rations with fresh venison, bear fat, and wild fowl.[36] Tribesmen could also turn their sights on more lucrative quarry, such as runaway livestock or truant infantrymen. Deserters might be tracked in any season and returned to commanders who paid up to £2 plus "plenty of ammunition & provisions"; similar rewards accrued when stray government animals were brought back to base.[37] Women too entered the cash economy by renting their horses for use as pack animals or selling surplus produce like corn and maple syrup to the needy troops.[38]

Caution was the watchword guiding British occupation policy since relations between the lower ranks and allied braves had not always been cordial in wartime encampments. Even though officers tried to separate the two parties by a cordon of armed sentinels, rumor-mongering, theft, fisticuffs, and other disturbances had still occurred.[39] Consequently, similar attempts were made at borderland posts to prevent any unsupervised contact between the races. Usually, only deputies from Sir William Johnson's Indian Department, the agency charged with Native management and welfare, or the various detachment heads were allowed to deal directly with visiting tribesmen at the larger bases. Unauthorized fraternization by those of lesser rank was discouraged.[40] Random strife arising from the callous behavior of enlisted personnel was settled according to the maxim

"Let no man injure an Indian unpunished & that before the Indian." When, for example, a first battalion soldier killed a horse that belonged to nearby Ottawas, he received a hundred lashes in public and the villagers accepted gifts of rum, blankets, ammunition, and a new steed as recompense.[41]

A great deal of forbearance was demonstrated whenever Crown interests were imperiled by the misconduct of Aboriginal youth. Intermittent livestock theft posed a security threat for garrison personnel who had to eat imported rations in the event that live cattle, oxen, sheep, and swine were unavailable for slaughter. Similarly, the theft of draught animals by braves jeopardized the overland supply lines that sustained redcoats in the backcountry.[42] Although shooting rustlers was an expedient, it only heightened tensions between the two communities if bereaved relatives did not receive condolence gifts to placate a departed's spirit. Army officials in due course rectified this problem by prohibiting the purchase of domesticated animals from tribesmen to lessen the demand side of the equation and imposing trade sanctions on refractory villagers.[43]

Physical abuse of the soldiery was a much more serious matter. Although some Indians had previously enjoyed the open hospitality of French commandants, Royal American officers tightened security measures as persistent gossip about insurrection filled the air. Accordingly, assaults on hapless personnel occurred whenever sentries tried to stop unauthorized people from entering a fort.[44] Injury could also occur if troops encountered warriors on "a frolick." Retaliation was discouraged in favor of the capture and temporary imprisonment of even those known to have killed redcoats in cold blood. British officials realized, like the French before them, that Native detainees were flashpoints for insurrection and thus were loath to bring them to trial. Malefactors instead were surrendered into the custody of clan elders at councils held to air the redcoats' grievances.[45]

American Indian unease about garrisons in their midst was heightened by the civilian tidal wave that surged over the Appalachian Mountains after the French withdrawal from the region. Pioneers rapidly moved westward along the army's supply lines to hunt or farm illegally on ancestral lands. Since these incursions violated Native sovereignty, regular troops were called on to evict squatters in compliance with the metropolitan government's edict against interior development.[46] Pittsburgh detachments became the most involved in these operations and turned over any of the chattel to villagers before buildings or crops were put to the torch. But the overstretched forces could not apprehend all trespassers. As one contemporary wag noted, "Not even a second Chinese wall, unless guarded by a million soldiers, could prevent the settlement of the Lands on the Ohio and its dependencies." Random attempts by small companies to preserve Native hunting grounds, however, demonstrated army resolve to maintain the peace, even at the colonists' expense.[47]

Royal American companies were also called on to safeguard Aboriginal enterprise in the fur trade after barter among trappers and vendors was restricted to garrison settings, where a neutral site encouraged fair exchange. Licensing by the Indian Department as well as a military pass system to regulate the flow of merchants and goods along major supply routes further checked the exploitation of tribesmen by avaricious peddlers.[48] Nevertheless, the importation of intoxicants by traders proved to be the Achilles heel of this ambitious program since the sale of rum guaranteed huge profits for retailers and it was a favored purchase of hunters despite the dire consequences of alcohol abuse.[49]

Redcoats made good-faith attempts to alleviate this horrible scourge. Alcohol sales to the Natives were initially forbidden at army bases, with senior officers empowered to revoke trading privileges and confiscate any contraband stocks. As with the case of squatters, bootleggers had their property seized and buildings demolished as further punishment for their misdeeds.[50] Despite these stiff penalties, entrepreneurs took every opportunity to circumvent the embargo. Some used the cover of darkness to evade vigilant sentries; others altered legitimate passes to state that they could exchange liquor for pelts; a few smugglers even established off-license hideouts, where there were no troops to regulate their activities.[51] Small squads easily eliminated these lairs, but time and distance precluded raids on all save the most infamous operations. Nevertheless, steady consumer appetite finally transformed the army's prohibition campaign into one of intense regulation. Rum sales became permissible in 1765 provided that distribution occurred under military supervision at least six miles away from the fort after trading had been completed.[52]

The December 1763 murders of twenty peaceful Indians by Pennsylvania vigilantes, known as the Paxton Boys, prompted an aggressive Royal American police action in defense of Native interests after first battalion elements became custodians of 140 Delaware-speaking refugees.[53] Although Benjamin Franklin and other local officials have received most of the plaudits for devising a diplomatic solution that halted the rabble's subsequent advance on Philadelphia, Captain John Schlosser's decision to secure his terrified charges behind barricaded walls and open fire on the frontiersmen was another key reason for the colonists' dispersal. Thomas Gage explained to superiors that the redcoats

> arrived in time to save the Indians who were under the Care and Support of the Province, as well as some of the Citizens, from the Fury of the Country People. Without the Interposition of the King's Troops, there is reason to believe, that much Blood would have been Spilt in that City; for as soon as the People heared, that the Indians were in the Barracks, under the Protection of the King's Forces, they halted at a few Miles from Philadelphia, Saying in that Case, they must look upon the Indians as under the Protection of the King, to which they should pay Respect, and would not on that Acct offer any Violence to them; but declared, if they had been only protected by the Legislature of the Province, that they would have put them all to Death.

The royal protection mentioned by the general included the eight artillery pieces that Schlosser had also entrenched around his position. None of the mob were willing to storm a building screened by cannons and the musketry of three infantry companies. As the accompanying 1764 engraving attests, supporters of the Paxton Boys' march were so outraged by the deployment of artillery against them that propagandists depicted Royal American gunners as rats in uniform.[54]

Humanitarian relief efforts were equally important examples of military support for Native communities under stress. Regimental surgeons or their mates furnished medical aid freely, though at considerable cost to the government. In one notable instance, the first battalion's Dr. James Milne provided services worth £58.13.2 paid for out of army extraordinary funds. Isabella Graham, the wife of the second battalion's surgeon, likewise recalled that her husband treated Indian patients at no charge during his tenure at Fort Niagara, as did garrison supervisors at more remote stations.[55] Much addi-

Royal American support for Native refugees is derided in this contemporary print by John Claypoole, Jr., entitled "An Indian Squaw King Wampum Spies." Note that Captain John Schlosser's men, prominent in the center of the panel, are being led by a Quaker and that those manning the artillery are depicted as rats. Courtesy of the Historical Society of Pennsylvania. (Bc 612 D326a)

tional documentary evidence suggests that post commanders willingly fed the hungry and clothed the threadbare when needy tribal members appeared before British gates. As with the case of presents, army headquarters sanctioned aid to transient hunting, trading, or war parties despite the fact that supplies reached the garrisons only after a great deal of intensive labor by the troops.[56] More than five tons of government-supplied beef and seven tons of flour were thus dispensed to Ohio Indians around Fort Pitt during the winter of 1762–63.[57] This support continued even after the war when traditional harvesting methods should have provided for the corporeal needs of local communities. As late as 1772, however, detachment heads were informing commanders that they were still "under the necessity of humouring" First Nations with provisions only recently delivered to the king's men. While government fare was not always of the highest quality, it was repeatedly given to villagers free of charge and in greater amounts than the soldiers themselves received for rations.[58] Straitened colonists, by contrast, had to purchase surplus victuals from the commissaries if they required food.[59]

Royal American benevolence toward the Native population cannot be ascribed solely to altruism or obedience to orders. Conceivably kinship obligations also motivated officers to deal benevolently with their neighbors because interracial marriage was an essential feature of backcountry life that astute commandants could not avoid. In arrangements brokered by clan matriarchs for "advantageous alliances," some military detachment heads cohabited with chieftains' daughters *à la façon du pays* (according to the manner of the country) to benefit from the indigenous knowledge, social connections, and companionship of their winter wives.[60] Faint paper trails confirm that this was the course of action followed by men including Ensign Robert Holmes at Fort Miami, Ensign Christopher Pauli at Fort Sandusky, and Captain James Stevenson at Fort Niagara. The latter developed the closest bonds with a Seneca woman whose father was a respected tribal leader. Their union lasted for more than a year until he was transferred to the Detroit garrison and had to leave his wife and mixed-blood son behind. Although raised by his maternal family as was customary, the child was never forgotten by his father, who subsequently left him a substantial legacy of £300.[61]

Greater affinity was fostered between Natives and another group of Royal American officers given joint appointment to the Indian Department. Preeminent among this cadre was Captain Daniel Claus, the son-in-law of Sir William Johnson, who eventually purchased a fourth battalion company after serving at a lesser grade throughout the war. Although he was granted a regular commission at the outset of the conflict, his regimental duties had not been onerous and he was allowed time to participate in conferences and join war parties raised to defend the northern frontiers. Because of his familiarity with the newly constituted "Seven Nations of Canada," Claus was given responsibility to manage that league's affairs between 1760 and 1775.[62] Comparable efforts among the Wyandot and Ottawa around Detroit became the responsibility of Lieutenant Jehu Hay, who had risen through the ranks of the first battalion. Active duty first brought this Pennsylvanian into the Great Lakes region, where he remained following the army's post–Treaty of Paris reduction in force. Next em-

A miniature of Daniel Claus (1727–87), who rose to the rank of captain in the forth battalion during the Seven Years' War. The son-in-law of Sir William Johnson, Claus served in the Northern Indian Department and was considered to be an expert in matters regarding Quebec's Seven Nations. Courtesy of Library and Archives Canada. (C-083515)

ployed by the Johnson organization, Hay initially functioned as a commissary there until 1769 and was finally assigned the weightier responsibilities of Indian agent in 1774. Ensign Thomas Hutchins's long association with the Ohio Indians followed a somewhat different course. After service in a provincial corps, he began working as George Croghan's assistant at Fort Pitt. Extensive travels and experience with western tribesmen contributed to an award of first battalion colors in 1762. Regular employment did not preclude further contact with the Natives, however, and his prescient observations about their numbers and settlements later appeared in published surveys of the hinterland. All three men applied the skills acquired in their dual roles to become effective mediators between whites and Indian villagers.[63]

Royal American advocacy on behalf of Eastern Woodland communities reached new heights after Major General John Stanwix returned to the United Kingdom in 1760. Native esteem for the officer was demonstrated when several prominent chiefs escorted Stanwix from Fort Pitt to Philadelphia before his embarkation that spring. The 60th commander's guidance was sought by metropolitan officials any time imperial policy decisions might affect tribesmen. Stanwix first attended the Board of Trade in an advisory capacity when Virginia's lieutenant governor requested that abandoned frontier properties be resettled by colonists.[64] The officer defended Native interests and stood foursquare against expansion, stating that "making settlements upon the lands to the westward of the Allegheny Mountains, would infallibly irritate and provoke the Indians, and might be attended with fatal consequences." As a parliamentarian, his vehement opposition helped slow hunting ground expropriations for another six years until part of the disputed territory was ceded, ironically, at the Fort Stanwix Treaty of 1768.[65]

The MP's lobbying efforts were complemented by a protégé, Captain Gavin Cochrane, who had spent five years in frontier outposts with the first battalion. Although he did not personally travel to England with Stanwix, the captain attempted to influence imperial policy with a detailed monograph entitled "Treatise on the Indians of North America." This manuscript, sent to the Board of Trade in early 1764—and too long overlooked by historians—was inspired by his positive encounters with various tribesmen while in charge of the Presque Isle blockhouse prior to Pontiac's Rebellion. Personal experience and concern for those Indians who had "behaved to me & my men, even with politeness, not only there, but whenever they met them" prompted the Royal American to write his perceptive report.[66]

Gavin Cochrane was well aware that contemporary prejudices against the American Indians flourished on both sides of the ocean because Britons had been inundated by disconcerting tales of warrior brutality throughout the Seven Years' War. Repeated outrages by France's Indian allies against British troops and the civilian population convinced the general public that Natives possessed an immutable barbarism that could not be redeemed.[67] His excursus thus offered a constructive analysis of tribal affairs infused with fragments of Enlightenment thought soon to coalesce in the theory of stadial human development. Like other Scottish intellectuals of his time, the captain believed that societies could advance from a nomadic subsistence phase to the pinnacle of merchant capitalism given time and proper circumstances. As Cochrane wrote to his aristocratic readers, this natural maturation process had only now been derailed by some young warriors in fear of dispossession. Their rational defense of hunting grounds against white encroachment had inadvertently revived "everything they ever had that was barbarous." Not all confederacies, though, had participated in the insurrection, nor had every Indian reverted to primal ways: a majority of Iroquois, Sauk, Menomonee, Fox, and Winnebago people had remained neutral or actually come to the aid of beleaguered redcoats. It was recommended that future policy decisions be devised with similar bright lights in mind.[68]

Members of the Board of Trade were then presented with a scheme for hinterland pacification in the final pages of Cochrane's essay. Drawing partly from the French occupation model and his own experience, the Royal American officer recommended the establishment of stronger alliances with Natives already sympathetic to metropolitan interests. These auxiliaries, sustained by presents and fair treatment, would punish other villagers who dared to break the peace, thereby eventually bringing dissident communities into line. Fearing further retribution, they, in turn, would constrain militant members by the rule of law, deemed an essential indicator of civilization. Influential leaders arising from these more politically mature groups could then be brought further within the British orbit through the influence of Protestant missionaries living among them. Evangelical Protestant clergymen were the ideal candidates for these positions, the captain believed, because Natives were naturally superstitious and would be more receptive to a fervent brand of Christianity.[69]

The introduction of European farming techniques into the Great Lakes region was the final element of Cochrane's prescription for détente. His improving sentiments, however, were not a resurrection of Puritan schemes to housebreak Natives through agricultural pursuits. Rather, they were based on personal observations that American Indians had a robust appetite for government bread rations. This craving for flour provided a lure to co-opt prominent chiefs with gifts of plowshares and horticultural instruction. Cochrane believed that the remaining villagers would soon be weaned from a nomadic existence as they tried to emulate their leaders' success at sowing and reaping. The company commander reminded government officials that a strategic advantage was also gained from the establishment of such agrarian settlements because farming communities made much easier targets for military expeditions should tribal revolts occur. Regulars would be able to strike quickly into the backcountry, if need be, to burn the farms and crops of those who had broken the king's peace and bring the disaffected back into line.[70]

This visionary assessment of First Nations' potential, which was eventually scrutinized by the Board of Trade before being presented to King George III, complemented a more detailed plan that Sir William Johnson had also sent to London. While both proposals were of similar tone in their concern for Native welfare, the Indian superintendent's carried greater weight and helped shape future government policy.[71] Certainly, pleas for the equitable treatment of tribal communities flowed easiest from the quills of those whose lives had rarely been at risk in skirmishes with enemy war parties for gentlemen captives were usually ransomed by the French. Those accorded preferential treatment, on the one hand, had the luxury of assessing Aboriginal society from a safe vantage point. Ordinary redcoats, on the other hand, maintained a less charitable view of martial opponents whose mode of waging war often threatened the infantrymen's survival.[72]

Adversaries

The adversarial relationship between regular troops and tribesmen has garnered most scholarly attention because it represents a culture clash of distinctive martial values. The rank and file's disparaging views of American Indian opponents were based on their unorthodox behavior that transgressed Western norms and interjected a particular element of horror into New World conflicts. Such hostile encounters were characterized by an abrupt chorus of disconcerting war cries; hails of fire directed by invisible assailants; an irresistible charge of tomahawk-wielding braves; hand-to-hand combat; and then mutilation of the fallen by scalping knives.[73] Reports spread by survivors of irregular actions contributed to blackened stereotypes that were reinforced by official pronouncements, which characterized the French auxiliaries as "savages . . . whose Trade is not War but Murder."[74] Common wisdom averred no less that a redcoat's survival odds were not great if captured since few adult males escaped ritualistic torture at nearby encampments or immolation at the hands of mourning villagers. Ordinary servicemen therefore had little time for highbrow sentiments about this ferocious enemy reputed to offer no quarter in battle.[75]

American Indian ruthlessness became fixed in public consciousness after the surrender of Fort William Henry to the Marquis de Montcalm in 1757. Despite the victor's assurance to protect the defeated garrison during withdrawal from the operational theater, eighteen hundred warriors assailed the British troop column as it moved toward Fort Edward the following day. A token French escort was unable to prevent the abduction of 600 parolees and the murder of perhaps as many as 185 others in cold blood.[76] Montcalm's disclaimer that European military customs could not be universally applied in the New World carried little weight with individuals who had capitulated in good faith according to accepted protocol. The ensuing slaughter of defenseless men and women, primarily for their scalps, was ample evidence of tribal perfidy and was not quickly forgotten by the redcoats.[77]

The rank and file, like other nominal Protestants who affirmed scriptural injunctions about physical resurrection and life in the age to come, were understandably outraged at the Indians' wont to "insult a dead body" by scalping it after battle.[78] It was of no consolation to the common men that scalps were originally used to restore the spiritual vibrancy of diminished clans; distinctions between sacred and secular pursuits had become blurred after French officials began paying warriors up to £5 for the tresses of every dead British subject.[79] Regardless of intent, scalp hunters were reviled by the redcoats who tried to retrieve wounded and dead comrades from the front lines to prevent their desecration. Line troops, unlike their provincial counterparts, were usually constrained from exacting like vengeance on insentient enemies by regimental discipline and more pressing duties in a combat zone.[80]

Control and restraint, both hallmarks of a trained soldier, were keys to success on New World battlefields, despite tales of redcoat incompetence that have saturated the public consciousness. Belief in Georgian regulars' inferiority against American Indian war parties certainly emerged prior to the time of Major General Edward Braddock's defeat, when his men were told that "if they engaged ye Indians in their European Manner of fighting, they would be beat."[81] Had history's clock stopped during the afternoon of 9 July 1755, then this homespun wisdom would have certainly been proven true. But time did not stand still, and within two years British officers had devised ways to neutralize the Native menace by deploying skirmishers to screen their ponderous infantry columns. Equipment and tactical modifications followed apace, enabling the king's men to counter insurgents with greater effectiveness.

Grizzled veterans recognized that both nature and nurture made tribesmen exceptional partisans. Raised from infancy to take up the hatchet, braves were inured to the physical demands of forest campaigns. Mobile war parties were particularly lethal despite being lightly armed with only bows or trade guns, clubs, and hatchets.[82] First Nations' proficiency in small-scale operations against isolated outposts and farmsteads was repeatedly demonstrated between the years 1755 and 1764. No other combatants could match such success in petite guerre operations, for which the Indians were justly acclaimed.[83] Nevertheless, the Seven Years' War invariably changed the blueprint for North American conflicts by normalizing the use of regular formations, linear tactics, systematized maneuvers, grand sieges, and climactic battles instead of the customary "traversing from place to place, either for the defence or attack of a few straggling forts in a woody country." Detachments of the 60th Foot thus encountered Aboriginal opponents in a variety of combat situations, including skirmishes, marine operations, sieges, set-piece battles, and major offensive campaigns. European methods ultimately prevailed through this transitional period, as signified by the capitulation of Shawnee, Mingo, and Delaware communities to Colonel Henry Bouquet's expeditionary force in 1764.[84]

Ambuscades and skirmishes were the forte of Natives who had refined the art of striking suddenly from concealed positions. Warriors favored these surprise onslaughts since the tactical advantage lay in the charge, rather than open-field showdowns, where firepower and regimental discipline favored the redcoats.[85] Traps sprung by small bands of forty or fewer braves usually carried the day. However, if defensive opposition stiffened, then tribesmen exerted greater force on a perceived weak point through a series of flanking maneuvers until resistance crumbled or they prudently withdrew to avoid further casualties. Secondary positions could then be established along retreat lines to waylay careless pursuers, transforming a military reverse into a triumph. Hit-and-run operations like these proved difficult for conventional forces to counter because the initiative usually lay with the attackers, who routinely disappeared into the woods if a sortie turned against them.[86]

It took considerable resourcefulness for regular troops to adjust to a new environment in which they initially played a reactive rather than a proactive role. The dispatch of rangers and light infantry screens to flush out potential assailants was a major step toward denying warriors the important element of surprise they needed to accomplish their designs.[87] Native capabilities were further diminished by other innovations calculated to improve the performance of even the lowliest soldier in wilderness campaigns. Simplified maneuvers and volley control expedited formation of an extended battle line. This, in turn, maximized the effect of British musketry while reducing opportunities for braves to overrun unprotected flanks as they instinctively tried to do.[88] Night marches across difficult terrain moved the regulars over unfavorable ground and then placed the redcoats near enemy encampments, which they could attack at dawn.[89] These combat skills sharpened by time and experience eventually produced veterans who behaved "with great steadiness against the Indians."[90]

American Indian tactics based on surprise and maneuver were equally effective against conventional forces that utilized the vast network of inland waterways for transport. In 1757 braves overwhelmed a New Jersey provincial flotilla navigating Lake George by trapping twenty-two whaleboats between forces on land and a large surreptitious fleet of canoes that cut off retreat to open water.[91] One efficient countermeasure implemented by the British after this disastrous loss included the conversion of unarmed bateaux into row galleys through the addition of small bow-mounted artillery pieces called "swivels." First battalion troops manned these diminutive ships to great effect during Pontiac's Rebellion, especially around Fort Detroit where the narrows invited periodic naval contests. The heavier firepower of British craft allowed crews relatively free movement in these actions. When challenged, redcoats used grapeshot to keep assailants at bay while continuing their passage or commencing offshore bombardment of enemy positions. Contemporaries believed that such aggressive riverine operations helped to dampen local support for Pontiac's ill-fated cause.[92]

The hinterland revolt of 1763–64 marked the nadir in relations between 60th detachments and many Eastern Woodland communities since first battalion personnel paid the price for the mistakes of others at army headquarters. A general spirit of tribal unease caused by protracted occupation of old Bourbon garrisons was heightened by improvident decisions made by Major General Jeffery Amherst that bred some early resentment toward the new regime. A case in point was the commander-in-chief's temporary arms embargo designed to protect his troops. This proved to be a double-edged sword: while it reduced the potential for unfriendly fire during the earliest days of British occupation, it inadvertently harmed Natives who had forsaken traditional hunting methods and were unable to provide for themselves without powder or ball. Disaffection therefore grew in areas where these items remained in short supply even after the ban was lifted and ammunition began reaching the interior through commercial networks by 1762.[93]

Indian perceptions about the high command's changing diplomatic sensibilities were a second major cause for concern. This "different manner of treating them" from the French was especially evident in the reduction of grand councils, at which time vast quantities of gifts were given, or in the sponsorship of smaller tribal assemblies when presents were distributed up to four times a year.[94] As discussed earlier, British authorities believed that fair trade would substitute for reliance on the king's generosity and therefore tried to ease gift expenditure in light of smaller postwar military budgets. Villagers, however, still expected to receive these gratuities since the redcoats had merely replaced Louis XV's troops in the forts that remained on their soil. Tribesmen felt slighted by this abrogation of convention that had recognized their sovereignty over unceded areas and affirmed that outsiders lived at the army establishments only at the sufferance of the original inhabitants.[95]

Land grievances were especially pronounced among Ohio Country residents and the Chenussio Senecas, who all resented an increased Anglo-colonial presence in their territories. The former were outraged by the appearance of hunters and settlers whose presence degraded vital hunting grounds, while the latter group opposed the launch of a freight-forwarding operation along the Niagara portage that challenged their traditional monopoly over this strategic supply route.[96] In both cases, community welfare would suffer from activities that eroded a resource base on which they relied for survival. Villagers registered complaints with garrison commanders, who reported these concerns to superiors but could do little to redress all grievances with their limited manpower or authority.[97]

Resolve to oust the British newcomers early took fire among the Senecas, who circulated war belts among surrounding nations. Tribal neighbors, however, proved unwilling to mobilize for two more years until word of France's huge territorial concessions made according to the 1763 Treaty of Paris finally reached the hinterland.[98] The Natives were left in a subservient role to the triumphant Anglo-Americans after the collapse of Bourbon power in the region. Understandably, such a new world order was anathema to disgruntled Delaware, Seneca, Shawnee, Ojibwa, and Ottawa warriors, who together with others launched a ferocious crusade against the intruders, catching the army by surprise. During the struggle, Colonel Henry Bouquet's command lost 141 soldiers, almost 20 percent of its strength, after few survivors returned from the small posts that were overrun in the conflict's earliest days.[99]

Pontiac's Rebellion lacked even the veneer of civility that was sometimes apparent during the Seven Years' War when French troops had been present to temper American Indian excess. There were no such constraints in 1763 as exasperated tribesmen vented their fury on the British regulars in very explicit ways. The mutilation of first battalion garrisons and the verbal insults to erstwhile neighbors suggest that Natives were actually nullifying recent kinship bonds that had developed between them and the whites.[100] The war kettle too was not a bygone memory, causing Royal Americans to fear the same fate as unfortunates like Captain Donald Campbell, Lieutenant Charles Robertson, and others who were eaten by the enemy.[101] Culturally prescribed violence of this nature, however, precipitated a major change in the redcoats' mentality when surrender was no longer an option by the late summer of 1763. Their do-or-die tenacity ultimately proved to be the most effective countermeasure against risk-averse braves since beleaguered servicemen who fought "to the Last Extremity" lost few rounds thereafter.[102]

In retrospect, repeated Native triumphs over isolated Royal American detachments were not remarkable since the first battalion's seven hundred men represented only a quarter of those believed necessary to defend all the frontier posts. By themselves, 60th servicemen were surrounded by a potential force of 6,860 warriors able to take the field against them.[103] The War Office had also jeopardized troop safety by not implementing a plan that called for the construction of substantial bases to protect their men. Instead, bureaucrats presumed that even dilapidated stockades would deter lightly equipped tribesmen who were believed to be afraid of "any thing that looks like works" (i.e., fortifications). The efficacy of Native guile, however, which ultimately proved as effective as any heavy ordnance, was never considered by cost-conscious administrators in their evaluation of tribal strengths.[104] Four positions— Michilimackinac, St. Joseph, Ouiatenon, and Miami—were taken by stealth with little gunpowder expended; nor could troops stationed at Sandusky, Presque Isle, Venango, and LeBoeuf prevent superior forces from overpowering them. Only the consequential garrisons at Detroit, Niagara, and Fort Pitt, which shielded anterior posts at Ligonier and Bedford, were able to foil inventive Indians.[105]

Events at Presque Isle illustrate how warriors combined innate martial abilities with skills acquired from French engineers during previous operations. Tribesmen overcame traditional fears about direct assaults on pallisaded defenses by burrowing underground à la Vauban to protect their advance from the redcoats' musketry. Once the covered approaches reached the curtain wall that linked the four bastions, a breach was made that permitted more than two hundred allied braves to enter the compound. Assailants methodically tightened their grip on the base during another day of intensive action designed to deny the Royal Americans access to the lone well situated on the exposed parade ground.[106] Concurrently, the Natives initiated negotiations designed to appeal to the self-preservation instincts of the subaltern in charge, promising safe passage to Fort Pitt in return for immediate surrender. Ensign John Christie capitulated despite the protests of the twenty-seven other squad members. The majority's instincts proved correct, however, as few survived the bloodbath once prisoners were taken. Only two men appeared to testify against their fainthearted leader at the military tribunal later convened to investigate his misconduct.[107]

American Indians faced greater challenges in their attempts to subdue major British emplacements. Even though twice damaged by spring floods, Fort Pitt's daunting bastions, with sixteen artillery pieces, remained a menace to besiegers not supported by the necessary cannon fire to demolish walls or keep armed defenders off the parapets. A night storm of the battlements would have minimized European technological advantages had not the regulars sowed the glacis and ditch with antipersonnel devices, such as metal leg traps used by fur traders, to thwart such attempts. These practical safeguards kept the 540 inhabitants secure within their cocoon despite being peppered with firebrands and musket balls. It was a different story beyond the pale, however, where insurgents' control of the countryside afforded them a decisive strategic advantage. There warriors enjoyed unlimited food supplies while garrison larders grew bare and marauders systematically attacked any foraging details that ventured into the open. Save for the appearance of a relief column, tribesmen simply had to maintain their blockade until the defenders were starved into submission.[108]

Psychological coercion was an effective American Indian technique used to attain military objectives with a minimum of casualties. War cries, scalp yells, and death halloos also were frequently heard by the besieged garrison as warriors attempted to wear down the redcoats' resistance. Bluff and deception followed at furtive parleys when Fort Pitt's officers were reminded that satellite detachments had already been annihilated by superior numbers soon to be arrayed against them. Assurances of an unimpeded withdrawal down Forbes's Road were proffered in return for a surrender.[109] It was in such an atmosphere of duplicity with tribal leaders "threatening, then soothing, and offering their cordial Advice" that Pittsburgh's commander, Captain Simeon Ecuyer, demonstrated a touch for the wiles of frontier Realpolitik. Having already learned that Royal American subordinates had been massacred after they grounded arms, the regular officer tried to demoralize opposing chiefs by exaggerating his troop strength and spreading misinformation about army intentions. He even distributed pox-infected blankets disguised as presents to those who threatened the lives of his dependents. This ruse was not a genocidal act aimed at all First Nations but a Machiavellian ploy well within the bounds of Native martial canons, which prized subterfuge. Chicanery was an art refined by people on both sides of the cultural divide at Michilimackinac as well as at Fort Pitt.[110]

Covert pathogens had no detrimental effect on war parties, whose strength and aggressiveness increased throughout the summer months. Their large numbers allowed a screen of tribesmen to remain in Fort Pitt's environs while a powerful band of at least 110 braves prepared to thwart British reinforcements from reaching Pittsburgh. As in earlier irregular actions, the initiative lay with the Natives who chose their ground carefully for an ambush near a small watercourse called Bushy Run.[111] Colonel Bouquet's soldiers were a scratch force of 450 men detached from the 42nd (Royal Highland) Regiment of Foot and the 77th (Montgomery's Highland) Regiment braced by a few Royal Americans stationed at Forts Bedford and Ligonier. Personnel of the 60th were in relatively good shape compared to the Scots, who were weakened by tropical diseases contracted during recent Caribbean operations and from their long forced march that had begun at New York. Portents augured well for the American Indian plan to waylay enervated troops because their crescent-shaped hunting formation had repeatedly crushed more formidable opposition.[112]

Events did not unfold according to plan when warriors sprang their trap on 5 August 1763. Instead of falling back in disorder, the British advance guard received assistance from the rest of the column, which formed into line and then drove ambushers from their front with fixed bayonets. Concern for the safety of the packhorses, though, obliged the soldiers to redeploy on Edge Hill, where they constructed a redoubt of flour bags to protect the wounded.[113] At first light, tribesmen resumed their attacks by trying to penetrate the British perimeter, now arranged in a large circle around the central strong point. The American Indians' aggressiveness proved to be their downfall since regular officers had already determined that exultant braves could be baited into the open by a feigned retreat.[114] Colonel Bouquet therefore withdrew some of his infantry from the firing line to a defile, where they could not be seen, and then ordered this same force to mount a surprise flank attack on the enemy, who had invariably pursued the mirage of fleeing redcoats. Measured volleys followed by a bayonet charge broke the opponents' will to continue the engagement after warriors scurried off into the woods, leaving some of their dead behind.[115]

The insurgents' "severe encounter" at Edge Hill was a catastrophic blow that became etched in their folk memory. The Natives' morale plummeted when they learned that death by enemy hands had prevented as many as sixty of their sons from attaining a paradisiacal afterlife.[116] The loss of at least three prominent chiefs during the summer months also affected the Indians' offensive capabilities since there were fewer mature leaders available to direct campaigns on the grand scale exhibited at Presque Isle, Fort Pitt, and Bushy Run. Consequently, no significant war parties appeared against British troops, nor were villages as secure without the presence of these experienced headman.[117] Subsequent evacuation of Delaware and Shawnee towns left warriors bereft of the forward support they needed to sustain prolonged campaigns. Raiders only infrequently appeared along Forbes's Road after 6 August 1763. Offensive momentum, by contrast, flowed to the British regulars at Pittsburgh who were strengthened by reinforcements of men and supplies after the siege had been lifted. Plans were soon afoot to crush hostile tribes with a punitive foray the following year.[118]

Pontiac's Rebellion concluded in November 1764 after the British applied military force to achieve their political ends. The expedition against Ohio tribesmen was commanded by Colonel Henry Bouquet, whose march into areas previously deemed inaccessible obliged the militants to sue for peace. British mastery of irregular warfare was demonstrated throughout the 130-mile advance from Pittsburgh to a fortified encampment constructed deep in the heart of Shawnee territory. A new tactical configuration moved invaders along three parallel paths, facilitating quick deployment into a hollow square when fired on. Such innovation protected both the troops and the vulnerable packhorses from surprise attack because enemy scouts shadowing the advance could find no perceptible weaknesses.[119]

Colonel Bouquet's approach hurried alarmed villagers to the negotiating table. Delaware messengers were the first to request a parley upon learning that confederates at Detroit had already reconciled with the British and agreed to turn the hatchet against them. The Royal American officer displayed his diplomatic skills by receiving Native emissaries courteously, but without affection. Even the troops showed a cold shoulder to emphasize the solemnity of the occasion. Daily orders forbade the rank and file "to hold any kind of friendly Intercourse with them by speaking shaking of hand or otherwise, But on the Contrary to look on them w^t utmost disdain and w^t Stern and Manly Indignation."[120] At a conference held on 17 October 1764, Delaware, Shawnee, and Mingo chiefs were censured for breaking the peace, killing innocent civilians, besieging Fort Pitt, and murdering diplomatic couriers. Old refrains—that warriors had been compelled to participate in the insurrection, or that backcountry raiders were beyond the control of community elders—fell on deaf ears. Colonel Bouquet assured his listeners that a new armistice would not be signed until all previous treaty obligations agreed to at Easton in 1758 were honored, especially those concerning the return of English captives. It is noteworthy that this last convention had been implemented by the French after their own seventeenth-century struggles against the Iroquois Confederacy.[121]

Approximately twenty-seven hundred colonists had begun the coercive march into forest exile through the war years. Survivors later recalled that few opportunities for escape had appeared along the warpath because those recaptured were invariably murdered in appalling displays of brutality as a warning to others. Blood again flowed as the less ambulatory were killed for their scalps. These distinctive trophies were then tanned openly and carried triumphantly home with the surviving captives, who were then forced to run through a gauntlet of scourgers before their fate was decided by village elders.[122] Those deemed societal assets, especially young women or children, were integrated into the community, while a male minority was dispatched in torturous rituals designed to restore spiritual equilibrium.[123] Few "White Indians" above a tender age, however, escaped the psychological scars of this traumatic initiation into Native society because scalps taken from family and friends were publicly displayed by villagers for years after the event.[124]

The greatest concentration of unredeemed captives lived among the Shawnee, who had been the most vehemently opposed to their release. Official attempts to recover British subjects by denying trade privileges to abductors while rewarding those who released adoptive kin were similarly ineffective.[125] Only the intimidating presence of Bouquet's fortified encampment near Muskingum Forks obliged the discharge of 207 prisoners and the surrender of six hostages as surety for a delivery of the balance.[126] Some joyous reunions began upon entry into the army's lines. Eyewitnesses noted the euphoria of "fathers and mothers recognizing and clasping their once-lost babes;

husbands hanging round the necks of their newly recovered wives; sisters and brothers unexpectedly meeting together after long separations, scarce able to speak the same language, or for some time, to be sure that they were children of the same parents! In all these interviews, joy and rapture inexpressible were seen." The colonists were first conducted to Fort Pitt under the care of a military escort and then returned to their home counties. The Shawnee released nine more prisoners within weeks of the task force's withdrawal to Fort Pitt; all but a few stragglers were finally delivered to the proper authorities in the spring of 1765.[127]

Rescue proved too daunting for some who did not want to return to their natural families. Apparently, the lure of nomadic life, regard for adoptive parents, and extensive kinship ties motivated these colonists to defy repatriation. But less benevolent forces were also at work in the transculturation process that had converted settlers into "White Indians."[128] Foremost was a dread of annihilation. This fear had lurked in the captives' subconscious from the moment of seizure and was heightened just before release when Shawnee chiefs had to be dissuaded from killing all of their prisoners. Such precarious circumstances cause a psychological response in many captives now referred to as Stockholm syndrome, whereby the victimized bond with assailants even though it is not in their long-term interests to do so. The combination of confinement, dislocation from familiar surroundings, prolonged interaction and dependence on abductors for physical support triggers this inner defense mechanism. Even supposed displays of affection between the subjugated and their oppressors can flow from duress instead of normal consensual relationships. Liberation by the army at least rectified this profound power imbalance, allowing adults the opportunity to decide for themselves in which community they eventually wanted to reside.[129]

Pennsylvania legislators, in a rare moment of equanimity, voted public thanks to Henry Bouquet for restoring peace to the western borders. Their address recognized the Royal American colonel's expertise in partisan warfare, citing his recent triumphs as concrete evidence of martial prowess. Assemblymen also acclaimed the rank and file who had defeated an elusive foe and vanquished them on their home court, where "even their Woods could not protect them." But it would be a mistake to view the achievements of the 60th Foot at Bushy Run and in the Muskingum River valley purely in a military sense. While it is true that the redcoats had confirmed that discipline and firepower could prevail over the freebooting skills of enemy warriors, Bouquet's success was predicated on an appreciation for American Indian communities that he and his subordinates had cultivated during their years of frontier duty. Certainly, the adversarial element was not a permanent feature of the 60th Regiment's long relationship with tribesmen, which was marked generally by peace and benevolence.[130]

Diplomatic relations were the cornerstone of the association forged between Royal American forces and First Nations. Sixtieth troops were originally exposed to the intricacies of backcountry life within a year of their deployment as ceremonial displays gave way to actual political engagement at meetings in Pennsylvania and South Carolina. Battalion commanders subsequently improved their negotiating skills in talks with tribal leaders about a wide range of topics, including warfare, trade, treaty obligations, prisoners, justice issues, and mutual responsibilities. Garrison principals weighed local grievances seriously and took what they believed to be the best course of action until headquarters' pleasure was known. Whether through personal testimony in London, essays penned to the Lords of Trade, or direct correspondence with New York superiors, men like Stanwix, Bouquet, Bosomworth, Brown, Campbell, Claus, Cochrane, Gorrell, Hay, Hutchins, Turnbull, and Walters, among others, became spokesmen for Aboriginal communities as their ambassadorial role grew. Such diligence by Royal American officers through 1772 placed British–American Indian alliances on the positive trajectory that benefited the Crown into the nineteenth century. Natives remembered them as the first redcoats to have "seated our chiefs and warriors at his table."

Extended duty throughout the pays d'en haut invariably led 60th personnel to interact with neighboring villagers. Commercial associations developed first, and then relations strengthened as the army undertook a number of initiatives to protect First Nation communities: eviction of squatters and poachers, supervision of trade transactions, armed defense of innocents, and distribution of humanitarian relief. Although unauthorized fraternization between ordinary soldiers and individual Indians was discouraged for security reasons, some commanders cohabited with local women as propriety obliged. Thus, the indigenous people and customs of the New World were no longer as alien to Royal American officers as they had once appeared, for cultures had merged in British garrison settings. The rank and file too had been transformed by their years of military duty and were now better prepared for the challenges that lay ahead after demobilization in the expanded empire they had helped to create.

6

"I SHALL SETTLE, MARRY AND TRADE HERE"

Royal Americans in the Postwar Empire

The United Kingdom emerged from the Seven Years' War as the principal European owner of the landmass between Hudson Bay and Florida. No subjects were more delighted to learn about these huge territorial gains than the redcoats who had filled their personal journals, family correspondence, and publications with glowing references to the places through which they had campaigned.[1] The 60th Regiment's personnel were no exception, for they too had seen the bountiful fisheries, thriving ports and cities, affluent provincial estates, flourishing backcountry farms, and the continent's abundant resources. Their bullish sentiments were summarized by one British officer who became mesmerized by the natural wealth and beauty he saw in the environs around Fort Niagara. Convinced, like other soldiers, that North America would offer so many more opportunities than those in his own native land, Captain Charles Lee resolved to remain in the colonies after the war and informed relatives that "I shall settle, marry and trade here."[2]

Captain Charles Lee's dream of starting life afresh in the New World was shared by other veterans who reestablished themselves after discharge, raised families, and prospered in their civilian pursuits. This story of successful adaptation to provincial life during the

1760s and 1770s—the redcoat as colonist—has unfortunately been overshadowed by another image: the regular soldier as occupier and a threat to personal liberty.[3] While both are legacies of Canada's final conquest, twenty more years would pass before King George III's empire was finally torn apart by political revolution. In the interim, army personnel contributed to the vibrancy of the British Atlantic system using skills, capital, and patronage networks developed while on active duty to aid in their adjustment to a postwar world.

Demobilization and Settlement

Although short-term enlistees began receiving their discharges as early as 1757, the 60th Regiment's demobilization only began in earnest during the late summer of 1763. Each of the senior battalions remaining on the American Establishment were reduced from 700 to 423 men, and the two junior elements were struck from War Office rolls.[4] The fourth battalion paraded its colors for the last time at Montreal on 24 August 1763. The third battalion, after surviving the hardships of the Caribbean campaign and the occupation of Pensacola, was disbanded after its return to New York City six months later.[5]

Mustering out of the army was far less involved than enlistment. Soldiers were first required to return their firelocks and associated equipment to the armory. Next, they settled financial matters with the battalion paymaster and company commanders. Troops were allowed to keep the uniforms on their backs and expected repayment for any unused clothing from the annual allotment. Swords, tomahawks, and other camp equipage turned in to the stores likewise earned additional recompense. Troops wishing to return to the United Kingdom were then allotted spaces aboard transports, while those staying in the New World were given two weeks' provisions to carry them on the road to civilian life.[6] Finally, each soldier was given a signed regimental discharge, stating his name, rank, length of service, and reason for release. Place and date of birth as well as occupation might also be recorded. Such certificates were designed to protect honest men from suspicion of desertion and would be needed to validate applications for the property that veterans were now entitled to receive.[7]

Seven years separated discrete metropolitan land grant programs colloquially termed "the king's reward." The metropolitan government's original 1756 measure had been designed to facilitate recruitment into the British land forces already stationed in the New World. This initiative guaranteed volunteers or their legal heirs rights to two hundred acres of land quitrent-free for ten years either in New York, New Hampshire, or Nova Scotia at war's end.[8] Governor William Shirley of Massachusetts, apparently on his own authority, briefly increased this entitlement to three hundred acres for those inducted into the line regiments since he was vying for men with provincial units already entitled to the basic allowance. Consequently, all Royal American enlistees who had joined the colors between July and November 1756 became beneficiaries of imperial largesse. A smaller number of soldiers later drafted into the 60th Foot from two broken colonial corps, the 50th and 51st regiments, expected the bonus acreage because of Shirley's special promise.[9]

A more ambitious plan for the benefit of all North American troops was formulated soon after Quebec's conquest. This measure proved most advantageous both to colonists who had enlisted in the regulars after 5 November 1756, when land-grant inducements were no longer offered to volunteers, and to the thousands of redcoats dispatched overseas during the course of the conflict. Discharged servicemen, in particular, became the focus of domestic concern because the mother country feared inundation by unemployed returnees if nothing was done to make them stakeholders in the expanded empire. Since officials believed that former redcoats could "get their Livelyhood in America by working easier than they can at home," Whitehall intervened to prevent them becoming either societal threats or burdens.[10] Economics aside, veterans were likewise perceived as more reliable subjects than the thousands of foreign Protestants who were expected to teem into the colonies once again, and metropolitan administrators believed that imperial interests would be advanced if former servicemen became hardworking provincials indemnified for faithful service to the Georgian kings.[11]

The Royal Proclamation of 7 October 1763, which established new governments in Quebec, Florida, and Grenada, also contained provisions for a broad land-allocation scheme. The pertinent decree, framed to spur habitation of undeveloped regions, authorized free distribution of vacant Crown land to both officers and men on a graduated scale. Field officers received 5,000 acres; captains 3,000 acres; subalterns and battalion staff 2,000 acres; NCOs and drummers 200 acres. The remainder qualified for 50 acres, the minimum believed requisite to support a family.[12] Those already entitled to the 1756 grants of 200 or 300 acres also shared in this additional benefaction. Such grants were exempt from normal taxation for the first ten years but had to be fully occupied within that time to prevent escheat to the government. Possession was demonstrated through completion of settlement duties, including the maintenance of three cattle for every fifty acres of marginal ground, the drainage of three acres for every fifty acres of marsh, or the planting of three acres for every fifty acres of cultivable soil. Speculation was deterred by giving owners only three years from the date of the grant to begin these improvements.[13]

Not all service personnel joined the frontier land rush. Those discharged between the years 1758 and 1762 with an established residence, and men with no interest in farming whatsoever, perceived little benefit in relocating to colonial frontiers. Nevertheless, military rights could be sold, a frequent practice after 1766, when attorneys began submitting mass petitions to New York's governor, Henry Moore.[14] Unimproved tracts in the Lake Champlain basin could be purchased for as little as fourteen pence per acre, furnishing soldiers with a minimum bonus of between £3 and £21 York currency (£1.14.0–11.8.0 sterling) as their entitlements warranted. Some properties, however, sold for up to twenty shillings an acre, inflating bounty values to much higher sums. Such windfalls were a godsend to the disbanded troops who eked out a living in the major port cities.[15] Major General Thomas Gage informed metropolitan officials: "The discharged soldiers too have not contributed a little to this Increase in Philadelphia, as well as in other Cities of the Continent. Instead of clearing uncultivated Lands, which it was expected they would do, they have for the most part crowded into the Towns to work at Trades, and help to Supply the Inhabitants with Necessarys, which should be imported from the Mother Country." Wartime duties had familiarized these men with many of the occupations they now pursued: mariner, laborer, carman, stevedore, carpenter, bricklayer, tailor, and various other vocations.[16] Former soldiers with the ability to read and write applied these talents to best advantage as clerks, while some with modest financial resources became storekeepers or innholders.[17]

New York became the residence of choice for most of the redcoats because the colony offered the best settlement prospects nearest their discharge points and was already a familiar haunt for men accustomed to duty along the watersheds of the Hudson and St. Lawrence rivers.[18] The property-acquisition process, moreover, was accelerated because soldiers did not have to extinguish Indian title to the land that they solicited, as prewar applicants had been required to do. Rather, veterans identified desirable locations and then petitioned the governor and council directly for a deed to the site. Official consent was necessary before surveyors could run rudimentary lines between different holdings and record coordinates in field books. This vital information was used to create plats of each tract, which were submitted to the colonial authorities for final approval. Military claimants could receive lot titles in as little as thirteen months and were required to pay surveying expenses but not the other attendant fees normally charged to civilians.[19]

Veterans accompanied provincial surveyors northward from Albany to their proposed holdings during the spring of 1764. Several considerations including soil quality, presence of meadows, amount of cleared ground, water supply, and proximity to local garrisons influenced lot selections. Satellite communities, sanctioned by the commander-in-chief because of their utility to the troops, already existed around key British posts and attracted those wanting to establish farms in the area.[20] Veterans knew that immediacy to regular bases afforded protection, access to government provisions in lean years, presence of milling equipment, part-time employment for those with specialized skills, and a ready market for surplus produce.[21] Choice locations around Fort Edward and Crown Point were the first to be settled. Other grants were issued on the eastern shores of Lake Champlain between Otter Creek and Onion River, where the area's natural fecundity and mild climate enticed veterans to a region aptly labeled the Soldiers' Patent by eighteenth-century cartographers.[22]

Life in the ranks had equipped the military pioneers "with that technical American knowledge," as de Crevecoeur put it, for many of the important homesteading tasks at hand. Veterans first turned practical experience gained from erecting supply sheds, hospitals, barracks, and blockhouses to the task of fabricating shelters for their families and livestock. Basic habitations could be built quickly by a few men from local resources: eighty logs provided house walls capped by a roof of boughs or shingles. As one European traveler commented on this frontier architectural style: "the new settlers are generally in such a hurry to get up their houses that they pile up round trees one above another, notching them at the corners to hinder them from falling, saw out a door and windows, and bind a roof, covering it with bark instead of shingles, and plaistering up the joints between the trees with clay and straw." Finally, field stones were fashioned into fireplaces to furnish warmth and light. Simpler shanties were then readied for farm animals unable to tolerate winter extremes.[23]

Subsistence farming was onerous work in the early years until enough arable land had been cleared to allow for easy planting and harvesting. Here too, veterans could apply the methods they had used on fatigue parties to girdle and fell trees for army encampments. Pioneers might labor for up to ten years until enough open ground allowed free tillage of the wheat, barley, oats, and potatoes that sustained each family. Native crops of corn, squash, and beans were grown in mounds among the stumps in the interim. Previous experience working in the large garrison gardens that flourished around every British base had prepared the redcoats for these horticultural pursuits.[24]

Livestock management was the final requisite skill for a backcountry existence. Assignment to the army's grass guard—charged with the care of horses, oxen, cattle, sheep, or swine—equipped even men from urban backgrounds with the essentials of animal husbandry since most stock on primitive farmsteads simply browsed in the woods. Pigs and beef cattle were especially hardy creatures that foraged on their own without much human handling; dairy animals were merely retrieved from the pasture and penned in before nightfall. Horses or oxen were kept on a much shorter leash and were used daily to pull plows, wagons, or sleds. Discharged troops needed only to wed common sense to their prior work with government livestock for an increase in the size and value of their own domestic herds.[25]

Military duty had already acclimated army homesteaders to the New World and the environmental challenges of a frontier life. Scurvy, once the plague of northern garrisons, had been practically eradicated by 1761 after the troops began to brew and consume spruce beer.[26] Survival skills too had been enhanced by prescient commanders who encouraged their men to hunt and fish when not on active duty.[27] Such worthwhile knowledge was augmented by those familiar with the fabrication and proper use of canoes, snowshoes, and toboggans. Some redcoats, particularly those formerly held captive by American Indians, shared information about the intricacies of maple syrup production and the harvesting of edible forest plants. Even fragmentary knowledge of these pursuits enhanced a veteran's odds for success in establishing a new frontier home.[28]

Few disbanded troops tried to establish farms by themselves. Rather, regimental confreres requested patents adjacent to one another for "the Convenience of Mutual Assistance" since they knew that many hands would be required to wrest a livelihood from the wilderness. Collaborative efforts were crucial during this embryonic settlement phase when natural reverses or crop failures could jeopardize the lives of all involved.[29] But the soldiers pulled together with positive results. One rare partial inventory of an NCO's farm reveals that his two-hundred-acre grant had been developed into a financial asset worth £653 York currency (£365 sterling) within a decade of settlement. It consisted of twenty acres of fenced land sowed with wheat, flax, and hay, a furnished home for ten people, a barn, livestock, agricultural implements, carpenter's tools, and a canoe. Certainly this former sergeant exemplified those servicemen who had made a successful transition to civilian life as envisioned by the metropolitan government.[30]

Other veterans took less personal risk by choosing tenancy on established manors. There were several factors influencing this pragmatic step into civilian life. First, Crown grants were most often located in an area claimed by the governments of New York, New Hampshire, and by Canadian seigneurs who avowed French title to choice parcels around Lake Champlain. Landholding or financial investment in this region was problematic until the king's ministers finished adjudicating all the complex boundary issues in 1776.[31] Most established plantations were located in more developed locales with existing roads and mills. Second, tenancy was also a sound economic decision because housing, livestock, and farming implements were often made available by proprietors who were anxious to develop uncultivated tracts. Since the demand for leaseholders far outstripped supply, agreements were negotiated on very liberal terms, allowing renters and their families perpetual occupation as well as the right to profit from any improvements made.[32] Generous incentives of this nature brought some of the rank and file into the orbit of Mohawk River valley proprietors including members of Sir William

Johnson's extended family or onto the lands of former officers who were establishing their own rural seats.[33]

Military gentry had already begun to acquire New World estates before the Seven Years' War ended.[34] As Colonel Henry Bouquet explained to a European confidant:

> the towns are growing in a surprising manner, commerce is flourishing, the people are thriving and becoming more refined, the arts are being introduced, and it can be prophesied that in a century or two, it will be equal to Europe. Now is the time to establish there. The price of land is increasing in proportion to the increase of the inhabitants, and by buying a reasonable amount of land one is sure of leaving an estate for posterity for a small price.

Western conventions equating wealth, power, and social status with the amount of property owned made such acquisitiveness understandable. This same principle underpinned the more substantial land grants given to officers and battalion staff by the Royal Proclamation.[35] Ranging between 2,000 and 5,000 acres, such rewards underscored George III's concern for those placed on half pay whose reduced government salaries might leave them in difficult circumstances. Title to greater properties at least ameliorated some of the financial pressures on warriors whose "half pay with age and infirmities contracted in the service is but a poor prospect." Those not willing to carve new homes out of the wilderness sold their rights to comrades with dreams of larger estates.[36]

Regimental duties had prepared gentlemen, upon demobilization, for the responsibilities of manor ownership in a number of ways. First, officers had developed basic managerial and horticultural skills as they directed the daily fatigue parties. Second, they had acquired a rudimentary sense of the logistical efforts needed to maintain a workforce in good physical condition. More important, strong ties had been forged with subordinate company personnel that proved advantageous for those in dire need of tenants. Major Philip Skeene, for instance, reported to superiors that it was his practice to "give provisions and cattle &c. to all discharged soldiers that settle: 270 men discharged at the Havana came with me to New York, the most of them waits my return to settle them."[37] Even small-scale operators like Ensign Duncan McVicar brought with him four subordinates willing to work on his holdings. It is not surprising that military affiliation bound these principals together in civilian life as unemployed soldiers once again became dependents of their social betters. Both parties profited from this symbiotic relationship in which character, expectations, and abilities were already known.[38]

Land Speculation

Ambitious officers did not let the terms of the Royal Proclamation limit their dreams of acquiring property in other areas. Having established primary residences in more genteel settings, they soon formed real estate consortia to exploit the uninhabited lands of Nova Scotia. This too was an area well trodden by army commanders who had served in the expeditions against Louisbourg and then suppressed French partisans occupying the St. John River valley.[39] British operational success allowed Governor Charles Lawrence to open the region for colonization in 1758. This swath of productive salt marshes "fit for the Culture of Hemp and Flax; and by its Nature and Situation will want no Manure, as it may be overflown by the Tides when exhausted," deserted Acadian farms, lavish timber stands, abundant game, and proximity to eastern markets all lured those anxious to profit from a still-desolate portion of the Atlantic littoral.[40]

The 60th Regiment's involvement in Maritimes development was championed by two foreign Protestant officers, Captain Samuel Holland and Lieutenant Joseph F. W. DesBarres, who were employed by metropolitan authorities to reconnoiter the new lands ceded to King George III by the Treaty of Paris. Holland, now a member of Quebec's new legislative council, was also named its first surveyor general and was charged with mapping the Island of St. John (now Prince Edward Island), the Magdalen Islands, and Cape Breton Island before large-scale settlement could begin. A detachment of fifteen Royal Americans from the second battalion worked as his chain bearers.[41] The Admiralty Office gave DesBarres complementary responsibilities, employing him to produce nautical charts of the seaboard from the Gulf of St. Lawrence to New York. These were subsequently published in his book *Atlantic Neptune*, which also featured the subaltern's drawings of more than 130 local scenes that many now regard as the "most important visual survey of Britain's new continental empire in North America." Both men rapidly became expert at evaluating the economic promise of the places through which they passed, and their personal observations formed the basis for regional investment advice shared with regimental colleagues.[42]

Samuel Holland became a charter member of the St. John's River Society when it was organized by members of the Montreal garrison in 1764. Two other Royal Americans, Captain Beamsley Glasier and Reverend John Ogilvie, joined the 44th Regiment's Captain Thomas Falconer as pivotal players in this group determined to open up 600,000 acres of Nova Scotian land for settlement. Falconer served as president for the committee of sixty investors, Ogilvie became treasurer, and Glasier officiated as the resident manager until recalled to active duty in 1767.[43] Their plan was quite simple: Each proprietor would pay an initial subscription of £30 plus a £15 yearly renewal fee to offset the costs of locating and improving the grants. Returns would accrue to shareholders as the price of cultivated lands increased and dividends were garnered from the sale of cured fish, potash, and lumber across the Atlantic world. Anticipated profits were so great that residents from as far away as New York, Boston, and Philadelphia became involved alongside colonial officials such as Thomas Hutchinson of Massachusetts Bay and Charles Morris of Halifax. Additional Royal American participants included Colonel Frederick Haldimand, Captain Daniel Claus, Lieutenant John Nordberg, and Lieutenant Daniel Wriesberg.[44]

Glasier ascended the St. John River in the spring of 1765. Strong ties to the provincial government assured acceptance of his land application as well as preferential treatment in the awarding of five desirable townships, subsequently named Burton, Conway, Gage, New-Town, and Sunbury in honor of senior associates. Michael Francklin, an influential merchant and future lieutenant governor of Nova Scotia, joined the partnership, covered initial patent expenses, and defended the group's interests against rival company agents at Halifax.[45] Prospective residents were lured to the area through the construction of a dam at the Great Rapids along the Nashwaak River—a major tributary—the arrival of milling equipment and oxen from Boston, and easy financial terms offered to those willing to buy or rent land from the manager. Plans were even afoot to speed development by the direct importation of families from Ireland, New England, Canso Bay, and Quebec.[46]

Fissures soon appeared within the partnership despite an auspicious beginning. What had initially seemed a feasible project among officers from nine different regiments proved more problematic after more than half of the military proprietors returned to Europe with their battalions following the Treaty of Paris. Their failure to appoint deputies with powers of attorney also complicated the decision-making process when important management issues had to be resolved promptly. The formation of a Boston oversight committee expedited administrative matters somewhat but still left the burden of settlement on those in Nova Scotia who thus resented such "indolent people who want estates & do nothing for it."[47]

Relations worsened when some consortium members began reneging on their promises to support the enterprise. Failure to remit initial subscription charges or yearly dues caused a premature capitalization crisis after bills of exchange signed by Captain Glasier for necessary expenses were returned unpaid.[48] Canadian entrepreneurs refused to pump more funds into the project when the Boston management group rebuffed their request for an account audit in 1767. The partnership dissolved shortly thereafter with investors assuming personal responsibility for the improvement of each lot apportioned to them. Established mills were held in common another sixteen years prior to becoming the exclusive property of titleholders in the township where they stood.[49]

The problems inherent with burdensome fraternities like the St. John's River Society were avoided by other 60th officers also keen to acquire Nova Scotian lands. While Glasier and his associates were staking claim to a portion of the Bay of Fundy's north shore, Captain George Adam Gmelin began a scheme to develop 100,000 acres along its eastern tidal rim. Before leaving North America for London in the fall of 1763, he resigned his active commission and solicited the sponsorship of wealthier men who had the financial means to underwrite his plantation. Official favor was curried by the Gmelin syndicate, which promised to pay all resettlement costs for the four hundred European homesteaders they planned to station on their grant. Included in this £10,000 outlay were salaries for agents needed to secure colonists from along the Rhine; fares for transatlantic passage; and money for the purchase of provisions, livestock, and farming implements.[50] Gmelin was confident of the venture's success since the valuable experience he had gained as a recruiter for Prevost's corps in 1756 could now serve his civilian purposes.[51]

The mercenary's plans went awry immediately after his London arrival because the Board of Trade was much more circumspect about sanctioning large Nova Scotian grants by the spring of 1764 than it had been earlier. The board's unhappy dealings with Captain Johann Henirich Christian von Stumpel, another foreign Protestant entrepreneur, was the reason for this policy change. Chaos followed in the wake of this erstwhile Hanoverian officer who had initially proposed to settle 4,000 Europeans at his own expense on 200,000 acres between the St. John and St. Croix rivers. When his plans began to unravel, however, von Stumpel fled the capital, leaving behind a number of retainers without any financial support.[52] Board members from then on discouraged flamboyant schemes, and Gmelin received only 20,000 acres instead. Yet even this modest property along the Napan River in Cumberland County proved too grand for rapid development because few pioneer families were willing to relocate there. The Royal American officer's downward spiral continued when he began to lose much of this holding to creditors in the late 1760s. He left Nova Scotia shortly thereafter to live out the remainder of his days in Europe.[53]

Officers of the 60th Regiment continued to gamble on land in the Maritimes despite the collapse of Gmelin's scheme. Undaunted by the failure of those without sufficient capital to establish viable manors, Colonels Henry Bouquet and Frederick Haldimand joined forces with merchants Hugh Wallace of New York, Adam Hoops from Philadelphia, and London's Peter Hasenclever to establish a township called Hopewell along the Petitcodiac River. Provincial officials granted these associates 100,000 acres upon agreement that 2,000 settlers would be in residence within twenty years of the patent date. Initially, all the necessary ingredients—capital, connections, and a viable tenant source—seemed to be in place for a flourishing enterprise. The labor problem was apparently overcome by recruiting Pennsylvanian homesteaders instead of Europeans.[54] Twenty German families transshipped from Philadelphia were the earliest arrivals to take up land in the fall of 1765. Frequent injections of cash to buy provisions and livestock kept the settlement going for two years until the first exports of produce, plaster of paris, and grindstones were ready for market. But costs continued to rise, making the venture less inviting to the principal investors as the township's population stagnated "for want of industrious people."[55]

The Hopewell settlement eventually failed as a speculative endeavor because the two field officers had not learned from their earlier misadventures with the Charles Town plantations a decade before. Most important, lack of direct personal oversight put the association at risk. Without the presence of at least one competent investor to manage daily activities, the consortium had to rely on the business acumen of an inexperienced overseer. In Nova Scotia the role of Andrew Fesch was reprised by Thomas Colhoon, a destitute fur trader who had left the Ohio Valley for a fresh start as township agent after being ruined by Pontiac's Rebellion. Predictably, Colhoon alienated the tenants, mismanaged affairs, and ran up large debts. He then had the audacity to sue employers for back wages and was joined in court by leaseholders who charged that terms of their contracts had been breached. Plaintiffs won both cases, resulting in further monetary loss to the partnership.[56]

Major personnel changes within the proprietary group also weakened enthusiasm for the Hopewell project. By 1772 only two of the original shareholders remained, Frederick Haldimand, now a brigadier general, and Peter Hasenclever. Haldimand had inherited Bouquet's 20 percent interest after the latter's death in 1765, and Adam Hoops's heirs were squabbling over the plantation's future six years later. Hasenclever was forced to give creditors his 20,000 acres in the township after being forced into bankruptcy by London business partners. Parcels of the original grant were then sold off periodically in vain attempts to prevent further financial hemorrhage until the provincial government finally expropriated the remaining property after the American Revolution for noncompliance with charter obligations.[57]

Colonization schemes based on foreign Protestant tenant sources miscarried after the Seven Years' War because immigrant numbers never returned to their 1750s levels. German households, once a mainstay, now found greater opportunities in Prussian and Hapsburg territories, leaving fewer families to chance an ocean passage. Accordingly, single males, who were not particularly well suited for homesteading projects, dominated the reconstituted Continental migration stream between the years 1763 and 1775.[58] Viable replacements might have been found among the Ulster Scots, but the Bay of

Fundy was far removed from the major shipping lanes between Irish ports and the eastern seaboard. Without such essential merchant traffic, there was little opportunity for these Presbyterian families to reach the Maritimes unless proprietors first hired recruiting agents and vessels specifically for that purpose. The eventual demise of the St. John's River Society and the enterprises of some other Royal American improvers suggests that these dynamics ruined those unable to adjust to the new Atlantic immigration patterns of the postwar world.[59]

Lieutenant Joseph F. W. DesBarres was an exception to this rule because he took an active interest in estate management. Two regimental colleagues, Captain Rudolph Fesch and Ensign Edward Barron, were deputized to act on his behalf in business matters only when duty took the surveyor out of the province. DesBarres's commitment to the principle of living and investing in the same region was demonstrated on an estate called "Castle Frederick" that served as the command center for his extensive operations. A portion of the £5,000 expenditure on DesBarres's Falmouth township site included an observatory "for determining the Degree of accuracy of . . . Astronomical Observations taken periodically in the course of . . . Surveys of the Coasts & Harbors of North America."[60]

It did not take the officer long to make further acquisitions. During the mid-1760s he received two grants that ultimately netted him another 27,000 acres. The largest, a 20,000-acre tract situated on the northeastern coast near Bay Verte, called Tatamagouche Manor, was conveyed by the Board of Trade in 1764. Its fine Atlantic harbor was one of the site's main attractions to the seventeen families who initially settled there the following year.[61] The remaining 7,000-acre parcel at Menaudie, in Cumberland County, was the lion's share of a larger 8,000-acre grant acquired by DesBarres and a few other Royal Americans in the spring of 1765. Seventeen families settled this fertile Bay of Fundy estate, known as Elysian Fields, and came under DesBarres's wing after his acquisition of majority interest from indifferent partners. More than 30,000 additional acres were also purchased over time from other military gentlemen anxious to sell their bounties.[62]

DesBarres's expansionist dreams were tempered solely by the financial constraints imposed by his governmental income of £450 per year. To increase these revenues from his half pay and surveying work

Joseph F. W. DesBarres (1721–1824) used his regimental connections and other government employment to amass a large estate in Nova Scotia. The lieutenant was also the author of the *Atlantic Neptune,* whose charts of eastern North American waters served the needs of the seafarers through the latter half of the nineteenth century. Courtesy of Library and Archives Canada. (C-135130)

for the Lords of the Admiralty, the officer recommended to British officials that he be allowed to raise a special pioneer corps of 150 men. Their deployment would guarantee his promotion to captain, more than double his army salary, and allow him to enjoy all the financial perquisites of a £3,000 command paid for by British taxpayers. His troops, in turn, would build roads throughout the province, improve existing infrastructure, and provide a disciplined defense force should another war occur. Metropolitan authorities, however, were in the process of reducing military expenditures in North America when DesBarres's 1763 proposal came to their attention, and they decided that regular troops already stationed in the Halifax garrison were sufficient for such tasks.[63]

The foreign Protestant officer was more successful at solving the plantation development puzzle. Since success was contingent on the number of tenants engaged to cultivate manor lands, the lieutenant found a providential solution to the dearth of migrant homesteaders: encouraging local families to tend his scattered holdings in their place. Acadian refugees, now deemed legal subjects provided they had taken an oath of allegiance, made a superlative workforce since they knew how to build the dikes that protected fertile loam from high Fundy tides.[64] Common natal ties with prewar Montbéliard immigrants also induced some of their number to relocate to the Tatamagouche grant. Yorkshire and Lowland Scots farmers also found new homes in Nova Scotia during the early 1770s by reestablishing themselves on the officer's holdings at negligible personal cost to the proprietor.[65]

Entrepreneurs of the 60th Regiment were also attracted to the vacant lands on the Island of St. John. London administrators had to apply Solomonic wisdom when dividing this spoil of war among the powerful political figures, military officers, and merchants who applied for grants there. John Perceval, Earl of Egmont, then First Lord of the Admiralty, became the key player. His proposal to establish large feudal baronies was supported by underlings hoping to lease these forty-thousand-acre properties for the nominal sum of £20 per year. Each of these major holdings, or Hundreds, would contain twenty estates further subdivided into 2,000-acre plots for rent.[66] Egmont pragmatically co-opted rival claimants and earned their support for his initiative by offering them stations as capital tenants or manor holders. Even this powerful coalition, however, could not prevail on the Board of Trade, which ultimately vetoed the entire scheme. Instead, the island was divided into sixty-seven lots of 20,000 acres each, which were granted to individual syndicates on the condition that one hundred Protestants be settled in each township within a decade. Seven Royal Americans, including Major General James Murray, Captains Thomas Bassett, Samuel Holland, William Ridge, and James Stevenson, together with Lieutenants Francis and Samuel Mackay, all became proprietors when parcels were distributed on 23 July 1767.[67]

Marriage

The appearance of the Mackay brothers among those grandees allocated land on the Island of St. John suggests that some veterans used marriage as a mechanism to improve their social and financial standing in the colonies. The Mackays' transformation from impoverished ensigns to substantial landowners exemplified the process. Younger sons of General Francis Mackay, an itinerant Scots mercenary, the pair had been given junior commissions with the Royal Americans by the Earl of Loudoun when the regiment was first established. Soon promoted to lieutenant's rank in the fourth battalion, they distinguished themselves during the Battle of Fort Ticonderoga but could not afford the £800 purchase price of higher company commands. When wild dreams of improving their financial position by marriage into wealthy American families did not materialize, they both fell to the charm offensive launched by Quebec belles soon after the Canadian conquest.[68] As one regular officer noted, "Their young Ladys take the utmost pains to teach the officers of our army French, with what view, I know not, if it is not that they might hear themselves praised, flattered, and courted without loss of time." Samuel wed Marguerite-Louise Herbin in 1761 at Montreal, and Francis was united to Marie-Anne Marchand de Lignery two years later—both by Protestant rites.[69]

What the new Mackay brides lacked in dowries was offset by the social connections, community standing, and modest property conveyed to the brothers in Quebec. Both women were daughters of renowned colonial officers of long standing in New France. Herbin had been the commandant of Louis XV's stronghold at Crown Point, a knight of St. Louis, and the son-in-law of Jean-Baptiste Boucher de

Niverville, seigneur of Chambly. Similarly, the Marchand de Lignery had overseen French interests in the Ohio Valley as Fort Duquesne's commander before dying of wounds received at Niagara in the summer of 1759.[70] The Mackays were quick to make use of these new family connections for their own benefit when Pontiac's Rebellion erupted in 1763. Facing retirement on the half-pay list, they offered to raise a corps of six hundred Canadian habitants to aid the army during its 1764 operations around the Great Lakes. Although deemed good campaign officers, their proposal was rejected by New York headquarters in favor of three hundred men dispatched by Quebec's new governor, James Murray.[71]

Loss of this lucrative employment did not derail some of the brothers' other schemes. Foremost was the development of their family property interests, the La Gauchtiere Patent, along Lake Champlain, which allowed both men to style themselves seigneurs of Pointe aux Roches by 1771.[72] Entrée into the noblesse was confirmed by appointments to the magistracy for the Montreal district and Francis's lucrative sinecure as surveyor general for the King's Woods. Samuel held the lesser office of deputy surveyor for the Royal Navy. The combination of both posts allowed them to collaborate in the commercial export of timber to Great Britain. The Mackays also enjoyed the patronage of Governor James Murray's family and Sir William Johnson, whose influence helped extend their operations from Quebec to the Island of St. John.[73]

The Scots mercenaries were not the only men to acquire Canadian brides as a result of growing contact between the redcoats and the local population. Those of higher rank, like Major John Wharton, also merged into the local elite through marriage. Wharton retired from active duty to an estate outside of Montreal shortly after solemnizing vows in 1771 before a Protestant clergyman with Marie-Anne de Belestre, the daughter of the last French commander at Detroit. Notarial documents suggest that even some of the rank and file followed their leaders' example in matrimonial concerns.[74] Regardless of romantic interests, foreign Protestant officers found themselves quite at home in a French-language environment and quickly began purchasing manors from vacating seigneurs. Three of the most eminent were Frederick Haldimand, later governor of the colony; Conrad Gugy, a legislative councillor; and Lewis de Mestral, who became a magistrate at Rivière-de-Loup. Facility with the local tongue and close ties to the new political regime assured their social ascendancy.[75]

The other foreign Protestant officer to become prominent in Quebec was Augustine Prevost (the elder), who assumed active management of the first battalion in 1767 and became temporary commander of all British forces there three years later. Unlike comrades who had married into the French-Canadian elite, however, Lieutenant Colonel Augustine Prevost wed Anne Margaret Grand, the daughter of a wealthy Lausanne banker, Viscount Isaac-Jean-Georges-Jonas Grand. He was therefore able to draw on his wife's ample financial resources to complement his modest regimental salary of £310 plus any returns from the £564.14.6 prize money earned at the capture of Havana.[76] In addition, Prevost, like the other military gentry stationed overseas, began to speculate heavily in North American lands. New York excited immediate interest as the place where he and his illegitimate eldest son, Lieutenant Augustine Prevost, jointly received a large entitlement astride Catskill Creek in Albany County. The field officer also joined a consortium that purchased a quarter million acres just south of Charlotte River in what was known as the Harper Patent.[77] Nova Scotia was the other region that added to his extensive real estate portfolio. In concert with other foreign Protestant mercenaries, including Lieutenant J. F. W. DesBarres, Augustine acquired an eight-thousand-acre grant at Menaudie in Cumberland County during the spring of 1765. Such judicious investments helped to increase the officer's net worth dramatically; when he died intestate after twenty-three years of further distinguished military service, his English country seat in Hertfordshire was conservatively appraised at £8,000.[78]

The more established provinces proved happier hunting grounds for military gentlemen in search of wealthy consorts. A brace of St. Clair officers improved their social stations here. The fourth battalion's lieutenant colonel, Sir John St. Clair, eventually married the eldest daughter of John Moland, a lawyer and provincial councillor in Pennsylvania. He retained his other post as the army's deputy quartermaster general after his fourth battalion was disbanded in 1763 and enjoyed a comfortable life with his new wife on a New Jersey manor, Belleville, located near Elizabeth Town. Sir John's subaltern nephew, Arthur, eclipsed his uncle through a match to the moneyed Bostonian Phoebe Bayard. She brought a £14,000 dowry to the union, which allowed the couple to develop a large estate near Fort Ligonier, Pennsylvania. Her birthright aided the advancement of the younger St. Clair's position in frontier society, where he enjoyed the Penn family's patronage as their proprietary agent and magistrate of Westmoreland County.[79]

Active duty was not a deterrent to profitable unions, which began occurring soon after the 60th Regiment was deployed in the colonies. The first instance occurred in Charles Town, South Carolina, when Captain Francis Lander married Elizabeth Simpson while his battalion formed a part of the town garrison in the fall of 1757. Another notable example was Captain John Brown's entrée into the prominent Livingston-Alexander circle through marriage to Molly Livingston shortly before the regiment embarked for the West Indies in 1772. She was one of ten surviving children born to Peter Van Brugh Livingston and Mary Alexander, whose combined family fortunes from military supply contracts and New York privateers exceeded £100,000.[80] This match proved to be a major advantage for an impecunious regular officer banished to the half-pay list for much of his career. Brown subsequently acquired a major's commission after taking post on Antigua thanks to his substantial in-laws, who had the necessary money and influence to secure military promotion.[81]

Captain James Mark Prevost, the youngest of the three Prevost brothers, also made great social strides by marrying the daughter of a prominent colonial attorney while still on active duty in 1763. He tended his family's regimental and financial interests for another four years prior to Augustine's arrival at Quebec to supervise the battalion. Paramus, New Jersey, then became the Prevost home until James Mark rejoined the Royal Americans in 1773.[82] Land speculation certainly engaged some of the captain's time while on half pay. He invested first in the same Nova Scotian patent as his brother at Elysian Fields, and then reinvested its sale proceeds to develop another twelve-thousand-acre grant located in Orange County, New York. Promotion soon followed the officer's return to active duty in the West Indies, with his elevation to major backdated to 23 July 1772. Distinguished conduct during the American Revolution resulted in Prevost's advancement to the rank of lieutenant colonel just prior to his death on the island of Jamaica about the year 1780.[83]

Even the social stigma of bastardy could be mitigated by an advantageous colonial marriage. Lieutenant Augustine Prevost (the younger), the illegitimate son of Lieutenant Colonel Augustine Prevost, had been attached to the fourth battalion throughout the war. He transferred into the first battalion during Pontiac's Rebellion and served as a subaltern with Colonel Henry Bouquet's force that marched into the Muskingum Valley in 1764. While posted at Lancaster, Pennsylvania, he met and married Susannah Croghan, the daughter of Sir William Johnson's Indian agent at Fort Pitt.[84] The Croghan association initially proved very beneficial to the young émigré. The lieutenant was able to retire on half pay in 1767 before establishing a residence on 6,000 acres of his father-in-law's New York lands. There, at the head of Lake Otsego, he built a substantial log house and constructed a sawmill for the use of tenants who began to populate his estate. Within a few years this property was worth about £3,000 York currency (£1,875 sterling). Social prestige was assured after Sir William obtained a field commission for the young officer in the local horse troop of the Albany County militia. Prevost retained this dignity until he returned to active duty in 1771.[85]

Captain Walter Rutherfurd trumped all his compatriots in the marital sweepstakes by solemnizing vows with Catherine Alexander on 21 December 1758. She was a younger daughter of the prominent New York lawyer James Alexander, whose fortune was based on revenue derived from government salaries, legal fees, land speculation, and assorted commercial interests. Catherine fell heir to a large share of family money in 1760, prompting the captain to resign his commission so that he could manage this windfall. Prior service as battalion paymaster and appointment to the audit board that cleared the 60th's regimental accounts had accustomed Rutherfurd to the demands of high finance. This inherited wealth combined with an extensive patronage network laid the basis for an ambitious postwar investment concern designed to exploit the natural wealth of the Great Lakes basin.[86]

Commercial Enterprises

The fur trade had always been an integral part of New York's export economy. Although in decline for several decades, prospects temporarily improved following the loss of French suzerainty over the northwestern interior in 1760. Walter Rutherfurd combined his family fortune, contacts at army headquarters, and personal knowledge of the hinterland to take advantage of this lucrative £100,000 prize once the redcoats established garrisons throughout the pays d'en haut. With little difficulty, the captain formed a consortium of like-minded adventurers with close ties to the military. The partnership, which included Lieutenant Colonel John Bradstreet, Lieutenant John Duncan, Lieutenant George Coventry, Alexander Coventry, Peter Van Brugh Livingston, James Syme, and John Porteous, planned to reap huge rewards by establishing a major trade presence in areas just vacated by the French.[87]

Rutherfurd's scheme, contingent upon monopoly of the strategic Niagara portage, was based on his understanding of army logistics, topography of the Great Lakes watershed, and equitable relations with military superiors. Both he and Duncan had first visited the area in 1759 as members of Brigadier General John Prideaux's expeditionary force. A year later, the two men accompanied the western army during its treacherous run down the St. Lawrence River toward Montreal; Rutherfurd had been promoted to brevet major of the massed grenadier formation as a sign of Major General Jeffery Amherst's favor prior to this last triumphant campaign. It was relatively easy, then, for the retired officer to secure the commander-in-chief's blessing for a settlement of five hundred families in proximity to Fort Niagara.[88] This entrepôt was intended to support the garrison, provide a workforce to transship goods between Lakes Ontario and Erie, and more important, provide a secure base for the storage of company wares. Headquarters sanctioned this enterprise because of its perceived benefit to the army before forwarding Rutherfurd's submission to Whitehall for final approval.[89]

Events moved smoothly at first. The syndicate's chief agent, James Sterling, established a residence at Detroit, leaving assistants behind at Niagara to construct a storehouse at the upper landing. By the end of 1761, he reported that trading had been brisk with good returns. Sixty-two packs of fur were sent east the first spring.[90] Diversified marketing targeted not only American Indian villagers, but British occupation forces and the French civilian community as well. Blankets, wampum, shirts, garters, ribbon, ornamental silver, scalping knives, and animal traps sold quickly to Native customers. Whites purchased surplus army provisions, especially salt pork, in addition to alcohol, spermaceti candles, condiments, delftware, china, and other overseas commodities.[91] Secondhand clothing sent to Detroit for disposal by Catherine Rutherfurd, however, met with less success. As Sterling informed her husband: "I am heartily sorry that it is not in my power to make remittance suitable to her expectation, having sold but few of the things they are in general so much soild & unfashionable that the Ladies don't seem fond of buying them tho I have sold a few of them & have got six martin skins with some other skins." These outmoded raiments were returned to New York accompanied by a small bundle of peltry. Undaunted and still bitten by the trading bug, Mrs. Rutherfurd dispatched another clothing consignment in hopes that it would be better received by the chic women at Detroit.[92]

The company's development plans and preferential use of the Niagara route did have its detractors. At the forefront were the Chenussio Senecas, who jealously guarded their territorial rights to this strategic passage and expected payment for any freight conveyed around the falls. Despite the promise of recompense for any lands utilized by the merchants, they remained uneasy and expressed their concern through Sir William Johnson.[93] An influential lobby of Albany peddlers also voiced discontent at what they perceived as undo control over access to their own trading facilities at Fort Niagara. They claimed that agents for a rival partnership intercepted potential customers at their storehouse above the falls while asserting sole right to traffic there. Exclusive possession of this vantage point threatened to bankrupt competitors since few villagers ventured farther east to the main garrison, where the Albany traders bartered for furs. Even Major William Walters, the interim post commander, complained that private ownership of lands around the base would deny soldiers access to requisite building materials, firewood, and pasture for the draught animals.[94]

Much of the consortium's early success was due to Rutherfurd's associations with senior staff officers in New York and with Royal American commandants managing scattered posts across the western theater. Despite the vociferous protests of opponents, Amherst gave the syndicate another full year of trade by directing their remonstrances to imperial officials instead of immediately terminating operations. Even after Whitehall canceled settlement plans and ordered the destruction of the forward magazine, army headquarters merely required the partners to vacate the new facility pending final word from the Privy Council.[95] Battalion colleagues likewise abetted the company's activities by winking at the occasional use of their men to labor on private building projects, guard valuable merchandise, or transport company wares between British posts. This last concession was especially important when a season's worth of furs had to be moved down the Great Lakes transportation system to Albany for disposal.[96] While other traders were required to pay high prices to convey their freight, Rutherfurd's packs and merchandise traveled gratis aboard military vessels.[97]

Further advantages also accrued to the enterprise because of its founder's past service with the Royal Americans. Erstwhile comrades took it upon themselves to warehouse expensive company property in their own quarters while managing business affairs in the absence of accredited representatives. Even officers at the remotest detachments aided the Rutherfurd initiative by collecting arrears from traders who had acquired items on account but absconded into the wilderness to avoid repayment. The New York partnership thus had one of the most effective recovery systems in the lawless Northwest since soldiers confiscated debtors' fur bales and marked them with the Rutherfurd blazon as a means of repayment.[98] Dispensations of this nature were curried with presents of pickled oysters, anchovies, and fine wine to grace the officers' mess or gifts of Native curiosities to important individuals, which garnered "favours that gold cannot purchase."[99]

Regimental gentry also supplemented their own wages by dabbling in the fur traffic. Isolated commanders were ideally placed to conduct business with little effort or capital expense. Trade goods could be obtained on credit from merchants at the larger bases and then bartered for furs when tribal members appeared at the remoter outposts to hold council. Moreover, since garrison principals were sources of government largesse and often enjoyed equitable relations with local American Indian communities, the groundwork was already laid for the establishment of profitable winter stores. Ensigns Robert Holmes and Edward Jenkins were two such ambitious redcoats who mixed business with active duty. Trade at Holmes's Miami garrison had an estimated annual value of 80,000 livres (£3,500 sterling), while commerce at Jenkins's charge, Fort Ouiatenon, was reckoned at 60,000 livres (£2,600 sterling).[100]

Officers without the time or inclination to participate directly in commerce could back enterprises begun by acquaintances. Foreign

Protestant stakeholders in the metropolitan-based Guinand merchant house, for instance, had a portion of their capital allocated to the Quebec fur trade.[101] Others also financed the entrepreneurial efforts of friends whose pursuits were aided by military benefactors. Frederick von Hambach, formerly a Royal American gentleman volunteer from Europe, relied on the patronage of Colonel Bouquet to ensure the viability of his fur trading career. The veteran first obtained £3,000 worth of goods on credit through the field officer's recommendation. Army-controlled supply networks were then utilized to ship the merchandise expeditiously from Philadelphia before competitors' goods could reach the same market.[102] Once in the backcountry, Von Hambach depended continually on the colonel's good graces to protect him from censure when he conducted business outside fort precincts, a practice that was contrary to official army policy.[103]

Even the lowly rank and file actively engaged in trade whenever the opportunity presented itself. American Indians made willing partners. Rum, clothing, and ammunition were all-important commodities bartered with villagers, who provided food or furs in return. The craze to make a profit raged even in the middle of combat operations when security matters should have been of chief concern. During Bouquet's 1764 Ohio Valley offensive, troops had to be warned in daily orders against trading with the Natives. Just after the momentous conference with the insurgents at Tuscarawas, the commander admonished his men against "purchasing or Exchanging anything whatsoever" with tribesmen who might be permitted entry into British lines. Clearly, trade followed the flag and was sometimes even conducted by those standard-bearers of empire as they marched through a combat zone.[104]

Military logistical support posed economic opportunities for Royal Americans not inclined to the fur trade. In 1764 Lieutenant Francis Pfister, who settled at the western end of the Niagara portage after reduction to half pay, quickly put his expertise and personal contacts to advantageous use. The stars were perfectly aligned when he became beneficiary of a government contract to transport army supplies and boats around the falls for an annual stipend of £100. As part of the agreement, all of the king's wagons and draught animals at Fort Niagara were relinquished to the veteran, allowing him to earn considerable income by charging traders a minimum of £10 York currency (£6 sterling) for every load carried by his teams.[105] Pfister, on his own volition, also constructed a sawmill above the falls to provide 60th garrisons with the lumber they needed to maintain their barracks, storehouses, and vessels. This endeavor increased the entrepreneur's yearly income by several hundred pounds. Both profitable concerns were retained even after the subaltern returned to active duty in 1767.[106]

The military's insatiable demand for salt provided Lieutenant Dietrich Brehm, an auxiliary engineer who was one of the first British officers to reconnoiter the Great Lakes basin, with another opportunity for lucrative enterprise. During his 1760 survey, Brehm recognized tremendous economic potential at the Detroit narrows after noting the presence of saline springs and adjacent woodlots. This essential preservative was essential for British installations when garrison livestock was slaughtered in the early winter months as pastures became bare.[107] The redcoat believed that he could enrich himself by provisioning the upper posts from local refining works to be built on the Rouge River since all supplies had to be imported along lengthy supply lines. Although small distillation operations could be quite simply performed with iron kettles set over a roaring fire, Brehm may have had more ambitious plans in mind. By the mid-eighteenth century, imposing production facilities had been established in Europe that utilized pumps, large boiling pans, and intricate graduation houses to concentrate the final yield. The lieutenant's request for substantial land grants around two promising sites and an exclusive contract to furnish the king's men from Fort Pitt to La Baye with salt presaged large-scale development.[108]

The Royal Americans' entrepreneurial activities were not restricted to the frontier. The regiment's expansive patronage and financial network sustained the "American Company" that was formed in 1763 to supply Britain's demand for raw materials. Led by the German merchant Peter Hasenclever, metropolitan elites purchased New Jersey iron mines and plantations in the Mohawk River valley, where export crops of hemp, flax, and madder would be grown. Although no complete shareholder list exists, it is likely that the foreign Protestant capitalist relied on James Prevost's favor at court to gain investors there. Moreover, the mercenary's influence was apparent by how quickly family intimates like Henry Bouquet and Frederick Haldimand welcomed Hasenclever into their New York fold.[109] Prevost's contacts in Europe, who had recruited volunteers for his corps at the outset of the Seven Years' War, were again called on to provide a subservient workforce for the company's fields and forges. It is no coincidence that the Fesch clan supervised the transportation of 535 German employees and dependents overseas since they had already performed meritoriously as recruiters when the Royal Americans were first formed.[110]

Peter Hasenclever aggressively developed four ironworks and subsidiary plantations shortly after his 1764 Atlantic crossing. Almost £60,000 was expended in the construction of new facilities at Cortland, New York, and at two other locations in New Jersey. These complexes were technological marvels by colonial standards. Observers noted that

> the dams and water-ways, the casting-house, bellows-house, wheel-house, ton-house, coal-house &c. are all well-contrived. . . . Here are also a number of dwelling-houses, storehouses, workshops and stables, necessary and convenient to the works; also a good saw-mill. This furnace when in blast is capable of making from twenty to twenty-five ton pig-iron per week, and can be worked at a small expence, as there is plenty of wood and ore at hand, and need never stop for want of water at any season of the year.

A ruined furnace adjacent to the Long Pond site in Passaic County, New Jersey, was also refurbished.[111] Supervision of the labor force was entrusted to former Royal American officers like Lieutenants Frederick von Weissenfells and Daniel Wriesberg whose abilities made them ideal managers at the company's larger ironworks. Military investors thus ensured that deserving colleagues received employment with firms in which they held significant interests as Britons developed their newly expanded empire.[112]

Royal American veterans were among the thousands of redcoats who hoped to "settle, marry, and trade here" after being discharged from the army at the close of the Seven Years' War. Military service aided their adjustment to civilian life primarily because the metropolitan government furnished the rank and file with modest land grants, allowing them to become freeholders. Most soldiers preferred ready money over backcountry homesteading and thus quickly disposed of their land rights to speculators, using the cash to improve their lot in the major colonial centers where they lived. A minority who chose to establish frontier farms, principally in northern New York, had already learned the rudiments of building weatherproof shelters, clearing and cultivating ground, and raising farm animals during their time with the colors. More important, battalion comrades became neighbors so that they could assist one another during the early years of settlement, while regular garrisons provided succor, provisions, and employment during hard times.

Officers and former redcoats could be bound together again after discharge once gentlemen engaged subordinates as leaseholders for their large estates. Some ex-servicemen who did not wish to hazard independence chose tenancy instead since they enjoyed an enviable bargaining position. A postwar landlord glut meant that veterans could negotiate favorable terms with their social betters, including a grubstake of buildings and livestock, perpetual leases with rights to sell improvements, and access to demesne mills at very little cost to themselves. Similarly, trusted soldiers were hired to manage daily operations in some business enterprises financed by half-pay officers or those with active commissions.

Long sojourns in the New World convinced many army commanders that the countryside through which they marched possessed amazing commercial potential. The province of Nova Scotia attracted particular interest because of its coastal access, diverse resource base, and government conveyance of immense township grants to qualified applicants. Attempts to develop plantations there met with mixed results. Consortia with competent resident managers or active landlords thrived best since they were able to react quickly to changing circumstances if initial projections did not prove true. Unfortunately for developers, Maritime holdings were not as inviting to tenants in light of changed foreign Protestant migration streams and the region's relative isolation.

The 60th Regiment's personnel did not limit investment opportunities solely to property development. Years of frontier service gave them the necessary experience and connections to profit from military occupation of the continental interior. The fur trade, salt production, iron manufacture, and army contracting were just a few of the diversified businesses controlled by enterprising officers. Battalion patronage or cronyism assured that active-duty personnel supported such endeavors through provision of storage, security, management, and transportation assistance when needed. Collateral for these projects came from a wide variety of sources, including funds from affluent colonial heiresses whom 60th officers courted with some success. Marriage into elite circles was a particularly effective way of gaining both wealth and supporters for personal advancement.

In retrospect, the redcoats' contribution to British North American expansion must be understood in terms other than mere annexation by conquest. Demobilized troops became part of mainstream colonial society through participation in farming, laboring, apprenticeships, and various commercial pursuits. Officers, in particular, were able to take advantage of superior financial resources by investing in plantations and business enterprises based on natural resource extraction. Success rates varied, but military patronage guaranteed the profitability of many such ventures that extended Royal American influence beyond the battlefield and into the very heart of the Atlantic world.

Conclusion

Atlantic Microcosm

Francois La Rochefoucauld-Liancourt published his favorable impressions of the new American republic at the dawn of the nineteenth century. Among the residents featured in the nobleman's travelogue was a benevolent New York squire, Augustine Prevost (the younger), who lived on a substantial freehold near Albany. Although a Genevan by birth, this soldier had accompanied his family to the New World with the 60th Regiment in 1756 and was still developing the property given to him for service during the Seven Years' War. Remarkably, neighbors did not disparage the gentleman farmer for his distinguished army career because Prevost's industriousness, charitable nature, and public spirit won acclaim from all around. The enterprising landlord, like so many officers before him, had beaten his sword into a ploughshare after more than twenty years with the colors and enjoyed a comfortable retirement on his large estate.[1]

La Rochefoucauld's glowing profile of this veteran Swiss mercenary has been overlooked by historians in their search for material links between Europe and the Americas. Regrettably, scholarly preoccupation with social, economic, and cultural issues diverts attention away from the redcoats whose activities are still believed to fall beyond the scope of an Atlantic realm inhabited chiefly by "traders, settlers, and migrants." As this study of the Royal Americans has demonstrated, however, soldiers were often engaged in the same pursuits as their civilian counterparts and enjoyed an equally "effective trust network" of regimental patronage that extended from European capitals to the North American backcountry. Far from being a countercurrent to mainstream life, the 60th Foot's cast of disparate faces was remarkably active in the far-flung places and transnational spaces that constituted the eighteenth-century Atlantic world.[2]

There can be no doubt that the first British Empire was an ethnic polyglot by the time of the Seven Years' War. Battalion muster rolls confirm such diversity and indicate that regimental personnel were an eclectic mix representative of "all corners of the Universe, and of all languages and dispositions." Foreign Protestants formed the largest single bloc, followed closely by English and Irish enlistees. The whole closely mirrored Pennsylvania's own variegated European population profile. Thus, a Leeds clothier, a Limerick laborer, a Norwegian wigmaker, and a cook from Anhalt-Dessau could all rub shoulders together, and perhaps even share the same tent, during their time in the ranks. This camaraderie might even extend beyond wartime as many veterans began the process of establishing new lives together in pioneer homesteads. The regimental community certainly incorporated more exotic faces over time. While blacks transferred into the corps from provincial units, some on active duty even took French-Canadian brides when stationed in Quebec; garrison commanders too are known to have wed American Indian women à la façon du pays. The Royal American Regiment's uniformity in appearance was provided by only the redcoat that the soldiers wore.[3]

Social stratification within the Crown's land forces also reflected contemporary realities. Notables such as the Earl of Loudoun, a Scottish peer; John Stanwix, a well-regarded soldier and parliamentarian; Robert Monckton and Charles Lawrence, colonial governors; and James Prevost, that ambitious Swiss courtier; formed the 60th Foot's upper echelon. All of these men enjoyed the wealth and influence that derived from close connections to the metropolitan power structure. Next on the ladder stood the career field officers and company commanders who made their living primarily through military service, benefiting from the sponsorship of those above them. The subaltern caste was filled by the sons of the lesser gentry, those whose fathers were already commissioned officers, or capable sergeants raised from the ranks. Enlisted personnel included volunteers for life, as well as short-timers who were backcountry farmers, indentured servants, redemptioners, provincial soldiers from all colonial regions, and others of the lesser sort—some with wives and children in tow— who found greater opportunity in the army than that afforded by immediate civilian pursuits. Battalion collectives thus emulated the dominant social order with all elements working together to achieve a common goal.[4]

Military duty was a cohesive activity from which a shared British identity evolved because allegiance to King George, observance of Protestant religious rites, and antipathy for Bourbon monarchs were already core values. Soldiers acknowledged their fealty to the Crown upon entry into the land forces and celebrated their royal associations on significant dynastic occasions, in recognition of battlefield triumphs, or through the frequent passwords that regulated camp access. Protestant profession was a prerequisite for admission into the ranks, with diligent exercise reinforced through weekly church parades held on the Lord's Day. Unlike civilians, whose patriotism grew in the reflected glory of their troops' military successes, the soldiers themselves fought against ruthless French and American Indian foes. Such violent confrontations with an enemy whose battlefield conduct was often the antithesis of their own furnished the redcoats with a measure against which they could construct a more positive self-image than that ascribed to Louis XV's forces. This new consciousness, in turn, provided an important linchpin for a combat community formed by servicemen born in England, Scotland, Ireland, or the colonies and was malleable enough to include foreign Protestant veterans, who were given expedited naturalization after the war.

As the definition of national identity grew more expansive, so too did public interest in the empire's distant lands and its newest subjects. Service personnel helped to satisfy curiosity about the United Kingdom's overseas conquests through personal correspondence, published accounts, plays, topographical drawings, and commercial engravings. Although official reports and maps never circulated much beyond governmental circles, artistic endeavors by Royal Americans like Lieutenant J.F.W. DesBarres were particularly useful for the dissemination of information about the New World to both the educated and illiterate alike. Such efforts helped to mold perceptions about

A view of Annapolis Royal, Nova Scotia, by Lieutenant Joseph F. W. DesBarres. This image was one of 130 North American scenes published by the Royal American officer in his *Atlantic Neptune*. Courtesy of Library and Archives Canada. (C-2705)

George III's newest domains at a time when the British people's own sense of self was crystallizing.[5]

The 60th Regiment's story also illustrates how military forces can provide a nexus for comparative studies of the Atlantic world since the troops operated in distant places throughout their deployments. Redcoats were among the eighteenth century's most mobile groups, especially during wartime when military operations took them beyond British territorial limits. The travels of some foreign Protestant volunteers assigned to the Royal Americans' third battalion are suggestive. Enlisted in the Holy Roman Empire during the spring of 1756, the troops marched overland from Frankfort to Hamburg prior to embarkation for New York in midsummer. They were subsequently captured by a French naval squadron in the Atlantic and carried off into captivity for almost a year before repatriation to Portsmouth, England. The recruits eventually began operations with the 1758 Louisbourg task force before reinforcing the Quebec garrison in 1761. The infantrymen then remained in Canada for several months before joining the Martinique expedition, where they were initiated into the hazards of Caribbean warfare. While the French at Fort Royal surrendered quickly, battalion members remained in the tropics for another twenty-four months, first at Havana and then at Pensacola, before returning to New York for disbandment. Thus, within the course of eight years, these soldiers spent time in Continental Europe, the British Isles, Canada, the Caribbean, and Florida before discharge from the regiment.[6]

Colonial marchlands were also scenes of prolonged Royal American activity following the 60th's occupation of frontier outposts between 1757 and 1772. For example, Captain Gavin Cochrane discharged his duties first at Carlisle, Pennsylvania (1757), and then at Fort Pitt (1759) before eventually taking command of the Presque Isle blockhouse in 1761. He remained in the Great Lakes basin through Pontiac's Rebellion and was then reassigned to oversee South Carolina's borderland defenses for four years.[7] By the time he and his men were reunited with the first battalion at Quebec in 1768, the second battalion had marched to garrison the Upper Country's strongholds until the spring of 1772. While there, the second, like its sister corps before it, participated in American Indian diplomacy, trade management, policing, construction, and other military duties. Redcoats thus remained an influential presence in the backcountry because their fortified bases provided natural meeting sites for Natives and newcomers to interact.[8]

Royal American contact with a wide assortment of locales is also evident in their diffuse residency patterns. Senior officers lived in major European centers, while their subordinates resided in provincial capitals or remote frontier outposts. Seasonal abodes were the norm for the redcoats during wartime as the battalions moved into operational theaters for the summer months and then retired to various stations in New England, the Middle Colonies, and the Upper Chesapeake with the onset of winter. Such travel gave veterans practical acquaintance with many regions within British North America, allowing them to make informed choices about their future civilian domiciles. Upon demobilization, most discharged veterans eventually found work in the bustling port cities, while others established themselves in smaller centers or on tenancies; some even occupied their frontier land grants and began the arduous task of homesteading, often in concert with former messmates. A regimental presence thus continued to bridge the divide between metropole and backcountry through the postwar activities of those who remained on duty, or had previously marched, in the 60th Foot.

Historians agree that the Atlantic world was essentially a commercial realm that engaged people and resources from many lands. Military service was no exception as evinced by the conduct of army personnel who pursued business opportunities even while in uniform. Colonel James Prevost became the Royal American Regiment's principal founder by combining venture capital from a Huguenot merchant firm with Whitehall's strategic defensive needs. Profits made from this endeavor were then reinvested by Prevost and his foreign Protestant confreres in a wide variety of other enterprises: first, in South Carolinian plantations with a large slave labor force; second, in privateers; third, in Nova Scotian lands; and finally, in Peter Hasenclever's "American Company" that supplied the United Kingdom with iron, flax, and hemp from New York and the Middle Colonies. Those outside Prevost's immediate circle also created business networks predicated on their time with the colors. The Rutherfurd consortium, for instance, staked its financial success on the ability to satisfy hinterland demand for European wares by using the army's extensive communications links to transport and store goods at negligible cost. This was a competitive advantage that purely civilian enterprises did not enjoy. Furs acquired through trade were then exported to the mother country. Estate ownership and property development were also considered to be fundamental wealth builders. Although not always successful, officers pooled their resources to speculate in New World real estate, particularly in Nova Scotia, where additional revenue could be generated through the sale of fish and timber to more populated consumer markets around the Atlantic seaboard.

The redcoats also operated in other dimensions of transnational space besides commerce. Certainly participation in the political world of imperial affairs was paramount because the battalions were raised at a time of national emergency and kept on the army establishment after the Treaty of Paris to defend British interests. This critical military function grew in importance during the latter half of the eighteenth century as different powers vied for control over

New World wealth and territories. Indeed, the Royal Americans ultimately became key players in the empire-expansion process through steady battlefield performance and by tapping foreign Protestant manpower resources for Whitehall's purposes when "periods of peace could almost be regarded as exceptions to the wartime norm" in Western history.[9]

The 60th's troops encountered a wide variety of opponents before prevailing over both line regiments and partisans alike. Each adversary in these contested imperial spaces provided its own set of unique challenges. Combat against French and Spanish regulars required the king's men to become adept at all facets of conventional warfare, including battlefield engagements, amphibious assaults, and the attack or defense of fortified places. This became a familiar environment because their opponents were a known quantity who generally fought according to established norms. By contrast, American Indian war parties habitually struck only when they had a tactical advantage and remained an elusive foe through the time of Pontiac's Rebellion. Commanders responded by attuning European tactics to New World realities with simplified maneuvers, speedier deployments, and screens of light infantry trained for petite guerre operations. Battlefield success resulted in profound changes to the Western balance of power and enormous territorial acquisitions for the British Empire when international boundaries were redrawn to include Canada, the Island of St. John, Cape Breton Island, disputed sites in the Great Lakes and Mississippi basins, and the Floridas.

Royal American garrisons also represented Protestant beachheads in ecclesiastical regions that had previously known only Roman observance. Because their Reformation faith traveled with the redcoats throughout the New World, the 60th Regiment carried both Anglican and Reformed chaplains on their muster rolls during the Seven Years' War. Whether by personal conviction or prescribed conduct, the British army was certainly Protestant in character with worship services held at least once a week in its garrisons. There the troops affirmed the principle of the priesthood of all believers by holding Sabbath observance even if no ordained clergyman was present. Marriage to influential Roman Catholic women by Protestant rites and a call for evangelical missionary activity among Eastern Woodland tribes were just two instances of modest proselytizing activity conducted by Royal American commanders after taking up residence in former French possessions.

Although military personnel might not be generally associated with the expansion of European intellectual space, those holding the king's commission formed an important constituency within enlightened society through their contributions of patronage, exploration, and personal observations. These scientific interests became evident when battalion gentry took it upon themselves to further John Bartram's 1761 quest for new botanical specimens in the Ohio Country. Besides logistical support, commanders willingly shared their own personal findings with the Royal Society's agent as well as data about the flora and fauna discovered during the course of their surveys of the Great Lakes basin. Cooperation came from the top down since Colonel Henry Bouquet was an avid plant collector who aspired to provide European friends with North American specimens "when we have more peaceable Times."[10] This engagement with modernity was evident among even those posted in isolated fortifications. While away from polite society, they remained current with the latest European news and intellectual musings through their personal associations or correspondence with luminaries on both sides of the Atlantic, including Benjamin Franklin, Edward Gibbons, Dr. Samuel Johnson, and Voltaire, among others.[11]

The observation that "war and migration were intertwined" during the eighteenth century is certainly true with respect to the 60th Foot since these two phenomena were responsible for its creation and deployment. However, it was not the negative "push" caused by political upheaval, but the "pull" of economic opportunity or family reunification that prompted at least a thousand foreign Protestant troops to enter the Atlantic migrant stream via military service in the Royal Americans. English, Irish, and Scots troops likewise found themselves in the New World, where many chose to remain. Regimental gentry also facilitated the chain migration process that moved people across international boundaries by enlisting relatives, retainers, tenants, or employees in their postwar development schemes. Such initiatives could be as modest as attempts to populate the banks of the Petitcodiac River with a score of German households or as significant as the relocation of several hundred foreign Protestant families to work for the "American Company" in New York and

New Jersey. In every instance, Royal American officers used their personal network of connections and funds to help establish others in British North America within a few years of their own arrival.[12]

The 60th Foot was a military community that exemplified the Atlantic experience during the mid-eighteenth century. The corps was not just a combat force; its influence extended far beyond the confines of the geopolitical sphere, where redcoats are generally thought only to have been of consequence. Archival sources confirm that these soldiers, from different ethnic stocks, performed their duties in varied places, which, in turn, facilitated involvement with the transnational spaces of commerce, imperial affairs, religion, enlightened thought, migration, and settlement. The Royal American Regiment was clearly an integral part of the Atlantic world because it was Atlantic in its cast, Atlantic in its contacts, and Atlantic in its conduct—in sum, a dynamic Atlantic microcosm.

Appendix

A Battalion List of Senior Royal American Officers

Colonels-in-Chief
John Campbell, Fourth Earl of Loudoun, 1755–57
Major General James Abercromby, 1758
Sir Jeffery Amherst, 1758–68
Major General Thomas Gage, 1768
Sir Jeffery Amherst, 1768–97

First Battalion
Colonels-Commandant
John Stanwix, 1755–61
James Prevost, 1761–76
Frederick Haldimand, 1776–91

Lieutenant Colonels
Henry Bouquet, 1755–65
Augustine Prevost, 1765–68
Gabriel Christie, 1768–69
Augustine Prevost, 1769–75

Second Battalion
Colonels-Commandant
Joseph Dusseaux, 1755–57
Robert Monckton, 1757–59
James Murray, 1759–68
Bigoe Armstrong, 1768–72
Frederick Haldimand, 1772–76

Lieutenant Colonels
Frederick Haldimand, 1755–72
Gabriel Christie, 1772–75

Third Battalion
Colonels-Commandant
Charles Jeffreys, 1755–57
George Augustus, Lord Viscount Howe, 1757
Charles Lawrence, 1757–60
William Haviland, 1760–63

Lieutenant Colonels
Russell Chapman, 1755–57
John Young, 1757–61
Augustine Prevost, 1761–63

Fourth Battalion
Colonels-Commandant
James Prevost, 1755–61
Marcus Smith, 1761–63

Lieutenant Colonels
Sir John St. Clair, 1756–63

Abbreviations Used in the Notes

AB	Abercromby Papers
Add. MSS	Additional Manuscripts, BL
ADM	Admiralty Correspondence and Papers
ALG	Department of State Application for Land Grants
Amherst Journal	John C. Webster, ed., *The Journal of Jeffery Amherst: Recording the Military Career of General Amherst in America From 1758 to 1763*
AMSS	Amherst Manuscripts
ANQ-M	Archives Nationales du Quebec, Montreal
APS	American Philosophical Society, Philadelphia
"Barton Journal"	William Hunter, ed., "Thomas Barton and the Forbes Expedition," *PMHB* 95 (1971)
BL	British Library, London
Bouquet Orderly Book, 1764	Edward G. Williams, ed., *The Orderly Book of Colonel Henry Bouquet's Expedition Against the Ohio Indians, 1764*
Bouquet Papers	Sylvester K. Stevens et al., eds., *The Papers of Henry Bouquet*

LIST OF ABBREVIATIONS

ChP	Chatham Papers
CKS	Centre for Kentish Studies, Maidstone, Kent
CN	Collections Notaries
CO	Colonial Office
"Croghan Journal"	Nicholas B. Wainwright, ed., "George Croghan's Journal," *PMHB* 71 (1947)
EAMC	Edward E. Ayer Manuscript Collection
Forbes Papers	Alfred P. James, ed., *Writings of General John Forbes Relating to His Service in North America*
Gage Correspondence	Clarence E. Carter, ed., *The Correspondence of General Thomas Gage with the Secretaries of State and with the War Office and the Treasury, 1763–1775*
Gates Papers	James Gregory and Thomas Dunnings, eds., *The Horatio Gates Papers*
GD	Gifts and Deposits
Hawks' Orderly Book	Hugh Hastings, ed., *Orderly Book and Journal of Major John Hawks on the Ticonderoga–Crown Point Campaign, under General Jeffery Amherst, 1759–1760*
"HBOB"	"Colonel Henry Bouquet Orderly Book, 17 June 1758–15 September 1758," in *Bouquet Papers*
HCSP	Sheila Lambert, ed., *House of Commons Sessional Papers of the Eighteenth Century*
HEH	Henry E. Huntington Library, San Marino, Calif.
Hervey Journals	William Hervey, *Journals of the Hon. William Hervey, in North America and Europe, from 1755 to 1814: With Order Books at Montreal, 1760–1763, with Memoir and Notes*
HM	Huntington Manuscripts
HQJF	Headquarters Papers of Brig. Gen. John Forbes
HSP	Historical Society of Pennsylvania, Philadelphia
Jenks' Diary	Samuel Jenks, *Diary of Captain Samuel Jenks, During the French and Indian War, 1760*
Johnson Papers	James Sullivan et al., eds., *The Papers of Sir William Johnson*

LIST OF ABBREVIATIONS

"Kenny Journal"	John W. Jordan, ed., "Journal of James Kenny, 1761–1763," *PMHB* 37 (1913)
LAC	Library and Archives Canada, Ottawa
"Lord Adam Gordon's Journal"	[Lord Adam Gordon], "Journal of an Officer Who Travelled in America and the West Indies in 1764 and 1765," in Newton D. Mereness, ed., *Travels in the American Colonies*
LO	Loudoun Papers
MassHS	Massachusetts Historical Society, Boston
MG	Manuscript Group
"MOB"	Captain Alexander Moneypenny, "The Moneypenny Orderly Book," *Bulletin of the Fort Ticonderoga Museum* 12 (1969–70): 328–57, 434–61, and 13 (1970–71): 89–116, 151–84
"Munster's List"	"A List of Recruits under Command of Captain Herbert B[a]r[on] de Munster Embark'd ye 4th of June [*sic*] Near Hamburg and Arrived ye 27th of August at New York, 1756"
NAS	National Archives of Scotland, Edinburgh
NBHS	New Brunswick Historical Society
NL	Newberry Library, Chicago
NYCD	Edmund B. O'Callaghan and Berthold Fernow, eds., *Documents Relative to the Colonial History of the State of New York*
NYHS	New York Historical Society, New York
NYSL	New York State Library, Albany
Pitt Correspondence	Gertrude S. Kimball, ed., *Correspondence of William Pitt When Secretary of State with Colonial Governors and Military and Naval Commissioners in America*
PRO	Public Record Office
RA	Royal Archives
"St. John's River Society Papers"	W[illiam] O. Raymond, ed., "Papers Relating to the St. John's River Society," NBHS, *Collections* 6 (1905)
SGM	Simon Gratz Manuscripts
Shirley Correspondence	Charles H. Lincoln, ed., *The Correspondence of William Shirley Governor of Massachusetts and Military Commander in America, 1731–1760*

SP	State Papers
Sterling Letterbook	James Sterling Letterbook
TGPAS	Thomas Gage Papers, American Series
TNA	The National Archives, Kew, Richmond, Surrey
"Trent's Journal"	Albert T. Volwiler, ed., "William Trent's Journal at Fort Pitt, 1763," *MVHR* 11 (1924)
TWML	Tracy W. McGregor Library, University of Virginia, Charlottesville
Washington Papers	William W. Abbot, ed., *The Papers of George Washington: Colonial Series*
WHS	Wisconsin Historical Society
WLCL	William L. Clements Library, Ann Arbor, Mich.
WO	War Office

Notes

INTRODUCTION

1. Knox, *Historical Journal*, 1:453 (entry of 31 July 1759); Virgil, *Aeneid*, 9.235; Mante, *History of the Late War*, 247; *Impartial History of the Late War*, 127–28; *Boston Post-Boy & Advertiser*, 5 May 1760, 1; *Gentleman's Magazine* 29 (1759): 481.

2. *New York Gazette and the Weekly Mercury*, 9 November 1772, 3; *London Chronicle or Universal Evening Post*, 12–14 February 1765, 155; Smith, *Bouquet's Expedition against the Ohio Indians*, i–35; *Boston Post-Boy & Advertiser*, 5 May 1760, 1; *Gentleman's Magazine* 29 (1759): 491; *Pennsylvania Gazette*, 3 August 1758, 3, and 2 August 1759, 2.

3. Cooper, *The Last of the Mohicans*, 38–71, 145; Hale, *Royal Americans*, 1–28; Lätt, "Schweizer Offiziers als Indianerkrieger und Instruktoren der englischen leichten Infanterie," 3–45; Hutton, *Colonel Henry Bouquet*, 1–37.

4. Plank, *Rebellion and Savagery*, 155–72; Anderson, *Crucible of War*, 139–49; 286–89, 410–14, 560–63, 647–51; Jennings, *Empire of Fortune*, 206–11, 220–22, 297–311; Leach, *Roots of Conflict*, 76–133; Parkman, *Conspiracy of Pontiac*, 1:224–28, 2:123–24, 157–61, 394–96; Bancroft, *History of the United States*, 4:189, 240–41, 258, 266–67.

5. Quotation from Wallace, *Rebellion in the Red River Settlement*, 37; Stanley, *Toil and Trouble*, 44–201; Wallace, *Regimental Chronicle*, 1–312.

6. Quotation from "The Royal Americans," in Craig, *The Olden Time*, 332; Fisher, "Brigadier-General Henry Bouquet," 121–43.

7. Quotation from Richards, *The Pennsylvania-German*, 494; Waddell and Bomberger, *French and Indian War in Pennsylvania*, 90–96; Lonergan, *Ticonderoga*, 235–36; M. C. Darlington, *History of Colonel Henry Bouquet*, 88–114; Cort, *Colonel Henry Bouquet and His Campaigns*, 1–4, 11–96.

8. Quotation from Butler and Hare, *Annals*, 1:3; Daniele Fiorentino, "'Those Red-Brick Faces': European Press Reactions to the Indians of Buffalo Bill's Wild West Show," in Feest, *Indians and Europeans*, 403–13; Billington, *Land of Savagery/Land of Promise*, 43–57; Butler and Hare, *Annals*, 1:ix.

9. Quotation from Fuller, *British Light Infantry*, 98; Reid, *J. F. C. Fuller*, 1–33, 102–104; Trythall, *'Boney' Fuller*, 1–29, 104–105; Fuller, "Revival and Training," 1187–1214.

10. Chet, *Conquering the American Wilderness*, 127; Starkey, *European and Native American Warfare*, 133; Fischer, *Well-Executed Failure*, 67; Johnson, *Militiamen, Rangers, and Redcoats*, 50; Strachan, *European Armies*, 28.

11. Ross, "Historical Consciousness in Nineteenth-Century America," 911–19; Canary, *George Bancroft*, 4–7, 31–48, 54–55; Bancroft, *History of the United States*, 4:1–15, 91–92, 108–26, 150–58, 172–75, 190, 215–16, 225–26, 310–14.

12. Nye, *George Bancroft, Brahmin Rebel*, 10, 16–18, *American National Biography*, s.v. "Bancroft, George."

13. Quotation from Bancroft, *History of the United States*, 4:196; Robertson, *Scottish Enlightenment and the Militia Issue*, 22–31; Cress, *Citizens in Arms*, 15–57; J. P. Reid, *In Defiance of the Law*, 79–85; Bancroft, *History of the United States*, 4:169–92, 226–42, 256–71, 290–324.

14. Butler, *Becoming America*, 1–224; Dederer, *War in America to 1775*, 112–37; Rogers, *Empire and Liberty*, 37–89.

15. Anderson, *Crucible of War*, 286–89, 370–72, 412–14; Titus, *Old Dominion at War*, 127; Dederer, *War in America to 1775*, 139–44; Jennings, *Empire of Fortune*, 206–11; Leach, *Roots of Conflict*, 107–33; Anderson, *People's Army*, 110–41.

16. Gale, *Francis Parkman*, 20–21; Wade, *Francis Parkman, Heroic Historian*, 3–7; Parkman, *Conspiracy of Pontiac*, 1:117–22, 127, 130; Parkman, *Montcalm and Wolfe*, 1:157–58, 225–28, 301–304, 319–20, 2:119–24.

17. Quotation from Parkman, *Conspiracy of Pontiac*, 1:141; Brig. Gen. George Townshend to William Pitt, 20 September 1760, in *Pitt Correspondence*, 2:164–69; Jennings, "Francis Parkman," 307–15.

18. Quotation from Parkman, *Conspiracy of Pontiac*, 1:182; Jennings, "Francis Parkman," 316–22; Eccles, "New France according to Francis Parkman," 172–73; Parkman, *Conspiracy of Pontiac*, 1:ix–x, 3–50, 148–57, 217–381, 2:3–31.

19. Dowd, *War under Heaven*, 5–9, 60–89, 162–68, 190; Richter, *Looking East from Indian Country*, 191–201; Matthew C. Ward, "The Microbes of War: The British Army and Epidemic Disease among the Ohio Indians, 1758–1765," in Skaggs and Nelson, *Sixty Years' War*, 63–78; Axtell, *The Invasion Within*, 305–307.

20. Dixon, *Never Come to Peace Again*, 76–84, 103–243; Sleeper-Smith, *Indian Women and French Men*, 54–56; Anderson, *Crucible of War*, 535–53, 617–37; Steele, *Warpaths*, 234–42; McConnell, *Country Between*, 146–49, 159–206; Jennings, *Empire of Fortune*, 438–49.

21. Carole Shammas, "Introduction," in Mancke and Shammas, *Creation of the British Atlantic World*, 1–16; David Armitage, "Three Concepts of Atlantic History," in Armitage and Braddick, *British Atlantic World*, 11–

27; Bernard Bailyn and Philip D. Morgan, "Introduction," in Bailyn and Morgan, *Strangers within the Realm*, 25–26; Brewer, *Sinews of Power*, 27–32; Houlding, *Fit for Service*, 8–12.

22. Quotation from "Commons Debate," 20 February 1756, in Simmons and Thomas, *Proceedings and Debates*, 1:156.

1. "MUCH REGARDED BY THE DUKE"

1. Quotation from Thomas Penn to William Allen, 15 September 1756, Thomas Penn Letterbooks, vol. 5, p. 2, HSP; Col. James Prevost to the Earl of Loudoun, 14 August 1756 and 17 January 1757, LO 1491 and 2678, HEH; Whitworth, *William Augustus, Duke of Cumberland*, 170–72; Pargellis, *Lord Loudoun*, 61–63.

2. Williams, "Prevosts of the Royal Americans," 14–38; Wainwright, "Turmoil at Pittsburgh," 111–17; *American National Biography*, s.v. "Bouquet, Henry"; s.v. "DesBarres, Joseph Frederick Wallet," in *Dictionary of Canadian Biography*, 6:192–97; s.v. "Haldimand, Sir Frederick," ibid., 5:887–902; s.v. "Holland, Samuel Johannes," ibid., 5:425–28.

3. Rare exceptions include Plank, *Rebellion and Savagery*, 1–191; Crowley, "Taken on the Spot," 1–28; Nelson, *General James Grant*, 1–159; Johnson, *John Nelson, Merchant Adventurer*, 30–141; Godfrey, *Pursuit of Profit and Preferment*, 1–270; Gwyn, *The Enterprising Admiral*, 1–202; Evans, *Uncommon Obdurate*, 3–98.

4. Hancock, *Citizens of the World*, 6–18.

5. "Minutes of Lord Loudoun's Meeting with Capt. [Francis Gabriel] De Ruvynes," 18 January 1758, Loudoun Notebooks, vol. 5, p. 11, HM 1717, HEH; Prevost, *Records of the Prevost Family* (n.p., 1949), 7–9, in "Select Papers Relating to Major General Augustine and Sir George Prevost and Family," MG 24-A9, LAC; Galiffe, *Notices généalogiques*, 2:361; R. Campbell, *The London Tradesman*, 250–53.

6. Prevost, *Records of the Prevost Family*, 11, LAC; Mackay, *Life of Lieut. General Hugh Mackay*, 185–86.

7. Wokeck, *Trade in Strangers*, 54–57; Migliazzo, "Tarnished Legacy Revisited," 232–52; Rowen, *Princes of Orange*, 158–92; Carter, *Dutch Republic*, 1–37.

8. John Calcraft to the Earl of Loudoun, 8 July 1757, Add. MSS 17,493, 128, BL; Anderson, *Crucible of War*, 11–65; Brecher, *Losing a Continent*, 1–88; Fregault, *Canada*, 68–92; *Scots Magazine* 17 (1755): 70–72.

9. Peter Wilson, "Warfare in the Old Regime, 1648–1789," in Black, *European Warfare, 1453–1815*, 78–81; Lynn, *Giant of the Grand Siècle*, 55–66; Campbell, *Present State of Europe*, 300–301; *American National Biography*, s.v. "Washington, George"; s.v. "Coulon de Villiers, Louis" in *Dictionary of Canadian Biography*, 3:148–49.

10. Quotation from *Complete History of the Present War*, 168; Black, *Britain as a Military Power*, 11–34, 40–43; Bowen, *War and British Society*, 40–48; Houlding, *Fit for Service*, 3–11, 412; Shy, *Toward Lexington*, 4–39.

11. Cadwallader Colden to the Earl of Halifax, 3 August 1754, and the Earl of Loudoun to the Duke of Cumberland, 29 August 1756, in Pargellis,

Military Affairs, 19, 232; William Johnson to Sir Thomas Robinson, 17 January 1756, in *Johnson Papers*, 220–21; Shea, *Virginia Militia in the Seventeenth Century*, 122–37; Ferling, *Wilderness of Miseries*; 8–17; Shy, *People Numerous and Armed*, 23–33; *American Magazine, and Monthly Chronicle of the British Colonies* 1 (1757): 71–75.

12. Gov. William Shirley to Lt. Gov. James De Lancey, 24 February 1755, and Shirley to Sir Thomas Robinson, 24 March 1755, in *Shirley Correspondence*, 2:133–38 and 144–52; Clayton, "Duke of Newcastle," 571–603; Mante, *History of the Late War*, 16–33; *American National Biography*, s.v. "Shirley, William"; s.v. "Pepperrell, Sir William," in *Dictionary of Canadian Biography*, 3:505–509.

13. Kopperman, *Braddock at the Monongahela*, 3–89; Hamilton, *Braddock's Defeat*, 9–121; McCardell, *Ill-Starred General*, 138–265.

14. Gov. William Shirley to Sir Thomas Robinson, 28 September 1755, in *Shirley Correspondence*, 2:289–96; "Extract of a Letter from Governor Charles Hardy to Halifax," 27 November 1755, in Pargellis, *Military Affairs*, 149–51; Gipson, *British Empire before the American Revolution*, 6:127–77.

15. "Journal of Colonel John Winslow of the Provincial Troops, While Engaged in the Siege of Fort Beausejour in the Summer and Autumn of 1755," in Nova Scotia Historical Society, *Collections* 4 (1885): 172–76 (entries of 26 May–22 June 1755); Capt. Lt. John Brewse to the Board of Ordnance, 18 October 1755, in Pargellis, *Military Affairs*, 146–48; Webster, *Forts of Chignecto*, 49–62.

16. Quotation from "Commons Debate," 28 January 1756, in Simmons and Thomas, *Proceedings and Debates*, 1:128; William Johnson to Gov. William Shirley, 9 September 1755, in *Shirley Correspondence*, 2:53–59; Peter Wraxall to Henry Fox, 27 September 1755, in Pargellis, *Military Affairs*, 137–40; Steele, *Betrayals*, 28–56; s.vv. "Dieskau, Jean-Armand, Baron de Dieskau," and "Johnson, Sir William," in *Dictionary of Canadian Biography*, 3:185–86 and 4:394–95.

17. "Account of the Capture of HMS *Blandford* by the French," n.d., William H. Lyttelton Papers, vol. 1, WLCL; Gov. William H. Lyttelton to the Duke of Newcastle, 7 September 1755, Add. MSS 32,859, 18–21, BL; King Louis XV to King George II, 21 October 1755, in *NYCD*, 10:379; John Yorke to Lord Hardwicke, 28 October 1755, Add. MSS 35,374, 125, BL; *Impartial History of the Late War*, 17–18; *Dictionary of National Biography*, s.v. "Lyttelton, William Henry."

18. Henry Fox to the Duke of Newcastle, 28 September 1755, and Newcastle to Sir Thomas Robinson, 5 October 1755, Add. MSS 32,859, 255–56, 386, BL; Davis, "British Newspaper Accounts of Braddock's Defeat," 310–28; *Scots Magazine* 17 (1755): 451–53.

19. "Bond of James Prevost of Geneva and Joseph and Henry Guinand of London for £2,000 Should Prevost not use the £1,000 Advanced to Him According to his Warrant," 2 January 1756, Treasury Board, T1/368/4, TNA; "Capitulation d'un Regiment Suisse & Allemand pour le Service de la Grand Bretagne levee parmy les Gens de cette Nation Sujets de Sa Majeste," n.d., Add. MSS 73,648, BL; Robert C. Nash, "Huguenot Merchants and the De-

velopment of South Carolina's Slave-Plantation and Atlantic Trading Economy," in Van Ruymbeke and Sparks, *Memory and Identity*, 219.

20. "Guinand Family," File 350, Henry Wagner Huguenot Pedigrees, Huguenot Society of London Library, University College, London; Murdoch, *Quiet Conquest*, x–xi, 108; Whitworth, *Field Marshal Lord Ligonier*, 196–202, 209; Ditchfield, "Family of Riou," 236–38.

21. Lt. Gen. James Oglethorpe to the Duke of Newcastle, 22 September 1755, Add. MSS 32,859, 185–86, BL; MacKillop, *"More Fruitful than the Soil,"* 43–46; Parker, *Scottish Highlanders in Colonial Georgia*, 38–98; Ivers, *British Drums on the Southern Frontier*, 1–214.

22. "Extract of a Memorial Intended to be Presented to His Majesty by Lieut. Genl. Oglethorpe," n.d., Add. MSS 32,859, 187, BL; Black, *Culloden and the '45*, 117; Ettinger, *James Edward Oglethorpe, Imperial Idealist*, 261–70, 280.

23. "Capitulation d'un Regiment Suisse & Allemand pour le Service de la Grand Bretagne levee parmy les Gens de cette Nation Sujets de Sa Majeste," n.d., Add. MSS 73,648, BL; John Yorke to Lord Hardwicke, 28 October 1755, Add. MSS 35,374, 126, BL; "A Copy of the first SCHEME for Employing Foreign Officers, &c.," n.d., in MacKinney, *Pennsylvania Archives*, 8th ser., 5 (1931): 4376–77; Sir Thomas Robinson to North American Governors, 23 January 1755, WO 34/71/48, TNA; Childs, *British Army of William III*, 102–103, 132–37; Childs, *The Army, James II, and the Glorious Revolution*, 1–14, 83–113; *Complete History of the Present War*, 33–37.

24. Quotation from Duke of Newcastle to Lord Holderness, 26 August 1755, Add. MSS 32,858, 292, BL; Newcastle to Holderness, 26 August 1755, Add. MSS 32,858, 289, BL; Newcastle to the Duke of Devonshire, 5 February 1756, Add. MSS 32,862, 370, BL; Graham, "British Intervention," 168–72, 331–43.

25. Sir Thomas Robinson to Maj. [James] Prevost, 28 October 1755, LO 665, HEH; "Colonel Prevost's Account from 1 October 1755 to 28 February 1756," WO 34/46B/18–19, TNA; Prevost to the Earl of Holderness, 4 February 1760, Egerton Manuscripts, 3,439, 115, BL.

26. "Etat des Officers Suisses et Allemands engagez en Hollande par Mssr. Prevost," n.d., Cumberland Papers, box 46, item 126, RA; Lt. Col. Henry Bouquet to Sir John St. Clair, 18 April 1757, and Bouquet to [?], 10 June 1759, in *Bouquet Papers*, 1:83 and 3:371–72; Sgt. George Eberhard to Maj. Gen. Jeffery Amherst, 10 March 1760, WO 34/82/75, TNA; John Jamet to Brig. Gen. John Forbes, n.d., Dalhousie Muniments, GD 45/2/32/75, NAS; *Scots Magazine* 17 (1755): 201.

27. Quotation from Duffy, *Military in the Age of Reason*, 33; Sir Thomas Robinson to Maj. [James] Prevost, 28 October 1755, and "Observations on Colonel Prevost's Account," 10 and 25 April 1758, LO 665 and 5805, HEH; *Pensylvanische Berichte*, 16 July 1756, 3.

28. Lt. Gen. James Oglethorpe to the Duke of Newcastle, 22 September 1755, Add. MSS 32,859, 185, BL; Caecilius Calvert to Lt. Gov. Horatio Sharpe, 23 December 1755, in Browne, *Archives of Maryland* 6 (1888): 327–28; Olsen, *Making the Empire Work*, 117–21, 158–59; Kammen, *Rope of Sand*, 1–107.

29. Robert Charles to Lord Barrington, 1 January 1756, in MacKinney, *Pennsylvania Archives*, 8th ser., 5 (1931): 4378; John Sharpe to the Duke of Newcastle, 8 January 1756, Add. MSS 32,862, 48, BL; Thomas Penn to the Earl of Loudoun, 21 January 1756, LO 764, HEH; "Commons Proceedings," 18 February 1756, in Simmons and Thomas, *Proceedings and Debates*, 1:139–41; Varga, "Robert Charles: New York Agent," 211–35; Appleton, "Richard Partridge: Colonial Agent," 293–309.

30. Henry Fox to the Duke of Newcastle, 27 December 1755, Add. MSS 32,861, 481, BL; Duke of Devonshire to Newcastle, 31 January 1756, and Newcastle to Devonshire, 5 February 1756, Add. MSS 32,862, 303, 370, BL; Alan J. Guy, "The Irish Military Establishment, 1660–1776," in Bartlett and Jeffrey, *Military History of Ireland*, 211–16.

31. Benjamin Franklin to Peter Collinson, 9 May 1753, in Labaree, *Papers of Benjamin Franklin*, 4:483–86; Sir Thomas Robinson to North American Governors, 23 January 1755, WO 34/71/48, TNA; Wokeck, *Trade in Strangers*, xxiii, 8, 37–56; Fogleman, *Hopeful Journeys*, 133–42; Schwartz, "A Mixed Multitude," 215–16, 237–42; Douglas Brymner, "Intercepted Letters to the Duke de Mirepoix, 1756," in Jameson et al., *Report of the Historical Manuscripts Commission*, 660–703; [Smith], *State of the Province of Pennsylvania*, 4, 15, 25–32, 35–36.

32. "A Copy of Lord Barrington's Letter to the Agent, Containing the Second SCHEME for Employing Foreign Officers, &c.," 14 January 1756, and Robert Charles to Lord Barrington, 17 January 1756, in MacKinney, *Pennsylvania Archives*, 8th ser., 5 (1931): 4378–80; Thomas Penn to William Allen, 14 February 1756, Thomas Penn Letterbooks, vol. 4, pp. 238–39, HSP; *Pennsylvania Gazette*, 29 April 1756, 2; Pargellis, *Lord Loudoun*, 39–41, 61–63.

33. "Commons Debate," 9 February 1756, in Simmons and Thomas, *Proceedings and Debates*, 1:135–37; Strachan, *Politics of the British Army*, 44–51; Brewer, *Sinews of Power*, 43–45; Harding, "Growth of Anglo-American Alienation," 170–74; Leach, *Roots of Conflict*, 50–61.

34. "An Estimate of the Charge of a Regiment of Foot of Four Battalions," n.d., and Lord Barrington to the Earl of Loudoun, 13 March 1756, LO 3813 and 926, HEH; "Commons Debate," 9 February 1756, in Simmons and Thomas, *Proceedings and Debates*, 1:135; "An Extract of a Letter from ROBERT CHARLES," 16 February 1756, in MacKinney, *Pennsylvania Archives*, 8th ser., 5 (1931): 4376; *Scots Magazine* 18 (1756): 149, 481; *American National Biography*, s.v. "Campbell, John, Earl of Loudoun."

35. "Commons Debate," 9 February 1756, in Simmons and Thomas, *Proceedings and Debates*, 1:135–36; Black, *Pitt the Elder*, 106–21; Middleton, *Bells of Victory*, 4–14; *Scots Magazine* 18 (1756): 47.

36. Statt, *Foreigners and Englishmen*, 114–19; Colley, *Britons*, 11–36, 105–32; Duffy, *The Englishman and the Foreigner*, 13–46; Guy, *Oeconomy and Discipline*, 3–8; Schwoerer, "No Standing Armies," 1–191.

37. Quotation from Horace Walpole to Sir Horace Mann, 23 February 1756, in Lewis et al., *Horace Walpole's Correspondence*, 20:531; "Commons Proceedings," 10 and 26 February 1756, and "Commons Debates," 10, 12, 18, 20, and 23 February 1756, in Simmons and Thomas, *Proceedings and Debates*, 1:137–43, 155–59, 169; "Minutes of America," n.d., and "Speech

in Opposition to Government Bill Enabling Foreign Officers to Hold Commissions in America for the Duration of the War," n.d., Charles Townshend Papers, box 8, bundle 4, items 3 and 4, WLCL; Black, *Pitt the Elder*, 106–10; Namier and Brooke, *Charles Townshend*, 41–45; Pickering, *Statutes at Large*, 21:330–31 [29 George II, c. 5].

38. "A List of 20 Officers Named by Messr. Prevost to go in the First Ship for America," 26 February 1756, LO 859, HEH; "HRH," 27 February 1756, Loudoun Notebooks, vol. 8, p. 43, HM 1717, HEH; Lt. Col. James Wolfe to Lt. Gen. Edward Wolfe, 21 March 1756, in Willson, *Life and Letters of James Wolfe*, 287; "Report of Mr. Attorney and Mr. Solicitor General on the American Regiment," 31 March 1756, Add. MSS 32,864, 107–110, BL; *Boston Weekly Newsletter*, 17 June 1756, 1.

39. Lord Barrington to Henry Fox, 10 January 1756, in Hayter, *Eighteenth-Century Secretary at War*, 158; *London Gazette*, 9 March 1756, 1; "62d or Royal American Regiment of Foot," 13 March 1756, WO 25/137/53–58, TNA; Maj. Gen. James Murray to Lt. Gen. Jeffery Amherst, 2 September 1763, WO 34/2/207, TNA.

40. "62d or Royal American Regiment of Foot," 13 March 1756, WO 25/137/53–58, TNA; "List of Lieutenants and Ensigns Prepared for the Royal American Regiment," 17 March 1756, LO 6749, HEH; Goldsbrow Baynar to Sir William Johnson, 8 June 1756, in *Johnson Papers*, 2:485; Childs, *Armies and Warfare in Europe*, 77–90; Guy, *Oeconomy and Discipline*, 1–15, 56–157; Houlding, *Fit for Service*, 99–116; Bruce, *Purchase System in the British Army*, 6–39.

41. Gov. William Shirley to Sir Thomas Robinson, 12 August 1755, in *Shirley Correspondence*, 2:225; "Abstract of Governor Charles Lawrence's Letter," 30 November 1755, Add. MSS 32,861, 140, BL; "Return of His Majesty's Forces in Nova Scotia, 30 November 1755, Cumberland Papers, box 46, item 103, RA; "HRH," 27 February 1756, Loudoun Notebooks, vol. 8, pp. 43–44, HM 1717, HEH.

42. Henry Fox to the Governors of Nova Scotia, Newfoundland, Pennsylvania, Maryland, Virginia, North Carolina, South Carolina, and Georgia, 13 March 1756, Cumberland Papers, box 46, item 186, RA; "Commons Proceedings," 15 March 1756, in Simmons and Thomas, *Proceedings and Debates*, 1:173; Maj. Gen. Daniel Webb to the Earl of Loudoun, 29 March 1756, LO 979, HEH.

43. "Observations on Colonel Prevost's Account," 10 and 25 April 1758, and Earl of Loudoun to Lord Barrington, 3 August 1758, LO 5805 and 5884, HEH; Loudoun to Maj. Gen. James Abercromby, 9 June 1758, and Col. James Prevost to Maj. Gen. Jeffery Amherst, 3 September 1760, WO 34/46B/16–21 and 34/83/9–10, TNA.

44. "HRH," 25 and 27 February 1756, and "Foreign Officers in the American Regiment now in Germany Recruiting," n.d., Loudoun Notebooks, vol. 8, pp. 41–42, and vol. 11, HM 1717, HEH; "Colonel Prevost's Plan for Recruiting," n.d., and "Colonel Prevost's Plan 2," LO 2576 and 2577, HEH.

45. Lord Barrington to John Calcraft, 14 March 1756, and "Remarks on Instructions to Colonel Prevost," 21 April 1756, LO 929 and 1069, HEH; "Additional Instructions to Colonel Prevost," 23 April 1756, and "Instruc-

tions for Colonel Prevost Relating to His Bringing over Planters from Germany," n.d., WO 34/76/19–21, TNA.

46. "Memorandum," 14 March 1757, and "Proposals for Colonel Prevost's Bargain," n.d., Loudoun Notebooks, vol. 2, p. 41, and vol. 9, p. 31, HM 1717, HEH; Viscount Howe to Arnold Nesbit, 1 September 1756, Treasury Board, T1/368/53, TNA; "A State of the Cash of the 62d or Royal American Regiment to Christmas, 1756," 25 December 1756, LO 2521, HEH; "Evidence of Jacob Eykel," 19 June 1757, WO 71/65/329–30, TNA; "Petition of German Recruits," 22 April 1758, and "Payments to Colonel Prevost on Account of Clothing, Contingencies, &c.," 5 March 1761, LO 5812 and 5859, HEH; Roderick McLeod to Col. Henry Bouquet, n.d., Add. MSS 21,658, 150, BL.

47. Maj. Gen. Daniel Webb to the Earl of Loudoun, 26 March 1756, and Sir David Ochterlony to Loudoun, 24 April 1756, LO 968 and 1076, HEH; *New York Mercury*, 21 June 1756, 3; *Pennsylvania Gazette*, 1 July 1756, 2.

48. Col. John Stanwix to the Earl of Loudoun, 27 August and 13 September 1756, LO 1594 and 1787, HEH; *Scots Magazine* 18 (1756): 194; *Gentleman's Magazine* 26 (1756): 388.

49. "Journal of the Siege of Oswego," n.d., in *NYCD*, 10:440–43; "An Account of the Strength of the Garrison, & State of the Works at Oswego, at the Time of Its Being Invested," n.d. in Pargellis, *Military Affairs*, 218–21; Lord Barrington to the Earl of Loudoun, 22 December 1756, LO 2384, HEH; Fregault, *Canada*, 124–36.

50. Quotation from "Copy of a Letter from Schenectady," 6 August 1756, Add. MSS 35,909, 266, BL; "Extracts of Letters from a General Officer in North America to his Friend in London," 30 August 1756, ChP, PRO 30/8/95/122, TNA.

51. Earl of Loudoun to Henry Fox, 8 October 1756, LO 1986B, HEH; Loudoun to Gov. Benning Wentworth, 21 November 1756, and "Subsistence to the Royal American Regiment Before its Division into Four Battalions," 27 November 1756, WO 34/24/5 and 34/99/163, TNA; Bougainville, *Adventure in the Wilderness*, 57–63 (entries of 18–26 October 1756); Anderson, *Crucible of War*, 141–46.

52. Col. James Prevost to the Earl of Loudoun, 14 August 1756 and 17 January 1757, LO 1491 and 2678, HEH; Loudoun to the Duke of Cumberland, 8 March 1757, in Pargellis, *Military Affairs*, 321; Loudoun to Lord Barrington, 8 July 1758, WO 1/1/129–31, TNA.

53. Thomas Penn to William Allen, 15 September 1756, Thomas Penn Letterbooks, vol. 5, p. 2, HSP; John Calcraft to the Earl of Loudoun, 13 November 1756, Add. MSS 17,493, 14, BL; Col. James Prevost to the Duke of Cumberland, 12 May 1757, in Pargellis, *Military Affairs*, 335.

54. Earl of Loudoun to the Duke of Cumberland, 26 December 1756, in Pargellis, *Military Affairs*, 264, 279–80; Col. James Prevost to Loudoun, 17 January 1756, LO 2678, HEH; Anderson, *Crucible of War*, 179–84.

55. Brig. Gen. James Wolfe to Lord George Sackville, 30 July 1758, in Willson, *Life and Letters of James Wolfe*, 391; Maj. James Robertson to the Earl of Morton, 19 December 1758, in Pargellis, *Military Affairs*, 432; John Calcraft to Lt. Col. Ralph Burton, 10 April 1759, Add. MSS 17,494, 146–47, BL.

56. Quotation from Earl of Loudoun to the Duke of Cumberland, 22 June 1757, in Pargellis, *Military Affairs*, 378; Loudoun to Col. James Prevost, 20 March 1757, Cumberland Papers, box 52, item 35, RA; Lt. Col. Henry Bouquet to Sir John St. Clair, 18 April 1757, in *Bouquet Papers*, 1:83; Richard Huck and William Russell to Loudoun, 25 April 1757, and Prevost to Loudoun, 1 May 1757, LO 3468A and 3521, HEH; Loudoun to Cumberland, 25 April–3 June 1757, in Pargellis, *Military Affairs*, 358–59; "Memorandum," 1 May 1757, Loudoun Notebooks, vol. 2, p. 66, HM 1717, HEH.

57. "Representation of Officers of the Fourth Battalion," 15 March 1757, and Col. John Stanwix to the Earl of Loudoun, 7 April 1757, LO 3401 and 3308, HEH; Loudoun to the Duke of Cumberland, 25 April–3 June 1757, in Pargellis, *Military Affairs*, 354–56; "Memorandum," 16 July 1757, Loudoun Notebooks, vol. 3, pp. 34–35, HM 1717, HEH.

58. Maj. John Young to the Earl of Loudoun, 2 September 1756, LO 1681, HEH; Loudoun to the Duke of Cumberland, 2 October 1756, 5 January 1757, and 25 April–3 June 1757, and Col. James Prevost to Cumberland, 23 May 1757, in Pargellis, *Military Affairs*, 241, 292, 356, and 340; "Memorandum," 15 and 29 March 1757, Loudoun Notebooks, vol. 2, pp. 42, 51, HM 1717, HEH; Comte de Gegenfeld to [?], 25 August 1757, WO 34/75/107, TNA.

59. "HRH," n.d., and "Memorandum," 3 March 1757, Loudoun Notebooks, vol. 8, pp. 7–8, and vol. 2, p. 34, HM 1717, HEH; "Observations on Colonel Prevost's Account," 10 and 25 April 1758, and Maj. James Robertson to the Earl of Loudoun, 3 February 1759, LO 5805 and 5978, HEH; "Catalogue of the Names of Officers Who Are Indebted to Colonel Prevost," n.d., Cumberland Papers, box 52, item 52A, RA; Odintz, "British Officer Corps," 178–80, 492–98.

60. Earl of Loudoun to the Duke of Cumberland, 8 March 1757, in Pargellis, *Military Affairs*, 317–18; "Intelligence from Cape Breton," 28 June 1757, in *NYCD*, 10:572–73; "Return of the Troops That Came from New York with Me," 7 July 1757, Loudoun Notebooks, vol. 3, p. 25, HM 1717, HEH; Loudoun to the Earl of Holderness, 5 August 1757, LO 4073B, HEH; *Conduct of a Noble Commander*, 37–39.

61. Knox, *Historical Journal*, 1:38–39 (entries of 24 and 31 July 1757); Earl of Loudoun to the Duke of Cumberland, 6 August 1757, in Pargellis, *Military Affairs*, 391–92; "Lord Charles Hay's Court Martial," 26 February 1760, Add. MSS 35,894, 32, BL; Pargellis, *Lord Loudoun*, 240–42; s.v. "Hay, Lord Charles," in *Dictionary of Canadian Biography*, 3:283–84.

62. Maj. Gen. Daniel Webb to the Earl of Loudoun, 11 August 1757, CO 5/48/312, TNA; Webb to Lord Barrington, 17 August 1757, and "The Strength of the Garrison at Fort Wm. Henry," n.d., WO 1/1/270 and 1/972/209, TNA; "Monthly Return of His Majesty's Forces in North America," 24 September 1756, Dalhousie Muniments, GD 45/2/13/1, NAS; Steele, *Betrayals*, 92–135; s.v. "Montcalm, Louis-Joseph De, Marquis de Montcalm," in *Dictionary of Canadian Biography*, 3:460–61.

63. Thomas Penn to Lt. Col. John Armstrong, 7 December 1756, Thomas Penn Letterbooks, vol. 5, p. 39, HSP; "The Petition of the Merchants, Traders, Planters, and Others Interested in the Trade & Prosperity of South Carolina & Georgia," 21 December 1756, William H. Lyttelton Papers, vol. 3,

WLCL; Earl of Halifax to the Earl of Loudoun, 11 March 1757, and Col. John Stanwix to Loudoun, 10 September 1757, LO 3018A and 4446, HEH; Loudoun to the Duke of Cumberland, 25 April–3 June 1757, in Pargellis, *Military Affairs*, 344; Stanwix to Lt. Col. Frederick Haldimand, 22 December 1757, Add. MSS 21,666, 16, BL.

64. Earl of Loudoun to the Duke of Cumberland, 25 April–3 June 1757, in Pargellis, *Military Affairs*, 345; Maj. John Tulleken to Loudoun, 28 January 1758, LO 5486, HEH; Brig. Gen. John Forbes to Col. Henry Bouquet, 14 February 1758, Add. MSS 21,640, 241, BL; Gov. William H. Lyttelton to Loudoun, 21 March 1758, in *Bouquet Papers*, 1:323.

65. Earl of Loudoun to the Duke of Cumberland, 25 April–3 June 1757, in Pargellis, *Military Affairs*, 356; Nash, "Huguenot Merchants," 208–19; Butler, *Huguenots in America*, 92–132; McCusker and Menard, *Economy of British America*, 169–88.

66. Gov. William H. Lyttelton to Maj. Gen. James Abercromby, 16 May 1758, AB, 259, HEH; "Letter of Attorney: Joseph and Henry Guinand to Colonel James Prevost and Colonel Henry Bouquet," 11 July 1760, Add. MSS 21,687, 26–28, BL; Egnal, *New World Economies*, 100–110; Chaplin, *Anxious Pursuit*, 190–208, 227–62; "Baptêmes L'Eglise de Londres (Threadneedle Street)," in Moens et al., *Publications of the Huguenot Society*, 23:75, 93, and 104; Lucas, *Deeds of South Carolina, and Charleston*, 512.

67. Quotation from *South Carolina Gazette*, 25 August 1758, 2; Austin, Laurens, and Appleby to Col. Henry Bouquet, 7 September 1761, and Bouquet to [?], 5 October 1761, in *Bouquet Papers*, 5:735, 808; Calhoun, Zierden, and Paysinger, "Spread of Charleston's Merchantile Community," 206; Stumpf, "South Carolina Importers," 8.

68. Quotations from "Mémoire sur la Guerre d'Amérique," n.d., in Pargellis, *Military Affairs*, 337 and 339; Col. James Prevost to the Duke of Cumberland, 12 May 1757, ibid., 336; "Memorandum," 29 October 1757, Loudoun Notebooks, vol. 4, p. 9, HM 1717, HEH.

69. John Calcraft to Col. John Stanwix, 11 November 1757, Add. MSS 17,493, 191, BL; Duke of Cumberland to the Earl of Loudoun, 26 November 1757, in Pargellis, *Military Affairs*, 410; Col. James Prevost to Loudoun, 22 January 1758, LO 5438, HEH; Whitworth, *William Augustus*, 184–203; Dann, *Hanover and Great Britain*, 111–16; Savory, *His Britannic Majesty's Army in Germany*, 1–46.

70. Quotation from John Calcraft to the Earl of Loudoun, 8 July 1757, LO 3913A, HEH; Col. James Prevost to the Duke of Cumberland, 23 May 1757, in Pargellis, *Military Affairs*, 340; Prevost to Maj. Gen. Robert Napier, 5 June 1757, Cumberland Papers, box 52, item 88, RA; Whitworth, *William Augustus*, 35, 44.

71. Col. James Prevost to the Duke of Cumberland, 17 March 1758, Cumberland Papers, box 57, item 109, RA; George Sackville to Maj. Gen. Jeffery Amherst, 8 May 1758, AMSS, U 1350/C63/2, CKS; John Calcraft to Lt. Col. Ralph Burton, 11 May 1758, Add. MSS 17,493, 303, BL; Maj. Gen. James Abercromby to Lord Barrington, 12 July 1758, AB 437, HEH; Pargellis, *Lord Loudoun*, 339–48.

72. *Amherst Journal*, 47–72 (entries of 8 June–27 July 1758); *Boston Weekly Advertiser*, 3 July 1758, 2; *Pennsylvania Gazette*, 13 July 1758, 3; Maj. Gen. Jeffery Amherst to William Pitt, 10 August 1758, in *Pitt Correspondence*, 1:313–14; Bruce W. Fry, "'An Appearance of Strength,' The Fortifications of Louisbourg," in Krause et al., *Aspects of Louisbourg*, 43–64; Hitsman and Bond, "Assault Landing at Louisbourg," 314–30.

73. Maj. Gen. Jeffery Amherst to Brig. Gen. Robert Monckton, 24 August 1758, CO 5/53/170–71, TNA; "Report of the Proceedings of the Troops on the Expedition up the St. Johns River in the Bay of Fundy under the Command of Colonel Monckton," n.d., WO 34/43/1–8, TNA; Plank, *Unsettled Conquest*, 150–52.

74. Brig. Gen. John Forbes to William Pitt, 1 May 1758, in *Forbes Papers*, 77; *Maryland Gazette*, 5 October 1758, 2–3; *Pennsylvania Journal and Weekly Advertiser*, 14 December 1758, 2; Ward, *Breaking the Backcountry*, 160–83; James and Stotz, *Drums in the Forest*, 41–56, 89–112; *American National Biography*, s.v. "Forbes, John."

75. Maj. Gen. James Abercromby to Maj. Gen. Jeffery Amherst, 10 July 1758, AMSS, U 1350/O32/1, CKS; Richard Huck to Brig. Gen. John Forbes, 2 August 1758, HQJF, item 437, TWML; s.v. "Abercromby, James," in *Dictionary of Canadian Biography*, 4:4–5.

76. Maj. Gen. James Abercromby to William Pitt, 12 July 1758, in *Pitt Correspondence*, 1:306–307; *Boston Weekly Advertiser*, 24 July 1758, 3; *Pennsylvania Gazette*, 3 August 1758, 1; "Journal of What Has Happened in the Army from the 5th of July to this Day," 19 August 1758, ChP, PRO 30/8/96/97–98, TNA; Anderson, *Crucible of War*, 240–49.

77. Col. James Prevost to Maj. Gen. James Abercromby, 1 and 17 March 1758, Cumberland Papers, box 57, item 110, RA; Brig. Gen. John Forbes to the Earl of Loudoun, 4 March 1758, LO 5692, HEH; John Appy to Prevost, 11 June 1758, AB 345, HEH; Lord Barrington to the Duke of Newcastle, 3 February 1760, Add. MSS 32,902, 44, BL; *Scots Magazine* 20 (1758): 23.

78. Lord Barrington to Maj. Gen. James Abercromby, 26 August 1758, and Barrington to Maj. Gen. Jeffery Amherst, 12 April 1760, AMSS, U 1350/O36/2 and 1350/O37/14, CKS; "Extrait dune Lettre du Brigadier Prevost au General Yorke," [?] October, 1758, ChP, PRO 30/8/76/107–108, TNA; Col. James Prevost to Charles Pratt, 12 November 1759, Add. MSS 35,635, 309, BL.

79. Maj. Gen. James Abercromby to Col. Frederick Haldimand, 27 March 1758, Add. MSS 21,666, 36, BL; Maj. William Eyre to Maj. Gen. Robert Napier, 10 July 1758, in Pargellis, *Military Affairs*, 420; Maj. Francis Halkett to Col. Henry Bouquet, 31 July 1758, in *Bouquet Papers*, 2:295.

80. *New York Mercury*, 4 October 1756, 3; *Boston Weekly Advertiser*, 3 July 1758, 1; Joseph Haynes to Col. Henry Bouquet, 23 January 1761, in *Bouquet Papers*, 5:258; Matson, *Merchants and Empire*, 269–70; McCusker, *Money and Exchange*, 164; Lydon, *Pirates, Privateers, and Profits*, 143, 156–59, 250–51, 272, 277. Some sources list the privateer's name alternatively as *Colonel Prevoost*.

81. Col. James Prevost to Maj. Gen. James Abercromby, 6 July 1758, WO 34/75/160, TNA; *Boston Weekly Advertiser*, 24 July 1758, 2; Maj. Fran-

cis Halkett to Col. Henry Bouquet, 31 July 1758, in *Bouquet Papers*, 2:295; Brig. Gen. James Wolfe to Lord George Sackville, 30 July 1758 in Willson, *Life and Letters of James Wolfe*, 391; "Case on Behalf of Colonel Prevost, and Other Foreign Officers, in the Royal American Regiment," n.d., Add. MSS 35,635, 317–18; BL.

82. "MOB," 12:446 (entry of 18 July 1758); Richard Huck to Brig. Gen. John Forbes, 2 August 1758, HQJF, item 437, TWML; Maj. Gen. James Abercromby to Col. James Prevost, 4 August 1758, AB 947, HEH; Abercromby to Lord Barrington, 19 August 1758, WO 1/1/232, TNA; Prevost to the Duke of Cumberland, 21 August 1758, in Pargellis, *Military Affairs*, 427; "Narrative," 16 September 1758, in NYHS, *Collections for 1871* 4 (1872): 13–15; Richard Huck to the Earl of Loudoun, 3 November 1758, LO 5969, HEH.

83. "Establishment of the General Officers," 30 November 1741, Add. MSS 33,046, 122, BL; Maj. Gen. James Abercromby to Brig. Gen. James Prevost, 9 August 1758, AB, 519, HEH; Prevost to Abercromby, 20 August 1758, WO 34/75/191, TNA; Prevost to the Duke of Cumberland, 21 August 1758, in Pargellis, *Military Affairs*, 427–28; Richard Huck to the Earl of Loudoun, 13 December 1758, LO 5971, HEH; Simes, *Military Medley*, 172, 176; Bland, *Treatise of Military Discipline*, 246.

84. Quotation from "The World and Colonel Blimp," in Low, *Low's Political Parade with Colonel Blimp*, n.p.; *Pennsylvania Gazette*, 6 July 1758, 2; *Maryland Gazette*, 20 July 1758, 3; *Boston Weekly Advertiser*, 24 July 1758, 2; Brumwell, *Redcoats*, 137–48; 191–263; Russell, "Redcoats in the Wilderness," 645–52.

85. Quotation from Richard Huck to the Earl of Loudoun, 13 December 1758, LO 5971, HEH; Huck to Loudoun, 10 September 1758, LO 5914; Anderson, *People's Army*, 112.

86. Col. James Prevost to Maj. Gen. James Abercromby, 23 July 1758, WO 34/76/221, TNA; Capt. James Cunningham to the Earl of Loudoun, 16 September 1758, and Richard Huck to Loudoun, 13 December 1758, LO 5922 and 5971, HEH; Abercromby to Prevost, 24 September and 14 October 1758, WO 34/76/222, 233, TNA; Abercromby to William Pitt, 25 November 1758, in *Pitt Correspondence*, 1:398.

87. Richard Huck to the Earl of Loudoun, 13 December 1758, LO 5971, HEH; Maj. James Robertson to Loudoun, 3 and 27 February 1759, LO 5978 and 6047, HEH; Maj. Gen. Jeffery Amherst to Lord Barrington, 28 February 1759, WO 1/5/49–50, TNA.

88. Maj. Gen. James Wolfe to William Pitt, 2 September 1759, in *Pitt Correspondence*, 2:149–58; McNairn, *Behold the Hero*, 135–47; Stacey, *Quebec, 1759*, 27–94.

89. Maj. Gen. James Wolfe to the Earl of Holderness, 9 September 1759, in Willson, *Life and Letters of James Wolfe*, 474; Brig. Gen. George Townsend to William Pitt, 20 September 1759, in *Pitt Correspondence*, 2:166–67; "Plan of Battle Concerning the Different Forces Engaged at Quebec, 1759," n.d., Add. MSS 21,686, 81, BL; "Return of the Strength of the Army the 13th of September 1759 at the Battle of Quebec," n.d., WO 34/43/32, TNA; Stacey, *Quebec, 1759*, 120–55.

90. *Amherst Journal*, 142–51 (entries of 22 July–14 August 1759); Maj. Gen. Jeffery Amherst to William Pitt, 27 July and 5 August 1759, in *Pitt Correspondence*, 2:143, 147; Anderson, *Crucible of War*, 340–43, 369; Gipson, *British Empire before the American Revolution*, 7:360–69.

91. Maj. Gen. Jeffery Amherst to Brig. Gen. John Prideaux, 17 May 1759, and Brig. Gen. Thomas Gage to Amherst, 18 November 1759, WO 34/46B/137 and 34/46A/61, TNA; "Plan of Oswego with a Projected Fort for to Contain 500 Men," 17 June 1759, CO 5/55/239, TNA; Maj. John Grant to Col. Henry Bouquet, 18 July 1759, in *Bouquet Papers*, 3:423; *Pennsylvania Gazette*, 2 August 1759, 2; "Interrogatoire de prisonniers," n.d., in Doughty and Parmelee, *Siege of Quebec*, 4:5–9; Dunnigan, *Siege—1759*, 15–83.

92. Earl of Loudoun to Maj. Gen. James Abercromby, 9 June 1758, and Loudoun to Lord Barrington, 3 August 1758, LO 5849 and 5884, HEH; Col. James Prevost to John Calcraft, [?] June 1760, WO 34/83/11, TNA; "Report of the Board of General Officers," 7 March 1761, LO 6304A, HEH; Lt. Gen. Jeffery Amherst to Col. Frederick Haldimand, 4 December 1762, WO 34/7/298, TNA.

93. Lord Barrington to Maj. Gen. Jeffery Amherst, 14 April 1759, AMSS, U 1350/O36/33, CKS; Sir John Ligonier to Amherst, n.d., Ligonier Manuscript Letterbook, 1759–60, 78, WLCL; John Calcraft to Lt. Col. Ralph Burton, n.d., Add. MSS 17,495, BL; Col. Henry Bouquet to Maj. Gen. Thomas Gage, 30 November 1764, in *Bouquet Papers*, 6:715; Guy, *Oeconomy and Discipline*, 20–22.

94. John Yorke to Lord Hardwicke, 28 October 1755, and 20 July 1760, Add. MSS 35,374, 125, 173, BL; "Extrait dune Lettre du Brigadier Prevost au General Yorke," [?] October 1758, ChP, PRO 30/8/76/107–108, TNA; Col. James Prevost to Hardwicke, 12 November 1759, Add. MSS 35,635, 309, BL; [Maj.] Baron [Herbert von] Munster to Lt. Gen. Jeffery Amherst, 14 November 1763, AMSS, U 1350/C54, CKS; *Dictionary of National Biography*, s.vv. "Pratt, Charles," and "Yorke, Joseph."

95. "Report of the Attorney & Solicitor General, to Lord Barrington, on the Case of the Foreign Officers in the Royal American Regiment," 11 December 1759, and Col. James Prevost to the Duke of Newcastle, 29 January 1760, Add. MSS 32,901, 518–21, BL; Schwartz, *"Mixed Multitude,"* 160–63; Kettner, *Development of American Citizenship*, 74–76; Pickering, *Statutes at Large*, 17:370–73 [13 George II, c. 6].

96. Lt. Col. Henry Bouquet to Sir John St. Clair, 18 April 1757, in *Bouquet Papers*, 1:83; Col. James Prevost to the Duke of Cumberland, 23 May 1757, in Pargellis, *Military Affairs*, 341; Prevost to Mr. [Robert?] Wood, 17 April 1759, ChP, PRO 30/8/76/117, TNA; "Case on Behalf of Colonel Prevost, and Other Foreign Officers, in the Royal American Regiment," 28 November 1759, Add. MSS 35,635, 317–18, BL; Prevost to the Earl of Holderness, 4 February 1760, Egerton Manuscripts, 3,439, 115, BL; Prevost to Lord Barrington, 26 June 1760, WO 1/1/378, TNA.

97. Col. James Prevost to Charles Pratt, 12 November 1759, Add. MSS 35,635, 310, BL; "The Humble Petition of James Prevost Esq. Colonel of a Battalion in the Royal American Regiment, on Behalf of Himself and the Other Foreign Officers of the Said Regiment," n.d., Add. MSS 32,901, 523, BL.

98. Lord Barrington to Maj. Gen. Jeffery Amherst, 12 April 1760, AMSS, U 1350/O37/14, CKS; Maj. Augustine Prevost to Col. Henry Bouquet, 10 May 1760, and Capt. Thomas Basset to Bouquet, 10 December 1763, in *Bouquet Papers*, 4:562 and 6:477; "Return of the Forces under the Command of Major-General Jeffery Amherst," 4 August 1760, WO 34/85/38, TNA; Anderson, *Crucible of War*, 387–88; Gipson, *British Empire before the American Revolution*, 7:448–63.

99. Maj. Gen. Jeffery Amherst to Lord Barrington, 19 May 1760, and Amherst to Col. James Prevost, 5 June 1760, WO 1/5/112–13, and 34/84/265, TNA; Richard Huck to the Earl of Loudoun, 19 May 1760, LO 6246, HEH; *Amherst Journal*, 245–48 (entries of 6–8 September 1760).

100. Col. James Prevost to Maj. Gen. Jeffery Amherst, 11 May and 11 August 1760, WO 34/82/185, 316–17, TNA; Amherst to Prevost, 11 May 1760 and 6 January 1761, WO 34/84/133 and 34/88/8, TNA; Prevost to Lord Barrington, 26 June 1760, WO 1/1/378, TNA; Col. Henry Bouquet to Maj. Gen. Robert Monckton, 5 October 1761, in *Bouquet Papers*, 5:801; Prevost to Amherst, 10 April 1762, Add. MSS 21,661, 189, BL; Whitworth, *Field Marshal Lord Ligonier*, 46, 225–37; s.v. "Amherst, Jeffery, 1st Baron AMHERST," in *Dictionary of Canadian Biography*, 4:20–21.

101. Capt. John Schlosser to Col. Henry Bouquet, 22 August 1761, in *Bouquet Papers*, 5:709; Sir William Johnson to Capt. Daniel Claus, 9 February 1762, in *Johnson Papers*, 3:629; Capt. Lt. Elias Meyer to Maj. Gen. Jeffery Amherst, n.d., and Maj. Gen. James Murray to Amherst, 2 September 1763, WO 34/2/191 and 34/2/207, TNA.

102. "Capitaines venus avec Mons. Le Coll. Prevost," n.d., and the Earl of Loudoun to Abraham Mortier, 21 May 1757, LO 2679 and 5943, HEH; "Petition of John de Noyelles to the Board of Trade," n.d., in NYHS, *Collections for 1921* 54 (1923): 394–95; John Pownall to Lt. Gov. Cadwallader Colden, 14 April 1761, in *NYCD*, 7:462–63; Statt, *Foreigners and Englishmen*, 33; Schwartz, "Mixed Multitude," 28–29; Kettner, *Development of American Citizenship*, 4–9, 112–28.

103. Quotation from Capt. Samuel Wllyamoz to Col. Henry Bouquet, 9 September 1761, in *Bouquet Papers*, 5:739; Anderson, *Crucible of War*, 415–20; Wilson, *Sense of the People*, 192–97; Whitworth, *William Augustus*, 209–13; Langford, *Polite and Commercial People*, 340–46.

104. "List of Promotions in the Royal American Regiment," n.d., AMSS, U 1350/O39/26A, CKS; Brig. Gen. James Murray to Lt. Gen. Jeffery Amherst, 9 March 1762, WO 34/1/22, TNA; Black, *Pitt the Elder*, 200–227; Ayling, *George the Third*, 63–68; Namier and Brooke, *Charles Townshend*, 64–67.

105. "The Humble Petition of James Prevost Esq. Colonel of a Battalion in the Royal American Regiment, on Behalf of Himself and the Other Foreign Officers of the Said Regiment," n.d., Add. MSS 35,635, 350–51, BL; Col. Henry Bouquet to Maj. Gen. Robert Monckton, 5 October 1761, in *Bouquet Papers*, 5:801; "Commons Debate," 10 March 1762, in Simmons and Thomas, *Proceedings and Debates*, 1:387.

106. "Commons Debate," 8 and 21 April 1762, and "Lords Proceedings," 21 April 1762, in Simmons and Thomas, *Proceedings and Debates*,

1:393–97; Col. James Prevost to Lt. Gen. Jeffery Amherst, 10 April 1762, Add. MSS 21,661, 189, BL; Kettner, *Development of American Citizenship*, 76–78; Pickering, *Statutes at Large*, 25:162–63 [2 George III, c. 25].

107. Lt. Gen. Thomas Gage to Lt. Col. Augustine Prevost, 15 September 1770, TGPAS, vol. 95, WLCL; Williams, "Prevosts of the Royal Americans," 20–27; s.v. "Claus, Christian Daniel," in *Dictionary of Canadian Biography*, 4:154–55; s.v. "Grass, Michael," ibid., 5:377–78; s.v. "Gugy, Conrad," ibid., 4:316–17.

108. Lt. Col. Henry Bouquet to Loudoun, 28 April 1757, and Capt. John Schlosser to Bouquet, 15 March 1764, in *Bouquet Papers*, 1:102–103 and 6:502; Col. James Prevost to Charles Yorke, 12 November 1759, Add. MSS 35,635, 309, BL; Lt. Francis Mckay to Bouquet, 12 May 1764, and Lt. Joseph F. W. DesBarres to Bouquet, 21 August 1764, Add. MSS 21,650, 194, 419, BL; Capt. George Etherington to Bouquet, 20 April 1765, in *Bouquet Papers*, 6:784; Brig. Gen. Frederick Haldimand to Hugh Wallace, 20 April 1768, Add. MSS 21,679, 46, BL.

109. Quotation from Webb, *On the Appointments of the Army*, 106; *New York Mercury*, 3 July 1758, 2; *Pennsylvania Gazette*, 3 August 1758, 1; Lt. James Grant to Col. Henry Bouquet, 20 February 1759, in *Bouquet Papers*, 3:137; *Pennsylvania Gazette*, 2 August 1759, 2; *Boston Post-Boy & Advertiser*, 10 September 1759, 2 (entry of 22 July 1759), and 5 September 1763, 3; Bourinot, *Account of Cape Breton*, 157–58.

110. Lt. Col. Augustine Prevost to Lt. Gen. Jeffery Amherst, 25 April 1761, WO 34/4/49, TNA; Capt. Thomas Barnsley to Col. Henry Bouquet, 28 July 1761, in *Bouquet Papers*, 5:666; Smelser, *Campaign for the Sugar Islands*, 13–154.

111. Col. William Haviland to Lt. Gen. Jeffery Amherst, 17 February 1762, WO 34/55/73, TNA; *Boston Post-Boy & Advertiser*, 12 April 1762, 2, and 26 July 1762, 3; Syrett, *Siege and Capture of Havana*, xiii–xxxv; Gipson, *British Empire before the American Revolution*, 8:191–96, 227–54; Mante, *History of the Late War*, 418–64.

112. Henry Fox to the Governors of New Hampshire, New York, Connecticut, Massachusetts Bay, New Jersey, and Rhode Island, 13 March 1756, WO 34/71/65, TNA; "Lieutenant John Schlosser's Advertisement for Recruits," 2 July 1756, Timothy Horsfield Papers, APS; Maj. Gen. Thomas Gage to Welbore Ellis, 10 March 1764, in *Gage Correspondence*, 2:224.

113. Quotation from Lt. Gov. Cadwallader Colden to the Lords Commissioners for Trade and Plantations, 8 February 1764, CO 5/1071/50, TNA; "By the King: A Proclamation," 7 October 1763, in Brigham, *British Royal Proclamations Relating to America*, 215; Maj. Gen. Thomas Gage to the Earl of Shelburne, 23 January 1768, in *Gage Correspondence*, 1:161; O'Callaghan, *Indorsed Land Papers*, 331–522.

114. "Plan of the Establishment of the Sixtieth or Royal American Regiment of Foot," 18 May 1763, AMSS, U 1350/O43/9B, CKS; Col. James Prevost to Welbore Ellis, 2 May 1763, and Ellis to Lt. Gen. Jeffery Amherst, 20 May 1763, WO 1/985/691 and 4/987/18, TNA; Lt. Gen. Jeffery Amherst to Maj. Gen. James Murray, 4 August 1763, WO 34/3/202–203, TNA; Bullion, "Ten Thousand in America," 646–57; Shy, *Toward Lexington*, 45–83.

115. "List of Royal American Officers Who Form the First and Second Battalions of the Royal American Regiment, Agreeable to the New Establishment," n.d., WO 34/100/49, TNA; Maj. Gen. Thomas Gage to Maj. Gen. James Murray, 17 February 1766, TGPAS, vol. 48, WLCL; Gage to Lord Barrington, 15 June 1766, in *Gage Correspondence*, 2:357.

116. Col. Henry Bouquet to Maj. Gen. John Stanwix, 9 October 1760, and Capt. Donald Campbell to Bouquet, 16 June 1761, in *Bouquet Papers*, 5:63–64, 555–56; Ens. Christopher Pauli to Maj. Gen. Thomas Gage, 6 June 1766, TGPAS, vol. 52, WLCL; Hinderaker, *Elusive Empires*, 144–57; McConnell, *Country Between*, 159–87; White, *Middle Ground*, 256–68.

117. Maj. William Walters to Col. Henry Bouquet, 15 September 1760, and Bouquet to Lt. Gen. Jeffery Amherst, 24 October 1763, in *Bouquet Papers*, 5:43 and 6:438; Draper, "Lieut. James Gorell's Journal," 26–28 (entries of 8 September 1761–23 May 1762); McConnell, *Army and Empire*, 82–99.

118. Capt. Donald Campbell to Maj. William Walters, 17 June 1761, and Lt. Gen. Jeffery Amherst to Col. Henry Bouquet, 6 June 1763, in *Bouquet Papers*, 5:560–61 and 6:209; John Adair to Amherst, 18 September 1762, AMSS, U 1350/O42/8A, CKS; Dowd, *War under Heaven*, 114–47; Peckham, *Pontiac and the Indian Uprising*, 130–242; s.v. "Pontiac," in *Dictionary of Canadian Biography*, 3:525–31.

119. Lt. Gen. Jeffery Amherst to Colonel Henry Bouquet, 2 July 1763, and Bouquet to Amherst, 6 August 1763, in *Bouquet Papers*, 6:283, 342–44; Maj. Gen. Thomas Gage to the Earl of Halifax, 13 December 1764, in *Gage Correspondence*, 1:45–46; Daudelin, "Numbers and Tactics," 153–79; Mante, *History of the Late War*, 484–542; Smith, *Bouquet's Expedition against the Ohio Indians*, 1–35.

120. Col. James Prevost to Welbore Ellis, 2 May 1763, and Lt. Gen. Jeffery Amherst to Maj. John Wilkins, 29 October 1763, WO 1/985/691 and 34/23/156, TNA; "Officers Kill'd or Murdered by the Indians," n.d., AMSS, U 1350/O14/155, CKS; "Return of Major-General James Prevost's Company, 1st Battalion Royal American Regiment of Foot," 12 August 1772, WO 12/6871/13, TNA; Galiffe, *Notices généalogiques*, 2:360–61.

121. "Establishment of the General Officers," 30 November 1741, Add. MSS 33,046, 122, BL; *Georgia Gazette*, 20 June 1765, 2; Langford, *First Rockingham Administration*, 8–12, 70–75, 97–98; Childs, *British Army of William III*, 265; Millan, *List of Officers* (1765), 3–4.

122. "List of Officers Who Came over on Transports Hired by Colonel Prevost," 4 February 1758, LO 5404, HEH; Col. Henry Bouquet to Richard Peters, 24 February 1760, and Bouquet to Maj. Gen. Robert Monckton, 12 June 1761, in *Bouquet Papers*, 4:466 and 5:545; Sophia Fesch to Bouquet, 16 August 1760, ibid., 4:696–97.

123. Quotation from "Private Diary of General Haldimand," in Brymner, *Report on Canadian Archives*, 137 (entry of 31 January 1786); "Letter of Attorney: Joseph and Henry Guinand to Colonel James Prevost and Colonel Henry Bouquet," 11 July 1760, and Capt. James Mark Prevost to Bouquet, n.d., Add. MSS 21,687, 26–28, and Add. MSS 21,650, 237, BL; Brig. Gen. Frederick Haldimand to Hugh Wallace, 30 November 1767, Add. MSS 21,679, 33, BL.

124. "List of Proprietors of British Canada Reconnaissances," 30 May 1769, SP 78/278/115, TNA; Capt. Lt. Frederick Spiesmacher to Lt. Gen. Thomas Gage, 19 June 1770, TGPAS, vol. 93, WLCL; Brig. Gen. Frederick Haldimand to Hugh Wallace, 7 October 1770, Add. MSS 21,679, 83, BL; Riley, *Seven Years' War and the Old Regime*, 189; Bosher, "French Government's Motives," 70, 77.

125. Lord Barrington to Maj. Gen. Thomas Gage, 12 December 1765 and 14 March 1767, WO 4/988/28, 70, TNA; "60th Regiment," 13 December 1765, Succession Books (Series 1) General, 1764–71, WO 25/210/3, TNA; Gage to Maj. Gen. James Murray, 17 February 1766, TGPAS, vol. 48, WLCL; Whitworth, *William Augustus*, 238; Hugh Wallace to Brig. Gen. Frederick Haldimand, 1 July and 17 October 1769, Add. MSS 21,679, 64 and 75, BL.

126. Earl of Rochford to Horace St. Paul, 16 July 1773, SP 78/289/60, TNA; Home, *Letters and Journals of Lady Mary Coke*, 158–59 (entry of 27 October 1769); Millan, *List of Officers* (1774), 116.

127. Lt. Gen. James Prevost to Sir Robert Murray Keith, 27 August 1773, Add. MSS 35,506, 79, BL; Horace Walpole to Sir Horace Mann, 10 August 1773, in Lewis et al., *Horace Walpole's Correspondence*, 23:502; Black, *The British Abroad*, 7–85; *Dictionary of National Biography*, s.v. "Henry Frederick, Duke of Cumberland."

128. *London Gazette*, 5 September 1775, 1; "Grant of Arms to Lieutenant-General James Mackay formerly Prevost," 27 September 1775, MS Grants 13.125, College of Arms, London, England.

129. "60th Foot," 11 January 1776, Succession Books (Series 1) General, 1771–80, WO 25/211, TNA; Galiffe, *Notices généalogiques*, 2:361; Mackay, *Life of Lieut. General Hugh Mackay*, 6, 185–86; Mackay, *House and Clan of Mackay*, 562–63. I am grateful to Sir Christopher Prevost of Rochester, Kent, for providing me with a transcript of Lt. Gen. James Prevost Mackay's will and other information about his immediate family. Personal communication with the author, 13 August 2002.

2. "A MEDLEY OF ALL CHARACTERS"

1. Quotation from Hamilton, *Duties of a Regimental Surgeon*, 1:110.

2. Brumwell, *Redcoats*, 57–60; Guy, *Oeconomy and Discipline*, 123–25; Cuthbertson, *Management and Oeconomy of a Battalion*, 40–48.

3. Steppler, "Common Soldier," 14–23; Simes, *Military Guide for Young Officers*, 1:241–45; "Rules and Articles for the Better Government of His Majesty's Horse and Foot Guards, and All Other His Forces in Great Britain and Ireland, Dominions beyond the Seas, and Foreign Parts, Anno 1749" (hereafter cited as "Rules and Articles") in *HCSP*, 16:384 [sec. 3].

4. Maj. Gen. Daniel Webb to the Earl of Loudoun, 26 March 1756, and Lt. Gen. Humphrey Bland to Loudoun, 1 April 1756, LO 968 and 999, HEH; "A State of the Cash of the 62d or Royal American Regiment to Christmas, 1756," n.d., LO 2521, HEH; Brumwell, *Redcoats*, 318.

5. "Return of the Strength of the 42d, Royal American, and General Otway's Regiments Embarked at Greenock," 8 June 1756, and David Hepburn

to the Earl of Loudoun, 10 November 1757, LO 2415 and 4802, HEH; "Evidence in the Claim of Donald Munro," in Fraser, *Second Report*, 344.

6. "General Memorandums," 25–28 February 1756, Loudoun Notebooks, vol. 8, pp. 41–44, HM 1717, HEH; Lt. George Brereton to the Earl of Loudoun, 8 April 1756, and "Return of Discharged Men," 21 March 1757, LO 1026 and 3117, HEH.

7. Henry Fox to the Lords of the Admiralty, 9 February and 4 June 1756, ADM 1/4120/109 and 1/4121/19, TNA; John Clevland to the Duke of Newcastle, 19 April 1756, Add. MSS 32,864, 343, BL; "His Majesty's Declaration Of War against the French King," 17 May 1756, in Brigham, *British Royal Proclamations Relating to America*, 203–206; *Impartial History of the Late War*, 17.

8. Maj. Gen. Robert Napier to the Earl of Loudoun, 8 May 1756, LO 1136, HEH; "HRH," n.d., and "Memorandum," 11 May 1756, Loudoun Notebooks, vol. 9, p. 55, and vol. 10, p. 15, HM 1717, HEH; *Gentleman's Magazine* 26 (1756): 388.

9. Quotation from Lt. Gov. Robert H. Morris to Sir John St. Clair, 17 February 1755, Letterbook of Sir John St. Clair, p. 55, TWML; Maj. John Rutherfurd to the Earl of Loudoun, 23 August 1756, LO 1549, HEH; Rutherfurd, *Family Records and Events*, 90–96.

10. "(62) or Royal American Regt of Foot," 13 March 1756, Notification Books to the Secretary of State, 1755–59, WO 25/137/53–58, TNA; "List of Commissions Given by His Excellency the Earl of Loudoun," 26 December 1756 and 5 June 1757, in Pargellis, *Military Affairs*, 283–85; 364–65; "60th Foot," Succession Books (Series 1) General, 1754–64, WO 25/209/194–98, TNA.

11. Henry Fox to North American Governors, 13 March 1756, WO 34/71/64–66, TNA; Thomas Penn to Lt. Gov. Robert H. Morris, 13 March 1756, Thomas Penn Letterbooks, vol. 4, p. 247, HSP; Harding, "Growth of Anglo-American Alienation," 161–79.

12. Maj. John Rutherfurd to Gov. William Shirley, 29 June 1756, in Hildeburn, "Sir John St. Clair," 8–9; Col. John Stanwix to Lt. Col. Frederick Haldimand, 6 and 27 August 1756, Add. MSS 21,666, 1–2, BL.

13. "Heads of Instructions for Colonel [Daniel] Webb," 23 February 1756, LO 848, HEH; Thomas Penn to Lt. Gov. Robert H. Morris, 22 March 1756, Thomas Penn Letterbooks, vol. 4, p. 259, HSP; "Royal Instructions to the Earl of Loudoun," 7 May 1756, WO 34/71/75, TNA.

14. *New York Mercury*, 14 and 21 June 1756, 2 and 3; Leach, *Roots of Conflict*, 49–61, 82–84; Kopperman, *Braddock at the Monongahela*, 14–15, 91; Rutherfurd, *Family Records and Events*, 198.

15. Quotation from Maj. Gen. Daniel Webb to the Earl of Loudoun, 29 March 1756, LO 979, HEH; Sir Charles Hardy to the Earl of Halifax, 7 May 1756, in Pargellis, *Military Affairs*, 170–75; Sir John St. Clair to the Commanding Officer of the Royal American Regiment, 4 July 1756, Letterbook of Sir John St. Clair, p. 298, TWML; *Pennsylvania Gazette*, 2 September 1756, 1; Rogers, *Empire and Liberty*, 41–44.

16. Lt. Gov. Robert H. Morris. to the Pennsylvania Assembly, 13 February 1756, in Reed, *Pennsylvania Archives*, 4th ser., 2 (1900): 583; Gov.

William Shirley to Henry Fox, 8 March 1756, in *Shirley Correspondence*, 2:414; Salinger, *"To Serve Well and Faithfully,"* 57–60.

17. Gov. William Shirley to Lt. Gov. Robert H. Morris, 29 February 1756, in *Shirley Correspondence*, 2:407; Cuthbertson, *Management and Oeconomy of a Battalion*, 42–43; *Gentleman's Magazine* 29 (1759): 125.

18. "An Account of the Several Augmentations of Troops Either Raised Here or Brought from Ireland to This Kingdom and for North America in the Years 1755 & 1756," n.d., Add. MSS 33,047, 22, BL; Gov. William Shirley to Lt. Gov. Horatio Sharpe, 5 March 1756, in Browne, *Archives of Maryland* 6 (1888): 348; Campbell, "Stand in the Face of Danger," 422–27.

19. Salinger, *"To Serve Well and Faithfully,"* 69–81; Richard S. Dunn, "Servants and Slaves: The Recruitment and Employment of Labor," in Greene and Pole, *Colonial British America*, 157–72, 180–82; Galenson, *White Servitude in Colonial America*, 3–13, 97–99.

20. Atkinson, "Free-Born Englishman Transported," 93–99; Smith, *Colonists in Bondage*, 68–86.

21. Klepp and Smith, *The Infortunate*, 87–97; Eddis, *Letters from America*, 35–38; Ekirch, *Bound for America*, 3–4, 146–52. Salinger notes that 80 percent of Pennsylvania servant-enlistees came from rural areas, where living conditions were at their worst. Salinger, *"To Serve Well and Faithfully,"* 106–107.

22. Coldham, *Emigrants in Chains*, 125; Salinger, *"To Serve Well and Faithfully,"* 107–108, Smith, *Colonists in Bondage*, 233–34; Williamson, *Treatise on Military Finance*, 19.

23. Henry Fox to Northern Governors, 13 March 1756, WO 34/71/64–65, TNA; Salinger, *"To Serve Well and Faithfully,"* 134; Smith, *Colonists in Bondage*, 238–41.

24. Quotation from Captain Robert Cholmley's Batman, 24 April 1755, in Hamilton, *Braddock's Defeat*, 12; Coldham, *Emigrants in Chains*, 125, 205–209; Ekirch, *Bound for America*, 59–63; Smith, *Colonists in Bondage*, 67–86.

25. Lt. Gov. Horatio Sharpe to John Sharpe, 24 May 1755, in Browne, *Archives of Maryland* 6 (1888): 211; Gov. William Shirley to Lt. Gov. Robert H. Morris, 20 February 1756, and "Copy of a Letter to Captain Samuel Hobson," n.d., in Hazard, *Pennsylvania Archives*, 1st ser., 2 (1853): 578 and 640–41; "Evidence of Richard Benson," 28 November 1761, WO 71/70/169, TNA.

26. Simmons and Thomas, *Proceedings and Debates*, 1:173, 176; Pickering, *Statutes at Large*, 21:497–502 [29 George II, c. 36].

27. "An Act for Raising Recruits for His Majesty's Service; and for Other Purposes Therein Mentioned," in Hening, *Statutes at Large*, 7:61–63; "An Act for the Relief of sundry Inhabitants of this Province who have had their Servants Enlisted into his Majesty's Service," 6 May 1757, in Browne, *Archives of Maryland* 55 (1938): 136–37.

28. Lt. Gov. Robert H. Morris to the Earl of Loudoun, 5 July 1756, and "List of Servants Belonging to the Inhabitants of Pennsylvania and Taken in His Majesty's Service, For Whom Satisfaction Has Not Been Made by the Officers according to [the] Act of Parliament," n.d., LO 1287 and 3415, HEH;

Benjamin Franklin to Isaac Norris, New York, 30 May 1757, in Labaree, *Papers of Benjamin Franklin*, 7:223–29.

29. Maj. John Rutherfurd to Gov. William Shirley, 29 June 1756, in Hildeburn, "Sir John St. Clair," 8; *Pennsylvania Gazette*, 1 July 1756, 2; Maj. John Rutherford to [Lt. Gov. Horatio Sharpe], 12 September 1756, Frank M. Etting Collection, Autographs, Colonial Wars, HSP; Fogleman, *Hopeful Journeys*, 100–119; Purvis, "Patterns of Ethnic Settlement," 116–18.

30. Quotation from *Pensylvanische Berichte*, 16 July 1756, 3; Col. John Stanwix to the Earl of Loudoun, 6 August 1756, LO 1425, HEH; Richard Peters to Thomas Penn, 4 September 1756, Penn Papers, Official Correspondence, vol. 8, p. 151, HSP; "Extract of Mr. Dulany's Letter from Maryland," 4 November 1756, ChP, PRO 30/8/95/125, TNA.

31. Thomas Ringgold to Edward Tilghman, 23 September 1756, MS 2018, Colonial Collection, Manuscripts Division, Maryland Historical Society, Baltimore; Earl of Loudoun to Col. John Stanwix, 9 November 1756, and "List of Officers Belonging to the Regiments in Nova Scotia upon Recruiting Duty," n.d., LO 2184 and 2186, HEH.

32. "Commons Proceedings," 19 January 1756, in Simmons and Thomas, *Proceedings and Debates*, 1:121–22; Lt. Gov. Horatio Sharpe to Lt. Gov. Robert Dinwiddie, 26 September 1756, in Browne, *Archives of Maryland* 6 (1888): 488; "A State of the Cash of the 62d or Royal American Regiment to Christmas, 1756," n.d., LO 2521, HEH; "General Remarks upon the State of the 50th Regiment," n.d., WO 1/972/451, TNA; Guy, *Oeconomy and Discipline*, 62–65.

33. Robert Turner to Messrs. Wolffinder and Birchinsha, [?] September 1756, Allen and Turner Letterbook, Library Company Collection, HSP; Wokeck, *Trade in Strangers*, 84–85, 150–52; Grubb, "Redemptioner Immigration to Pennsylvania," 407–18; Smith, *Colonists in Bondage*, 20–25.

34. Lewis Evans to the Honourable Committee, 13 December 1754, Miscellaneous Manuscripts on Indian Affairs, 1737–75, APS; Joseph Turner to Jacob Bosanquat, [?] September 1756, Allen and Turner Letterbook, Library Company Collection, HSP.

35. Conrad Weiser to William Parsons, 28 October 1755, Timothy Horsfield Papers, APS; Ward, *Breaking the Backcountry*, 64–70, 96–97; Stephenson, "Pennsylvania Soldiers," 196–202; Hunter, *Forts on the Pennsylvania Frontier*, 184–97.

36. Quotation from "Petition of Some American Soldiers," 31 January 1758, LO 5550, HEH; "Evidence of Daniel Nangle," 25 November 1761, WO 71/70/165–66, TNA; Williamson, *French and Indian Cruelty*, 38–39.

37. Richard Peters to Timothy Horsfield, 30 June 1756, Timothy Horsfield Papers, APS; "Officers of the Provincial Service—1755," in Linn and Egle, *Pennsylvania Archives*, 2nd ser., 2 (1890): 443; "Etat des Officers Suisses et Allemands Engagez en Holland par Mr. Prevost, 1756," n.d., Cumberland Papers, box 46, item 126, RA.

38. "Lieutenant Schlosser's Advertisement for Recruits," 2 July 1756, Timothy Horsfield Papers, APS; Timothy Horsfield to William Parsons, 3 July 1756, and Parsons to Horsfield, 3 July 1756, ibid., APS.

39. Maj. Gen. James Abercromby to the Earl of Loudoun, 22 June 1756, LO 1237, HEH; Simler, "Tenancy in Colonial Pennsylvania," 550, 560–65; Lemon, *Best Poor Man's Country*, 67–70, 87–93.

40. "General Return of the Royal American Regiment," 16 August 1756, LO 1500, HEH; "Evidence of Matthew Wassirman," and "Evidence of Andrew Snyder," 9 June 1757, WO 71/65/320, 322, TNA; "Recruits Enlisted for the Royal American Regiment from 25 June 1756 to 24 June 1758, Inclusive," n.d., WO 34/99/171, TNA.

41. Richard Peters to Thomas Penn, 26 June 1756, Penn Papers, Official Correspondence, vol. 8, p. 123, HSP; Maj. John Rutherfurd to the Earl of Loudoun, n.d., and "Memorial of the State of the Forces in Pennsylvania," 22 July 1756, LO 1473 and 1328, HEH.

42. Edward Shippen to Major James Burd, 29 June 1756, and John Inglis to Burd, 3 July 1756, Shippen Family Papers, vol. 2, APS; Shippen to [Capt.] Joseph Shippen, 15 July 1756, Correspondence of Edward and Joseph Shippen, 1750–78, Edward Shippen Papers, APS; Thomas Penn to James Hamilton, 7 September 1756, Thomas Penn Letterbooks, vol. 4, pp. 349–50, HSP.

43. Earl of Loudoun to the Duke of Cumberland, 20 August 1756, in Pargellis, *Military Affairs*, 223–30; Fregault, *Canada*, 124–36; Pargellis, *Lord Loudoun*, 132–66.

44. Quotation from Daniel Dulany to [?], 9 December 1755, in Dulany, "Military and Political Affairs," 16; Col. John Stanwix to the Earl of Loudoun, 6 August 1756, LO 1425, HEH; *Pennsylvania Gazette*, 2 September 1756, 2; Edmund Atkin to Gov. William H. Lyttelton, 15 October 1756, William H. Lyttelton Papers, vol. 2, WLCL.

45. Richard Peters to Thomas Penn, 4 September 1756, Penn Papers, Official Correspondence, vol. 8, p. 151, HSP; Penn to Peters, 11 December 1756, Thomas Penn Letterbooks, vol. 5, p. 43, HSP; Ward, "Army of Servants," 76–79.

46. Earl of Loudoun to the Governors of New Jersey, Pennsylvania, Maryland, Virginia, North Carolina, South Carolina, & Georgia, 20 August 1756, and Loudoun to Henry Fox, 21 August 1756, LO 1524 and 1543, HEH.

47. Gov. Jonathan Belcher to the Earl of Loudoun, 2 September 1756, LO 1685, HEH; Gov. Arthur Dobbs to the Board of Trade, 31 October 1756, in Saunders, *Colonial Records of North Carolina*, 5:638–40; Gov. John Reynolds to Loudoun, 24 November 1756, and Gov. William H. Lyttelton to Loudoun, 16 December 1756, LO 2274 and 2365, HEH.

48. Lt. Gov. Horatio Sharpe to Lord Baltimore, 3 October 1756, and Sharpe to John Sharpe, 10 October 1756, in Browne, *Archives of Maryland* 6 (1888): 489, 495.

49. Thomas Robinson to Lt. Gov. Horatio Sharpe, 5 July 1754, in Browne, *Archives of Maryland* 31 (1911): 52–53; Sharpe to William Sharpe, 2 May 1756, in ibid. 6 (1888): 398–99; Sharpe to Sharpe, 6 July 1757, in ibid. 9 (1890): 48; *American National Biography*, s.v. "Sharpe, Horatio."

50. "A Proclamation," 16 July 1756, in Browne, *Archives of Maryland* 31 (1911): 154; *Maryland Gazette*, 22 July 1756, 3; Thomas Ringgold to Edward Tilghman, 23 September 1756, MS 2018, Colonial Collection, Manu-

scripts Division, Maryland Historical Society, Baltimore; Lt. Gov. Horatio Sharpe to Cecilius Calvert, 4 February 1757, in Browne, *Archives of Maryland* 6 (1888): 524.

51. Earl of Loudoun to Lt. Gov. Horatio Sharpe, 20 August 1756; Sharpe to John Sharpe, 15 September 1756, and Sharpe to Loudoun, 12 October 1756, in Browne, *Archives of Maryland* 6 (1888): 463, 486, 497.

52. "An Account of Services Incurred during the War, in His Majesty's Colonies in North America," 12 March 1749/50, in Stock, *Proceedings and Debates of Parliament*, 5:414; "An Act for his Majesty's Service, and further Defence and Security of this Province," 8 October 1756, in Browne, *Archives of Maryland* 52 (1935): 650-51; Lt. Gov. Horatio Sharpe to Cecilius Calvert, 4 February 1757, in ibid. 6 (1888): 523-24; Sharpe to Col. John Stanwix, 15 November 1757, in ibid. 9 (1890): 103.

53. Col. George Washington to Lt. Gov. Robert Dinwiddie, 14 August 1756, and Washington to the Earl of Loudoun, 10 January 1756, in *Washington Papers*, 3:330 and 4:86-87; Titus, *Old Dominion at War*, 37-72.

54. *Virginia Gazette*, 3 September 1756, 3; Lt. Gov. Robert Dinwiddie to the Earl of Loudoun, 8 September 1756, and Loudoun to Dinwiddie, 25 October 1756, LO 1734 and 2087, HEH.

55. "Council Minutes," 3 September 1756, in McIlwaine et al., *Executive Journals*, 6:13-14; Lt. Gov. Robert Dinwiddie to the General Assembly, 20 September 1756, in Brock, *Official Records of Robert Dinwiddie*, 2:513-14.

56. Lt. Gov. Robert Dinwiddie to the Earl of Loudoun, 6 October and 16 November 1756, LO 1977 and 2228, HEH; *Pennsylvania Gazette*, 7 October 1756, 3.

57. "Memorandum," 24 February 1757, Loudoun Notebooks, vol. 2, p. 28, HM 1717, HEH; Earl of Loudoun to the Duke of Cumberland, 8 March 1757, in Pargellis, *Military Affairs*, 319; Convicts in Woodstreet Compton to Lord Barrington, n.d., WO 1/974/179, TNA; Conway, "Recruitment of Criminals," 48-52.

58. Lt. Gov. Robert Dinwiddie to the Earl of Loudoun, 5 April 1757, in Brock, *Official Records of Robert Dinwiddie*, 2:605; Lt. David Ochterlony to Loudoun, 9 April 1757, and Col. John Stanwix to Loudoun, 12 May 1757, LO 3328 and 3600, HEH; Ward, *Breaking the Backcountry*, 98; Titus, *Old Dominion at War*, 59-65.

59. "Memorandums," n.d., Loudoun Notebooks, vol. 8, pp. 7, 25, and vol. 9, p. 25, HM 1717, HEH; Glatfelter, *Pastors and People*, 1:42; Hinke, *Ministers of the German Reformed Congregations*, 374-76.

60. *Pennsylvania Gazette*, 24 June and 18 November 1756, 2 and 2; Gov. William H. Lyttelton to the Earl of Loudoun, 5 November 1756 and 19 February 1757, LO 2162 and 2865, HEH; Wood, *Slavery in Colonial Georgia*, 115-24.

61. Quotation from Lt. Col. Henry Bouquet to Loudoun, 16 October 1757, in *Bouquet Papers*, 1:215; Bouquet to Loudoun, 25 August 1757, ibid., 1:172; *Pensylvanische Berichte*, 13 April 1757, 3; "Memorandum," 28 April 1757, Loudoun Notebooks, vol. 2, p. 64, HM 1717, HEH; Higginbotham, "Martial Spirit in the Antebellum South," 9.

62. Earl of Loudoun to Maj. Edward Brice Dobbs, 2 September 1756, and Loudoun to Gov. Arthur Dobbs, 22 September 1756, LO 1677 and 1879, HEH; Gov. Arthur Dobbs to the Board of Trade, 31 October 1757, in Saunders, *Colonial Records of North Carolina*, 5:640.

63. Quotation from Earl of Loudoun to Gov. Arthur Dobbs, 28 October 1756, LO 2100, HEH; Loudoun to the Duke of Cumberland, 22 November 1756, in Pargellis, *Military Affairs*, 267.

64. "HRH," 25 February 1756, Loudoun Notebooks, vol. 8, pp. 41–42, HM 1717, HEH; "Payments Made to Colonel Prevost on Account of Clothing, Contingencies, &c.," n.d., LO 5859, HEH; *Complete History of the Present War*, 72–73.

65. Quotation from "Commons Debate," 7 December 1770, in Simmons and Thomas, *Proceedings and Debates*, 3:351; Wilson, "German 'Soldier Trade,'" 757–92; Parker, *Thirty Years' War*, 191–97; Casparis, "Swiss Mercenary System," 593–642.

66. Quotation from "Colonel Prevost's Plan for Recruiting," n.d., LO 2576, HEH; "Proposals for Col. Prevost's Bargain," n.d., Loudoun Notebooks, vol. 9, p. 31, HM 1717, HEH.

67. Earl of Loudoun to the Earl of Albemarle, 21 April 1756, LO 1068; "Memorandum," 23 April 1756, and "Memorandum," n.d., Loudoun Notebooks, vol. 1, p. 32, and vol. 9, p. 39, HM 1717, HEH; "Instructions for Colonel Prevost Relating to His Bringing over Planters from Germany," n.d., WO 34/76/20-21, TNA.

68. "Extraits des Differentes Lettres ecrites au Col. Prevost au Sujet des Recrues a faire en Allemagne," n.d., LO 2575, HEH; Sir Joseph Yorke to the Earl of Holderness, 10 January 1755, SP 84/468, TNA; Wilson, *German Armies*, 12–67, 165–201; Vann, *Making of a State*, 142–57, 179–88.

69. George Cressener to the Earl of Holderness, 25 March and 7 April 1756, SP 81/128, TNA; Vattel, *Law of Nations*, 363–64 [bk. 3, chap. 2, sec. 15].

70. "General Memorandum," 23 April 1756, and "Foreign Officers in the American Regiment Now in Germany Recruiting," n.d., Loudoun Notebooks, vol. 1 and vol. 11, HM 1717, HEH; "Munster's List," 27 August 1756, LO 1607, HEH; Maj. John Tulleken to Col. Henry Bouquet, 15 April 1759, in *Bouquet Papers*, 3:244–45.

71. Sir Joseph Yorke to Maj. Gen. Robert Napier, 23 March 1756, LO 959, HEH; *Pennsylvania Gazette*, 3 June 1756, 1.

72. "Munster's List," 27 August 1756, LO 1607, HEH; Wokeck, *Trade in Strangers*, 2–3; George Fertig, "Transatlantic Migrations from the German-Speaking Parts of Central Europe, 1600–1800: Proportions, Structures, and Explanations," in Canny, *Europeans on the Move*, 192–235. Munster's list records the presence of a small number of Scots and Poles among the Holy Roman Empire recruits.

73. Sir Joseph Yorke to Maj. Gen. Robert Napier, 23 March 1756, LO 959, HEH; George Cressener to the Earl of Holderness, 25 March 1756, SP 81/128, TNA; "Memorandum," 14 March 1757, Loudoun Notebooks, vol. 2, p. 41, HM 1717, HEH; "Evidence of Corporal Henry Dorman," 20 August

1757, WO 71/66/57–58, TNA; Duffy, *Instrument of War*, 198, 206; Duffy, *Army of Frederick the Great*, 54; Corvisier, *L'armée Française*, 1:171–78.

74. "Lieutenant [John] Schlosser's Advertisement for Recruits," 2 July 1756, Timothy Horsfield Papers, APS; "Munster's List," 27 August 1756, LO 1607, HEH. I am grateful to Helmut Radday of the Oberharzer Berwerksmusem for information about Clausthal's economic problems in the mid-1750s. Personal communication with the author, 4 May 2000.

75. Quotation from "Extraits des Differentes Lettres ecrites au Col. Prevost au Sujet des Recrues a faire en Allemagne," n.d., LO 2575, HEH; Wokeck, *Trade in Strangers*, 9–17, 86, 118–28; Fertig, "Transatlantic Migrations," 203–17.

76. "Colonel Prevost's Plan for Recruiting," n.d., LO 2576, HEH; Mayer, *Belonging to the Army*, 5–15; Kopperman, "British High Command and Soldiers' Wives," 14–34.

77. Quotation from Col. John Stanwix to the Earl of Loudoun, 6 August 1756, LO 1425, HEH; "Additional Instructions to Colonel Prevost Relating to His Bringing over Planters from Germany," 23 April 1756, WO 34/76/20–21, TNA; Maj. John Young to Loudoun, 2 September 1756, LO 1681, HEH; Cuthbertson, *Management and Oeconomy of a Battalion*, 9.

78. Lt. Gen. Humphrey Bland to the Earl of Loudoun, 6 May 1756, and Loudoun to Maj. Gen. Daniel Webb, 7 September 1756, LO 1114 and 1731, HEH; *Pennsylvania Journal and Weekly Advertiser*, 14 October 1756, 3; *South Carolina Gazette Supplement*, 4 August 1757, 1.

79. Earl of Loudoun to the Duke of Cumberland, 22 November 1756, in Pargellis, *Military Affairs*, 268; *Gentleman's Magazine* 26 (1756): 547; Lord Barrington to John Clevland, 2 September 1757, ADM 1/4323, TNA; "Memorandum," 8 December 1757, Loudoun Notebooks, vol. 4, p. 44, HEH; John Calcraft to Loudoun, 9 December 1757, LO 4978, HEH; "Petition of German Non-Commissioned Officers and Private Men Held Prisoner in France," n.d., WO 34/99/182, TNA.

80. Henry Fox to the Lords of the Admiralty, 15 September 1756, ADM 1/4121/80, TNA; Col. James Prevost to the Earl of Loudoun, 17 January 1757, LO 2678, HEH; "Affidavit of John Pell," 14 February 1757, CO 5/48/129–31, TNA.

81. "Parole of Captain George Gmelin," 10 January 1757, LO 2662, HEH; Gov. Charles Hardy to William Pitt, 26 February 1757, in *Pitt Correspondence*, 1:12; Lord Barrington to John Clevland, 19 October 1757, ADM 1/4323, TNA.

82. Col. Henry Bouquet to Brig. Gen. Robert Monckton, 29 December 1760, in *Bouquet Papers*, 5:217; Lt. Gen. Jeffery Amherst to Maj. Alexander Duncan, 26 September 1762, WO 34/20/116, TNA.

83. *Pennsylvania Gazette*, 3 August 1758, 2; Maj. Gen. Jeffery Amherst to William Pitt, 10 August 1758, CO 5/53/152, TNA; "Evidence of Gaspard Peter," 11 May 1762, WO 71/48/291–92, TNA; Wright, "Sieges and Customs of War," 643.

84. George Cressener to Lord Holderness, 20 June 1756, SP 81/128, TNA; Duke de Belleisle to Peirenne de Moras, 13 February 1757, in *NYCD*,

10:526; Adm. Edward Boscawen to William Pitt, 14 August 1758, in *Pitt Correspondence*, 1:315.

85. Earl of Loudoun to the Duke of Cumberland, 5–6 January 1757, in Pargellis, *Military Affairs*, 290–92; Loudoun to Lt. Col. Henry Bouquet, 7 September 1757, in *Bouquet Papers*, 1:184; Guy, *Oeconomy and Discipline*, 126–27; Houlding, *Fit for Service*, 48–50, 120–25.

86. Quotation from Col. James Prevost to the Duke of Cumberland, 12 May 1757, in Pargellis, *Military Affairs*, 335; John Calcraft to the Earl of Loudoun, 12 February 1757, and "List of Men Unfit for Service with the 4th Battalion, Royal American Regiment," 22 April 1757, LO 2821A and 3433, HEH.

87. Lord Barrington to the Earl of Loudoun, 22 December 1756, and John Berry to Loudoun, n.d. LO 2384 and 5507, HEH; Loudoun to Gov. Charles Lawrence, 22 February 1757, WO 34/11/162, TNA; "Return of the Sergeants, Corporals, Drummers, Private Men, and Deserters from the 50th and 51st Regiments, Turned over to the 62d Regiment," 7 March 1757, WO 1/1/83, TNA.

88. Earl of Loudoun to Col. John Stanwix, 2 September 1756, WO 34/45/144, TNA; Jeremiah Gridley to Loudoun, 6 June 1757, LO 3797, HEH; Selesky, *War and Society in Colonial Connecticut*, 103–19, 168; Anderson, *People's Army*, 39–44, 59–60; Pencak, *War, Politics, and Revolution in Massachusetts*, 136, 154.

89. Earl of Loudoun to Henry Fox, 8 February 1757, CO 5/48/106, TNA; Capt. Harry Charteris to Loudoun, 11 June 1757, and Lt. Col. John Young to Loudoun, 12 June 1757, LO 3816B and 3821, HEH; "Recruits Enlisted for the Royal American Regiment," n.d., WO 34/99/171, TNA; Brumwell, *Redcoats*, 76; Vickers, *Farmers and Fishermen*, 129–33, 156–57, 229–32; Jones, *Village and Seaport*, 42–52.

90. "Memorandum," 26 February 1757, Loudoun Notebooks, vol. 2, p. 29, HM 1717, HEH; Earl of Loudoun to John [sic] Pitt, 10 March 1757, in *Pitt Correspondence*, 1:16; "Subsistence to the Royal American Regiment," n.d., WO 34/99/163–68, TNA.

91. "Recruiting Instructions," 15 November 1756 and [?] November 1757, LO 2221 and 6761, HEH; "List of Servants Belonging to the Inhabitants of Pennsylvania...," n.d., LO 3415, HEH.

92. "Observations on the Value and Rates of the Gold and Silver to Be Provided for the Use of His Majesty's Forces in North America," 25 October 1756, in Pargellis, *Military Affairs*, 248; Col. John Stanwix to the Earl of Loudoun, 20 April 1757, and "Recruiting Instructions," [?] November 1757, LO 3407 and 6761, HEH; *New York Gazette or the Weekly Post Boy*, 26 March 1759, 1; Knoblauch, "Mobilizing Provincials for War," 156–57; Ward, "Army of Servants," 79; Selesky, *War and Society*, 149–53; Anderson, *People's Army*, 38–39.

93. Quotation from "Memorandum," 15 March 1757, Loudoun Notebooks, vol. 2, p. 43, HM 1717, HEH; Col. John Stanwix to the Earl of Loudoun, 20 April and 12 October 1757, LO 3407 and 4629, HEH; "A List of the Officers of the Pennsylvania Regiment, for the Year 1760," in Linn and Egle, *Pennsylvania Archives*, 2nd ser., 2 (1890): 519.

94. Lt. Col. Henry Bouquet to Capt. Charles [sic] Busse, 9 April 1757, in *Bouquet Papers*, 1:77; Lord Barrington to the Earl of Loudoun, 13 May 1757, WO 34/71/159, TNA; "Return of the Five Companies of the 1st Battalion 60th or Royal American Regiment of Foot," 26 December 1757, LO 6877, HEH.

95. Brumwell, *Redcoats*, 73–75, 318; Wokeck, *Trade in Strangers*, 44–45, 172; Fischer, *Albion's Seed*, 420–31; Purvis, "European Ancestry of United States Population," 98.

96. John Berry to the Earl of Loudoun, n.d., and "A Return of the Men of the 4th Battn. Royal American Regiment of Foot Whose Time of Service is Expired or Will Expire before May Next," 21 January 1758, LO 5507 and 6909, HEH; Maj. Gen. John Stanwix to Maj. Gen. Jeffery Amherst, 20 November 1759, WO 34/45/115, TNA.

97. Lt. Gov. Horatio Sharpe to Col. John Stanwix, 17 December 1757, in Browne, *Archives of Maryland* 9 (1890): 109–10; Lt. Col. Henry Bouquet to Stanwix, 26 April 1759, in *Bouquet Papers*, 3:257; "A List of Men That Were Formerly in the Maryland Service and Are Now in the Royal American Regt," n.d., Add. MSS 21,651, 118, BL.

98. "Return of Captain Lewis Steiner's Company of the 4th Battalion, Royal American Regiment," 31 October 1757, and "Return of Captain Marcus Prevost's Company, of the 4th Battalion, Royal American Regiment," 24 April 1758, WO 12/7033/8, 17, TNA; Gov. Jonathan Belcher to the Earl of Loudoun, 3 January 1757, LO 2630, HEH; Lt. Beamsley Glazier to Maj. Gen. Jeffery Amherst, 24 April 1760, WO 34/82/143, TNA.

99. Col. James Prevost to Richard Peters, 18 April 1758, SGM, case 4, box 8, "Colonial Wars," HSP; Martin Heydler to Maj. Gen. Jeffery Amherst, 4 April 1760, and Maj. Gen. John Stanwix to Amherst, 25 April 1760, WO 34/82/109 and 34/45/141, TNA.

100. Quotation from Capt. Gavin Cochrane to Col. Henry Bouquet, 3 March 1760, in *Bouquet Papers*, 4:480; Cochrane to Maj. Gen. John Stanwix, 17 January 1760, ibid., 424–25. "List of the Men That Has [sic] Been Exchanged for Provincials, of the 1st Battalion Royal American Regiment," 13 October 1762, WO 34/22/81, TNA.

101. Quotation from "List of the Men Discharged by Major Gladwin Belonging to the 1st Battalion of the Royal American Regiment & the Men by Whom They Were Replaced," 1762, Add. MSS 21,648, 482, TNA; Padeni, "Forgotten Soldiers," 152–69; Knoblauch, "Mobilizing Provincials for War," 162; Titus, *Old Dominion at War*, 88; *Reflections on Reducing the Rebels*, 21.

102. Maj. Gen. Jeffery Amherst to Lord Barrington, 18 October 1760, WO 1/5/133, TNA; Barrington to Amherst, 2 December 1760, and "New Establishment," 20 March 1761, AMSS, U 1350/O37/36 and 1350/O14/109, CKS.

103. William Pitt to Maj. Gen. Jeffery Amherst, [?] January 1760, in *Pitt Correspondence*, 2:247–49; "Petition of Soldiers in the 1st Battalion, Royal American Regiment," 5 April 1761, WO 34/21/139, TNA; "Recruiting Account of the 3rd Battalion, Royal American Regiment from June 1758," 5 August 1761, WO 34/199/334, TNA; Maj. Thomas Oswald to Amherst,

19 October 1761, and Amherst to Brig. Gen. James Murray, 10 June 1762, WO 34/4/70 and 34/3/147, TNA.

104. Brig. Gen. Thomas Gage to Maj. Gen. Jeffery Amherst, 18 November 1759, and "Regimental Returns in Light of the New Establishment," 20 March 1761, WO 34/46A/61 and 34/88/106, TNA.

105. James Pitcher to the Earl of Loudoun, 5 August 1757, LO 4082, HEH; Col. Henry Bouquet to Maj. Gen. Jeffery Amherst, 24 June 1760, in *Bouquet Papers*, 4:604–605; Amherst to John Calcraft, 21 July 1761, WO 34/99/153, TNA.

106. Capt. Gavin Cochrane to Col. Henry Bouquet, 30 June 1761, in *Bouquet Papers*, 5:601; "Evidence of Lieutenant Daniel McAlpin," 11 May 1762, WO 71/48/292, TNA.

107. Lt. Gen. Jeffery Amherst to Col. Frederick Haldimand, 4 December 1762, WO 34/7/298, TNA; Brumwell, *Redcoats*, 130–32.

108. Col. Henry Bouquet to Maj. William Walters, 10 June 1761, in *Bouquet Papers*, 5:537; Lt. Gen. Jeffery Amherst to Brig. Gen. James Murray, 9 April 1762, WO/34/3/139, TNA.

109. Lord Egremont to Lt. Gen. Jeffery Amherst, 12 December 1761, AMSS U 1350/O41/3, CKS; *Amherst Journal*, 279–80 (entry of 19 February 1762); Lt. Cols. James Robertson and William Amherst to Amherst, 20 February 1762, WO 34/92/47, TNA.

110. Lt. Gen. Jeffery Amherst to Maj. Gen. Thomas Gage, 21 May 1762, and "Account of the Number of Recruits Enlisted," n.d., WO 34/7/94 and 34/92/108, TNA; "State of the Recruits Raised by the Several Provinces for the Regular Corps Serving in North America," [?] September 1762, AMSS, U 1350/O40/12A,CKS.

111. Lt. Gen. Jeffery Amherst to Maj. Gen. James Murray, 4 May 1763, WO 34/3/194, TNA; "Plan of the Establishment of the Sixtieth or Royal American Regiment of Foot," 18 May 1763, AMSS, U 1350/O43/9B, CKS; Bullion, "Ten Thousand in America," 646–57; Shy, *Toward Lexington*, 45–83, 118.

112. Lt. Gen. Jeffery Amherst to Maj. Gen. James Murray, 30 July 1763, WO 34/3/200, TNA; Gov. Guy Carleton to Maj. Gen. Thomas Gage, 20 July 1768, TGPAS, vol. 79, WLCL; "Account of Extraordinary Services," 6 March 1769, in Simmons and Thomas, *Proceedings and Debates*, 3:127.

113. Lt. Gen. Jeffery Amherst to Maj. John Wilkins, 29 October 29 1763, WO 34/23/156, TNA; Col. Henry Bouquet to Maj. Gen. Thomas Gage, 20 May 1764, in *Bouquet Papers*, 6:544; Maj. Gen. Thomas Gage to Lord Barrington, 21 December 1765, in *Gage Correspondence*, 2:330.

114. Lt. Gen. Jeffery Amherst to Charles Townshend, 27 January 1763, and Welbore Ellis to Amherst, 12 November 1763, WO 1/5/277 and 4/987/29, TNA.

115. Quotation from Western, *English Militia in the Eighteenth Century*, 298; Welbore Ellis to Philip Stephens, 26 April 1765, ADM 1/4327, TNA; Maj. Gen. Thomas Gage to Capt. Lt. Ralph Phillips, 12 October 1766, TGPAS, vol. 58, WLCL.

116. Wokeck, *Trade in Strangers*, 44–48; Fogleman, *Hopeful Journeys*, 28–32.

117. Quotation from the Enlistment Certificate of Johann Cristian Klepper, 14 August 1766, Fort Pitt Museum, FP2003.6.1, Pittsburgh; Lord Barrington to Maj. Gen. Thomas Gage, 25 June 1766, WO 4/988/59–60, TNA; Gage to Barrington, 15 January 1767, in *Gage Correspondence*, 2:403; Lt. Col. Augustine Prevost to Gage, 27 April 1771, TGPAS, vol. 102, WLCL; Brumwell, *Redcoats*, 133–35.

3. "CANADA BELONGS TO THE KING"

1. Quotation from Maj. Gen. Jeffery Amherst to Sir Joseph Yorke, 8 September 1760, WO 34/85/81, TNA; *Amherst Journal*, 244–48 (entries of 4–10 September 1760); Mante, *History of the Late War*, 300–343; s.v. "Amherst, Jeffery, 1st Baron Amherst," in *Dictionary of Canadian Biography*, 4:23–24.

2. Starkey, *European and Native American Warfare*, 133; Williams, *Redcoats along the Hudson*, 79–80; Johnson, *Militiamen, Rangers, and Redcoats*, 50; Smith, *Bouquet's Expedition against the Ohio Indians*, 1–35; *American National Biography*, s.v. "Bouquet, Henry."

3. Brig. Gen. Charles Lawrence to Maj. Gen. James Abercromby, 12 April 1758, AB 147, HEH; Brig. Gen. John Stanwix to Abercromby, 20 August 1758, and Brig. Gen. Robert Monckton to Maj. Gen. Jeffery Amherst, 9 July 1760, WO 34/45/10 and 34/43/70, TNA.

4. Wilson, "Warfare in the Old Regime," in Black, *European Warfare 1453–1815*, 88–94; Parker, *Military Revolution*, 16–24; 159–61; Childs, *Armies and Warfare in Europe*, 37, 105–108, 123–30.

5. Parker, *Military Revolution*, 45–81; Steele, *Warpaths*, 151–247; Brewer, *Sinews of Power*, 29–190; Duffy, *The Fortress*, 262–74; Childs, *Armies and Warfare in Europe*, 15–30; Houlding, *Fit for Service*, 293–96.

6. Quotation from Lamb, *Memoirs*, 62; "Length of the Barrel, Diameter of the Bore, and the Total Weight of Small Arms in the Year 1756," 4 September 1757, LO 6683, HEH.

7. "Minutes of a Regimental Court Martial," 29 July 1761, Add. MSS 21,682, 44, BL; Capt. Richard Mather to Col. Henry Bouquet, 23 August 1760, in *Bouquet Papers*, 4:699–700; "The Platoon Exercise," 18 April 1756, LO 1060B, HEH; Houlding, *Fit for Service*, 160, 259–64, 281; Darling, *Redcoat and Brown Bess*, 11.

8. Quotation from "Reflections on the General Principles of War," in *Annual Register* 9 (1766): 173; *Amherst Journal*, 273 (entries of 25 September–5 October 1761); Houlding, *Fit for Service*, 91–93.

9. Col. John Stanwix to the Earl of Loudoun, 9 May 1757, LO 3583, HEH; Nosworthy, *Anatomy of Victory*, 55–61; Houlding, *Fit for Service*, 284, 318–21; Hughes, *Firepower*, 10–11, 26–28.

10. Houlding, *Fit for Service*, 324; Duffy, *Military Experience in Age of Reason*, 144–47.

11. *Scots Magazine* 20 (1758): 246; Houlding, *Fit for Service*, 334–42; Bland, *Treatise of Military Discipline*, 101–31; Smith, *Universal Military Dictionary*, s.v. "Brigade."

12. "Extract from a Letter from Schenectady Camp," 2 July 1756, Add.

MSS 35,909, 263, BL; Knox, *Historical Journal*, 1:38–39 (entries of 24–31 July 1758); Houlding, *Fit for Service*, 293–96; Duffy, *The Fortress*, 1–148; Bland, *Treatise of Military Discipline*, 304–33.

13. "Clothing Delivered for the Royal American Regiment of Foot by Galfridus Mann," 4 May 1756, LO 1108A, HEH; "Memorandum from Orders and Advices," 14 May 1756, Loudoun Notebooks, vol. 10, p. 14, HM 1717, HEH; Rogers, *Whigs and Cities*, 184; Pargellis, *Lord Loudoun*, 68–70.

14. Capt. Archibald Kennedy to the Earl of Loudoun, 17 August 1756, and Col. John Stanwix to Loudoun, 27 August 1756, LO 1507 and 1594, HEH; *Gentleman's Magazine* 26 (1756): 388.

15. Quotation from "Extract from a Letter from Schenectady Camp," 2 July 1756, Add. MSS 35,909, 263, BL; Col. John Stanwix to the Earl of Loudoun, 30 August 1756, and Lt. Col. Henry Bouquet to Loudoun, 11 October 1756, LO 1628 and 1998, HEH; Loudoun to the Duke of Cumberland, 3 October 1756, in Pargellis, *Military Affairs*, 239; "General Orders of the Earl of Loudoun, 21 August 1756–30 November 1756" (entry of 22 October 1756), LO 1538, HEH.

16. Earl of Loudoun to Col. John Stanwix, 9 November 1756, and "A List of His Majesty's 62d or Royal American Regiment," n.d., LO 2184 and 6952, HEH; "Subsistence to the Royal American Regiment," n.d., WO 34/99/163, TNA.

17. Quotations: ("Raw men") Maj. John Young to the Earl of Loudoun, 2 September 1756, LO 1681, and ("to qualify them for the Service of the Woods") Loudoun to the Commanding Officers of the 62d or Royal American Regiment, 28 December 1756, LO 2421, HEH; "Short Exercise Proposed for the Use of the Four Battalions till Further Orders," n.d., and Loudoun to Col. James Prevost, 20 March 1757, LO 2445 and 3108, HEH; Loudoun to the Duke of Cumberland, 6 January 1757, in Pargellis, *Military Affairs*, 291–92.

18. Anderson, *Crucible of War*, 166–67, 181; Jennings, *Empire of Fortune*, 298–305; Leach, *Roots of Conflict*, 87–98; Pargellis, *Lord Loudoun*, 186–210.

19. Quotation from "Memorandum," 25 February 1757, in *Bouquet Papers*, 1:50; Earl of Loudoun to Lt. Gov. Horatio Sharpe, 28 October 1756, LO 2097, HEH; Loudoun to the Duke of Cumberland, 25 April–3 June 1757, in Pargellis, *Military Affairs*, 343–45, 348–49; Cuthbertson, *Management and Oeconomy of a Battalion*, 23–25.

20. Quotation from Col. James Prevost to the Earl of Loudoun, 23 April 1757, LO 3438, HEH; "Memorandum Regarding Barracks to Be Built at Charleston," 21 July 1757, in *Bouquet Papers*, 1:150; "Troops under Lord Loudoun's Immediate Command," 24 July 1757, WO 1/1/102, TNA.

21. Brig. Gen. James Wolfe to Lord George Sackville, 24 May 1758, in Willson, *Life and Letters of James Wolfe*, 368–69; "Intelligence from Cape Breton," 28 June 1757, in *NYCD*, 10:572–73; Mante, *History of the Late War*, 100–101; *Conduct of a Noble Commander*, 38–41.

22. "General Orders for the Army, 7 May 1757–19 October 1757," n.p. (entries of 7–10 July 1757), LO 3576, HEH; *Gentleman's Magazine* 28 (1758): 169–70.

23. Quotation from Knox, *Historical Journal*, 1:38 (entry of 24 July 1757); "A Return of the Service, Size, Age, and Country of Commissioned, Non-Commissioned Officers and Private Soldiers of the Second Battalion of His Majesty's Royal American Regiment," 1 July 1757, and "Return of the Service, Size, Age & Country of the Commissioned, Non-Commissioned, Officers & Private Soldiers of the 4th Battalion Royal Americans," 3 July 1757, LO 1345 and 4068, HEH.

24. Quotation from "Extracts of Letters from a General Officer in North America to a Friend in London," 28 July 1756, ChP, PRO 30/8/95/121, TNA; Earl of Loudoun to the Duke of Cumberland, 3 October 1756 and 5 January 1757, in Pargellis, *Military Affairs*, 242–43, 292. For a discussion of the decrepit state of British regulars on the Irish Establishment, see Guy, "Irish Military Establishment," in Bartlett and Jeffrey, *Military History of Ireland*, 211–30; Thomas Bartlett, "Army and Society in Eighteenth-Century Ireland," in Maguire, *Kings in Conflict*, 173–85.

25. Quotation from Col. John Stanwix to the Earl of Loudoun, 9 May 1757, LO 3583, HEH; Thomas Penn to Lt. Col. John Armstrong, 7 December 1756, Thomas Penn Letterbooks, vol. 5, p. 39, HSP; "The Petition of the Merchants, Traders, Planters and Others Interested in the Trade & Prosperity of South Carolina & Georgia," 21 December 1756, William H. Lyttelton Papers, vol. 3, WLCL; William Pitt to Loudoun, 4 February 1757, WO 34/71/108, TNA; Houlding, *Fit for Service*, 269–70.

26. *South Carolina Gazette*, 23 June 1757, 2; Lt. Col. Henry Bouquet to Gov. Henry Ellis, 17 September and 12 November 1757, and "Representation of Field Officers Regarding Troops," 2 December 1757, in *Bouquet Papers*, 1:201, 238, 248–50; Greene, "South Carolina Quartering Dispute," 193–204.

27. Lt. Col. Henry Bouquet to Gov. William H. Lyttelton, 20 July 1757, and Bouquet to the Earl of Loudoun, 16 October 1757, in *Bouquet Papers*, 1:147, 217–18; Capt. George Mercer to Col. George Washington, 17 August 1757, in *Washington Papers*, 4:372; *Boston Weekly Advertiser*, 23 January 1758, 2.

28. Earl of Loudoun to the Duke of Cumberland, 23 April 1757, in Pargellis, *Military Affairs*, 344; Col. John Stanwix to Loudoun, 10 September 1757, LO 4446, HEH; Stotz, *Outposts of the War for Empire*, 108–109.

29. Quotation from Brig. Gen. John Stanwix to Maj. Gen. James Abercromby, 20 August 1758, WO 34/45/10, TNA; Stanwix to Lt. Gov. William Denny, 18 July 1757, SGM, case 4, box 8, "Colonial Wars," HSP; Stanwix to Richard Peters and Stanwix to Lt. Gov. William Denny, 25 July 1757, in Hazard, *Pennsylvania Archives*, 1st ser., 3 (1853): 239, 241; Ward, "Fighting the 'Old Women,'" 306–308.

30. Brig. Gen. Charles Lawrence to Maj. Gen. James Abercromby, 12 April 1758, AB, 147, HEH; "Memorandum," 15 March 1757, Loudoun Notebooks, vol. 2, p. 42, HM 1717, HEH; Wallace, *Regimental Chronicle*, 68.

31. Earl of Loudoun to the Duke of Cumberland, 4 October 1756, in Pargellis, *Military Affairs*, 239; Loudoun to William Pitt, 10 March 1757, in *Pitt Correspondence*, 1:18; "A Return of the Service, Size, Age, and Country of the Commission'd, Non-Commission'd Officers, and Private Soldiers of

His Majesty's 35th Regimt., the 3rd Battalion of the 60th Regiment, and Four Independent Companies," 15 July 1757, LO 6616, HEH.

32. "Extract from a Letter from Schenectady Camp," 2 July 1756, Add. MSS 35,909, 260, BL; Earl of Loudoun to the Duke of Cumberland, 3 October 1756, and Loudoun to Maj. Gen. Daniel Webb, 20 June 1757, in Pargellis, *Military Affairs*, 242, 370–71; Steele, *Betrayals*, 75–77; Middleton, *Bells of Victory*, 1–10.

33. William Pitt to the Earl of Loudoun, 17 March 1757, LO 3076, HEH; Bougainville, *Adventure in the Wilderness*, 118–54 (entries of 26 June–29 July 1757); Maj. Gen. Daniel Webb to Loudoun, 5 August 1757, CO 5/48/304, TNA; Anderson, *Crucible of War*, 169–79; Steele, *Betrayals*, 78–96; Pargellis, *Lord Loudoun*, 228–32.

34. Lt. Col. Ralph Burton to the Earl of Loudoun, 27 August 1756, CO 5/47/325, TNA; Ford, *General Orders of 1757*, 33, 42, 48 (entries of 28 June, 9 July, and 21 July 1757); Starbuck, *Great Warpath*, 76–77.

35. Ford, *General Orders of 1757*, 54 (entry of 24 July 1757); "Journals of Col. James Montresor," NYHS, *Collections for 1881* 14 (1882): 22–25 (entries of 24 July–2 August 1757); Maj. Gen. Daniel Webb to the Earl of Loudoun, 5 August 1757, CO 5/48/304, TNA. The drafting of the most experienced soldiers is suggested by contemporary muster rolls that note only a few men from each company were casualties or under capitulation following the siege. "Return of the Officers to the Detachments from Several Corps, Who Are Included [in] the Capitulation Articles of Fort William Henry," 9 August 1757, LO 4170, HEH; "Returns of the 3rd Battalion, Royal American Regiment of Foot," 24 October 1757, WO 12/6998/2–7, TNA.

36. Maj. Gen. Daniel Webb to the Earl of Loudoun, 11 August 1757, CO 5/48/312, TNA; Capt. Louis-Antoine de Bougainville to Marquis de Paulmy, 19 August 1757, in *NYCD*, 10:611–14; Steele, *Betrayals*, 93–110.

37. Lt. Col. John Young to Lt. Col. George Munro, 4 August 1757, and Marquis de Montcalm to the Earl of Loudoun, 9 August 1757, LO 4056 and 4182, HEH; Ford, *General Orders of 1757*, 66 (entry of 12 August 1757); *Pennsylvania Gazette*, 18 August 1757, 3; Maj. Gen. James Abercromby to [?], 25 June 1758, WO 34/76/144, TNA.

38. "Extract from a Letter from Schenectady Camp," 2 July 1756, Add. MSS 35,909, 263, BL; Duke of Cumberland to the Earl of Loudoun, 2 December 1756, in Pargellis, *Military Affairs*, 255–56; "Evidence of Henry Garman," 9 July 1757, WO 71/65/336–37, TNA; Brumwell, *Redcoats*, 215–17; Steele, *Betrayals*, 84–88; Pargellis, *Lord Loudoun*, 94–102, 300–304.

39. "Memorial of Volunteers in the Ranger Service," n.d., LO 5172, HEH; Brumwell, *Redcoats*, 211–14; Loescher, *History of Rogers Rangers*, 1:184–93; Rogers, *Journals of Major Robert Rogers*, 55–71.

40. Lt. Col. Thomas Gage to the Earl of Loudoun, n.d., WO 34/46A/1, TNA; Loudoun to William Pitt, 14 February 1758, in *Pitt Correspondence*, 1:191; Brumwell, *Redcoats*, 228–29; s.v. "Gage, Thomas," in *Dictionary of Canadian Biography*, 4:278–81.

41. Capt. George Scott to the Earl of Loudoun, 13 February 1758, LO 6927, HEH; Maj. Gen. Jeffery Amherst to Pitt, 11 June 1758, in *Pitt Correspon-*

dence, 1:273; Stephen E. Patterson, "Colonial Wars and Aboriginal Peoples, 1744–1763," in Buckner and Reid, *Atlantic Region to Confederation*, 125–49; s.v. "Scott, George," in *Dictionary of Canadian Biography*, 3:589–90.

42. William Pitt to the Earl of Loudoun, 30 December 1757, in *Pitt Correspondence*, 1:133–34; Daniel J. Beattie, "The Adaptation of the British Army to Wilderness Warfare," in Ultee, *Adapting to Conditions*, 56–74; Middleton, *Bells of Victory*, 15–51; Pargellis, *Lord Loudoun*, 279–306, 337–47.

43. Quotation from William Pitt to Maj. Gen. James Abercromby, 30 December 1757, in *Pitt Correspondence*, 1:143; Brig. Gen John Forbes to Col. Henry Bouquet, 14 February 1758, in *Bouquet Papers*, 1:301; Knox, *Historical Journal*, 1:162–66 (entry of 30 April 1758); Anderson, *Crucible of War*, 232–36; Pargellis, *Lord Loudoun*, 356–58.

44. Quotation from Col. Henry Bouquet to Maj. Gen. Jeffery Amherst, 13 March 1759, in *Bouquet Papers*, 3:194; Maj. Gen. James Abercromby to Brig. Gen. John Stanwix, 15 March 1758, AB 41, HEH; Brig. Gen. John Forbes to William Pitt, 1 May 1758, in *Pitt Correspondence*, 1:237; "Distribution of Troops to Penetrate into Canada," n.d., and "Distribution of Troops for Fort Du Quesne," n.d., CO 5/50/49, 51, TNA; Stanwix to Abercromby, 20 August 1758, and Stanwix to Amherst, 7 January 1759, WO 34/45/10, 34, TNA.

45. "Return of the Present State of His Majesty's Forces under the Immediate Command of His Excellency Major-General Abercrombie at Lake George," 26 June 1758, WO 34/76/145, TNA; Richard Huck to Brig. Gen. John Forbes, 9 July 1758, HQJF, item 359, TWML; Mante, *History of the Late War*, 144–45.

46. Capt. W[illiam] Forbes to Brig. Gen. John Forbes, 16 July 1758, item 378, HQJF, TWML; "Extract of a Letter from Saratoga," *Boston Weekly Advertiser*, 24 July 1758, 3; "Journal of What Has Happened in the Army from the 5th of July to This Day," 19 August 1758, ChP, PRO 30/8/96, TNA; Cardwell, "Mismanagement," 248–66.

47. Quotation from "Journal of What Has Happened in the Army from the 5th of July to This Day," 19 August 1758, ChP, PRO 30/8/98, TNA; Bougainville, *Adventure in the Wilderness*, 221–31 (entries of 30 June–8 July 1758); Maj. Gen. James Abercromby to Maj. Gen. Jeffery Amherst, 10 July 1758, AMSS; U 1350/O32/1, CKS; Richard Huck to Brig. Gen. John Forbes, 2 August 1758, HQJF, item 437, TWML.

48. Maj. Gen. James Abercromby to William Pitt, 12 July 1758, in *Pitt Correspondence*, 1:300; *Boston Weekly Advertiser*, 24 July 1758, 3; *Pennsylvania Gazette*, 3 August 1758, 1; Knox, *Historical Journal*, 1:191 (entry of 20 August 1758).

49. Maj. Gen. James Abercromby to Maj. Gen. Jeffery Amherst, 10 July 1758, AMSS, U 1350/O32/1, CKS; Maj. William Eyre to Robert Napier, 10 July 1758, in Pargellis, *Military Affairs*, 420. A sketch of the British battle line by John Bremner made shortly after the action indicates the precise positions of the various regiments; see John Bremner's Diary and Memorandum Book, 1756–64, p. 47, NYHS.

50. Quotation from "A Particular Account of the Action at Ticonderoga," in *Scots Magazine* 20 (1758): 698–99; *Hervey Journals*, 50 (entry of

8 July 1758); Maj. Gen. James Abercromby to Lord Barrington, 12 July 1758, AB 437, HEH; *Pennsylvania Gazette*, 3 August 1758, 1.

51. Bougainville, *Adventure in the Wilderness*, 232–34 (entry of 8 July 1758); Maj. Gen. James Abercromby to William Pitt, 12 July 1758, in *Pitt Correspondence*, 1:300; Richard Huck to Brig. Gen. John Forbes, 2 August 1758, HQJF, item 437, TWML; Capt. Walter Rutherfurd to the Earl of Loudoun, n.d., in Rutherfurd, *Family Records and Events*, 95.

52. "Return of the Present State of His Majesty's Forces under the Immediate Command of His Excellency Major General Abercrombie at Lake George," 26 June 1758, WO 34/76/145, TNA; *Boston Weekly Advertiser*, 24 July 1758, 3.

53. Lt. Gov. Horatio Sharpe to William Sharpe, 27 August 1757, in Browne, *Archives of Maryland* 9 (1890): 253; William Cotterell to the Earl of Loudoun, 20 September 1758, LO 5927, HEH; *Gentleman's Magazine* 28 (1758): 446.

54. Quotation from Maj. William Eyre to Robert Napier, 10 July 1758, in Pargellis, *Military Affairs*, 420; Pouchot, *Memoirs*, 146 (entry of 8 July 1758); Bougainville, *Adventure in the Wilderness*, 232–34 (entry of 8 July 1758); Maj. Gen. James Abercromby to Lord Barrington, 12 July 1758, AB 437, HEH.

55. Maj. Gen. James Abercromby to William Pitt, 12 July and 19 August 1758, in *Pitt Correspondence*, 1:300–301, 327; Ray, "Journal of Dr. Caleb Rea," 177 (entry of 3 August 1758).

56. Maj. Gen. James Abercromby to Col. James Prevost, 4 August 1758, AB 947, HEH; "MOB," 12:458–61 (entries of 4–7 August 1758); Brig. Gen. James Wolfe to Lt. Gen. Edward Wolfe, 7 August 1758, in Willson, *Life and Letters of James Wolfe*, 393.

57. Brig. Gen. John Forbes to Col. Henry Bouquet, 2 August 1758, in *Bouquet Papers*, 2:303–304; Forbes to Maj. Gen. James Abercromby, 3 August 1758, in *Forbes Papers*, 168; Lt. Gov. Horatio Sharpe to Lord Baltimore, 27 August 1757, in Browne, *Archives of Maryland* 9 (1890): 256; s.v. "Forbes, John," in *Dictionary of Canadian Biography*, 3:218–19.

58. Brig. Gen. John Forbes to William Pitt, 17 June 1758, in *Pitt Correspondence*, 1:280; Col. Henry Bouquet to Forbes, 8 August 1758, in *Bouquet Papers*, 2:337; "Barton Journal," 449–50 (entry of 12 August 1758); Russell, "Redcoats in the Wilderness," 641, 646.

59. "Barton Journal," 471 (entry of 11 September 1758); Col. Henry Bouquet to Brig. Gen. John Forbes, 17 September 1758, in *Bouquet Papers*, 2:517–18.

60. Maj. James Grant to Brig. Gen. John Forbes, n.d., and "An Inventory, of ye Officers & Soldiers Effects, That Are Missing Since ye Last Engagement, at Fort Du Quesne," 20 September 1758, in *Bouquet Papers*, 2:499–503, 531–32; Col. George Washington to Lt. Gov. Francis Fauquier, 28 September 1758, in *Washington Papers*, 6:52; *Maryland Gazette*, 5 October 1758, 2; Nelson, *General James Grant*, 21–23.

61. Col. Henry Bouquet to Brig. Gen. John Forbes, 17 September 1758, in *Bouquet Papers*, 2:519; "A List of the Officers and Soldiers Killed and

Missing in the Action near Fort du Quesne," 4 September 1758, WO 34/44/181, TNA; *Pennsylvania Gazette*, 12 October 1758, 2; *Boston Weekly Advertiser*, 30 October 1758, 1.

62. Quotation from "A Letter from an Officer Who Attended Brigadier Gen. Forbes," in *Gentleman's Magazine* 9 (1759): 174; Brig. Gen. John Forbes to Maj. Gens. James Abercromby and Jeffery Amherst, 26 November 1758, in *Forbes Papers*, 262; McConnell, *Country Between*, 113–41; White, *Middle Ground*, 240–56; Stotz, *Outposts of the War for Empire*, 127–36.

63. Quotation from Capt. John Joseph Schlosser to Col. Henry Bouquet, 19 April 1760, in *Bouquet Papers*, 4:523; Brig. Gen. John Stanwix to Maj. Gen. Jeffery Amherst, 7 January 1759, and Amherst to Stanwix, 5 April 1759, WO 34/45/34 and 34/45/210, TNA; Amherst to William Pitt, 19 June 1759, in *Pitt Correspondence*, 2:125.

64. Earl of Loudoun to the Earl of Holderness, 5 August 1757, LO 4073B, HEH; Baker, *Campaign of Amateurs*, 5–53; McNeill, *Atlantic Empires of France and Spain*, 81–85, 95.

65. Quotation from George William Fairfax to Col. George Washington, 25 July 1758, in *Washington Papers*, 5:328; *Pennsylvania Gazette*, 27 July 1758, 3; Fregault, *Canada*, 215–18; Mante, *History of the Late War*, 113–14.

66. Maj. Gen. Jeffery Amherst to William Pitt, 11 June 1758, in *Pitt Correspondence*, 1:273; Capt. [George] Fletcher to [?], 22–29 June 1758, HQJF, item 324, TWML; *Pennsylvania Gazette*, 29 June 1758, 2; "Orders before Landing at Louisbourg, 1758," n.d., AMSS, U 1350/O30/1, CKS; Hitsman and Bond, "Assault Landing at Louisbourg," 323–27.

67. Quotation from "Extract of the Proceedings of the Navy and Army upon the Expedition against Louisbourg," in *Boston Weekly Advertiser*, 3 July 1758, 2; Gordon, "Journal of the Siege of Louisbourg," 129–31 (entry of 8 June 1758); [?] to [?], 23 June 1758, WO 34/11/168, TNA; *Pennsylvania Journal & Weekly Advertiser*, 7 September 1758, 2; Brumwell, *Redcoats*, 240–41.

68. "Orders before Landing at Louisbourg, 1758," n.d., AMSS, U 1350/O30/1, CKS; *Amherst Journal*, 51–69 (entries of 9 June–22 July 1758); Webster, *Journal of William Amherst*, 14–30 (entries of 9 June–22 July 1758); Fry, "An Appearance of Strength," 1:148–50. Capt. Lt. Samuel Holland's detailed map of the British operations indicates that the redcoats advanced overland without the benefit of protective approaches; see "Plan of Louisbourg, The Harbour, Part of the Coast with the French Entrenchments along the Same and the Attack of the British Troops under the Command of Major General Amherst." n.d., National Map Collection, 109811, H3/249/Louisbourg 1758, LAC.

69. Knox, *Historical Journal*, 1:220 (entry of 9 June 1758); Sumner, "Standing Orders for the Army," 196–99; Bland, *Treatise of Military Discipline*, 245–62; s.v. "Drum," in Simes, *Military Medley*.

70. Gordon, "Journal of the Siege of Louisbourg," 119; "Journals of Capt. John Montresor," NYHS, *Collections for 1881* 14 (1882): 159–65 (entries of 9 June–3 July 1758); Knox, *Historical Journal*, 1:224, 236–37 (entries of 12 June, and 2 July 1758); Anderson, *People's Army*, 80; Duffy, *Fire and Stone*, 91, 104; Bland, *Treatise of Military Discipline*, 307–309.

71. Webster, *Journal of William Amherst*, 19-20 (entries of 27-30 June 1758); "Journals of Capt. John Montresor," NYHS, *Collections for 1881* 14 (1882): 162-65 (entries of 21 June-1 July 1758); Knox, *Historical Journal*, 1:225-26 (entries of 12-13 June 1758); s.v. "Siege," in Smith, *Universal Military Dictionary*, 233.

72. Webster, *Journal of William Amherst*, 28-29 (entries of 17-19 July 1758); "Journals of Capt. John Montresor," NYHS, *Collections for 1881* 14 (1882): 169-71 (entries of 15-22 July 1758); Duffy, *Fire and Stone*, 107-23; Vauban, *Siegecraft and Fortification*, 58-60; Williamson, *Treatise on Military Finance*, 61-63.

73. Webster, *Journal of William Amherst*, 30-32 (entries of 22-26 July 1758); Gordon, "Journal of the Siege of Louisbourg," 147-48 (entries of 22-26 July 1758); "Journals of Capt. John Montresor," NYHS, *Collections for 1881* 14 (1882): 170-72 (entries of 22-26 July 1758); Knox, *Historical Journal*, 1:249-50 (entries of 22-23 July 1758).

74. *Gentleman's Magazine* 28 (1758): 389; "Letters from a French Officer," in Knox, *Historical Journal*, 3:112-14; Mante, *History of the Late War*, 140; s.v. "Boschenry de Drucour, Augustin de," in *Dictionary of Canadian Biography*, 3:73.

75. Capt. James Cuninghame to the [Earl of Loudoun?], 30 May 1758, in McLennan, *Louisbourg*, 239; *Boston Weekly Advertiser*, 3 July 1758, 2; *Pennsylvania Gazette*, 13 July 1758, 3; "Distribution of Troops for the Siege of Louisbourg," n.d., and "Return of the Killed & Wounded in the Several Regiments on the Island of Cape Breton from June 8 to July 26, 1758," 27 July 1758, CO 5/50/50 and 5/53/143, TNA; Wallace, *Regimental Chronicle*, 66.

76. Webster, *Journal of William Amherst*, 15-16, 27-28 (entries of 18 June, and 16 July 1758); Andrew Oliver to William Pitt, 14 August 1758, in *Pitt Correspondence*, 1:315-16; "A Journal," n.d., in *Northcliffe Collection*, 70; Dickason, *Louisbourg and the Indians*, 64-108.

77. Maj. Gen. Jeffery Amherst to Brig. Gen. Robert Monckton, 25 August 1758, CO 5/53/170-71, TNA; Capt. James Abercrombie to the Earl of Loudoun, 17 December 1758, LO 5977, HEH.

78. "Report of the Proceeding of the Troops on the Expedition up the St. Johns River in the Bay of Fundy under the Command of Colonel Monckton," n.d., and "Return of the Forces Under the Command of the Honble: Colo. Robt. Monckton," 24 September 1758, WO 34/43/1-8, 19, TNA; Knox, *Historical Journal*, 1:268-69 (entry of 6 October 1758); Brig. Gen. Robert Monckton to Maj. Gen. James Abercromby, 12 November 1758, CO 5/54/57-62, TNA; Raymond, "Brigadier General Monckton's Expedition," 113-65.

79. Gordon, "Journal of the Siege of Louisbourg," 152 (entry of 30 August 1758); William Pitt to Maj. Gen. Jeffery Amherst, 9 September and 27 December 1758, in *Pitt Correspondence*, 1:346, 432-41; John Calcraft to the Earl of Loudoun, 14 September 1758, LO 5921, HEH; Brig. Gen. John Stanwix to Amherst, 13 May 1759, WO 34/45/63, TNA.

80. *Maryland Gazette*, 20 July 1758, 3; Knox, *Historical Journal*, 1:285-86, 352-53 (entries of 12 December 1758, and 31 May 1759); Maj. John Tulleken to Col. Henry Bouquet, 5 March 1759, in *Bouquet Papers*, 3:177; Brig.

Gen. Edward Whitmore to Maj. Gen. Jeffery Amherst, 20 April 1759, WO 34/17/10, TNA.

81. Maj. Gen. Jeffery Amherst to Sir John Ligonier, 18 January 1759, AMSS, U 1350/O35/5, CKS; Maj. John Tulleken to Col. Henry Bouquet, 22 February 1759, and Capt. Gavin Cochrane to Bouquet, 10 March 1759, in *Bouquet Papers*, 3:140, 183–84; "Orderly Book Kept by Lieut. Joseph Bull, 1st New York Regiment, 25 May 1759–1 November 1759," 27 (entry of 14 June 1759), HM 687, HEH; Knox, *Historical Journal*, 1:400 (entry of 5 July 1759); Frederick the Great, *Military Instructions*, 65; Brumwell, *Redcoats*, 229–31.

82. Quotation from Peter Burroughs, "An Unreformed Army? 1815–1863," in Chandler and Beckett, *Illustrated History of the British Army*, 180; Knox, *Historical Journal*, 1:487 (entry of 9 July 1759); Webster, *Journal of William Amherst*, 40–42 (entry of 10 July 1759); "Ordres du G. Amherst pr. la revue," 3 August 1760, Add. MSS 21,661, 80, BL; Houlding, *Fit for Service*, 370–73; Kopperman, *Braddock at the Monongahela*, 51–71; Russell, *Great War with Russia*, 147.

83. Quotation from Robert Leake to Christopher Gist, 5 August 1759, in *Bouquet Papers*, 3:497; Richard Huck to the Earl of Loudoun, 17 April 1759, LO 6091, HEH; Maj. Gen. James Wolfe to William Pitt, 2 September 1759, in *Pitt Correspondence*, 2:149–58; Fregault, *Canada*, 246–52. Five hundred men from Monckton's and Lawrence's battalions remained in the Halifax garrison during the 1759 campaign. "Garrisons and Winter Quarters of His Majesty's Forces in North America," 15 December 1759, WO 1/1/355, TNA.

84. "Journal of the Voyage to America and the Campaign against Quebec, 1759," in Doughty and Parmelee, *Siege of Quebec*, 5:254 (entry of 31 July 1759); *Boston Post-Boy & Advertiser*, 10 September 1759, 3; Stacey, *Quebec, 1759*, 65–75.

85. "Journal of Major Moncrief," in Doughty and Parmelee, *Siege of Quebec*, 5:41–43 (entry of 31 July 1759); "Return of the Killed, Wounded, & Missing in the River St. Lawrence," 2 September 1759, CO 5/51/86, TNA; Lt. James Grant to Col. Henry Bouquet, 15 September 1759, in *Bouquet Papers*, 4:96; *Boston Post-Boy & Advertiser*, 17 September 1759, 2; Mante, *History of the Late War*, 243–48.

86. "Narrative of the Siege of Quebec, Published by the French," in *NYCD*, 10:999 (entry of 21 July 1759); "Extracts from Journal of the Particular Transactions during the Siege of Quebec" (entry of 21 July 1759) and "Letter of James Gibson" (entry of 22 July 1759), in Doughty and Parmelee, *Siege of Quebec*, 5:65, 173; Gouin and Brault, *Les Panet de Québec*, 197 (entry of 21 July 1759); "Return of the Killed, Wounded, & Missing in the River St. Lawrence," 2 September 1759, CO 5/51/86, TNA.

87. "Extracts from Journal of the Particular Transactions during the Siege of Quebec," in Doughty and Parmelee, *Siege of Quebec*, 5:177–82 (entries of 8–18 August 1759); "A Private Journal of the Siege of Quebec, 1759," by Edward Coats (entries of 7–21 August 1759), MG 18-N46, LAC; *Pennsylvania Gazette*, 18 October 1759, 2.

88. "Genuine Letters from a Volunteer in the British Service at Quebec," in Doughty and Parmelee, *Siege of Quebec*, 5:17 (entry of 4 July 1759); Wolfe, *Instructions to Young Officers*, 105–106.

89. Quotation from "Memoirs of the Siege of Quebec and Total Reduction of Canada in 1759 and 1760 by John Johnson Clerk and Quarter Mas'r Sergeant to the 58th Reg't," in Doughty and Parmelee, Siege of Quebec, 5:97; "A Journal of the Expedition Up the River St. Lawrence by the Sergeant-Major of Gen. Hopson's Grenadiers," ibid., 5:2 (entry of 8 July 1759); "Journal of the Voyage to America and the Campaign against Quebec, 1759," ibid., 5:242-45 (entry of 8 July 1759); Knox, Historical Journal, 2:38-40 (entry of 18 August 1759).

90. Quotation from Maj. Gen. James Wolfe to William Pitt, 2 September 1759, in Pitt Correspondence, 2:158; "Journal of Major Moncrief," in Doughty and Parmelee, Siege of Quebec, 5:48-52 (entries of 10-13 September 1759); Knox, Historical Journal, 2:94-98 (entry of 13 September 1759); "Return of the Strength of the Army the 13th of September 1759 at the Battle of Quebec," n.d., WO 34/43/32, TNA; Lt. Daniel McAlpin to Maj. Gen. Thomas Gage, n.d., WO 1/7/27, TNA; Stacey, Quebec, 1759, 102-11.

91. "Journal of Major Moncrief," in Doughty and Parmelee, Siege of Quebec, 5:52-53 (entry of 13 September 1759); "Journal of Malcolm Fraser," in Wrong, Canadian Manor, 256-59 (entry of 13 September 1759); Brig. Gen. George Townshend to William Pitt, 20 September 1759, in Pitt Correspondence, 2:166-67; "Return of the Strength of the Army the 13th of September 1759 at the Battle of Quebec," n.d., WO 34/43/32, TNA; "An Account of the Action Which Happened near Quebec, 13th September 1759," in Pargellis, Military Affairs, 438. A contemporary sketch of this battle in the Haldimand Collection highlights the second battalion's activities; see "Plan of Battle Concerning the Different Forces Engaged at Quebec, 1759," n.d., Add. MSS 21,686, 81, BL.

92. Quotation from Brig. Gen. James Murray to Maj. Gen. Jeffery Amherst, 30 April 1760, CO 5/58/192, TNA; "Journal of Major Moncrief," in Doughty and Parmelee, Siege of Quebec, 5:54-55 (entries of 14-18 September 1759); Murray to William Pitt, 25 May 1760, in Pitt Correspondence, 2:292; "The Present Situation of the Town of Quebec with a Description of it and its Environs," n.d., in "Journals of Capt. John Montresor," NYHS, Collections for 1881 14 (1882): 234-35; Eccles, France in America, 203-204; Fregault, Canada, 254-56; s.v., "Ramezay, Jean-Baptiste-Nicolas-Roch De," in Dictionary of Canadian Biography, 4:651-52.

93. Quotation from Bougainville, Adventure in the Wilderness, 321 (entry of 18 September 1759); Brig. Gen. George Townshend to William Pitt, 20 September 1759, in Pitt Correspondence, 2:168; Knox, Historical Journal, 2:246 (entry of 29 October 1759).

94. Amherst Journal, 142-64 (entries of 22 July-3 September 1759); Col. Francois-Charles de Bourlamaque to Marshal Fouquet de Belle-Isle, 1 November 1759, in NYCD, 10:1055; Beattie, "General Jeffery Amherst," 137-59; "Lord Adam Gordon's Journal," 443-44.

95. Maj. Gen. Jeffery Amherst to Brig. Gen. John Prideaux, 17 May 1759, WO 34/46B/137, TNA; "Plan of Oswego with a Projected Fort for to Contain 500 Men," 17 June 1759, CO 5/55/239, TNA; Maj. James Grant to Col. Henry Bouquet, 18 July 1759, in Bouquet Papers, 3:423; Dunnigan, Siege—1759, 24-30.

96. Pouchot, *Memoirs*, 190–229 (entries of 6–25 July 1759); Capt. [James] De Lancey to Lt. Gov. James De Lancey, 25 July 1759, in *NYCD*, 7:402–403; Dunnigan, *Siege—1759*, 39–84.

97. "Haldimand: Orders to Several Posts," 5 July 1759, in *Bouquet Papers*, 3:392; *Pennsylvania Gazette*, 26 July 1759, 2; "Relation de la Campagne de M. le Chevalier De la Corne À Chougen," in Casgrain, *Collections des mansucrits du Maréchal de Lévis*, 11:215–18; MacLeod, *Canadian Iroquois*, 133–36.

98. Quotation from "Camp at Lake Ontario," in *Pennsylvania Gazette*, 2 August 1759, 2; "General Return of the Fourth Battalion Royal Americans and Second Battalion New York Regiment," 6 July 1759, Add. MSS 2,1687, 9, BL; Maj. James Grant to Col. Henry Bouquet, 18 July 1759, in *Bouquet Papers*, 3:423; *Amherst Journal*, 207 (entry of 6 June 1760).

99. Quotation from Knox, *Historical Journal*, 2:352 (entry of 1 March 1760); Murray, *Governor Murray's Journal*, 13–26 (entries of 3 December 1759–26 April 1760); Brig. Gen. James Murray to Maj. Gen. Jeffery Amherst, 25 January 1760, Add. MSS 32,902, 170–71, BL; "Journal of Happenings at Quebec by an Officer of the Royal Americans," in Pargellis, *Military Affairs*, 440–43; Charbonneau et al., *Québec the Fortified City*, 59–61, 151–53.

100. Murray, *Governor Murray's Journal*, 26–27 (entry of 28 April 1760); Brig. Gen. James Murray to Maj. Gen. Jeffery Amherst, 30 April 1760, CO 5/58/192–93, TNA.

101. Knox, *Historical Journal*, 2:390–96 (entry of 28 April 1760); Joseph Fournerie de Vezon, "*Eventments de la Guerre en Canada depuis Le 13 7bre 1759 Jusqu' au 14 Juillet 1760*," in *Rapport de L'Archiviste de la Province de Quebec, pour 1938–1939*, 6–7 (entry of 28 April 1760); "Return of the Non Comd. Officers, Rank and File Killed, Wounded &c.," 30 April 1760, CO 5/58/196, TNA; "Letter from an Officer of the Royal American Regiment," 24 May 1760, in *Gentleman's Magazine* 30 (1760): 314; Brumwell, *Redcoats*, 255–61; Mahon, *Life of James Murray*, 219–36.

102. "Return of the Non Comd. Officers, Rank and File Killed, Wounded &c.," 30 April 1760, CO 5/64/18, TNA; Knox, *Historical Journal*, 2:450–53, 463 (entries of 28 April–22 May, and 2 July 1760); Anderson, *Crucible of War*, 397–401; Beatson, *Naval and Military Memoirs*, 3:263–64.

103. *Amherst Journal*, 227–34 (entries of 10–18 August 1760) Pouchot, *Memoirs*, 302–303 (entry of 18 August 1760); *Gentleman's Magazine* 30 (1760): 459–60; MacLeod, "Fight at the West Gate," 172–85.

104. *Amherst Journal*, 234–40 (entries of 19–26 August 1760); Pouchot, *Memoirs*, 303–15 (entries of 19–26 August 1760); "Return of the Killed & Wounded in the Army from the 16th to the 25th August Inclusive, 1760," n.d., WO 34/85/59, TNA; MacLeod, "Fight at the West Gate," 187–90.

105. William Pitt to Maj. Gen. Jeffery Amherst, 7 January 1761, in *Pitt Correspondence*, 2:384–86; Anderson, *Crucible of War*, 308–14, 490; Smelser, *Campaign for the Sugar Islands*, 13–154; Wallace, *Regimental Chronicle*, 66.

106. Quotation from *Amherst Journal*, 273 (entry of 29 September 1761); "General Return of the Troops Ordered on the Expedition under the

Command of His Excellency Major-General Monckton," 27 November 1761, CO 5/61/162, TNA.

107. Quotation from "Extract of Two Letters from an Officer at Martinique, to a Gentleman in This Town," in *Boston Post-Boy & Advertiser*, 12 April 1762, 2; "Return of the Killed, Wounded, and Missing of the Army under the Command of His Excellency Major-General Robt: Monckton &c. at the Attack of the Enemy's Redoubts, Intrenchments & Breastworks between Casca Naviere & Morne Tartenson," 24 January 1762, and Maj. Gen. Robert Monckton to Lt. Gen. Jeffery Amherst, 11 February 1762, WO 34/55/53, 58, TNA.

108. Quotation from "Journal of Lieutenant John Grant, 42nd Foot, 1758–1762," p. 77, Alexander Turnbull Library, Wellington, New Zealand; Henry Pringle Letterbook, MG 18-L18, 115–17 (entry of 5 February 1762), LAC; Col. William Haviland to Lt. Gen. Jeffery Amherst, 17 February 1762, WO 34/55/73, TNA; "Proceedings of the Force against Martinique," in *Gentleman's Magazine* 32 (1762): 125. I am grateful to Lt. Col. Ian McCulloch for bringing my attention to the Grant and Pringle material.

109. "Return of the Killed, Wounded, and Missing of the Army under the Command of His Excellency Major-General Robt: Monckton &c. When the Enemy Attacked on the Evening of the 27th Jan: 1762," 27 January 1762, WO 34/55/60, TNA; "Abstract of the General Return of HM's Forces under the Command of Lt. General Earl of Albemarle," 23 May 1762, CO 117/1/77, TNA; Brumwell, *Redcoats*, 156–57; Mante, *History of the Late War*, 358–82.

110. Anderson, *Crucible of War*, 487–90; Harding, *Amphibious Warfare*, 123–37; John R. McNeill, "The Ecological Basis of Warfare in the Caribbean, 1700–1804," in Ultee, *Adapting to Conditions*, 26–38; McNeill, *Atlantic Empires of France and Spain*, 100–103; Syrett, *Siege and Capture of Havana*, xiii–xxii.

111. Quotation from "Narrative & Remarks upon the Siege of Havana and Isle of Cuba by Admiral Sir Charles Knowles, Bart., in 1761 and 1762," Add. MSS 23,678, 17, BL; Lydenberg, *Archibald Robertson*, 54–62 (entries of 12 June–22 July 1762); "The Chief Engineer's Journal of the Siege of the Moro Fort & the Havana," CO 117/1/110–18, TNA (entries of 7 June–14 August 1762).

112. Earl of Albemarle to the Earl of Egremont, 13 July 1762, CO 117/1/79, TNA; "General Return of His Majesty's Forces under the Command of Lt. Gen. The Earl of Albemarle," 17 July 1762, and "Return of the Killed Wounded and Missing and Dead since the Army Landed on Cuba," 13 August 1762, CO 117/1/95, 107, TNA; Lt. Gen. Jeffery Amherst to Charles Townshend, 20 October 1762, AMSS, U 1350/O40/13, CKS.

113. Welbore Ellis to the Earl of Egremont, 17 March 1763, WO 4/987/6, TNA; Gov. William Keppel to Egremont, 3 July 1763, CO 117/1/225, TNA; Maj. Gen. Thomas Gage to Welbore Ellis, 10 March 1764, in *Gage Correspondence*, 2:224; Mante, *History of the Late War*, 406.

4. "NO END TO THEIR FATIGUES"

1. Quotation from Col. Henry Bouquet to Maj. Gen. Robert Monckton, 12 June 1761, in *Bouquet Papers*, 5:544; Bouquet to Capt. Donald Campbell,

9 July 1761, ibid., 623; Maj. Gen. Thomas Gage to Lord Barrington, 13 July 1766, in *Gage Correspondence*, 2:360; "An Account of a Conversation, Chiefly Relative to the Army," in Langworthy, *Memoirs of Charles Lee*, 69.

2. Col. Henry Bouquet to Lt. Col. Sir John St. Clair, 30 June 1758, in *Bouquet Papers*, 2:149; McConnell, *Army and Empire*, xvi–xvii, 82–99; Anderson, *Crucible of War*, 411–13; Rogers, *Empire and Liberty*, 66–67.

3. Brumwell, *Redcoats*, 137–38, 140–50; Beattie, "Adaptation to Wilderness Warfare," in Ultee, *Adapting to Conditions*, 56–68.

4. "Clothing Delivered for the Royal American Regiment of Foot by Galfridus Mann," 4 May 1756, LO 1108A, HEH; Maj. Gen. John Stanwix to Col. Henry Bouquet, 18 January 1760, in *Bouquet Papers*, 4:430; Guy, *Oeconomy and Discipline*, 147–51; Cuthbertson, *Management and Oeconomy of a Battalion*, 50–56.

5. Quotation from Simes, *Military Guide for Young Officers*, 1:244; Col. Henry Bouquet to Brig. Gen. John Stanwix, 21 February 1758, and "First Royal American Battalion: Disbursements," 1 July 1759, in *Bouquet Papers*, 1:308–309 and 3:387–88; Maj. James Robertson to the Earl of Loudoun, 27 February 1759, LO 6047, HEH.

6. "Memorandum," 14 May 1756, Loudoun Notebooks, vol. 10, p. 14, HM 1717, HEH; Lt. Col. Henry Bouquet to Maj. John Young, 10 December 1756, and Bouquet to Brig. Gen. John Stanwix, 26 April 1759, in *Bouquet Papers*, 1:33 and 3:256; Knox, *Historical Journal*, 1:92–93 (entry of 17 October 1757); Houlding, *Fit for Service*, 138–49.

7. "General Return of Stores Received & Delivered Out to the 62d, or Royal American Regiment," 27 December 1756, LO 2532, HEH; "Estimate for Camp Necessaries for the 40th Regt of Foot," 22 November 1758, WO 1/978/93, TNA; Capt. John Schlosser to Col. Henry Bouquet, 5 May 1760, in *Bouquet Papers*, 4:550–51; s.v. "CAMP-*Utensils*," in Smith, *Universal Military Dictionary*, 45.

8. Maj. Gen. James Abercromby to William Pitt, 29 June 1758, and Maj. Gen. Jeffery Amherst to Pitt, 21 June 1760, in *Pitt Correspondence*, 1:284–85, and 2:305–308; Anderson, *Crucible of War*, 795.

9. Earl of Loudoun to Lt. Lewis Ourry, 3 April 1757, LO 3277, HEH; Lt. Col. Sir John St. Clair to Lt. Gov. William Denny, 4 September 1757, in Hazard, *Pennsylvania Archives*, 1st ser., 3 (1853): 266; "HBOB," in *Bouquet Papers*, 2:660 (entry of 26 June 1758); "Return of the Weight for the Clothing, Arms, Accouterments, Ammunition, Provision, Necessary's &c of a Grenadier, upon a March," 28 August 1762, Add. MSS 21,648, 341, BL; Guy, *Oeconomy and Discipline*, 72.

10. "A Proportion of Brass Ordnance, Howitzers and Store for the Intended Expedition to North America," 12 October 1754, in Pargellis, *Military Affairs*, 479–87; James Appy to Robert Wood, 2 July 1758, CO 5/50/188–89, TNA; West, *Gunpowder, Government and War*, 100–115.

11. Quotation from Col. James Prevost to Maj. Gen. James Abercromby, 29 October 1758, WO 34/75/263, TNA; Abercromby to William Pitt, 22 May 1758, in *Pitt Correspondence*, 1:250; Hughes, *British Smooth-Bore Artillery*, 28–31; Duncan, *Royal Regiment of Artillery*, 1:203; LeBlond, *Treatise of Artillery*, 9–11.

12. "General Orders of the Earl of Loudoun, 7 May 1757–28 September 1757," (entry of 17 May 1757), LO 3576, HEH; "Orderly Book, Expedition to Martinique: 15 November 1761–18 January 1762," in *Gates Papers*, reel 18, frames 188, 192, 196 (entries of 7, 12 November, and 1 December 1761); Rodger, *Wooden World*, 40–42; Cuthbertson, *Management and Oeconomy of a Battalion*, 134–35.

13. Earl of Loudoun to William Pitt, 25 April 1757, in *Pitt Correspondence*, 1:40; "Lord Adam Gordon's Journal," 416–17; Beattie, "Adaptation to Wilderness Warfare," 62–65; Pargellis, *Lord Loudoun*, 291–98.

14. *Hervey Journals*, 26 (entry of 3 June 1756); Maj. Gen. James Abercromby to William Pitt, 29 June 1758, in *Pitt Correspondence*, 1:285; *Amherst Journal*, 195 (entry of 1 December 1759).

15. Kalm, *Travels in North America*, 1:333 (entry of 13 June 1749); s.v. "Bateau," in Gallay, *Colonial Wars of North America*, 62.

16. Quotation from "A Dialogue between the Earl of Stair and General Wolfe," in the *London Chronicle or Universal Evening Post* 17 (1765): 156; "MOB," 12:336–38 (entries of 11–15 May 1758); Maj. Gen. James Abercromby to William Pitt, 22 May 1758, in *Pitt Correspondence*, 1:251; Dawes, *Journal of General Rufus Putnam*, 84–85 (entries of 1–5 June 1759).

17. Quotation from *Amherst Journal*, 115 (entry of 4 June 1759); "Minutes of the Time & Method in Which the Army Took the Field Last Campaign & of Getting Up the Stores & Provisions to the Lake, & the Order of March on the Lake," 10 April 1759, TGPAS, vol. 2, WLCL; *Amherst Journal*, 134 (entry of 11 July 1759); "A Return of Provisions in Store at Fort Pitt," n.d., WO 34/40/205, TNA.

18. Quotation from Williamson, *French and Indian Cruelty*, 47; *Hervey Journals*, 5–11 (entries of 18 July–5 August 1756); "Orderly Book Kept by Lieutenant Joseph Bull, First New York Regiment, 25 May–1 November 1759," 4–26 (entries of 25 May–13 June 1759), HM 687, HEH; Lt. Gen. Thomas Gage to Capt. John Carden, 31 March 1772, TGPAS, vol. 109, WLCL; Livingston and Smith, *Review of Military Operations*, 53.

19. Quotation from Maj. James Abercrombie to the Earl of Loudoun, 6 August 1760, LO 6259, HEH; "The Prideaux and Johnson Orderly Book," in *Johnson Papers*, 3:48–55 (entries of 21–26 June 1759); *Amherst Journal*, 213–17 (entries of 24 July–9 August 1760); Livingston and Smith, *Review of Military Operations*, 54.

20. Maj. William Walters to Maj. Gen. Jeffery Amherst, 25 July 1760, and Capt. Henry Balfour to Amherst, 29 December 1761, WO 34/21/67 and 34/40/131–32, TNA; Col. Henry Bouquet to Walters, 25 April 1761, in *Bouquet Papers*, 5:444.

21. Quotation from Maj. William Walters to Col. Henry Bouquet, 8 October 1760, in *Bouquet Papers*, 5:59; Walters to Lt. Gen. Jeffery Amherst, 5 and 30 April 1761, WO 34/21/137, 149, TNA; Capt. Gavin Cochrane to Bouquet, 6 May 1761, in *Bouquet Papers*, 5:465; Kirk, *Memoirs and Adventures*, 64.

22. Capt. Joshua Loring to Lt. Gen. Jeffery Amherst, 24 July 1762, and "A List of Vessels on the Different Lakes in North America," November 1762, WO 34/65/101, 109, TNA; John Bremner's Diary and Memorandum Book,

1756–64, pp. 127–32 (entries of 12–29 July 1763), NYHS; "Journals of Capt. John Montresor," NYHS, *Collections for 1881* 14 (1882): 321–22.

23. Quotation from "A Dialogue between the Earl of Stair and General Wolfe," in the *London Chronicle or Universal Evening Post* 17 (1765): 156; Col. Henry Bouquet to Brig. Gen. Robert Monckton, 11 August 1760, and Lt. Elias Meyer to Bouquet, 22 October 1761, in *Bouquet Papers*, 4:685–86 and 5:835; Capt. Donald Campbell to Lt. Gen. Jeffery Amherst, 9 August 1761, and Capt. Henry Balfour to Amherst, 24 November 1761, WO 34/49/46, 66, TNA; Carver, *Travels through North America*, 168.

24. "Orderly Book of Major Gates on the March from Carlisle to Pittsburgh, 16 July 1759–2 September 1759," in *Gates Papers*, reel, 18, frames 85–86 (entries of 19–22 August 1759); Col. Henry Bouquet to Maj. Gen. John Stanwix, 9 October 1760, in *Bouquet Papers*, 5:63; "Distances from Philadelphia to the Following Places," n.d., AMSS, U 1350/O53/10, CKS; Waddell and Bomberger, *French and Indian War in Pennsylvania*, 38–49, 57.

25. Col. Henry Bouquet to Brig. Gen. Robert Monckton, 9 July 1760, and "Journal of March from Fort Pitt to Presque Isle," 17 July 1760, in *Bouquet Papers*, 4:626, 640–42; Anderson and Williams, "Venango Path," 1–18, 141–54.

26. Quotation from Lt. Elias Meyer to Col. Henry Bouquet, 1 September 1761, in *Bouquet Papers*, 5:726; Brig. Gen. Robert Monckton to Bouquet, 18 October 1760, and Bouquet to Monckton, 4 November 1760, ibid., 5:74, 94; "Bouquet: Orders to Buckner," 1 December 1760, and "Bouquet: Orders to Shryock," 17 March 1761, ibid., 5:136, 347; Capt. Donald Campbell to Lt. Gen. Jeffery Amherst, 22 May 1761, WO 34/49/36, TNA.

27. Ford, *General Orders of 1757*, 62 (entry of 2 August 1757); "MOB," 12:446 (entry of 15 July 1758); *Amherst Journal*, 217 (entry of 10 July 1760); s.v. "QUARTER-*master-general*," in Smith, *Universal Military Dictionary*, 219.

28. Ford, *General Orders of 1757*, 34 (entry of 1 July 1757); Ray, "The Journal of Dr. Caleb Rea," 111 (entry of 17 July 1758); Cuthbertson, *Management and Oeconomy of a Battalion*, 29.

29. Anderson, *People's Army*, 90–98; Priestly, "Army Life, 1757," 199–200; Bland, *Treatise of Military Discipline*, 291–94.

30. "Account of Sundry Goods &c. Being the Effects of the Late Colonel Joseph Dusseaux Esqr. Sold at Auction at Carlisle," 20 October 1757, Add. MSS 21,687, 5–7, BL; Capt. Lt. Lewis Ourry to Col. Henry Bouquet, 21 February 1760, in *Bouquet Papers*, 4:461.

31. Cobb, "Journal," 20 (entry of 18 July 1758); Col. Henry Bouquet to Brig. Gen. Robert Monckton, 18 July 1760, in *Bouquet Papers*, 4:644; "Letters and Papers Relating to the Siege of Quebec in the Possession of the Marquess Townshend," in Doughty and Parmelee, *Siege of Quebec*, 5:244–45.

32. "Report of the Works Carried On in the Several Undermentioned Places, with Their Present State," 1 October 1757, LO 6754, HEH; "MOB," 12:446–47 (entries of 17–18 July 1758); Stotz, *Outposts of the War for Empire*, 62–66.

33. Ford, *General Orders of 1757*, 34 (entry of 30 June 1757); "Orderly Book Kept at Oneida Station, 18 August 1758–12 October 1758," in *Gates*

Papers, reel 18, frames 8, 46 (entries of 20 August, and 30 September 1758); Wallace, "Regimental Routine," 13 (entry of 5 May 1759).

34. Ford, *General Orders of 1757*, 39, 72–73 (entries of 5 July, and 24 August 1757); "Earl of Loudoun's Orderly Book, Halifax, 25 July 1757–12 August 1757," 3 (entry of 28 July 1757), LO 3993, HEH; "MOB," 12:356 (entry of 28 June 1758); "HBOB," in *Bouquet Papers*, 2:664, 666 (entries of 10, 19 July 1758); "Rates & Prices Settled upon Sutlers at Rays Town," 10 August 1758, ibid., 2:352–53; Bland, *Treatise of Military Discipline*, 294–95.

35. Quotation from Knox, *Historical Journal*, 1:140 (entry of 25 February 1758); *Hawks' Orderly Book*, 31, 45 (entries of 11, 24 July 1759); "Major Gates' Orderly Book, 6 June 1760–5 July [sic], 1760," in *Gates Papers*, reel 18, frame 130 (entry of 5 July 1760); Anderson, *People's Army*, 84–88; Simes, *Military Medley*, 272–73.

36. Knox, *Historical Journal*, 1:50, 102–103, 233, 400, 435 (entries of 14 August, and 1–3 November 1757; 6 September 1758; 5 and 22 July 1759); *Jenks' Diary*, 7, 30 (entries of 24 June, and 12 September 1760).

37. Knox, *Historical Journal*, 1:211 (entry of 6 September 1758); Grant, *Memoirs of an American Lady*, 177.

38. Knox, *Historical Journal*, 1:71–72, 235, 2:19 (entries of 10 September 1757, 26 June 1758, and 6 August 1759); Shammas, *Pre-Industrial Consumer*, 137.

39. *Hervey Journals*, 42–43 (entries of 7, 13 October 1756); Ford, *General Orders of 1757*, 23, 63, 73 (entries of 13 June, and 4, 26 August 1757); "MOB," 12:352 (entry of 21 June 1758) and 13:98 (entry of 2 September 1758); de Peyster, *Commissary Wilson's Orderly Book*, 21 (entry of 11 June 1759); "Orderly Book of Major Gates on the March from Carlisle to Pittsburgh," in *Gates Papers*, reel 18, frame 87 (entry of 23 August 1759).

40. Lt. Col. Henry Bouquet to the Earl of Loudoun, 11 October 1756, in *Bouquet Papers*, 1:12; Maj. Gen. Jeffery Amherst to Lt. [Bernard] Ratzer and Ens. [Charles] Rivez, 8 June 1759, and Amherst to Major [John] Hawke, 27 May 1760, WO 34/80/6 and 34/84/215, TNA; Taylor, *Military Roads in Scotland*, 32–37; James and Stotz, *Drums in the Forest*, 91–94.

41. Lt. Col. [Ralph] Burton to the Earl of Loudoun, 27 August 1756, CO 5/47/324–25, TNA; "MOB," 13:89, 107 (entries of 8 August, and 30 September 1758); Col. Henry Bouquet to Lt. Col. Sir John St. Clair, 23 August 1758, and Bouquet to Ens. Louis Duplessis, 17 June 1760, in *Bouquet Papers*, 2:409 and 4:598; Webster, *Journal of William Amherst*, 40 (entry of 8 July 1759).

42. Earl of Loudoun to Henry Fox, 8 October 1756, CO 5/47/394, TNA; "General Orders of the Earl of Loudoun, 21 August–30 November 1756," (entry of 22 October 1756), LO 1538, HEH; Maj. Gen. James Abercromby to William Pitt, 19 August 1758, in *Pitt Correspondence*, 1:318–21; Andre Doreil to Marshal Fouquet de Belle-Isle, 31 August 1758, in *NYCD*, 10:818–19; MacLeod, *Canadian Iroquois*, 120–27; Steele, *Betrayals*, 84–86.

43. Quotation from Lt. Col. Thomas Lloyd to Col. Henry Bouquet, 23 May 1759, in *Bouquet Papers*, 3:310; "MOB," 12:445 (entry of 16 July 1758); "Convoys," n.d., TGPAS, vol. 1, WLCL; Capt. Gavin Cochrane to Maj. John Tulleken, 12 July 1759, in *Bouquet Papers*, 3:405–406.

44. Quotation from Col. Henry Bouquet to Richard Peters, 8 August 1759, in *Bouquet Papers*, 3:512; "Croghan's Journal," 314–15 (entry of 12 May 1759).

45. Lt. Col. Thomas Lloyd to Brig. Gen. John Stanwix, 23 May 1759, and Col. Henry Bouquet to Lt. Col. Hugh Mercer, 26 May 1759, in *Bouquet Papers*, 3:310, 326–27; Stanwix to Maj. Gen. Jeffery Amherst, 14 August 1759, WO 34/45/86, TNA.

46. Ford, *General Orders of 1757*, 31–32, 74 (entries of 27 June, and 28 August 1757); "MOB," 13:89, 99 (entries of 9 August, and 4 September 1758); "Orderly Book Kept at Oneida Station," in *Gates Papers*, reel 18, frame 8 (entry of 20 August 1758); de Peyster, *Commissary Wilson's Orderly Book*, 125 (entry of 9 August 1759); "Orderly Book of Silas Brown's Company, Timothy Ruggles's Regiment of Massachusetts Provincials, 31 August 1760–12 November 1760," (entry of 12 November 1760), Silas Brown Collection, MassHS.

47. Ford, *General Orders of 1757*, 39, 74 (entries of 5 July, and 29 August 1757); Maj. Gen. Jeffery Amherst to Brig. Gen. John Prideaux, 17 May 1759, WO 34/46B/137, TNA; Capt. Robert Stewart to George Washington, 28 September 1759, in *Washington Papers*, 6:360; "Bouquet: Order for Meyer," 12 August 1761, in *Bouquet Papers*, 5:691; Waddell and Bomberger, *French and Indian War in Pennsylvania*, 53–57.

48. Quotation from Wallace, "Regimental Routine," 18 (entry of 24 June 1759); "MOB," 12:341–43 (entries of 24–28 May 1758); *Hawks' Orderly Book*, 25–26, 59, 73 (entries of 29–30 June, and 7 August 1759; and 18 June 1760); *Amherst Journal*, 222 (entry of 28 July 1760).

49. Ford, *General Orders of 1757*, 31 (entry of 27 June 1757); "MOB," 12:332 (entry of 16 April 1758); "Return of the Contractors, Carpenters, Absent and Present with the Number of All the Artificers of Different Regiments and Trade, Employ'd This Day by the Engineer," 23 August 1759, TGPAS, vol. 3, WLCL.

50. "Journal (No. 2) of Col. James Montresor, Saratoga," NYHS, *Collections for 1881* 14 (1882): 41–43 (entries of 23 August–7 September 1757); "Report of the Works Carried On in the Several Undermention'd Places, with Their Present State," 1 October 1757, LO 6754, HEH; Maj. [Alexander] Duncan to Lt. Gen. Jeffery Amherst, 19 October 1763, WO 34/19/271, TNA; Dunnigan, *Necessity of Regularity in Quartering Soldiers*, 47–52.

51. "State of the Works at Fort Edward," 15 August 1757, and "Report of the Works Carried On in the Several Undermention'd Places, with Their Present State," 1 October 1757, LO 4235A and 6754, HEH; John Bremner's Diary, pp. 26–27 (entry of 4 August 1759), NYHS; Stotz, *Outposts of the War for Empire*, 152–67.

52. Quotation from Col. Henry Bouquet to Maj. Gen. Robert Monckton, 12 June 1761, in *Bouquet Papers*, 5:544; "Journal (No. 2) of Col. James Montresor," NYHS, *Collections for 1881* 14 (1882): 44 (entries of 10–13 September 1757); "Kenny Journal," 14, 27 (entries of 21 July, and 19 November 1761); "A Report of the Works Done at this Garrison [Fort Niagara]," 24 October 1762, WO 34/22/88–89, TNA.

53. John Bremner's Diary, p. 28 (entry of 14 March 1759), NYHS; Guy, *Oeconomy and Discipline*, 65–70.

54. "HBOB," in *Bouquet Papers*, 2:661 (entry of 2 July 1758); "Orderly Book Kept at Oneida Station," in *Gates Papers*, reel 18, frames 9–10 (entry of 22 August 1758); Brig. Gen. Robert Monckton to Col. Henry Bouquet, 28 July 1760, in *Bouquet Papers*, 4:660; Pargellis, *Lord Loudoun*, 281–84.

55. *New York Mercury*, 23 August 1756, 1; "Extract out of the Orderly Books," 13 September 1756, LO 1791C, HEH; "Orderly Book Kept at Oneida Station," in *Gates Papers*, reel 18, frame 10 (entry of 23 August 1758); *Hawks' Orderly Book*, 71 (entry of 4 June 1760).

56. Ford, *General Orders of 1757*, 15, 48–49 (entries of 31 May, and 21–22 July 1757); *Hawks' Orderly Book*, 14, 19, 22 (entries of 16, 20, and 24 June 1760); Sumner, "Standing Orders for the Army," 197; Bland, *Treatise of Military Discipline*, 245–48.

57. Ford, *General Orders of 1757*, 90 (entry of 20 September 1757); *Hawks' Orderly Book*, 21, 24, 81 (entries of 22, 26 June 1759, and 2 July 1760); Bland, *Treatise of Military Discipline*, 246–50.

58. Ford, *General Orders of 1757*, 15–16, 20–22, 24, 67, 89 (entries of 31 May; 7, 8, and 19 June; 14 August; and 19 September 1757); *Hawks' Orderly Book*, 17 (entry of 18 June 1759); de Peyster, *Commissary Wilson's Orderly Book*, 62 (entry of 7 July 1759); Wolfe, *Instructions to Young Officers*, 96; Bland, *Treatise of Military Discipline*, 254–62.

59. "Captain Orme's Journal," in Sargent, *Expedition against Fort Du Quesne*, 333 (entry of 11 June 1755); Ford, *General Orders of 1757*, 70, 129 (entries of 19 August, and 5 November 1757); "Evidence of Captain [Samuel] Wllyamoz, Sergeant Andreas Hartman, and Private William Beamond," 22 June 1758, WO 71/66/332–33, TNA; *Hawks' Orderly Book*, 9, 17, 25 (entries of 8, 18, and 29 June 1759); Wolfe, *Instructions to Young Officers*, 78, 82–83, 97.

60. Sumner, "Standing Orders for the Army," 197; "HBOB," in *Bouquet Papers*, 2:656 (entry of 17 June 1758); Brumwell, *Redcoats*, 104; Gilbert, "Why Men Deserted," 554–56.

61. "Evidence of William Macqueed," 18 July 1757, WO 71/65/383–84, TNA; Ford, *General Orders of 1757*, 56, 83, 129 (entries of 26 July, 7 September, and 5 November 1757); "MOB," 12:340 (entry of 19 May 1758); Knox, *Historical Journal*, 1:384 (entry of 29 June 1759); *Hawks' Orderly Book*, 25, 27 (entries of 29 June, and 3 July 1759).

62. Knox, *Historical Journal*, 1:227 (entry of 6 September 1758); de Peyster, *Commissary Wilson's Orderly Book*, 21 (entry of 11 June 1759); "Evidence of George Rush," 16 November 1759, WO 71/46/4, TNA.

63. "Rules and Articles," in *HCSP*, 16:383–84, 387–88; "Trial of Matthew Wassirman," 9 June 1757, WO 71/65/318–19, TNA; Guy, *Oeconomy and Discipline*, 120–21, 127–28, 141; Childs, *Armies and Warfare in Europe*, 67–68.

64. "The Journal of Captain Robert Chomley's Batman," in Hamilton, *Braddock's Defeat*, 19–20 (entry of 8 June 1755); "Trials of Walrade Winter

and Jacob Eykel," 19 June 1757, WO 71/65/327–30, TNA; Bougainville, *Adventure in the Wilderness*, 279–80 (entry of 25 September 1758); Knox, *Historical Journal*, 2:103 (entry of 13 September 1759); *Hawks' Orderly Book*, 55 (entry of 3 August 1759).

65. Quotation from Cuthbertson, *Management and Oeconomy of a Battalion*, 86; "Proceedings of a Regimental Court Martial," 4 November 1756, and "HBOB" (entry of 1 August 1758), in *Bouquet Papers*, 1:19–22 and 2:669; Ford, *General Orders of 1757*, 43, 87 (entries of 12 July, and 17 September 1757).

66. *Hawks' Orderly Book*, 29 (entry of 6 July 1759); Gridley, *Luke Gridley's Diary of 1757*, 30–31, 38 (entries of 25 May, and 26 June 1757); Knox, *Historical Journal*, 1:128–29 (entry of 14 December 1757); Steppler, "British Military Law," 859–81; Gilbert, "Regimental Courts-Martial," 51–56; Wolfe, *Instructions for Younger Officers*, 76.

67. Ford, *General Orders of 1757*, 41, 79–81, 114–16 (entries of 9 July, 3 September, and 19 October 1757); *Hawks' Orderly Book*, 3 (entry 26 May 1759); "Trial of Thomas Higgins," 17 July 1760, WO 71/46/306–308, TNA; Cuthbertson, *Management and Oeconomy of a Battalion*, 88–89.

68. *Hervey Journals*, 14, 20–21 (entries of 3 September 1755, and 19–25 May 1756); "Trial of Reynard Anthis," 9 July 1757, WO 71/65/346–48, TNA; Ford, *General Orders of 1757*, 81, 116 (entries of 3 September, and 19 October 1757); *Amherst Journal*, 222–23, 226 (entries of 30 July, and 9 August 1760); Gilbert, "Why Men Deserted," 556–59; s.v. "COURT-*martial*," in Smith, *Universal Military Dictionary*, 68–69.

69. *Hawks' Orderly Book*, 5, 74 (entries of 28 May 1759, and 20 June 1760); Morgan and Rushton, *Rogues, Thieves, and Rule of Law*, 132–38; Briggs et al., *Crime and Punishment in England*; 80–84; Frey, *British Soldier in America*, 90–92.

70. De Peyster, *Commissary Wilson's Orderly Book*, 25, 51 (entries of 14, 28 June 1759); *Hervey Journals*, 70, 135 (entries of 6 June, and 8 November 1760); Hamilton, *Duties of a Regimental Surgeon*, 2:27–61; Cuthbertson, *Management and Oeconomy of a Battalion*, 87–88.

71. Ford, *General Orders of 1757*, 117 (entry of 4 September 1757); de Peyster, *Commissary Wilson's Orderly Book*, 28–29 (entry of 15 June 1759); *Hawks' Orderly Book*, 55 (entry of 3 August 1759).

72. *Hervey Journals*, 14, 20–21, 91–92 (entries of 3 September 1755, 19 May 1756, and 29–30 July 1760); Ford, *General Orders of 1757*, 82 (entry of 4 September 1757); Cobb, "Journal," 25 (entry of 28 August 1758); Maj. Gen. Jeffery Amherst to Col. Frederick Haldimand, 29 July 1760, Add. MSS 21,661, 78, BL.

73. Butler, *Becoming America*, 127–29; Anderson, *Crucible of War*, 286–89, 370–72, 412–14; Titus, *Old Dominion at War*, 127; Jennings, *Empire of Fortune*, 207–11, 220–22; Anderson, *People's Army*, 111–41; Rogers, *Empire and Liberty*, 59–74.

74. Quotation from Leach, *Roots of Conflict*, 106; Landsman, *From Colonials to Provincials*, 1–148, 176–80; Bowen, *Elites, Enterprise*, 103–46; Koehn, *Power of Commerce*, 50–52; Bushman, *Refinement of America*, 1–203; Olson, *Making the Empire Work*, 1–125; Shammas, *Pre-industrial Con-*

sumer, 52–113; Breen, "Empire of Goods," 467–99; O'Brien, "Transatlantic Community of Saints," 811–32.

75. McConnell, *Army and Empire,* 57–59; Brumwell, *Redcoats,* 73–75, 318; Bailyn and Morgan, "Introduction," in *Strangers within the Realm,* 20–25; Fischer, *Albion's Seed,* 31–50, 212–55, 420–55, 605–39.

76. Quotation from Colonel Joseph Williams's Orderly Book, in "The Expedition to Fort Craven, Oneida Great Carrying Place, and Frontenac in 1758," *Colonial Wars* 1 (1914): 190 (entry of 28 July 1758); Maj. William Eyre to Sir Joseph Yorke, 23 January 1756, Add. MSS 35,357, 21, BL; Sir Charles Hardy to the Earl of Halifax, 7 May 1756, in Pargellis, *Military Affairs,* 170–71; "Barton Journal," 458 (entry of 26 August 1758); Shannon, *Indians and Colonists,* 108–109, 175–92; Ward, *"Unite or Die,"* 37–40, 74–81, 113–14, 192–214.

77. Lt. Col. [Ralph] Burton to the Earl of Loudoun, 27 August 1756, CO 5/47/323–25, TNA; Lt. Col. Sir John St. Clair to Maj. Gen. Robert Napier, 24 November 1756, Letterbook of Sir John St. Clair, 308–309, TWML; Brig. Gen. James Wolfe to Lord George Sackville, 30 July 1758, in Willson, *Life and Letters of James Wolfe,* 392; Greene, *Pursuits of Happiness,* 1–209; Anderson, *People's Army,* 167–95. By the end of the war, even some New England officers had become ashamed of their men's predilection for desertion; see Col. [Nathan] Whiting to Gov. Thomas Fitch, 2 July 1761, WO 34/51/156, TNA.

78. "Trial of John Thomas," 21 January 1757, WO 71/44/240, TNA; Ford, *General Orders of 1757,* 20, 25–26 (entries of 6, 20 June 1757); "Trial of Matthew Wassirman," 9 June 1757, WO 71/65/318–19, TNA; Dawes, *Journal of General Rufus Putnam,* 30, 83 (entries of 17 June 1757, and 24 May 1759); "MOB," 12:340 (entry of 22 May 1758).

79. Capt. George Mercer to Col. George Washington, 17 August 1757, in *Washington Papers,* 4:372; Lt. Col. John Bradstreet to Maj. Gen. Jeffery Amherst, 15 August 1758, WO 34/57/4, TNA; Lt. Col. Henry Bouquet to Brig. Gen. John Forbes, 20 August 1758, in *Bouquet Papers,* 2:397; Knox, *Historical Journal,* 2:538 (entry of 9 August 1760).

80. *Boston Weekly Advertiser,* 21 August 1758, 3, and 30 October 1758, 1; "Barton Journal," 457 (entry of 24 August 1758); "Orderly Book, 21 September–24 November 1758," in *Washington Papers,* 6:27–98 (entries of 21 September–30 October 1758).

81. Capt. Robert Stewart to George Washington, 16 January 1759, in *Washington Papers,* 6:188; Maj. Gen. John Stanwix to Capt. [Gavin] Cochrane, 24 August 1759, WO 34/45/132, TNA; Col. Henry Bouquet to Maj. Gen. Jeffery Amherst, 20 December 1760, and Amherst to Bouquet, 2 March 1761, in *Bouquet Papers,* 5:179, 324.

82. Quotation from Brig. Gen. John Forbes to Lt. Gov. Francis Fauquier, 5 November 1758, in Reese, *Official Papers of Francis Fauquier,* 1:102; Conway, "From Fellow-Nationals to Foreigners," 73–80; Gould, *Persistence of Empire,* 5–34; Colley, *Britons,* 1–236.

83. "Barton Journal," 457 (entry of 24 August 1758); Rev. Henry True to Mrs. Ruth True, 30 July 1759, in Barrett, *Rev. Henry True of Hampstead,* 20; Peter J. Marshall, "A Nation Defined by Empire, 1755–1776," in Grant and Stringer, *Uniting the Kingdom,* 208–22; Wilson, *Sense of the People,* 190–99.

84. Brumwell, *Redcoats*, 179–84; Harold E. Selesky, "Colonial America," in Howard, Andreopoulos, and Shulman, *Laws of War*, 70–74; Woodward, *Sermon Preached October 9, 1760*, 8–26; Adams, *Songs of Victory*, 21–26.

85. Sir John St. Clair to the Duke of Richmond, 22 December 1755, Letterbook of Sir John St. Clair, 193–94, TWML; *Hervey Journals*, 40 (entry of 22 September 1756); "Orders before Landing at Louisbourg, 1758," n.d., AMSS, U 1350/O30, CKS; Ian K. Steele, "Surrendering Rites: Prisoners on Colonial North American Frontiers," in Taylor, Connors, and Jones, *Hanoverian Britain and Empire*, 137–57; Geoffrey Parker, "Early Modern Europe," in Howard, Andreopoulos, and Shulman, *Laws of War*, 40–58; Grotius, *Rights of War and Peace*, 361–63, 366 [bk. 3, chap. 11, secs. 7–16; and chap. 12, sec. 4].

86. *Pennsylvania Gazette*, 13 July 1758, 3, and 27 July 1758, 3; *Boston Weekly Advertiser*, 25 December 1758, 1; Knox, *Historical Journal*, 1:387–89, 2:78–79 (entries of 28 June, and 7 September 1759); *Gentleman's Magazine* 32 (1762): 126; *Boston Post-Boy & Advertiser*, 15 August 1763, 2.

87. Quotation from Maj. Gen. Jeffery Amherst to Sir Joseph Yorke, 8 September 1760, WO 34/85/81, TNA; Eliot, *Sermon Preached October 25th, 1759*, 20–35; Foxcroft, *Grateful Reflections*, 24–35; Marshall, *Making and Unmaking of Empires*, 115–18; Conway, "From Fellow-Nationals to Foreigners," 77–100; Anderson, *Crucible of War*, 373–76; Bowen, *Elites, Enterprise*, 76–78.

88. Brumwell, *Redcoats*, 117–18; Kopperman, "Religion and Religious Policy," 390–405; Anderson, *People's Army*, 117–18; Frey, *British Soldier in America*, 115–17.

89. "Rules and Articles," in *HCSP*, 16:381–82; Sumner, "Standing Orders for the Army," 198; Knox, *Historical Journal*, 1:30 (entry of 30 June 1757); de Peyster, *Commissary Wilson's Orderly Book*, 17 (entry of 10 June 1759); Procter, "Diary Kept at Louisbourg," 44 (entry of 27 July 1760); Simes, *Military Medley*, 3.

90. "Earl of Loudoun's Orderly Book, Halifax, 25 July 1757–12 August 1757," 7 (entry of 1 August 1757), LO 3993, HEH; "MOB," 12:353 (entry of 24 June 1758); "HBOB," in *Bouquet Papers*, 2:665 (entry of 15 July 1758).

91. Michael Schlatter to the Earl of Loudoun, 4 February 1758, LO 5538, HEH; Maj. Gen. Thomas Gage to Lt. Gen. Jeffery Amherst, 10 March 1763, WO 34/5/285, TNA; Hinke, *Ministers of the German Reformed Congregations*, 37–47; Pargellis, *Military Affairs*, 283, 333.

92. Quotation from "Rules and Articles," in *HCSP*, 16:384; Procter, "Diary Kept at Louisbourg," 32 (entry of 10 November 1759); "Amherst Order Book," AMSS, U 1350/O16/2 (entry of 19 July 1763), CKS; Guy, *Oeconomy and Discipline*, 19–22, 149.

93. Quotation from Capt. Lt. Lewis Ourry to Col. Henry Bouquet, 5 June 1761, in *Bouquet Papers*, 5:530; *Amherst Journal*, 189 (entry of 10 November 1759); (St. James's): "MOB," 13:154 (entry of 18 November 1758); (King George): *Hawks' Orderly Book*, 47 (entry of 27 July 1759); (King George and Queen Charlotte) and (Prince of Wales): *Hervey Journals*, 158, 174 (en-

tries of 1 February, and 26 October 1762); s.v. "PAROLE," in Smith, *Universal Military Dictionary*, 199.

94. *Hervey Journals*, 15, 39, 123, 152, 155, 162, 172 (entries of 18 September 1755; 8 September 1756; 8 September 1760; 16 August, and 22 October 1761; 26 April, and 19 September 1762); Cobb, "Journal of Captain Samuel Cobb," 25 (entry of 28 August 1758); "MOB," 13:101 (entry of 11 September 1758); *Hawks' Orderly Book*, 50 (entry of 28 July 1759).

95. *Hervey Journals*, 15, 123, 152, 155, 162, 172 (entries of 18 September 1755; 8 September 1760; 16 August, and 22 October 1761; 26 April, and 19 September 1762); Cleaveland, "Journal," 215–16, 221 (entries of 28 August, and 11 September 1758); "Barton Journal," 465 (entry of 1 September 1758); Cobb, "Journal of Captain Samuel Cobb," 27 (entry of 11 September 1758); Bland, *Treatise of Military Discipline*, 98–100; s.v. "REJOICING-*fire*," in Smith, *Universal Military Dictionary*, 223.

96. Ford, *General Orders of 1757*, 47 (entry of 19 July 1757); Hamilton, "Diary of the Reverend John Ogilvie," 379 (entries of 30 September, and 2–4 November 1757); *Pennsylvania Gazette*, 15 March 1759, 2; Webster, *Journal of William Amherst*, 53 (entry of 28 July 1759).

97. "Barton Journal," 452 (entry of 19 August 1758); Fort Stanwix Orderly Books, Rose of Kilravock Muniments, GD 125/34/7, 2 (entry of 11 November 1758), NAS; Cuthbertson, *Management and Oeconomy of a Battalion*, 114–15; s.v. "BURIALS," in Smith, *Universal Military Dictionary*, 37.

98. "Rules and Articles," in *HCSP*, 16:406 [sec. 18]; "MOB," 13:101 (entry of 10 September 1758); Maj. John Tulleken to Col. Henry Bouquet, 5 March 1759, in *Bouquet Papers*, 3:176; "Receipt of Capt.-Lt. William Winepress," 18 December 1761, SGM, case 4, box 9, "Colonial Wars," HSP; "Kenny Journal," 45 (entry of 18 March 1762); "Affidavit of Henry Babcock," 26 July 1763, Frank M. Etting Collection, Autographs, American and British Army Officers, HSP.

99. Ford, ed., *General Orders of 1757*, 18–19 (entry of 4 June 1757); "MOB," 13:98, 105 (entries of 3 and 23 September 1758); Knox, *Historical Journal*, 1:430 (entry of 19 July 1759); *Hawks' Orderly Book*, 24, 33 (entries of 26 June, and 14 July 1759).

100. "Evidence of James Wiley," 10 October 1756, WO 71/44/154, TNA; Ford, *General Orders of 1757*, 92, 111 (entries of 21 September, and 15 October 1757); "HBOB," in *Bouquet Papers*, 2:663 (entry of 6 July 1758); *Hawks' Orderly Book*, 24 (entry of 26 June 1759); Lamb, *Memoirs of His Own Life*, 74; Cuthbertson, *Management and Oeconomy of a Battalion*, 94.

101. "Evidence of John Stephens," 10 October 1756, WO 71/44/155, TNA; "HBOB," in *Bouquet Papers*, 2:659, 664 (entries of 25 June, and 11 July 1758); "MOB," 12:441 (entry of 7 July 1758).

102. Ford, *General Orders of 1757*, 101–104, 120 (entries of 3–5 and 23 October 1757); *Amherst Journal*, 170–72, 183, 193 (entries of 19, 20, and 22 September; 21 October; and 24 November 1759); Anderson, *People's Army*, 189–92.

103. Ford, *General Orders of 1757*, 106 (entry of 9 October 1757); "MOB," 13:102 (entry of 13 September 1758); *Jenks' Diary*, 37 (entry of

27 October 1760); Cuthbertson, *Management and Oeconomy of a Battalion*, 30–31; Monro, *Account of the Diseases*, 315–20.

104. Lt. Col. Arthur Morris to Col. John Forbes, 13 November 1757, Dalhousie Muniments, GD 45/2/21/8, NAS; Piper, *Diary and Journal of Seth Metcalf*, 14 (entries of 8–16 November 1757); *Amherst Journal*, 91–92 (entries of 5–6 October 1758); "MOB," 13:114–15 (entries of 23–24 October 1758); "Journal of Warren Johnson," in *Johnson Papers*, 13:200 (entry of 23 January 1761).

105. "List of Quarters in America," n.d., LO 4450, HEH; Anderson, *People's Army*, 68–74, 108.

106. Kalm, *Travels in North America*, 1:115–25 (entries of 27–30 October 1748); "Quarters," 29 October 1757, Loudoun Notebooks, vol. 4, p. 10, HM 1717, HEH; Lt. Gen. Jeffery Amherst to Lt. Col. Augustine Prevost, 18 August 1761, WO 34/89/205, TNA; "Routes Southwestward," n.d., John Bremner's Diary, p. 89, NYHS.

107. Lt. Gov. Horatio Sharpe to the Earl of Loudoun, 15 November 1756, in Browne, *Archives of Maryland* 6 (1888): 509; Loudoun to Henry Fox, 22 November 1756, CO 5/48/2, TNA; "Route of March for the Royal American Regiment in the Province of Pennsylvania," 10–22 September 1757, in Hazard, *Pennsylvania Archives*, 1st ser., 3 (1853): 267; "Note of Distances from Stage to Stage on the Road from Pittsburgh on the Ohio to New York," n.d., Dalhousie Muniments, GD 45/2/72, NAS.

108. Hazard, *Provincial Council of Pennsylvania*, 7:374 (entry of 26 December 1756); "Return of the First Battalion of the 62d Regiment," 24 December 1756, and Lt. Lewis Ourry to Lt. Col. Henry Bouquet, 26 December 1756, in *Bouquet Papers*, 1:40, 42; Zimmerman, "Governor Denny and the Quartering Act," 266–81.

109. Pennsylvania Assembly to Lt. Gov. William Denny, 26 December 1756, LO 2404; Richard Peters to Thomas Penn, 26 December 1756 and 10 January 1757, Penn Papers, Official Correspondence, vol. 8, p. 211, and Penn Papers, Additional Miscellaneous Letters, vol. 1, p. 100, HSP; Fenn, *Pox Americana*, 15–20.

110. Earl of Loudoun to the Duke of Cumberland, 3 October 1756, in Pargellis, *Military Affairs*, 241; *Pennsylvania Gazette*, 7 April 1757, 3; Loudoun to Lord Barrington, 17 October 1757, WO 1/1/120, TNA; Cuthbertson, *Management and Oeconomy of a Battalion*, 23–27.

111. Lt. Gov. Horatio Sharpe to Cecilius Calvert, 4 February 1757, in Browne, *Archives of Maryland* 6 (1888): 523–24; William Wethered to the Earl of Loudoun, 26 February 1757, and Col. John Stanwix to Loudoun, 9 November 1757, LO 2928 and 4789, HEH.

112. Edward Shippen to James Hamilton, 15 December 1757, Burd-Shippen Collection, APS; Lt. Gov. Horatio Sharpe to the Earl of Loudoun, 22 December 1757, in Browne, *Archives of Maryland* 9 (1890): 114; Leach, *Roots of Conflict*, 87–98; Pargellis, *Lord Loudoun*, 186–210.

113. Maj. Gen. James Abercromby to Lt. Gov. James DeLancey, 12 October 1758, and Maj. Gen. Jeffery Amherst to Brig. Gen. Thomas Gage, 2 October 1759, WO 34/30/36 and 34/46A/184, TNA; "Monthly Return

of His Majesty's Forces in North America," 23 July 1765, and Gage to Maj. Gen. Frederick Haldimand, 3 October 1772, TGPAS, vols. 40 and 114, WLCL.

114. Quotation from Col. Henry Bouquet to Maj. Gen. Thomas Gage, 4 February 1764, in *Bouquet Papers*, 6:495; Maj. Gen. Jeffery Amherst to Brig. Gen. John Stanwix, 5 April 1759, WO 34/45/210, TNA; Stanwix to Lt. Gov. Francis Fauquier, 6 January 1760, in Reese, *Official Papers of Francis Fauquier*, 1:307; Bouquet to Amherst, 24 October 1763, in *Bouquet Papers*, 6:438; McConnell, *Army and Empire*, 118–29.

115. Maj. Robert Stewart to Capt. Lt. Mordecai Buckner, 23 December 1760, and James Stevenson to Col. Henry Bouquet, 27 March 1761, in *Bouquet Papers*, 5:202, 374; Monro, *Account of the Diseases*, 312–18, 354.

116. Quotation from Capt. Lewis Steiner to Brig. Gen. Thomas Gage, 24 March 1760, TGPAS, vol. 5, WLCL; "Monthly Return of His Majesty's Forces at Oswego," 24 August 1759, and "Monthly Return of His Majesty's Forces in the District of Albany," 24 March 1760, TGPAS, vols. 3 and 5, WLCL; "Present State of the Garrison of Fort Ontario," 13 March 1760, WO 34/46A/100–101, TNA; "Journal of Happenings at Quebec by an Officer of the Royal Americans," in Pargellis, *Military Affairs*, 446.

117. Quotation from Monro, *Account of the Diseases*, 250; Jonathan Rogers to Brig. Gen. Thomas Gage, 16 February 1760, and Capt. Lewis Steiner to Gage, 14 March 1760, TGPAS, vol. 5, WLCL; Brig. Gen. James Murray to William Pitt, 25 May 1760, in *Pitt Correspondence*, 2:291–92; *Amherst Journal*, 207 (entry of 6 June 1760).

118. Richard Brocklesby and Robert Adair to Lord Barrington, n.d., AMSS, U 1350/O37/24A, CKS; Capt. Lt. Lewis Ourry to Col. Henry Bouquet, 6 March 1760, in *Bouquet Papers*, 4:488; Lt. Col. William Eyre to Maj. Gen. Jeffery Amherst, 28 April 1760, WO 34/21/37, TNA; *Jenks' Diary*, 7 (entry of 24 June 1760); "Major Gates' Orderly Book," in *Gates Papers*, reel 18, frame 132 (entry of 9 July 1760); Grant, *Memoirs of an American Lady*, 204–206.

119. Maj. Gen. Thomas Gage to Lt. Gen. Jeffery Amherst, 2 May 1761, WO 34/5/135, TNA; Ford, *British Officers Serving in America*, 71; Grant, *Memoirs of an American Lady*, 199–206.

120. Lt. Col. Sir John St. Clair to Col. Henry Bouquet, 21 August and 2 October 1761, in *Bouquet Papers*, 5:705, 792–93; "Kenny Journal," 20–23 (entries of 14–23 September 1761); Bouquet to John Bartram, 3 February 1762, and Bartram to Bouquet, 3 May 1762, in Berkley and Berkley, *Correspondence of John Bartram*, 547, 555–57.

121. "Trial of Anthony Shoultz," 13 May 1761, Add. MSS 21,682, 40–41, BL; Col. Henry Bouquet to Officers at Niagara, 10 September 1761, in *Bouquet Papers*, 5:741; "A Catalogue of Ens. Robert Johnstone of the 2d Battl. Exploits," n.d., in May, *Doctor's Secret Journal*, 36–37; Kopperman, "British High Command and Soldiers' Wives," 14–34.

122. "MOB," 12:338–39 (entries of 14, 19 May 1758); Lt. Col. William Amherst to Post Commanders from Albany to Niagara, 1 June 1760, Add. MSS 21,678, 7, BL; Maj. Robert Stewart to Col. Henry Bouquet, 4 September 1760, in *Bouquet Papers*, 5:19; McConnell, *Army and Empire*, 65–71; Brumwell, *Redcoats*, 122–26; Bethune, *Power of Faith*, 17.

123. Quotation from Grant, *Memoirs of an American Lady*, 199; "Report of the Works Carried On in the Several Undermention'd Places, with Their Present State," 1 October 1757, LO 6754, HEH; "Present State of Fort Pitt and Posts Depending," 24 December 1760, in Stevens and Kent, *Wilderness Chronicles*, 202; Maj. Gen. Thomas Gage to James Glassford, 1 April 1765, in *Gage Correspondence*, 2:275; Starbuck, *Great Warpath*, 69–76.

124. Draper, "Lieut. James Gorell's Journal," 26 (entry of 12 October 1761); Capt. John Schlosser to Col. Henry Bouquet, 24 October 1761, in *Bouquet Papers*, 5:839; Capt. John Brown to Maj. Gen. Thomas Gage, 1 September 1766, and Capt. Lewis Fuser to Gage, 16 April 1767, TGPAS, vols. 56 and 63, WLCL; Gage to Lord Hillsborough, 4 March 1769, in *Gage Correspondence*, 1:219.

125. "Plan of the Establishment of the Sixtieth or Royal American Regiment of Foot," 18 May 1763, AMSS, U 1350/O43/9B, CKS; "Return of the Garrison of the Detroit and Posts Depending," 5 September 1762, WO 34/49/107, TNA; Capt. John Brown to Maj. Gen. Thomas Gage, 17 November 1766, and Capt. George Turnbull to Gage, 1 August 1771, TGPAS, vols. 59 and 105, WLCL.

126. "Orders for the Main Guard by Brigadier-General [John] Stanwix," 25 November 1758, TGPAS, vol. 1, WLCL; Lt. Edward Jenkins to Col. Henry Bouquet, 21 August 1761, in *Bouquet Papers*, 5:704; Lamb, *Memoirs*, 90; Bland, *Treatise of Military Discipline*, 182–89.

127. Col. Henry Bouquet to Brig. Gen. Robert Monckton, 14 January 1761, and Capt. Richard Mather to Bouquet, 13 February 1761, in *Bouquet Papers*, 5:246 and 294–95; "Journal of Warren Johnson," in *Johnson Papers*, 13:200 (entry of 23 January 1761); Capt. John Brown to Lt. Gen. Thomas Gage, 12 November 1770, TGPAS, vol. 98, WLCL.

128. Knox, *Historical Journal*, 1:292 (entry of 1 February 1759); *Gentleman's Magazine* 30 (1760): 312; Maj. William Walters to Maj. Gen. Jeffery Amherst, 2 February and 5 April 1761, WO 34/21/123, 138, TNA; "Kenny Journal," 29 (entry of 30 November 1761); Capt. Gavin Cochrane to Lt. Gen. Thomas Gage, 16 October 1771, TGPAS, vol. 107, WLCL; McConnell, *Army and Empire*, 94.

129. Quotation from Capt. John Brown to Lt. Gen. Thomas Gage, 26 June 1771, TGPAS, vol. 104, WLCL; Fort Stanwix Orderly Books, Rose of Kilravock Muniments, GD 125/34/7/14–15, 30 (entries of 4–5 December 1758, and 2 January 1759), NAS; "General Orders," 22 October 1760, in *Bouquet Papers*, 5:83; Draper, "Lieut. James Gorell's Journal," 27 (entry of 12 October 1761); Brown to Gage, 25 February 1770, TGPAS, vol. 90, WLCL; Stotz, *Outposts of the War for Empire*, 133.

130. "Kenny Journal," 436 (entry of 9 August 1759); "Petition of Royal American Soldiers," n.d., and Maj. William Walters to Lt. Gen. Jeffery Amherst, 13 April 1762, WO 34/2/239 and 34/22/15, TNA; Capt. Francis Legge to [?], 24 August 1764, SGM, case 4, box 7, "Colonial Wars," HSP; Childs, *Armies and Warfare in Europe*, 58–59.

131. Knox, *Historical Journal*, 1:137 (entry of 8 February 1758); Maj. Gen. Thomas Gage to Lt. Gen. Jeffery Amherst, 29 August 1763, WO 34/

5/313, TNA; "Petition of NCOs and Private Men of the 60th Regiment at Niagara," 20 June 1771, TGPAS, vol. 104, WLCL.

132. *New York Mercury*, 23 August 1756, 1; Lt. Gen. Jeffery Amherst to Col. Henry Bouquet, 11 January 1763, in *Bouquet Papers*, 6:142–43; "Amherst Order Book," AMSS, U 1350/O16/2 (entries of 22 September, and 29 October 1763), CKS; Maj. Gen. Thomas Gage to Welbore Ellis, 10 August 1765, and Gage to Lord Barrington, 6 May 1771, in *Gage Correspondence*, 2:299, 582; Way, "Rebellion of the Regulars," 761–92; Kopperman, "Stoppages Mutiny of 1763," 241–54.

5. "HE SEATED OUR CHIEFS AND WARRIORS AT HIS TABLE"

1. Quotation from Atwater, *Tour to Prairie Du Chien*, 122; Draper, "Lieut. James Gorell's Journal," 25–48 (entries of 8 September 1761–18 July 1763); Kappler, *Indian Affairs*, 2:300–303.

2. Dowd, *War under Heaven*, 62–89, 162–68, 189–90; Ward, *Breaking the Backcountry*, 202–51; Richter, *Facing East from Indian Country*, 191–201; McConnell, *Country Between*, 146–206; Jennings, *Empire of Fortune*, 438–49; Axtell, *Invasion Within*, 305–308.

3. Merritt, *At the Crossroads*, 229–63; Shannon, *Indians and Colonists*, 132–73; Merrell, *Into the American Woods*, 221–24.

4. Quotation from "Conference Minutes," 8 November 1756, in Hazard, *Provincial Council of Pennsylvania*, 7:314; Lt. Gov. William Denny to Sir William Johnson, 6 December 1756, in *Johnson Papers*, 9:564–66.

5. Col. John Stanwix to the Earl of Loudoun, 13 September 1756, LO 1787, HEH; "Conference Minutes," 14–17 November 1756, in Hazard, *Provincial Council of Pennsylvania*, 7:326–30; "Instructions to George Croghan," 16 February 1757, in *Johnson Papers*, 9:609; *Pennsylvania Gazette*, 17 April 1760, 3; Merritt, *At the Crossroads*, 19–49, 224–28; Ward, *Breaking the Backcountry*, 123–41.

6. Quotation from Col. John Stanwix to the Earl of Loudoun, 9 May 1757, LO 3583, HEH; Maj. Herbert von Munster to Stanwix, 7 May 1757, LO 3575, HEH; "Conference Minutes," 20 May 1757, in *Johnson Papers*, 9:760–62; Ward, *Breaking the Backcountry*, 149–51.

7. Col. John Stanwix to Lt. Gov. Horatio Sharpe, 12 May 1757, LO 3609A, HEH; Stanwix to Lt. Gov. William Denny, 18 July 1757, SGM, case 4, box 8, "Colonial Wars," HSP; Ward, "Fighting the 'Old Women,'" 306–308.

8. "Conference Minutes," 17–21 May 1757, and George Croghan to Sir William Johnson, 24 May 1757, in *Johnson Papers*, 9:750–62, 771; Cornelius Jaenen, "The Role of Presents in French-Amerindian Trade," in Cameron, *Canadian Economic History*, 231–50; Jacobs, *Diplomacy and Indian Gifts*, 13–18; s.v. "Stanwix, John," in Namier and Brooke, *House of Commons*, 3:473.

9. Lt. Gov. Horatio Sharpe to Lt. Gov. Robert Denny, 8 May 1757, in Browne, *Archives of Maryland* 6 (1888): 552; "Journal of George Croghan, and the Treaty of Easton, &c., 1757," in *NYCD*, 7:280–84 (entries of 2, 21 June, and 3 July 1757); George Croghan to Lt. Gen. Jeffery Amherst, 12 October

1761, in *Johnson Papers*, 3:550; Ward, *Breaking the Backcountry*, 141–45; Merrell, *Into the American Woods*, 186–92.

10. Lt. White Outerbridge to Gov. William H. Lyttelton, 22 October 1756, and Old Warrior of Tomotley to Capt. Raymond Demere, 9 November 1756, in McDowell, *Documents Relating to Indian Affairs*, 2:210–11, 244–45; "The Petition of the Merchants, Traders, Planters and Others Interested in the Trade & Prosperity of South Carolina & Georgia," 21 December 1756, William H. Lyttelton Papers, vol. 3, WLCL; Morris, *Bringing of Wonder*, 107–25.

11. *South Carolina Gazette*, 23 June 1757, 2; Gov. Henry Ellis to the Board of Trade, 20 September 1757, in Coleman and Ready, *Colonial Records of Georgia*, 69; s.v. "REVIEW," in Smith, *Universal Military Dictionary*, 225.

12. Lt. Col. Henry Bouquet to the Earl of Loudoun, 28 April 1757, and Loudoun to Bouquet, 5 May 1757, in *Bouquet Papers*, 1:103, 106; Loudoun to Gov. William H. Lyttelton, 13 February 1758, William H. Lyttelton Papers, vol. 6, WLCL; "A List of His Majesty's 62d or Royal American Regiment," n.d., LO 6952, HEH; Morris, *Bringing of Wonder*, 39–53; s.v. "Musgrove, Mary" in Gallay, *Colonial Wars of North America*, 463–65.

13. Earl of Loudoun to Capt. Abraham Bosomworth, 15 February 1758, LO 5606, HEH; Bosomworth to Brig. Gen. John Forbes, 8 April 1758, HQJF, item 110, TWML; Alden, *John Stuart*, 76–78.

14. Quotation from "Calculation of Expense for Indian Warriors," 23 July 1758, in *Bouquet Papers*, 2:260; "List of Goods Bought by Capt. Bosomworth and William West for the Cherokee Indians," [?] May 1758, and William Trent to Brig. Gen. John Forbes, 22 May 1758, HQJF, items 163 and 242, TWML; Murray, *Indian Giving*, 116–40; Jacobs, *Diplomacy and Indian Gifts*, 46–58.

15. "Speech of Captain Bosomworth to the Headmen, Chiefs, and Warriors of His Majesty's Faithful Friends, and Allies the Cherokees and Catawbas," 21 April 1758, and "The Answer of Captain Bosomworth to the Tallassey Warrior's Speech, 23 April 1758, HQJF, item 133, TWML.

16. Capt. Abraham Bosomworth to Col. Henry Bouquet, 5 June 1758, HQJF, item 295, TWML; Bosomworth to Bouquet, 16 June 1758, and Bouquet to Brig. Gen. John Forbes, 16 June 1758, in *Bouquet Papers*, 2:92–93, 95–96; Gregory E. Dowd, " 'Insidious Friends': Gift Giving and the Cherokee-British Alliance in the Seven Years' War," in Cayton and Teute, *Contact Points*, 114–50.

17. Col. Henry Bouquet to Brig. Gen. John Forbes, 28 June and 3 August 1758, in *Bouquet Papers*, 2:143, 313; Bouquet to Lt. Col. Sir John St. Clair, 30 June 1758, ibid., 149; Bouquet to Capt. Abraham Bosomworth, 3 September 1758, in NYHS, *Collections* 54 (1923): 257–58.

18. Quotation from Brig. Gen. John Forbes to William Pitt, 17 June 1758, in *Forbes Paper*, 117; Lt. Gov. William Denny to Col. George Washington, 25 March 1758, in *Washington Papers*, 5:106–108; "The Journal Of Christian Frederick Post, from Philadelphia to the Ohio, on a Message from the Government of Pennsylvania to the Delaware, Shawnees, and Mingo Indians, Settled There [15 July 1758–22 September 1758]," in Thwaites, *Early Western Travels*, 1:212 (entry of 28 August 1758); Thomas Penn to Col. Henry

Bouquet, 14 April 1759, in *Bouquet Papers*, 3:243; McConnell, *Country Between*, 126–35.

19. Lt. Col. Adam Stephen to Col. Henry Bouquet, 6 June 1758, and Brig. Gen. John Forbes to Bouquet, 25 October 1758, in *Bouquet Papers*, 2:41, 586; Merrell, *Indians' New World*, 92–122, 134–50.

20. Col. Henry Bouquet to Brig. Gen. John Forbes, 3 June 1758, in *Bouquet Papers*, 2:15; Merritt, *At the Crossroads*, 55–61; Merrell, *Indians' New World*, 139; Axtell, *Invasion Within*, 314–16; Henry, *Travels and Adventures*, 99–102; Kirk, *Memoirs and Adventures*, 9–11.

21. Col. George Washington to Col. Henry Bouquet, 24 August 1758, in *Washington Papers*, 5:417; "Barton Journal," 459 (entry of 27 August 1758); Brig. Gen. John Forbes to Col. George Washington, 20 November 1758, in *Forbes Papers*, 259.

22. Quotation from Sir William Johnson to the Earl of Loudoun, 17 September 1756, in *Johnson Papers*, 9:531; "Bouquet: Conference with the Delaware Indians," 4 December 1758, in *Bouquet Papers*, 2:621–24; "Casteogain's Report," 4 January 1759, in Stevens and Kent, *Wilderness Chronicles*, 134–35.

23. "The Journal of Christian Frederick Post, on a Message from the Governor of Pennsylvania, to the Indians on the Ohio, in the Latter Part of the Same Year [25 October 1758–10 January 1759]," in Thwaites, *Early Western Travels*, 1:282–85 (entry of 4 December 1758); Col. Henry Bouquet to Richard Peters, 8 August 1759, and "Bouquet: Speech to the Delawares, Shawnees, and Ohio Senecas," 20 October 1764," in *Bouquet Papers*, 3:513 and 6:673.

24. "Bouquet: Conference with the Delaware Indians," 4 December 1758, in *Bouquet Papers*, 2:621–23; "Casteogain's Report," 4 January 1759, in Stevens and Kent, *Wilderness Chronicles*, 135–37; White, *Middle Ground*, x, 1–93, 97, 179.

25. Maj. Gen. Jeffery Amherst to William Pitt, 16 April 1759, in *Pitt Correspondence*, 2:88–90; "James Hamilton's Narrative," n.d., in Reese, *Official Papers of Francis Fauquier*, 2:603–605.

26. Brig. Gen. John Stanwix to Maj. Gen. Jeffery Amherst, 13 May 1759, WO 34/45/64, TNA; Col. Henry Bouquet to Capt. George Croghan, 13 July 1759, and Col. Hugh Mercer to Bouquet, 28 July 1759, in *Bouquet Papers*, 3:408, 462; Stanwix to William Pitt, 20 November 1759, in *Pitt Correspondence*, 2:212; Ward, *Breaking the Backcountry*, 190–93.

27. Quotation from Col. Henry Bouquet to Col. James [sic] Mercer, 13 July 1759, in *Bouquet Papers*, 3:409; Maj. Gen. John Stanwix to Maj. Gen. Jeffery Amherst, 17 September 1759, CO 5/56/241, TNA; Hinderaker, *Elusive Empires*, 146–47; Wainwright, *George Croghan*, 162–68.

28. Quotation from Maj. John Tulleken to Col. Henry Bouquet, 20 August 1759, in *Bouquet Papers*, 3:592; "The Journal Of Christian Frederick Post...," in Thwaites, *Early Western Travels*, 1:208 (entry of 26 August 1758); "Croghan Journal," 335–39, 388 (entries of 5–8 August 1759, and 5 November 1760); "Kenny Journal," 26 (entry of 1 November 1761); White, *Middle Ground*, 34–40, 176–85.

29. "Croghan Journal," 347–50, 358–59 (entries of 3 September, and 24–26 October 1759); Brig. Gen. Robert Monckton to Col. Henry Bouquet, 7 July

1760, in *Bouquet Papers*, 4:620–21; "Conference Minutes," 12–17 August 1760, in Hazard, *Pennsylvania Archives*, 1st ser. 3 (1853): 744–52; "Disposition of His Majesty's Forces in North America," 4 October 1760, WO 1/5/127, TNA.

30. "Disposition of His Majesty's Forces in North America," 4 October 1760, WO 1/5/127, TNA; "Garrison Return of the Small Posts Depending upon Fort Pitt," 24 October 1761, WO 34/40/114, TNA; "Disposition of His Majesty's Troops Serving in North America," 1 January 1762, AMSS, U 1350/O42/1D, CKS; *Boston Post-Boy & Advertiser*, 22 August 1763, 3; McConnell, *Army and Empire*, 23–24, 29, 32–35.

31. Maj. William Walters to Maj. Gen. Jeffery Amherst, 3 August 1760, WO 34/21/74, TNA; Capt. Donald Campbell to Amherst, 22 May 1761 and 10 April 1762, WO 34/49/36, 82, TNA; Richter, *Facing East from Indian Country*, 174–77; White, *Middle Ground*, 128–40.

32. "Croghan Journal," 406, 432 (entries of 25 May 1761, 30 November, and 6 December 1762); "Kenny Journal," 21 (entry of 18 September 1761); Draper, "Lieut. James Gorell's Journal," 26–38 (entries of 14 October 1761–1 September 1763); Lt. Gen. Jeffery Amherst to Capt. Donald Campbell, 24 October 1762, WO 34/49/316, TNA; Maj. Gen. Thomas Gage to Capt. George Turnbull, 9 April 1770, TGPAS, vol. 91, WLCL.

33. Quotation from Ens. Christopher Pauli to Maj. Gen. Thomas Gage, 6 June 1766, TGPAS, vol. 52, WLCL; Capt. Donald Campbell to Col. Henry Bouquet, 1 June 1761, in *Bouquet Papers*, 5:517; Campbell to Lt. Gen. Jeffery Amherst, 21 June 1762, WO 34/49/94, TNA; Capt. George Turnbull to Gage, 30 September 1769, TGPAS, vol. 87, WLCL; McCusker, *Money and Exchange*, 165.

34. Maj. Gen. Robert Monckton to Col. Henry Bouquet, 5 April 1761, and Capt. Donald Campbell to Bouquet, 21 May 1761, in *Bouquet Papers*, 5:392, 492; Campbell to Lt. Gen. Jeffery Amherst, 8 November 1761, and Amherst to Campbell, 31 December 1761, WO 34/49/62, 290, TNA; Hinderaker, *Elusive Empires*, 147–48; McConnell, *Country Between*, 163–65.

35. Quotation from Capt. Simeon Ecuyer to Col. Henry Bouquet, 8 January 1763, in Darlington, *Fort Pitt*, 111; "Queries from Bouquet with J. Amherst's Answers," 10–11 January 1763, and Bouquet to Ecuyer, 18 February 1763, in *Bouquet Papers*, 6:147–48, 165; Lt. Gen. Thomas Gage to Capt. George Turnbull, 9 April 1770, and Gage to Capt. Beamsley Glazier, 9 June 1770, TGPAS, vols. 91 and 92, WLCL.

36. Quotation from Merritt, *At the Crossroads*, 38; "Ormsby and Hutchins: Account of Provisions," 17 December 1759, and Col. Henry Bouquet to Lt. Stair Campbell Carre, 15 October 1761, in *Bouquet Papers*, 4:366, 5:832; Capt. Donald Campbell to Lt. Gen. Jeffery Amherst, 14 February 1761, WO 34/49/17, 20, TNA; "Order Book: 3 November 1760–29 October 1763," AMSS, U 1350/O16/2 (entry of 22 September 1763), CKS; McConnell, *Country Between*, 153–55.

37. Quotation from Jean Baptiste de Couagre to Sir William Johnson, 6 December 1762, in *Johnson Papers*, 3:958; Maj. William Walters to Maj. Gen. Jeffery Amherst, 15 September 1760, and Maj. John Wilkins to Amherst,

7 December 1762, WO 34/21/98 and 34/22/95-96, TNA; Capt. Lewis Ourry to Col. Henry Bouquet, 2 June 1761, in *Bouquet Papers*, 5:523.

38. Lt. Col. William Eyre to Maj. Gen. Jeffery Amherst, 15 April 1760, WO 34/21/31, TNA; "Mather: Account of Indian Services," 21 March 1761, and "Payments to Indians for Deliveries at Venango," 1 April 1761, in *Bouquet Papers*, 5:373, 387-88.

39. "HBOB," in *Bouquet Papers*, 2:659, 664, 684 (entries of 25 June, 11 July, and 29 August 1758); "Barton Journal," 460 (entry of 28 August 1758); *Amherst Journal*, 219, 222 (entries of 17, 29 July 1760); "Croghan Journal," 365, 417-18 (entries of 25 January 1760, and 24 November 1761); Brumwell, *Redcoats*, 167-68.

40. "Memorandum," 2 August 1756, and "Instructions for the Officers Commandg at Michilmackinack, St. Joseph, &ca Relative to Their Conduct with the Indians," 8 September 1761, in *Johnson Papers*, 9:490 and 3:473; "Copy of Instructions Given the Officers Commanding at Several Posts Depending on the Detroit," 21 April 1762, WO 34/49/87, TNA.

41. Quotation from Capt. Gavin Cochrane to Maj. Gen. Thomas Gage, 20 July 1764, TGPAS, vol. 21, WLCL; "Conference Minutes," 3 October 1761, and Lt. Gen. Jeffery Amherst to Sir William Johnson, 6 July 1762, in *Johnson Papers*, 10:329 and 3:825; Col. Henry Bouquet to Lt. Stair Campbell Carre, 15 October 1761, in *Bouquet Papers*, 5:822-23; "Croghan Journal," 418, 421 (entries of 24 November 1761, and 15 February 1762); Capt. George Turnbull to Gage, 29 June 1770, TGPAS, vol. 93, WLCL.

42. "Bouquet: Speech to the Indians," 29 June 1761, and Capt. Gavin Cochrane to Col. Henry Bouquet, 27 July 1761, in *Bouquet Papers*, 5:590-92, 662; "Croghan Journal," 419 (entries of 3, 10 January 1762); Capt. John Brown to Maj. Gen. Thomas Gage, 25 June 1767, TGPAS, vol. 66, WLCL.

43. Col. Hugh Mercer to Col. Henry Bouquet, 15 August 1759, in *Bouquet Papers*, 3:566; "Orders Concerning Pittsburgh Inhabitants," 9 May 1761, and "Order Limiting Trade with Shawnees," 13 May 1761, ibid., 5:470, 477; "Croghan Journal," 415 (entries of 27-28 August 1761); Maj. William Walters to Lt. Gen. Jeffery Amherst, 30 May 1762, WO 34/22/34, TNA; Capt. George Turnbull to the Inhabitants of Detroit, 22 May 1768, TGPAS, vol. 77, WLCL; Henry, *Travels and Adventures*, 44-45.

44. Capt. Donald Campbell to Col. Henry Bouquet, 2 December 1760, and George Croghan to Ens. Thomas Hutchins, 25 October 1761, in *Bouquet Papers*, 5:142, 842; "Kenny Journal," 179 (entry of 29 December 1762); Capt. George Turnbull to Maj. Gen. Thomas Gage, 17 February 1767, TGPAS, vol. 62, WLCL; Dixon, *Never Come to Peace Again*, 85-100; McConnell, *Country Between*, 171-75.

45. Quotation from Lt. Townshend Guy to Col. Henry Bouquet, 1 June 1761, and Bouquet to Lt. Stair Campbell Carre, 15 October 1761, in *Bouquet Papers*, 5:522, 823; Maj. Gen. Thomas Gage to Capt. George Turnbull, 18 September 1770, TGPAS, vol. 96, WLCL; Capt. John Brown to Gage, 2 November 1770, and "Proceedings of Indian Council at Niagara," 2 November 1770, TGPAS, vol. 97, WLCL; Grabowski, "French Criminal Justice," 405-29.

46. Maj. Gen. Jeffery Amherst to Lt. Gov. James Hamilton, 30 March 1760, in *Johnson Papers*, 3:205; "Plantations General," 2 December 1761, in

Journal of the Commissioners for Trade and Plantations [1759–63], 230; "Kenny Journal," 152, 193 (entries of 12 April 1762, and 27 March 1763); McConnell, *Country Between*, 167–69; Sosin, *Whitehall and the Wilderness*, 105–10, 122–26.

47. Quotation from *Virginia Gazette* [Rind], 14 January 1773, 3; "Bouquet: Proclamation against Settlers," 31 October 1761, and Col. Henry Bouquet to Lt. Gov. Francis Fauquier, 8 February 1762, in *Bouquet Papers*, 5:844 and 6:44–45; "Croghan Journal," 420–21 (entries of 5, 7 February 1762); "Kenny Journal," 40 (entry of 5 February 1761).

48. Lt. Gen. Jeffery Amherst to Sir William Johnson, 22 February and 9 August 1761, in *Johnson Papers*, 3:343–45, 515; "Indian Trade Regulations, Fort Pitt," 18 September 1761, in *Bouquet Papers*, 5:762; Dunn, *Frontier Profit and Loss*, 29–41; Sosin, *Whitehall and the Wilderness*, 39–42.

49. Col. Henry Bouquet to Maj. Gen. Robert Monckton, 28 March 1761, and Lt. Gen. Jeffery Amherst to Bouquet, 2 May 1762, in *Bouquet Papers*, 5:375 and 6:82; "Kenny Journal," 16 (entry of 4 August 1761); "[Major] Henry Balfour's Conference with Indians," 29 September 1761, and Amherst to Sir William Johnson, 30 December 1761, in *Johnson Papers*, 3:544–45, 597–98; Mancall, *Deadly Medicine*, 42–100.

50. "Burd: General Orders," 8 October 1760, and "Orders Concerning Pittsburgh Inhabitants," 9 May 1761, in *Bouquet Papers*, 5:62, 470; "Kenny Journal," 28, 44, 155 (entries of 21 November 1761, 15 March, and 7 June 1762); "Garrison Orders," 30 March 1762, WO 34/22/14, TNA.

51. Col. Henry Bouquet to Maj. Gen. Robert Monckton, 22 April and 4 May 1761, in *Bouquet Papers*, 5:436, 459; Maj. Gen. Thomas Gage to Maj. John Wilkins, 7 October 1762, Thomas Gage Letterbook, vol. 1, WLCL; Lt. Gen. Jeffery Amherst to Wilkins, 24 October 1762, WO 34/23/111, TNA.

52. Lt. Gen. Jeffery Amherst to Maj. John Wilkins, 21 November 1762, WO 34/23/113, TNA; "Orders for Regulation of Trade," 16 January 1765, in *Johnson Papers*, 11:535; Mancall, *Deadly Medicine*, 160–67.

53. Lt. Gov. John Penn to Sir William Johnson, 5 January 1764, in *Johnson Papers*, 11:1–2; Maj. Gen. Thomas Gage to Penn, 6 January 1764, TGPAS, vol. 12, WLCL; Dowd, *War under Heaven*, 191–96; Dunbar, *Paxton Papers*, 16–38.

54. Quotation from Maj. Gen. Thomas Gage to the Earl of Halifax, 12 May 1764, in *Gage Correspondence*, 1:26; Capt. John Schlosser to Gage, 31 January 1764, TGPAS, vol. 13, WLCL; Lt. Gov. John Penn to Sir William Johnson, 17 February 1764, in *Johnson Papers*, 4:327; Dixon, *Never Come to Peace Again*, 247–51; Merritt, *At the Crossroads*, 285–94; Richter, *Facing East from Indian Country*, 203–206.

55. "Ourry: Account of Expenditures," 8 July 1758, in *Bouquet Papers*, 2:172; Fort Pitt Cash Book, 23 October 1760, p. 8, APS; Lt. Gen. Jeffery Amherst to Lt. Col. William Amherst; 3 August 1763, AMSS, U 1350/C81/7, CKS; Bethune, *Power of Faith*, 18.

56. "Croghan Journal," 406, 419–20, 422, 432 (entries of 18 May, and 1–3 December 1761; 16–17 January, 29 March, 30 November, and 6 December 1762); George Croghan to Ens. Thomas Hutchins, 25 October 1761, and Col. Henry Bouquet to Lt. Thomas Roskruge," 15 November 1762, in *Bouquet*

Papers, 5:841–42 and 6:129–30; Maj. John Wilkins to Lt. Gen. Jeffery Amherst, 29 September 1762, WO 34/22/74, TNA.

57. "Return of Provisions at Fort Pitt," 24 December 1762, 24 February, and 24 March 1763, WO 34/40/205, 215, 222, TNA.

58. Quotation from Maj. George Etherington to Lt. Gen. Thomas Gage, 12 May 1772, TGPAS, vol. 110, WLCL; Capt. Gavin Cochrane to the Earl of Halifax, [?] January 1764, EAMC, 176, NL; "Journals of Capt. John Montresor," NYHS, *Collections for 1881* 14 (1882): 303 (entry of 3 October 1764); Gage to Maj. Robert Bayard, 21 June 1766, TGPAS, vol. 53, WLCL; Capt. John Brown to Gage, 25 April 1770, in *Johnson Papers*, 7:583.

59. Lt. Gen. Jeffery Amherst to Col. Henry Bouquet, 2 May 1762, in *Bouquet Papers*, 6:82; Maj. Gen. Thomas Gage to Capt. Robert Bayard, 27 May 1765, TGPAS, vol. 37, WLCL.

60. Quotation from Lafitau, *Customs of the American Indians*, 1:341; James Sterling to Ens. [Francis] Schlosser, 12 June 1762, Sterling Letterbook, WLCL; Capt. John Brown to Sir William Johnson, 25 August 1771, in *Johnson Papers*, 8:235; Morris, *Bringing of Wonder*, 28; White, *Middle Ground*, 15–18, 60–74; Van Kirk, *Many Tender Ties*, 28–33, 75–86; Brown, *Strangers in Blood*, 62–68, 81–96.

61. "Court of Enquiry," 6 July 1763, Add. MSS 21,682, 55, BL; Capt. James Stevenson to Sir William Johnson, 18 May 1770, 8 May 1772, and 1 April 1774, in *Johnson Papers*, 7:681–82 and 8:469, 1108; "Power of Attorney: Major James Stevenson to John Stevenson," 3 May 1796, EAMC, 832, NL; Morris, *Miscellanies in Prose and Verse*, 17.

62. "Journal of Indian Affairs," 1 August 1757 and 2 July 1758, in *Johnson Papers*, 9:809, 942; "Return of Captain Samuel Wllyamoz's Company, Fourth Battalion, Sixtieth (Royal American) Regiment of Foot," 24 April 1758, WO 12/7003/20, TNA; Maj. Gen. Thomas Gage to Lt. Gen. Jeffery Amherst, 8 March 1762, WO 34/5/68, TNA; "Canadian Indians to Western Indians," 25 August 1763," in *Johnson Papers*, 10:792; s.v. "Claus, Christian Daniel," in *Dictionary of Canadian Biography*, 4:154–55.

63. *Maryland Gazette*, 11 August 1757, 3; George Croghan to Sir William Johnson, 10 May 1762, and "Journal and Report of [Ensign] Thomas Hutchins, 4 April–24 September 1762," in *Johnson Papers*, 3:733 and 10:521–29; Hutchins, *Topographical Description*, 101, 104, 108–109, 135–37; s.v. "Hay (Hayes, Hays), Jehu (John)," in *Dictionary of Canadian Biography*, 4:336–37; *American National Biography*, s.v. "Hutchins, Thomas."

64. Maj. Gen. Jeffery Amherst to William Pitt, 8 March 1760, in *Pitt Correspondence*, 2:261; *Pennsylvania Gazette*, 17 April 1760, 3; Board of Trade to Lt. Gov. Francis Fauquier, 17 February 1761, and Fauquier to the Board of Trade, 29 August and 30 November 1761, in Reese, *Official Papers of Francis Fauquier*, 2:479, 563, 596–602; Sosin, *Whitehall and the Wilderness*, 42–48.

65. Quotation from "Virginia," 7 April 1762, in *Journal of the Commissioners for Trade and Plantations* [1759–63], 271; Board of Trade to Lt. Gov. Francis Fauquier, 8 April 1762, in Reese, *Official Papers of Francis Fauquier*, 2:714–15; "Proceedings of Sir William Johnson with the Indians at Fort Stanwix to Settle a Boundary Line," 24 October–6 November 1768, in *NYCD*,

8:111–37; McConnell, *Country Between*, 244–54; Sosin, *Whitehall and the Wilderness*, 136–86.

66. Quotation from Capt. Gavin Cochrane to the Earl of Halifax, [?] January 1764, EAMC, 176, NL; "Croghan Journal," 347 (entry of 3 September 1759); Cochrane to Lt. Gen. Jeffery Amherst, n.d., WO 34/100/8, TNA.

67. David Milobar, "Aboriginal Peoples and the British Press, 1720–1763," in Taylor, Connors, and Jones, *Hanoverian Britain and Empire*, 73–77; Selesky, "Colonial America," in Howard, Andreopoulos, and Shulman, *Laws of War*, 66–74; Childs, *Armies and Warfare in Europe*, 22–27.

68. Quotation from Cochrane, "Treatise," chap. 3, EAMC, 176, NL; Draper, "Lieut. James Gorell's Journal," 38–46 (entries of 14 June–12 July 1763); Ferguson, *History of Civil Society*, xviii–xx, 75, 80–94; Meek, *Social Science and the Ignoble Savage*, 1–176; George W. Stocking, Jr., "Scotland as the Model of Mankind: Lord Kames' Philosophical View of Civilisation," in Thoresen, *Towards a Science of Man*, 73–81.

69. Cochrane, "Treatise," chap. 7, EAMC, 176, NL; White, *Middle Ground*, 25–27, 66–68, 142–85, 215–31; Trigger, *Natives and Newcomers*, 226–68, 289–96; Dickason, *Myth of the Savage*, 251–70; Lehmann, *Henry Home, Lord Kames*, 175–212.

70. Cochrane, "Treatise," chap. 7, EAMC, 176, NL; Capt. Richard Mather to Col. Henry Bouquet, 29 January 1761, in *Bouquet Papers*, 5:273; Axtell, *Invasion Within*, 148–58, 162–67.

71. Sir William Johnson to the Lords of Trade, 13 November 1763, in *NYCD*, 7:578–81; Capt. Gavin Cochrane to Maj. Gen. Thomas Gage, 25 May 1764, and Gage to Cochrane, 23 June 1766, TGPAS, vols. 19 and 53, WLCL; Daniel K. Richter, "Native Americans, the Plan of 1764, and a British Empire That Never Was," in Olwell and Tully, *Cultures and Identities*, 284–92; Sosin, *Whitehall and the Wilderness*, 73–77.

72. François Le Marchand, Sieur de Ligneris, to Col. Henry Bouquet, 22 September 1758, in *Bouquet Papers*, 2:534; "Major [James] Grant's Account of Money Paid to the Officers & Men Who Were Prisoners of War in Canada," n.d., WO 34/198/28, TNA; Ian K. Steele, "Surrendering Rites: Prisoners on Colonial North American Frontiers," in Taylor, Connors, and Jones, *Hanoverian Britain and Empire*, 140–43; Steele, *Betrayals*, 14–18; 118–22, 130–32; Ferling, *Wilderness of Miseries*, 34–35, 48–54.

73. Starkey, *European and Native American Warfare*, 26–30; Carver, *Travels through North America*, 312; Smith, *Bouquet's Expedition against the Ohio Indians*, 44–45; Rogers, *Concise Account of North America*, 227–30.

74. Quotation from "Orders before Landing at Louisbourg, 1758," n.d., AMSS, U 1350/O30, CKS; Dawes, *Journal of General Rufus Putnam*, 34–35, 39 (entries of 4, 29 July 1757); Peckham, "Thomas Gist's Indian Captivity," 293–94 (entry of 14 September 1758); Knox, *Historical Journal*, 1:290, 2:47 (entries of 21 January, and 25 August 1759); "Kenny Journal," 160 (entry of 30 June 1762).

75. Maj. Gen. Daniel Webb to the Earl of Loudoun, 11 August 1757, CO 5/48/312, TNA; Maj. Gen. James Wolfe to William Pitt, 2 September 1759, in *Pitt Correspondence*, 2:155; "Journal of Major Moncrief," in Doughty and

Parmelee, *Siege of Quebec*, 5:47 (entry of 3 September 1759); Quaife, *Siege of Detroit*, 114–15 (entry of 30 May 1763); Kirk, *Memoirs*, 8–9; Rogers, *Concise Account of North America*, 233–36.

    76. "List of Indians with the Marquis de Montcalm's Army," in Bougainville, *Adventure in the Wilderness*, 150–51 (entry of 28 July 1757); "Garrison of Fort William Henry," 9 August 1757, and "An Account of the Campaign of 1757 in North America," n.d., in *NYCD*, 10:624, 643; Steele, *Betrayals*, 110–19, 143–44.

    77. Marquis de Montcalm to the Marquis de Paulmy, 15 August 1757, and Maj. Gen. James Abercromby to Gov. Pierre de Rigaud de Vaudreuil, 26 June 1758, in *NYCD*, 10:598, 772; *Scots Magazine* 19 (1757): 598–99; "Major General James Abercromby to Commanding Officers of the Army," 25 June 1758, WO 34/76/144, TNA; Knox, *Historical Journal*, 1:267 (entry of 28 September 1758); Carver, *Travels through North America*, 316–26; Brumwell, *Redcoats*, 179–87.

    78. Quotation from Alexander, "Capture of Quebec," 141 (entry of 2 July 1759); "Memoirs of the Siege of Quebec and Total Reduction of Canada in 1759 and 1760 by John Johnson Clerk and Quarter Mas'r Sergeant to the 58th Reg't," in Doughty and Parmelee, *Siege of Quebec*, 5:164–66; Peter Linebaugh, "The Tyburn Riot against the Surgeons," in Hay et al., *Albion's Fatal Tree*, 102–109.

    79. Abler, "Scalping, Torture, Cannibalism, and Rape," 6–9; Lafitau, *Customs of the American Indians*, 2:153–54; Jaenen, *Friend and Foe*, 122–27; Kirk, *Memoirs*, 56; Hanway, *Society for the Encouragement of British Troops*, 56.

    80. Knox, *Historical Journal*, 1:395 (entry of 1 July 1759); Maj. Gen. Jeffery Amherst to Maj. Gen. James Wolfe, 7 August 1759, WO 34/46B/312, TNA; "Accurate and Authentic Journal," in Doughty and Parmelee, *Siege of Quebec*, 4:289 (entry of 15 August 1759); *Gentleman's Magazine* 29 (1759): 481; "Trent's Journal," 398 (entry of 15 June 1763); Col. Henry Bouquet to Amherst, 6 August 1763, in *Bouquet Papers*, 6:343.

    81. Quotation from "Inquiry into the Behaviour of the Troops at the Monongahela," 21 November 1755, CO 5/46/135, TNA; [Benjamin Franklin], "To the Printer of the London Chronicle," 9 May 1759, in Labaree, *Papers of Benjamin Franklin*, 8:345; Brumwell, *Redcoats*, 2–4; Jennings, *Empire of Fortune*, 151–59, 214.

    82. Sir John St. Clair to the Duke of Richmond, 22 December 1755, Letterbook of Sir John St. Clair, 193, TWML; "Extract of a Letter from Schenectady Camp," 2 July 1756, Add. MSS 35,909, 262–63, BL; "Journal of Warren Johnson," in *Johnson Papers*, 13:188 (entry of 25 November 1760); Cochrane, "Treatise," chaps. 5–6, EAMC, 176, NL; 28; Carver, *Travels through North America*, 293–97; Smith, *Bouquet's Expedition against the Ohio Indians*, 38–40.

    83. "Abstract of Despatches Received from Canada," 4 June 1756, and Andre Doreil to Marshal Fouquet de Belle-Isle, 31 August 1758, in *NYCD*, 10:408, 818–19; Lt. Col. Adam Stephen to Brig. Gen. John Stanwix, 25 May 1759, in *Bouquet Papers*, 3:318–19; Ward, *Breaking the Backcountry*, 47–51, 58–73.

84. Quotation from *Scots Magazine* 20 (1759): 245; Bougainville, *Adventure in the Wilderness*, 252 (entry of 29 July 1758); Col. Henry Bouquet to Maj. Gen. Thomas Gage, 15 November 1764, in *Bouquet Papers*, 6:703–704; *Pennsylvania Gazette*, 6 December 1764, 3; Anderson, *Crucible of War*, 77–625; Steele, *Warpaths*, 131–247.

85. Col. Henry Bouquet to Col. George Washington, 27 June 1758, and Bouquet to Brig. Gen. John Forbes, 20 August 1758, in *Bouquet Papers*, 2:134, 397; Lafitau, *Customs of the American Indians*, 2:139–42; Smith, *Account of the Remarkable Occurrences*, 157–58; Williamson, *French and Indian Cruelty*, 94–95; Carver, *Travels through North America*, 309–11.

86. Eid, "A Kind of Running Fight," 148–55; Adair, *History of the American Indians*, 384–86; Smith, *Bouquet's Expedition against the Ohio Indians*, 39, 45–46; Rogers, *Journals of Major Robert Rogers*, 62–63.

87. Brumwell, *Redcoats*, 208–15, 228–36; Beattie, "Adaptation to Wilderness Warfare," in Ultee, *Adapting to Conditions*, 68–77; Russell, "Redcoats in the Wilderness," 645–51.

88. "Barton Journal," 449–50 (entries of 10, 12 August 1758); Webster, *Journal of William Amherst*, 40–42 (entry of July 10, 1759); Brumwell, *Redcoats*, 251–55; Houlding, *Fit for Service*, 373.

89. Peckham, "Thomas Gist's Indian Captivity," 291 (entry of 13 September 1758); Capt. Gavin Cochrane to Maj. John Tulleken, 12 July 1759, and Col. Henry Bouquet to Lt. Gen. Jeffery Amherst, 5 August 1763, in *Bouquet Papers*, 3:405–406 and 6:339; *Pennsylvania Gazette*, 8 September 1763, 2.

90. Quotation from Col. Henry Bouquet to Richard Peters, 8 August 1759, in *Bouquet Papers*, 3:513; Cohen, "Triumph on the St. Lawrence," 252 (entry of 13 July 1759); "A Journal of the Siege of Quebec," in Doughty and Parmelee, *Siege of Quebec*, 4:268; Capt. Simeon Ecuyer to Bouquet, 2 August 1763, in *Bouquet Papers*, 6:332; *Boston Post-Boy & Advertiser*, 12 September 1763, 1; Maj. Gen. Thomas Gage to Lt. Gov. Guy Carleton, 3 April 1768, and Carleton to Gage, 4 July 1770, TGPAS, vols. 75 and 93, WLCL.

91. Andre Doreil to the Marquis de Paulmy, 31 July 1757, in *NYCD*, 10:594; "Journal of the Expedition against Fort William Henry," 12 July–16 August 1757, ibid., 599 (entries of 21, 24 July 1757); Maj. Gen. Daniel Webb to the Earl of Loudoun, 1 August 1757, CO 5/48/200, TNA; *Pennsylvania Gazette*, 4 August 1757, 3; Steele, *Betrayals*, 87–88.

92. *Amherst Journal*, 138 (entry of 15 July 1759); "Journal of the Siege of Detroit," n.d., WO 34/49/8–11 (entries of 31 July, and 2 October 1763), TNA; *Pennsylvania Gazette*, 8 September 1763, 2; Hough, *Diary of the Siege of Detroit*, 73–74 (entry of 2 October 1763); James Sterling to John Duncan, 6 October 1763, Sterling Letterbook, WLCL; Webster, "John Montresor's Expedition to Detroit," 23 (entry of 13 October 1763); *Pennsylvania Gazette*, 22 and 29 December 1763, 2–3 and 3; *Pennsylvania Journal & Weekly Advertiser*, 29 December 1763, 2.

93. Maj. Gen. Jeffery Amherst to Maj. William Walters, 2 November 1760, and Amherst to Capt. Donald Campbell, 31 December 1761, WO 34/23/45 and WO 34/49/290, TNA; Dixon, *Never Come to Peace Again*, 78–84.

94. Quotation from Capt. Donald Campbell to Col. Henry Bouquet, 11 December 1760, in *Bouquet Papers*, 5:171; Lt. Thomas Hutchins to

George Croghan, n.d., WO 34/39/295, TNA; Dowd, *War under Heaven*, 62–75.

95. Maj. William Walters to Maj. Gen. Jeffery Amherst, 14 August 1760, and Capt. Donald Campbell to Amherst, 16 February 1762, WO 34/21/84 and 34/49/75, TNA; McConnell, *Country Between*, 163–65.

96. Col. Henry Bouquet to Maj. Gen. Robert Monckton, 20 March 1761, in *Bouquet Papers*, 5:354–55; Sir William Johnson to Maj. Gen. Jeffery Amherst, 29 July 1761, WO 34/39/200, TNA; Dowd, *War under Heaven*, 78–82.

97. Col. Henry Bouquet to Fort Major James Livingston, 31 October 1761, and 6 February 1762, in *Bouquet Papers*, 5:847 and 6:43; Maj. William Walters to Maj. Gen. Amherst, 20 June 1762, WO 34/22/40, TNA; McConnell, *Army and Empire*, 21–25.

98. Capt. Donald Campbell to Maj. William Walters, 17 June 1761, in *Bouquet Papers*, 5:560; "Journal of Indian Affairs," 4 July–4 August 1763, and Sir William Johnson to Maj. Gen. Jeffery Amherst, 6 October 1763, in *Johnson Papers*, 10:769, 866–68; Steele, *Warpaths*, 236–38.

99. Sir William Johnson to the Lords of Trade, 13 November 1763, in *NYCD*, 7:577; *Boston Post-Boy & Advertiser*, 15 August 1763, 2; Maj. Gen. Jeffery Amherst to Maj. John Wilkins, 29 October 1763, WO 34/23/156, TNA; Dowd, *War under Heaven*, 114–31; Anderson, *Crucible of War*, 535–50.

100. *Pennsylvania Gazette*, 17 July 1760, 3; "Court of Enquiry," 6 July 1763, Add. MSS 21,682, 54–55, BL; John Bremner's Diary and Memorandum Book, 1756–64, pp.129–30 (entries of 21, 27 July 1763), NYHS; *Boston Post-Boy & Advertiser*, 15 August and 12 September 1763, 2 and 1; Merritt, *At the Crossroads*, 177–80.

101. Quaife, *Siege of Detroit*, 229, 235; Hough, *Diary of the Siege of Detroit*, 41 (entry of 5 July 1763); *Boston Post-Boy & Advertiser*, 15 and 22 August 1763, 2 and 3; Henry, *Travels and Adventures*, 102–103.

102. Quotation from Lt. Gen. Jeffery Amherst to Col. Henry Bouquet, 7 July 1763, in *Bouquet Papers*, 6:300; *Pennsylvania Gazette*, 1 September and 13 October 1763, 2 and 2; Smith, *Remarkable Occurrences*, 158–59; Dowd, *War under Heaven*, 136–68.

103. "New Establishment," 20 March 1761, AMSS, U 1350/O14/109, CKS; "A List of the Number of Fighting Men of the Different Indian Nations," 5 October 1762, in *Johnson Papers*, 10:544–45; "Return of the Number of Men Necessary to Garrison the Following Posts, in Case They Were Threaten'd to Be Attacked by an Enemy," 24 November 1762, WO 34/93/215, TNA.

104. Quotation from Capt. Gavin Cochrane to Col. Henry Bouquet, 9 July 1761, in *Bouquet Papers*, 5:625; Maj. Gen. Jeffery Amherst to Brig. Gen. John Forbes, 25 December 1758, WO 34/44/236, TNA; Amherst to Brig. Gen. Robert Monckton, 29 April 1760, Add. MSS 21,678, 5, BL; Amherst to Bouquet, 19 June 1763, in *Bouquet Papers*, 6:240.

105. "Extract of a Court of Enquiry," 6 July 1763, Add. MSS 21682, 54–55, BL; *Boston Post-Boy & Advertiser*, 15 August 1763, 2; Dixon, *Never Come to Peace Again*, 106–67; Steele, *Warpaths*, 236–39.

106. Lt. Elias Meyer, "Map of the Country Showing Fort Presque Isle on Lake Erie ... and Fort Cumberland in Maryland," 1 December 1760, in Maps

and Plans Extracted from War Office Records, 346, Pennsylvania, 1760, TNA; "Present State of Fort Pitt and Posts Depending," 24 December 1760, in Stevens and Kent, *Wilderness Chronicles*, 202; Ens. John Christie to Col. Henry Bouquet, 10 July 1763, in *Bouquet Papers*, 6:301–302; Malone, *Skulking Way of War*, 14; Carver, *Travels through North America*, 82–83.

107. Col. Henry Bouquet to Capt. Lewis Ourry, 4 July 1763, and Ens. John Christie to Bouquet, 10 July 1763, in *Bouquet Papers*, 6:296, 302; Lt. Gen. Jeffery Amherst to Sir William Johnson, 7 July 1763, in *Johnson Papers*, 10:733; "Court of Enquiry," 12 September and 20 December 1763, Add. MSS 21,682, 62, 65, BL.

108. Capt. Simeon Ecuyer to Col. Henry Bouquet, 2, 16, 26 June, and 2 August 1763, in *Bouquet Papers*, 6:202, 231–32, 259–60, 332–33; Stotz, *Outposts of the War for Empire*, 127–39.

109. "Trent's Journal," 398–99, 407, 410 (entries of 10 and 17 June, 24 and 26 July, and 4 August 1763); "Discourse between Delawares and Ecuyer," 24 June 1763, in *Bouquet Papers*, 6:261; *Boston Post-Boy & Advertiser*, 5 September 1763, 3; Brumwell, *Redcoats*, 201; Ward, *Breaking the Backcountry*, 55–56.

110. Quotation from "Extract of a Letter from Fort Pitt," in *Boston Post-Boy & Advertiser*, 12 September 1763, 1; "Trent's Journal," 394, 398, 400, 401 (entries of 30 May, and 7, 24, and 26 June 1763); Capt. Simeon Ecuyer to Col. Henry Bouquet, 16 and 26 June 1763, and "Ecuyer: Reply to Indians," 27 July 1763, in *Bouquet Papers*, 6:231, 260, 336–37; Ranlet, "The British, the Indians, and Smallpox" 431–36.

111. "Trent's Journal," 408–10 (entries of 28 July–4 August 1763); Capt. Simeon Ecuyer to Col. Henry Bouquet, 2 August 1763, in *Bouquet Papers*, 6:341; *Boston Post-Boy & Advertiser*, 12 September 1763, 1; "Journal of Indian Affairs," 2 March 1765, in *Johnson Papers*, 11:618; Dixon, *Never Come to Peace Again*, 181–85.

112. John Adair to Lt. Gen. Jeffery Amherst, 18 September 1762, AMSS, U 1350/042/8A, CKS; Amherst to Col. Henry Bouquet, 16 June 1763, and Lt. Gov. James Hamilton to Bouquet, 29 August 1763, in *Bouquet Papers*, 6:227, 376; Dixon, *Never Come to Peace Again*, 167–70; Eid, "A Kind of Running Fight," 155–66; Daudelin, "Numbers and Tactics," 157–61.

113. Col. Henry Bouquet to Lt. Gen. Jeffery Amherst, 5 August 1763, in *Bouquet Papers*, 6:339; *Boston Post-Boy & Advertiser*, 12 September 1763, 1; Daudelin, "Numbers and Tactics,"162–63; Smith, *Bouquet's Expedition against the Ohio Indians*, viii–ix.

114. Knox, *Historical Journal*, 1:400 (entry of 5 July 1759); "Journal of Major Moncrief," in Doughty and Parmelee, *Siege of Quebec*, 5:39–40 (entry of 26 July 1758); Frederick the Great, *Military Instructions*, 65.

115. Col. Henry Bouquet to Lt. Gen. Jeffery Amherst, 6 August 1763, in *Bouquet Papers*, 6:342–44; *Pennsylvania Gazette*, 1 September 1763, 2; Daudelin, "Numbers and Tactics," 164–68.

116. Quotation from Klinck and Talman, *Journal of Major John Norton*, 268; "Bouquet to Officer Commanding at Presque Isle, 28 August 1763, and Capt. William Grant to Col. Henry Bouquet, 15 May 1764, in *Bouquet Pa-*

pers, 6:375, 541; *Boston Post-Boy & Advertiser*, 5 September 1763, 3; Richter, "War and Culture," 535–36.

117. *Pennsylvania Gazette*, 25 August and 1 September 1763, 2; Eid, "'National' War among Indians," 125–54; Carver, *Travels through North America*, 299–307; Rogers, *Concise Account of North America*, 220–22, 228–29.

118. "Trent's Journal," 411–12 (entries of 14 August–16 September 1763); Capt. Lewis Ourry to Col. Henry Bouquet, 27 August 1763, and Bouquet to Maj. Henry Gladwin, 29 September 1763, in *Bouquet Papers*, 6:371, 403; Dixon, *Never Come to Peace Again*, 193–97; Smith, *Bouquet's Expedition against the Ohio Indians*, 2, 11.

119. Williams, *Bouquet Orderly Book, 1764*, 14–18, 21–22, 27, 38 (entries of 2, 7, 13, and 26 October 1764); Smith, *Bouquet's Expedition against the Ohio Indians*, 7–9, 17.

120. Quotation from Williams, *Bouquet Orderly Book, 1764*, 28 (entry of 13 October 1764); "Pontiac to Gladwin and the Reply," 1 November 1763, and "Bouquet to Delawares," 15 October 1764, in *Bouquet Papers*, 6:449, 661–62; *Pennsylvania Journal & Weekly Advertiser*, 29 December 1763, 2; Sir William Johnson to Maj. Gen. Thomas Gage, 22 August 1764, in *Johnson Papers*, 11:336–37; "Journals of Capt. John Montresor," NYHS, *Collections for 1881* 14 (1882): 307–12 (entries of 13–18 October 1764); Godfrey, *Pursuit of Profit and Preferment*, 175–205.

121. "Conference between Chevalier de Callières and the Iroquois at Montreal," 18 July 1700, in *NYCD*, 9:208–10; *Conferences, Held at Easton*, 6, 10, 14, 15, 21; Williams, *Bouquet Orderly Book, 1764*, 31, 34–40 (entries of 16 and 21–29 October 1764); Col. Henry Bouquet to Maj. Gen. Thomas Gage, 21 October 1764, in *Bouquet Papers*, 6:676–77; Dixon, *Never Come to Peace Again*, 237–40; Smith, *Bouquet's Expedition against the Ohio Indians*, 14–16.

122. Darlington, *Christopher Gist's Journals*, 39 (entry of 26 December 1750); Col. Henry Bouquet to Brig. Gen. Robert Monckton, 15 September 1760, in *Bouquet Papers*, 5:39; Steele, "Surrendering Rites," 141; Lafitau, *Customs of the American Indians*, 2:148–49, 152–57; Mrs. E. M. Davis, "Capture and Captivity of David Boyd," 28–30; "Narrative of Marie LeRoy and Barbara Leininger," in Linn and Egle, *Pennsylvania Archives*, 2nd ser. 7 (1891): 429–30; Seaver, *DEH-HE-WA-MIS*, 29–39.

123. Steele, "Surrendering Rites," 137–40; Calloway, "Uncertain Destiny," 194–95; Richter, "War and Culture," 530–33; Kirk, *Memoirs*, 36.

124. Matthew J. Friedman and Anthony J. Marsella, "Posttraumatic Stress Disorder: An Overview of the Concept," in Marsella et. al., *Ethnocultural Aspects of Posttraumatic Stress Disorder*, 11–32; Leo Eitinger, "The Effects of Captivity," in Ochberg and Soskis, *Victims of Terrorism*, 73–93; Lafitau, *Customs of the American Indians*, 2:153–54.

125. "Croghan Journal," 406–407 (entries of 28 May, and 12–19 June 1761); Col. Henry Bouquet to Maj. Gen. Robert Monckton, 24 July 1761, and Bouquet to Lt. Gen. Jeffery Amherst, 11 July 1762, in *Bouquet Papers*, 5:654–55 and 6:100.

126. "Minutes: Conference with Shawnees," 14 November 1764, in *Bouquet Papers*, 6:700–703; "Captives Delivered to Colonel Bouquet," 3 December 1764, and "Conference Minutes," 9–11 May 1765, in *Johnson Papers*, 11:484–91, 723–28; Smith, *Bouquet's Expedition against the Ohio Indians*, 17–26, 33–35.

127. Quotation from Smith, *Bouquet's Expedition against the Ohio Indians*, 26; Williams, *Bouquet Orderly Book, 1764*, 40 (entry of 29 October 1764); Col. Henry Bouquet to Capt. Charles Lewis, 4 November 1764, and "Prisoners Delivered by the Shawnees," 5 January 1765, in *Bouquet Papers*, 6:683–84, 753–54; *Pennsylvania Gazette*, 17 January 1765, 1; *Maryland Gazette*, 31 January 1765, 2–3; Alvord and Carter, "George Croghan's Journals, February 28, 1765–May 11, 1765," *Collections of the Illinois State Historical Library* 11 (1916): 7, 9–14 (entries of 28 April, and 2, 5, 7, and 9 May 1765).

128. Ward, "Redeeming the Captives," 174–75, 181–83; Vaughan, *Roots of American Racism*, 232–36, 251–52; Derounian-Stodola and Levernier, *Indian Captivity Narrative*, 5–7, 73–85, 159–65; Axtell, *Invasion Within*, 306–309; Smith, *Bouquet's Expedition against the Ohio Indians*, 29.

129. Col. Henry Bouquet to Maj. Gen. Thomas Gage, 15 November 1764, in *Bouquet Papers*, 6:704; Graham, Rawlings, and Rigsby, *Loving to Survive*, 24–61; Thomas Strentz, "The Stockholm Syndrome: Law Enforcement Policy and Hostage Behavior," in Ochberg and Soskis, *Victims of Terrorism*, 149–63; Seaver, *DEH-HE-WA-MIS*, 74–76; Smith, *Bouquet's Expedition against the Ohio Indians*, 21.

130. Quotation from *Pennsylvania Gazette*, 6 December 1764, 3; ibid., 14 February 1765, 1; *Virginia Gazette* [Purdie and Dixon], 13 August 1767, 2.

6. "I SHALL SETTLE, MARRY AND TRADE HERE"

1. Knox, *Historical Journal*, 1:51, 54, 83–84, 309–20 (entries of 14, 21 August, and 12 October 1757; 11 June, and 24 July 1758; and 5 May 1759); John Bremner's Diary and Memorandum Book, 1756–64, p. 120 (entry of 22 July 1763), NYHS; "Lord Adam Gordon's Journal," 394–453; Anderson, *Crucible of War*, 503–506; Kirk, *Memoirs and Adventures*, 3, 69–70, 92–94; Rogers, *Concise Account of North America*, v–vi, 20–23, 28–30, 160, 168–70.

2. Quotation from Capt. Charles Lee to Miss Sidney Lee, 30 July 1759, in NYHS, *Collections for 1871* 4 (1872): 19–20; "Lieut. [Dietrich] Brehm's Report to His Excellency General Amherst of a Scout Going from Montreal . . . to Detroit," 23 February 1761, WO 34/49/21–24, TNA; "Lt. DesBarres: Remarks for Nova Scotia," 1 December 1763, WO 34/12/415–16, TNA; "Journal of Captain Harry Gordon, 1766," in Mereness, *Travels in the American Colonies*, 464–89.

3. Marshall, *Making and Unmaking of Empires*, 274–338; Anderson, *Crucible of War*, 647–51; Jennings, *Empire of Fortune*, 459–64; Countryman, *People in Revolution*, 36–47, 63–67; Shy, *Toward Lexington*, 45–83, 181–320.

4. "Return of the First Battalion of the Royal American Regiment," 26 December 1757, and "Court of Enquiry," 20 January 1758, LO 6877 and 5428,

HEH; Welbore Ellis to Lt. Gen. Jeffery Amherst, 20 May 1763, WO 4/987/17–18, TNA; "New Establishment," 20 March 1761, and "Plan of the Establishment of the Sixtieth or Royal American Regiment of Foot," 18 May 1763, AMSS, U 1350/014/109 and 1350/O43/9B, CKS.

5. Gov. William Keppel to the Earl of Egremont, 3 July 1763, CO 117/1/55–59, TNA; Maj. Gen. Thomas Gage to Lt. Gen. Jeffery Amherst, 29 August 1763, WO 34/5/312, TNA; Gage to Welbore Ellis, 10 March 1764; in *Gage Correspondence*, 2:224.

6. "Abstract of Royal Orders to Reduce the Army," 18 May 1763, and "Instructions to Reduce the 42d Regiment," 7 August 1763, in *Bouquet Papers*, 6:186–88, 354–55; Maj. Gen. Thomas Gage to Lt. Gen. Jeffery Amherst, 29 August 1763, WO 34/5/313, TNA.

7. "Mackay's Discharge," 24 April 1760, in *Bouquet Papers*, 4:536–37; "Discharge of Sergeant Moses Campbell," 21 December 1763, Lower Canada Land Papers, Record Group 1-L3L, vol. 54, p. 27452, LAC; "Discharge of Sergeant Lutwig Simon," 20 February 1764; ALG, AO 272/17/77, NYSL; Cuthbertson, *Management and Oeconomy of a Battalion*, 97–98.

8. Quotation from Lt. Gov. Cadwallader Colden to the Lords of Trade, 8 February 1764, in *NYCD*, 7:608; Henry Fox to Northern Governors, 13 March 1756, WO 34/71/65, TNA; "Lieutenant Schlosser's Advertisement for Recruits," 2 July 1756, Timothy Horsfield Papers, APS.

9. Webster, "Journal of Abijah Willard," 57–59 (entries of 7–8 October 1755); *Boston Evening Post*, 12 July 1756, 1; Earl of Loudoun to Gov. Charles Lawrence, 22 February 1757, n.d., WO 34/11/162, TNA.

10. Quotation from Lt. Gen. Jeffery Amherst to Maj. Gen. James Murray, 4 August 1763, WO 34/3/203, TNA; "Recruiting Instructions," 15 November 1756, LO 2221, HEH; Brumwell, *Redcoats*, 20, 31, 33, 44, 290–97; McLynn, *Crime and Punishment*, 320–31; Hanway, *Society for the Encouragement of British Troops*, 67–72.

11. "Settlement of German Families in English Colonies," 5 November 1761, in Redington and Roberts, *Home Office Papers of George III*, 1:75; Earl of Egremont to the Lords of Trade, 14 July 1763, in Shortt and Doughty, *Documents Relating to Constitutional History*, pt. 1, 149; Lt. Gen. Jeffery Amherst to Maj. Gen. James Murray, 6 October 1763, WO 34/3/212, TNA.

12. "By the King: A Proclamation," 7 October 1763, in Brigham, *British Royal Proclamations Relating to America*, 215; "Petition of Daniel Crowther, et al.," 30 June 1766, ALG, AO 272/21/50, NYSL; Merchant, *Ecological Revolutions*, 183; Sosin, *Whitehall and the Wilderness*, 52–65.

13. "Instructions to Governor [James] Murray," 7 December 1763, in Shortt and Doughty, *Documents Relating to Constitutional History*, pt. 1, 195–97; "Evidence on the Claim of John Mebus," 11 July 1787, in W. Antliff, *Loyalist Settlements*, 296–97.

14. John Watts to Messrs. Lasselles, Clarke, and Dalling, 11 October 1764, and Watts to Maj. Gen. Robert Monckton, 16 March 1765, in NYHS, *Collections for 1928* 61 (1928): 294, 338; John Bowles to Gov. Henry Moore, 9 June 1766, and "Assignment from Philip Harvey, et. al. to Robert Buchanan," 21 January 1767, ALG, AO 272/21/7 and 272/22/164, NYSL;

"Petition of James Duane in Behalf of Private Philip Daulton, et al.," 4 February 1767, ALG, AO 272/23/19–20, NYSL; "Evidence on the Claim of Donald McIntosh," 24 June 1787, in Antliff, *Loyalist Settlements*, 121.

15. "Evidence on the Claim of Donald Fisher," 16 June 1787, in Antliff, *Loyalist Settlements*, 105–106; "Evidence on the Claim of Donald Munro," 5 March 1788, in Fraser, *Second Report*, 344–45; Smith, *The "Lower Sort,"*, 64–84, 109–25; McCusker, *Money and Exchange*, 165; Nash, *Urban Crucible*, 246–60.

16. Quotation from Maj. Gen. Thomas Gage to the Earl of Shelburne, 23 January 1768, in *Gage Correspondence*, 1:161; *Pennsylvania Gazette*, 12 February 1761 and 17 May 1764, 4 and 3; *Virginia Gazette* [Purdie and Dixon], 6 August 1772, 2; "Evidence on the Claim of Daniel Fraser," [?] November 1783, and "Evidence on the Claim of Thomas Mills," 8 December 1785, in Coldham, *American Loyalist Claims*, 166–67, 349.

17. Capt. Lewis Ourry to Lt. Gov. James Hamilton, 26 August 1763, Burd-Shippen Collection, APS; "Evidence on the Claim of John Chisholm," 11 July 1787, in Fraser, *Second Report*, 326; "Evidence on the Claim of John Driver," 21 July 1787, in Antliff, *Loyalist Settlements*, 323.

18. *New London Summary; or The Weekly Advertiser*, 21 September 1759, 3; Lt. Gov. Cadwallader Colden to the Lords of Trade, 8 February 1764, in *NYCD*, 7:608; O'Callaghan, *Indorsed Land Papers*, 331–522.

19. "Council Minutes," 2 February 1764, CO 5/1071/55–59, TNA; "Petition of Sergeant Moses Campbell, et al.," 6 February 1764, and "Return of Survey for Sergeant Moses Campbell," 25 March 1765, ALG, AO 272/17/67, 149, NYSL; Maj. Gen. Thomas Gage to Lt. Henry Munro, 28 September 1764, TGPAS, vol. 25, WLCL; Taylor, *William Cooper's Town*, 44–45.

20. Articles for the Western Department," n.d., and Col. Henry Bouquet to Maj. Gen. Robert Monckton, 22 April 1761, in *Bouquet Papers*, 5:228, 437; "Private Instructions for Fort Pitt," n.d., Add. MSS 21,657, 28, BL; Lt. Gen. Jeffery Amherst to William Sharpe, 20 October 1762, WO 34/74/155–56, TNA; "James Hamilton's Narrative," n.d., in Reese, *Official Papers of Francis Fauquier*, 2:605; Mayer, "From Forts to Families," 5–43; Taylor, "Great Change Begins," 274–77.

21. Capt. Lewis Ourry to Lt. Gov. James Hamilton, 10 June 1763, Burd-Shippen Collection, APS; Maj. Gen. Thomas Gage to the Earl of Halifax, 14 April 1764, in *Gage Correspondence*, 1:24–25; Gage to Capt. Robert Bayard, 27 May 1765, and Capt. Gavin Cochrane to Gage, n.d. [March 1772], TGPAS, vols. 37 and 109, WLCL.

22. Claude J. Sauthier, "A Choriographical Map of the Province of New York," 1779, CO 700, New York, no. 40, TNA; "Evidence in the Claim of Rebecca Woods," 20 July 1787, in Antliff, *Loyalist Settlements*, 319–20; "Evidence on the Claim of Thomas Sparham," 27 February 1788, in Fraser, *Second Report*, 447–48; Klyza and Trombulak, *Story of Vermont*, 37–39; "Lord Adam Gordon's Journal," 446.

23. Quotations: ("technical American knowledge") from Crevecoeur, *Letters from an American Farmer*, 86; and ("the new settlers") from Bridenbaugh, "Patrick M'Roberts Tour," 172; "Journal (No. 2) of Col. James Mon-

tresor, Saratoga," and "Journals of Capt. John Montresor," NYHS, *Collections for 1881* 14 (1882): 41–45, 276 (entries of 23 August–21 September 1757, and 24 July 1764); Williams, *Americans and Their Forests*, 72–74; Weslager, *Log Cabin in America*, 13–21, 133.

24. Lt. Col. William Eyre to Maj. Gen. Jeffery Amherst, 28 April 1760, WO 34/21/37, TNA; Jenks, *Diary*, 7 (entry of 24 June 1760); Taylor, "Great Change Begins," 278–85; Merchant, *Ecological Revolutions*, 155–62; Williams, *Americans and Their Forests*, 60–65; Grant, *Memoirs of an American Lady*, 204–206.

25. "HBOB," in *Bouquet Papers*, 2:666, 680 (entries of 20 July, and 21 August 1758); *Hawks' Orderly Book*, 29, 67, 83 (entries of 8 July 1759, 30 May, and 7 July 1760); Merchant, *Ecological Revolutions*, 169–70, 181–82; Williams, *Americans and Their Forests*, 67–69.

26. *Hawks' Orderly Book*, 3–4 (entry of 11 June 1759); Dr. James Stevenson to Col. Henry Bouquet, 27 March 1761, and Bouquet to Maj. William Walters, 10 June 1761, in *Bouquet Papers*, 5:374, 536–37.

27. Ford, *General Orders of 1757*, 75 (entry of 30 August 1757); "HBOB," in *Bouquet Papers*, 2:665 (entry of 14 July 1758); *Hawks' Orderly Book*, 58 (entry of 7 August 1759); Lt. Col. William Eyre to Brig. Gen. Thomas Gage, 20 April 1760, TGPAS, vol. 6, WLCL; Grant, *Memoirs of an American Lady*, 234.

28. Capt. John Schlosser to [?], 2 February 1759, TGPAS, vol. 1, WLCL; Lt. Col. William Eyre to Maj. Gen. Jeffery Amherst, 15 April and 27 May 1760, WO 34/21/31, 46, TNA; Peckham, "Thomas Gist's Indian Captivity," 296 (entry of 20 September 1758); Kirk, *Memoirs*, 119–20; Grace, *Life and Sufferings of Henry Grace*, 24–27.

29. Quotation from "Petition of Corporal Henry Urkley, et al.," 7 March 1764, ALG, AO 272/17/92, NYSL; Taylor, "Great Change Begins," 285–86; Taylor, *Liberty Men and Great Proprietors*, 82–84.

30. "Evidence on the Claim of Elizabeth Campbell," 6 March 1787, Audit Office 13/12/18–20, TNA; "Evidence on the Claim of Saml. Richardson," 20 July 1787, in Antliff, *Loyalist Settlements*, 320; "Evidence on the Claim of Andr. Coulter," 2 August 1787, and "Evidence on the Claim of Donald Munro," 21 August 1787, in Fraser, *Second Report*, 336, 344–45; McCusker, *Money and Exchange*, 165.

31. Gov. Henry Moore to the Earl of Shelburne, 8 November 1766, and "Representation of the Lords of Trade on the New Hampshire Grants," 3 December 1772, in *NYCD*, 7:875 and 8:330–37; Moore to the Board of Trade, 4 April 1767, CO 5/1073/3, TNA; Board of Trade to the Committee of the Privy Council, 13 February 1776, in O'Callaghan, *History of the State of New-York*, 1:585–86; Bellesiles, *Revolutionary Outlaws*, 27–32, 70–111.

32. Lt. Col. John Reid to [Sir William Johnson], 1 June 1773, SGM, case 4, box 8, "Colonial Wars," HSP; Kierner, *Traders and Gentlefolk*, 92–105; Mancall, *Valley of Opportunity*, 105–14; Kim, *Landlord and Tenant*, 162–72, 242–46, 261–70.

33. *New York Mercury*, 2 April 1764, 4; "Evidence on the Claim of Alexander Young," 12 July 1787, in Antliff, *Loyalist Settlements*, 298–99; "Evidence on the Claim of Anthony Walliser," and "Evidence on the Claim of

John Fraser," 30 October 1787, in Fraser, *Second Report*, 354–55; "Evidence on the Claim of Peter McGregor," 12 November 1787, and "Evidence on the Claim of John Farlinger," 14 February 1788, ibid., 369, 406–407.

34. Barnabas Hughes to Col. Henry Bouquet, 28 March 1760, and Capt. Harry Gordon to Bouquet, 24 May 1761, in *Bouquet Papers*, 4:502–503, 5:502; Lt. Gov. Cadwallader Colden to the Lords of Trade, 30 August 1760, in *NYCD*, 7:445–46; "Indenture between William Allen of Philadelphia and Colonel Henry Bouquet," 3 March 1763, Add. MSS 21,685, 18–19, BL.

35. Quotation from Col. Henry Bouquet to [?], 10 June 1759, in *Bouquet Papers*, 3:371–72; Hancock, *Citizens of the World*, 285–94; Langford, *Public Life and the Propertied Englishman*, 1–70; Mingay, *English Landed Society*, 3–288.

36. Quotation from Capt. John Carden to Lt. Gen. Thomas Gage, 21 December 1771, TGPAS, vol. 108, WLCL; Capt. Lt. Elias Meyer to Lt. Gen. Jeffery Amherst, n.d., WO 34/2/191, TNA; Ens. Thomas Ellis to Maj. Gen. Thomas Gage, 22 July 1764, TGPAS, vol. 22, WLCL; Thomas Swords to George Cockburn, 9 November 1765, Ferdinand J. Dreer Autograph Collection, box 46, "Officers Serving in America before the American Revolution," HSP; Grant, *Memoirs of an American Lady*, 233.

37. Quotation from Maj. Philip Skene to Secretary [John] Pownall, 12 March 1764, in *NYCD*, 7:616; "Petition of Sergeant Frederic Hartel," 21 April 1764, ALG, AO 272/17/122, NYSL; "Calculation of Provisions for 100 Men for One Year," 20 March 1765, and Capt. Thomas Falconer to Members of the St. John's River Society at Boston, 19 April 1765, St. John's River Society Records, items 6 and 7, MassHS; Grant, *Memoirs of an American Lady*, 205–206.

38. Lt. Rudolph Bentinck to Col. Henry Bouquet, 8 April 1759, in *Bouquet Papers*, 3:235; *New York Mercury*, 9 September 1765, 4; "Evidence on the Claim of Donald McIntosh," 24 June 1787, in Antliff, *Loyalist Settlements*, 120–21; "Evidence on the Claim of Wm. Ferguson," 26 July 1788, and "Evidence on the Claim of John Pickle," 21 February 1788, in Fraser, *Second Report*, 391–92, 424; Grant, *Memoirs of an American Lady*, 233–35.

39. "Report of the Proceeding of the Troops on the Expedition up the St. John's River in the Bay of Fundy under the Command of Colonel Monckton," n.d., WO 34/43/1–8, TNA; "Nova Scotia," 2 December 1762, in *Journal of the Commissioners for Trade and Plantations* [1759–63] (London, 1920–38), 307; Maj. Joseph Gorham to the King's Most Excellent Majesty in Council, 31 May 1766, CO 323/22/39, TNA; Raymond, *River St. John*, 177–86, 206–207.

40. Quotation from Lt. J. F. W. DesBarres to Col. Henry Bouquet, 21 August 1764, Add. MSS 21,650, 419, BL; Capt. Beamsley Glasier to the St. John's River Society at Montreal, 14 December 1764, in "St. John's River Society Papers," 310–12; *Pennsylvania Gazette*, 5 February 1767, 1, and 17 March 1768, 4; Elizabeth Mancke, "Corporate Structure and Private Interest: The Mid-Eighteenth-Century Expansion of New England," in Conrad, *They Planted Well*, 163–77; Rawlyk, *Nova Scotia's Massachusetts*, 217–28.

41. Maj. George Etherington to Lt. Gen. Thomas Gage, 5 February 1772, TGPAS, vol. 109, WLCL; Thomson, *Men and Meridians*, 1:97–105; Chip-

man, "Major Samuel Holland," 22-37; s.v. "Holland, Samuel Johannes," in *Dictionary of Canadian Biography*, 5:425-27.

42. Quotation from Crowley, "Taken on the Spot," 20; Lt. J. F. W. DesBarres to Col. Henry Bouquet, 21 August 1764, Add. MSS 21,650, 419, BL; Hugh Wallace to Col. Frederick Haldimand, 10 April 1765 and 11 January 1767, Add. MSS 21,679, 5, 18, BL; "Power of Attorney: Lt. Col. Augustine Prevost and Capt. James M. Prevost to Joseph DesBarres," 3 August 1769, DesBarres Papers, MG 23-F1, ser. 5, vol. 15, 2944, LAC; Evans, *Uncommon Obdurate*, 11-26; s.v. "DesBarres, Joseph Frederick Wallet," in *Dictionary of Canadian Biography*, 6:193-94.

43. Capt. Beasmley Glasier to John Fenton, 1 March 1765, and Capt. Thomas Falconer to Members of the St. John's River Society at Boston, 19 April 1765, St. John's River Society Records, items 5 and 7, MassHS; "St. John's River Society Papers," 302-303; s.v. "Glasier, Beamsley Perkins," in *Dictionary of Canadian Biography*, 4:300.

44. "List of Officers of the 60th Regiment Reduced," 24 August 1763, WO 1/1/420, TNA; Capt. Beasmley Glasier to the St. John's River Committee at Montreal, 14 December 1764, and James Porteous to Nathaniel Rogers, 7 October 1766, in "St. John's River Society Papers," 310-13, 333; Capt. Thomas Falconer to Members of the St. John's River Society at Boston, 19 April 1765, St. John's River Society Records, item 7, MassHS; Glasier to [?], 13 February 1766, in W. I. Morse, *Canadian Collection*, 95, 97; "St. John's River Society Papers," 302.

45. Capt. Beasmley Glasier to John Fenton, 1 March 1765, and Charles Morris, Jr., to Nathaniel Rogers, n.d., St. John's River Society Records, items 5 and 30, MassHS; Michael Francklin to Glasier, 22 July 1765, in "St. John's River Society Papers," 319-20; s.v. "Francklin, Michael," in *Dictionary of Canadian Biography*, 4:272-74.

46. "List of Tools &c Fix'd upon to be Bought at Boston," n.d., and Capt. Beamsley Glasier to Nathaniel Rogers, 30 June and 12 May 1766; St. John's River Society Records, items 1, 33, and 34, MassHS; James Simonds to Glasier, 20 August, 1765, and Charles Morris, Jr., to Rogers, n.d., in "St. John's River Society Papers," 321, 326.

47. Quotation from Capt. Beamsley Glasier to [?], 13 February 1766, in Morse, *Canadian Collection*, 92; Glasier to Nathaniel Rogers, 13 February 1766, and James Jameson to Rogers, 25 July 1767, St. John's River Society Records, items 31 and 56, MassHS; Glazier to Rogers, 10 April 1766, in "St. John's River Society Papers," 327.

48. "Protested Bill of Exchange for £250," 14 January 1766, and Rev. John Ogilvie to Nathaniel Rogers, 27 July 1767, St. John's River Society Records, items 26 and 57, MassHS; "Minutes of the Meeting of New York Members of the St. John's River Society," 3 June 1766, in "St. John's River Society Papers," 328-29.

49. James Porteous to Nathaniel Rogers, 18 February and 24 August 1767, St. John's River Society Records, items 49 and 58, MassHS; D.Murray Young, "Planter Settlements in the St. John Valley," in Conrad, *They Planted Well*, 33-35; "St. John's River Society Papers," 339-49.

50. Capt. G[eorge] A[dam] Gmelin to Maj. Gen. Jeffery Amherst, 29 October 1760, WO 34/4/33, TNA; "Memorial of Michael Francklin, Joseph Pernette, and J. F. W. DesBarres on Behalf of Themselves, George A. Gmelin and Others," 3 September 1763, CO 217/20/267, TNA; Maj. Gen. James Murray to Amherst, 17 October 1763, WO 34/2/248, TNA; "Nova Scotia," 23 January 1764, in *Journal of the Commissioners for Trade and Plantations* [1764–67], 6.

51. "Foreign Officers in the American Regiment Now in Germany Recruiting," n.d., in Loudoun Notebooks, vol. 11, HM 1717, HEH; Capt. George Gmelin to the Earl of Loudoun, 10 May 1757, LO 3592, HEH; Count de Gegenfeld to [?], 25 August 1757, and G.A. de Reicke to Lt. Gen. Jeffery Amherst, 7 May 1762, WO 34/75/107 and 34/55/224, TNA.

52. "Nova Scotia," 30 August and 25 November 1763, in *Journal of the Commissioners for Trade and Plantations* [1759–63], 380–81, 412; "Nova Scotia," 18 and 21 July 1764, in *Journal of the Commissioners for Trade and Plantations* [1764–67], 101, 105; Selig, "Emigration, Fraud, Humanitarianism," 1–23.

53. "Nova Scotia," 5 June 1764, in *Journal of the Commissioners for Trade and Plantations* [1764–67], 64; "Plan of Part of Nova Scotia Referred to in Colonel McNutt's Memorial of 5 April 1766," n.d., CO 700, Nova Scotia, no. 43, TNA; "Notice of Auction on Debt of George Adam Gmelin," 27 November 1771," DesBarres Papers, MG 23-F1, ser. 5, vol. 15, 2953–54, LAC; Cahill, "A Man and his Lawyer," 102–103.

54. Hugh Wallace to Col. Frederick Haldimand, 4 February 1765 and 19 May 1766, Add. MSS 21,679, 1, 8, BL; Ells, "Philadelphia Merchants and the Petitcodiac," 104–107.

55. Quotation from Raymond, "Sketch of Nova Scotia," 150; "Copy of a Letter from Mr. Adam Hoops," 14 December 1767, and Hugh Wallace to Brig. Gen. Frederick Haldimand, 15 June 1768, Add. MSS 21,679, 35, 50–51, BL; Allison, "Notes on 'A General Return . . . ,' " 57.

56. "Colhoon: Indian Intelligence from Tuscarawas," 1 June 1763, in *Bouquet Papers*, 6:197–98; Hugh Wallace to Brig. Gen. Frederick Haldimand, 10 July 1767, Add. MSS 21,679, 25, BL; Bailyn, *Peopling of British North America*, 80; Wright, *Petitcodiac*, 26–37.

57. "Bouquet: Last Will and Testament," 25 June 1765, in *Bouquet Papers*, 6:795; Hugh Wallace to Brig. Gen. Frederick Haldimand, 3 August 1771 and 6 February 1775, Add. MSS 21,679, 95, 133, BL; "Private Diary of General Haldimand," in Brymner, *Report on Canadian Archives*, 289 (entry of 13 June 1787); Wright, *Petitcodiac*, 59–61; s.v. "Haldimand, Sir Frederick," in *Dictionary of Canadian Biography*, 5:902.

58. Wokeck, *Trade in Strangers*, 8–9, 39–55; Fertig, "Transatlantic Migrations," 202–203; Fenske, "International Migration," 332–47.

59. "Petition of Lieutenant Hugh Wallace," 24 December 1763, ALG, AO 272/17/40, NYSL; Capt. Beamsley Glasier to Nathaniel Rogers, 12 May 1766, and Capt. Thomas Falconer to Rogers, 14 September 1766, St. John's River Society Records, items 34 and 38, MassHS; Griffin, *People with No Name*, 1–97; Wokeck, *Trade in Strangers*, 167–69, 175–217.

60. Quotation from "Estates and Property, Seized by Mr. Sparrow in Nova Scotia," n.d., DesBarres Papers, MG 23-F1, ser. 7, item 21, LAC; Kernaghan, "Most Eccentric Genius," 43–45; Evans, *Uncommon Obdurate*, 33; Bell, *The "Foreign Protestants,"* 517; Ford, *British Officers Serving in America*, 13, 37.

61. "Nova Scotia," 5 June 1764, in *Journal of the Commissioners for Trade and Plantations* [1764–67], 64; "Plan of Part of Nova Scotia Referred to in Colonel McNutt's Memorial of 5 April 1766," n.d., CO 700, Nova Scotia, no. 43, TNA; "Estimate of Estates Belonging to Lieutenant Governor Desbarres," n.d., DesBarres Papers, MG 23-F1, ser. 7, item 23, LAC.

62. "Purchase in Elysian Fields from George Faesch," 2 February 1768, and "Purchase in Elysian Fields from Jacob Muller," 14 April 1768, DesBarres Papers, MG 23-F1, ser. 5, 2922–27, LAC; "Purchase in Elysian Fields from Marcus and Augustine Prevost," 7 May 1773, ibid., 2985–89, LAC; "Estimate of Estates Belonging to Lieutenant Governor Desbarres," n.d., DesBarres Papers, MG 23-F1, ser. 7, item 23, LAC; Evans, *Uncommon Obdurate*, 32–33.

63. "Proposals for the Effectual Settlement of the Valuable Colony of Nova Scotia by Lt. J[oseph] F.W. DesBarres," n.d., AMSS, U 1350/057, CKS; Maj. Gen. Thomas Gage to Lord Barrington, 14 May 1768, in *Gage Correspondence*, 2:470; DesBarres, *Statement Submitted*, 2–3; Williamson, *Treatise on Military Finance*, 19.

64. "Nova Scotia," 16 July 1764, in *Journal of the Commissioners for Trade and Plantations* [1764–67], 100; Capt. Beamsley Glasier to the St. John's River Committee at Montreal, 14 December 1764, in "St. John's River Society Papers," 313; "Acquisition, Improvements & Settlement of Menaudie," n.d., DesBarres Papers, MG 23-F1, ser. 5, vol. 17, 3187–99, LAC.

65. Bailyn, *Voyagers to the West*, 372–90, 401–19; Punch, "Montbéliard," 74–92; Bell, *The "Foreign Protestants,"* 550–51.

66. "An Account of a Conversation, Chiefly Relative to the Army," in Langworthy, *Memoirs of Charles Lee*, 71; Purceval, *Memorial of John Earl of Egmont*, 1–32.

67. "Island of St. John," 8 and 23 July 1767, in *Journal of the Commissioners for Trade and Plantations* [1764–67], 400–406, 413–15; Bumsted, *Land, Settlement, and Politics*, 15–26; Clark, *Three Centuries and the Island*, 42–48; Ford, *British Officers Serving in America*, 76, 13, 55, 85, 95, 69.

68. Ensigns Francis and Samuel Mackay to the Earl of Loudoun, 1 April 1756, LO 996, HEH; *Pennsylvania Gazette*, 3 August 1758, 1; Lt. Gen. Jeffery Amherst to Col. Frederick Haldimand, 13 June 1761, and Maj. Gen. Thomas Gage to Amherst, 3 March 1762, WO 34/9/197 and 34/5/60, TNA; Papineau, "Le général Francis Mackay," 105.

69. Quotation from Alexander Campbell to John Lloyd, 22 October 1759, in *Historical Magazine, and Notes*, 4 (1860): 149; Maj. Gen. Thomas Gage to Lt. Gen. Jeffery Amherst, 26 October 1761, WO 34/5/235, TNA; Papineau, "Le général Francis Mackay," 108.

70. Greer, *People of New France*, 51–52; Harris, *Seigneurial System in Early Canada*, 46–55; s.vv. "Boucher de Niverville, Jean-Baptiste" and "Le Marchand de Lignery, François-Marie," in *Dictionary of Canadian Biography*, 3:82–83, 378–79.

71. Maj. Gen. Thomas Gage to Lt. Gen. Jeffery Amherst, 11 June 1762, WO 34/5/151–52, TNA; Lts. Francis and Samuel Mackay to [Col. Ralph Burton], n.d., and Gage to Col. Henry Bouquet, 14 May 1764, TGPAS, vols. 11 and 18, WLCL; Gage to the Earl of Halifax, 13 February 1764, in *Gage Correspondence*, 1:17; Trudel, *La régime militaire*, 181–91.

72. "A Chart of Lake Champlain Exhibiting at One View, the Claims of the French . . . and the Grants Made to the English Reduc'd Officers and Disbanded Soldiers . . .," n.d., CO 700, New York, no. 26, TNA; "Concession d'une terre . . . par François de Mackay . . . et Samuel de Mackay," 24 April 1771, CN, 601-229 (Lalanne), ANQ-M; Palmer, *History of Lake Champlain*, 53–57, 93.

73. Benjamin Roberts to Sir William Johnson, 31 August 1771, in *Johnson Papers*, 8:243–44; "Vente d'un emplacement . . . à François Mackay," 15 October 1765, and "Obligation . . . à Samuel Mackay," 17 September 1768, CN, 601-229 (Lalanne), ANQ-M; Everest, *Moses Hazen*, 18–19; Papineau, "Le général Francis Mackay," 105–106; s.v. "Price, Benjamin," in *Dictionary of Canadian Biography*, 3:542.

74. "Vente d'une part de terre . . . par Jean-Frédéric Heyser . . . et Elisabeth Migneron," 27 October 1761, and "Quittance de Pierre Mée . . . et Marie-Françoise Bedard," 27 March 1764, CN, 601-362 (Sanguinet, pere), ANQ-M; Lt. Col. Augustine Prevost to Lt. Gen. Thomas Gage, 27 April 1771, TGPAS, vol. 102, WLCL; Fernand Ouellet, "The British Army of Occupation in the St. Lawrence Valley, 1760–74: The Conflict between Civil and Military Society," trans. A.Kern, in Prete and Ion, *Armies of Occupation*, 23; Trudel, *La régime militaire*, 43–44; s.v. "Picoté de Belestre, Françoise-Marie," in *Dictionary of Canadian Biography*, 4:633–34.

75. "Concession . . . par Conrad Gugy," 25 June 1764, CN, 401-73 (Pillard), ANQ-M; Lt. Gov. Guy Carleton to Maj. Gen. Thomas Gage, 28 May 1767, TGPAS, vol. 65, WLCL; Fernand Ouellet, "Propriétés seigneuriale et groupes sociaux dans la vallé du Saint-Laurent (1663–1840)," in Savard, *Mélanges d'histoire du Canada Français*, 197–98; Ford, *British Officers Serving in America*, 72; s.vv. "Haldimand, Sir Frederick," and "Gugy, Conrad," in *Dictionary of Canadian Biography*, 5:891, 902, and 4:316–17.

76. Maj. Gen. Thomas Gage to Gov. Guy Carleton, 15 January 1767, TGPAS, vol. 61, WLCL; Gage to the Earl of Hillsborough, 8 September 1768, in *Gage Correspondence*, 1: 269–70; "Private Diary of General Haldimand," in Brymner, *Report on Canadian Archives*, 181 (entry of 11 May 1786); Guy, *Oeconomy and Discipline*, 92; Williams, "Prevosts of the Royal Americans," 33–34; Beatson, *Naval and Military Memoirs*, 3:407.

77. Claude J. Sauthier, "A Choriographical Map of the Province of New York," 1779, CO 700, New York, no. 40, TNA; O'Callaghan, *Indorsed Land Papers*, 439, 446, 459. I am grateful to Sir Christopher Prevost of Rochester, Kent, for providing me with detailed genealogical information about Lt. Col. Augustine Prevost's family. Personal communication with the author, 13 August 2002.

78. Maj. Gen. Thomas Gage to Lt. Col. Augustine Prevost, 15 September 1770, TGPAS, vol. 95, WLCL; "Purchase in Elysian Fields from Augustine Prevost," 7 May 1773, and "Estates and Property, Seized by Mr. Sparrow in

Nova Scotia," DesBarres Papers, MG 23-F1, ser. 5, 2988–89, and ser. 7, item 21, LAC; "Private Diary of General Haldimand," in Brymner, *Report on Canadian Archives*, 179–81 (entries of 4 and 7 May 1786); Butler and Hare, *Annals*, 1:208–18, 323–26.

79. Maj. Gen. John Stanwix to Maj. Gen. Jeffery Amherst, 25 April 1760, WO 34/45/141, TNA; Shy, *Toward Lexington*, 356; Keith, *Provincial Councilors of Pennsylvania*, 417–18; Hildeburn, "Sir John St. Clair," 1–14; *American National Biography*, s.v. "St. Clair, Arthur."

80. Lt. Col. Henry Bouquet to Col. John Stanwix, 18 October 1757, in *Bouquet Papers*, 1:222; Kierner, *Traders and Gentlefolk*, 66–75; Thayer, "Army Contractors," 31–46; Rutherfurd, *Family Records and Events*, 63; *New York Journal; or the General Advertiser*, 18 June 1772, 651; *American National Biography*, s.vv. "Alexander, William," and "Livingston, Peter Van Brugh."

81. "Lieutenant [John] Brown," 9 February 1756, Notification Books to the Secretary of State, 1755–1759, WO 25/137/56, TNA; "List of Officers of the 60th Regiment Reduced," 24 August 1763, WO 1/1/420, TNA; Butler and Hare, *Annals*, 1:201; Wallace, *Regimental Chronicle*, 73, 85, 96.

82. Capt. James Mark Prevost to Col. Henry Bouquet, 17 October 1763 and 19 April 1765, Add. MSS 21,649, 407, and Add. MSS 21,651, 263, BL; "60th Regiment," 8 November 1766, Succession Books (Series 1) General, 1764–71, WO 25/210, TNA; Williams, "Prevosts of the Royal Americans," 14–16.

83. "Purchase in Elysian Fields from Marcus Prevost," 7 May 1773, DesBarres Papers, MG 23-F1, ser. 5, 2985–86, LAC; "60th Foot, First Battalion, 1773," 13 September 1773, Succession Books (Series 1) General, 1771–80, WO 25/211, TNA; Butler and Hare, *Annals*, 326–27; Wallace, *Regimental Chronicle*, 93; O'Callaghan, *Indorsed Land Papers*, 615, 619–20.

84. "Ensign Augustine Prevost," 24 July 1758, and "Lieutenant Augustine Prevost," 6 May 1761, Succession Books (Series 1) General, 1754–64, WO 25/209/198, 200, TNA; Williams, "Prevosts of the Royal Americans," 21–25.

85. Lt. Augustine Prevost to Lt. Gov. Guy Carleton, 17 July 1767, TGPAS, vol. 67, WLCL; Sir William Johnson to Goldsbrow Banyar, 30 March 1770, in *Johnson Papers*, 12:811; Smith, *Tour*, 100 (entry of 15 May 1769); Wainwright, "Turmoil at Pittsburgh," 130 (entry of 9 September 1774); Williams, "Prevosts of the Royal Americans," 25–26; Wainwright, *George Croghan*, 242–44, 255–68; McCusker, *Money and Exchange*, 165.

86. Capt. Walter Rutherfurd to Lt. Gen. Jeffery Amherst, 13 February 1761, and Lt. Col. Roger Morris to Amherst, 23 February 1761, WO 34/86/69 and 34/99/155, TNA; Valentine, *Lord Stirling*, 7–45; Rutherfurd, *Family Records and Events*, 3–5, 91, 106–107, 272; *American National Biography*, s.v. "Alexander, James."

87. Walter Rutherfurd to Lt. Gen. Jeffery Amherst, 28 April 1761, and John Porteous to Amherst, 30 March 1762, WO 34/21/147 and 34/49/79, TNA; Sir William Johnson to Capt. Daniel Claus, 20 May 1761, in *Johnson Papers*, 10:270; "Extract of a Letter to Governor Murray from Albany," 10 August 1761, Add. MSS 35,913, 151, BL; Matson, *Merchants and Empire*, 93–96, 222–27; Norton, *Fur Trade in Colonial New York*, 198–203.

88. Maj. Gen. Jeffery Amherst to Lord Barrington, 10 August 1759, WO 1/5/62, TNA; Walter Rutherfurd to Amherst, 9 April 1761, and "A Proclamation," 10 April 1761, WO 34/74/161–62, TNA; Maj. John Wilkins to Amherst, 20 September 1762, WO 34/22/72, TNA; Dunnigan, *Siege—1759*, 36, 98.

89. Walter Rutherfurd to Sir William Johnson, 12 May 1761, in *Johnson Papers*, 10:265; John Duncan to Lt. Gen. Jeffery Amherst, 9 July 1762, and Amherst to William Sharpe, 20 October 1762, WO 34/91/29 and 34/74/155–56, TNA.

90. James Sterling to John Duncan, 8 July 1761 and 14 April 1762, and Sterling to Messrs. Rutherfurd and Livingston, 12 February 1762, Sterling Letterbook, WLCL; s.v. "Sterling, James," in *Dictionary of Canadian Biography*, 4:722.

91. "Invoice of Goods for Detroit," 30 March 1762, WO 34/49/80, TNA; James Sterling to [Robert] Callbeck, 14 April 1762, Sterling Letterbook, WLCL; Sterling to John Duncan, 26 August 1762, and Sterling to Messrs. Livingston and Rutherfurd, 25 January 1763, ibid.

92. Quotation from James Sterling to Walter Rutherfurd, 27 [?] 1761, Sterling Letterbook, WLCL; Sterling to James Syme, 14 April 1762, and Sterling to Rutherfurd, 15 July 1762, ibid.

93. Lt. Gen. Jeffery Amherst to Sir William Johnson, 7 May 1761, and Johnson to Amherst, 29 July 1761, in *Johnson Papers*, 3:387 and 10:322; Maj. William Walters to Amherst, 20 June 1762, WO 34/22/40, TNA; Eccles, "Fur Trade and Eighteenth-Century Imperialism," 358–59.

94. Maj. William Walters to Lt. Gen. Jeffery Amherst, 30 July 1761, WO 34/21/185–86, TNA; "Petition of Merchants of Albany to the Lords of Trade," 25 January 1762, in *NYCD*, 7:488–89; Sir William Johnson to Amherst, 6 February 1762, in *Johnson Papers*, 3:623.

95. "New York," 27 May 1762, in *Journal of the Commissioners for Trade and Plantations* [1759–63], 281; "Report of the Lords of Trade on the Memorial of the Albany Merchants," 3 June 1762, in *NYCD*, 7:502–503; Lt. Gen. Jeffery Amherst to Maj. John Wilkins, 17 October 1762, and Amherst to William Sharpe, 20 October 1762, WO 34/22/163 and 34/74/155–56, TNA.

96. James Sterling to John Duncan, 8 July 1761, and Sterling to James Syme, 10 January 1762, Sterling Letterbook, WLCL; Maj. John Wilkins to Lt. Gen. Jeffery Amherst, 17 January 1763, WO 34/22/101, TNA; Capt. Francis Legge to [?], 24 August 1764, SGM, case 4, box 7, "Colonial Wars," HSP.

97. James Sterling to John Duncan, 26 August and 2 October 1762, Sterling Letterbook, WLCL; Henry Bostwick to James Beekman, 10 December 1764, in White, *Beekman Mercantile Papers*, 2:952–53; Hough, *Diary of the Siege of Detroit*, 144.

98. James Sterling to Capt. George Etherington, 31 May 1762, Sterling Letterbook, WLCL; Sterling to James Syme [?] June 1762, and Sterling to Lt. William Leslye, 3 June 1762, ibid.; Sterling to Lt. Edward Jenkins, 14 April 1763, ibid.; "Petition of English and French Traders at Detroit," 24 July 1767, TGPAS, vol. 67, WLCL.

99. Quotation from James Sterling to John Duncan, 26 August 1762, Sterling Letterbook, WLCL; Sterling to Commodore Joshua Loring, 19 August 1762, and Sterling to Henry Van Schaack, 7 October 1762, ibid.

100. "Extract of a Letter to Governor Murray from Albany, 10 August 1761," Add. MSS 35,913, 151, BL; James Sterling to Ens. Robert Holmes, 28 April and 6 July 1762, and Sterling to Lt. Edward Jenkins, 14 April 1763, Sterling Letterbook, WLCL; Andrews, *Eighteenth-Century Europe*, 359.

101. "Memorial of Sundry Merchants of the City of London Interested in the Trade of the Province of Quebec," n.d., CO 323/25/11-12, TNA; Capt. Lt. Frederick Spiesmacher to Lt. Gen. Thomas Gage, 19 June 1770, TGPAS, vol. 93, WLCL.

102. Col. James Prevost to Richard Peters, 18 April 1758, SGM, case 4, box 8, "Colonial Wars," HSP; Frederick von Hambach to Col. Henry Bouquet, 13 February and 22 March 1761, in *Bouquet Papers*, 5:294, 362; Alexander Lunan to Bouquet, 7 March 1761, and Capt. Donald Campbell to Bouquet, 21 May 1761, ibid., 337, 492.

103. Frederick von Hambach to Col. Henry Bouquet, 24 May 1761, in *Bouquet Papers*, 5:503; "A List of Traders Trading from Pennsylvania to the Westward," n.d., and von Hambach to Bouquet, 6 May 1764, Add. MSS 21,654, 183, 186, BL.

104. Quotation from "Headquarters at the 15th Camp," 24 October 1764, in Williams, *Bouquet Orderly Book, 1764*, 37; "Camp at Wills's Creek," 23 May 1755, in Hamilton, *Braddock's Defeat*, 92; "HBOB," in *Bouquet Papers*, 2:659, 684 (entries of 25 June, and 29 August 1758); Lt. Gen. Jeffery Amherst to [?] Campbell, 28 November 1762, WO 34/93/232, TNA.

105. Maj. Gen. Thomas Gage to Col. John Bradstreet, 17 March 1766, TGPAS, vol. 49, WLCL; "Journal of John Lees of Quebec, Merchant," 8 (entry of 27 June 1768), MG 21, Add. MSS 28,605, LAC; McCusker, *Money and Exchange*, 165.

106. "Francis Phister," 9 October 1767, Succession Books (Series 1) General, 1764-71, WO 25/210, TNA; Capt. John Brown to Maj. Gen. Thomas Gage, 6 November 1768, TGPAS, vol. 82, WLCL; Gage to Brown, 19 December 1768, Add. MSS 21,678, 122, BL.

107. Maj. Gen. Jeffery Amherst to Lt. Dietrich Brehm, 12 September 1760, and "Lieut. Brehm's Report," 21 February 1761, WO 34/50/191 and 34/49/22, TNA; Adam Hoops to Col. Henry Bouquet, 4 November 1760, in *Bouquet Papers*, 5:100; Bouquet to Maj. Gen. Thomas Gage, 15 June 1764, TGPAS, vol. 20, WLCL.

108. Capt. Donald Campbell to Col. Henry Bouquet, 11 December 1760, in *Bouquet Papers*, 5:172; Lt. Col. John Campbell to Maj. Gen. Thomas Gage, 31 October 1765, and Lt. Dietrich Brehm to Campbell, 3 November 1765, TGPAS, vol. 45, WLCL; Multhauf, *Neptune's Gift*, 7, 27, 36-38, 49, 71-92.

109. "Plantations General," 10 January 1764, in *Journal of the Commissioners for Trade and Plantations* [1764-67], 3; Hugh Wallace to Col. Frederick Haldimand, 4 February 1765, Add. MSS 21,679, 1, BL; Neu, "Iron Plantations," 11-12; Spieler, "Peter Hasenclever, Industrialist," 231-36; Hasenclever, *Remarkable Case*, 1-10.

110. "Extraits des Differentes Lettres ecrites au Col. Prevost au Sujet des Recrues a faire en Allemagne," n.d., LO 2575, HEH; "Foreign Officers in the American Regiment Now in Germany Recruiting," n.d., Loudoun Note-

books, vol. 11, HM 1717, HEH; Neu, "Iron Plantations," 17; Hasenclever, *Remarkable Case*, 36.

111. Quotation from *New York Gazette and Weekly Mercury*, 21 September 1772, 1; "Petition of Peter Hasenclever & Company, of London, to the Earl of Shelburne," 28 January 1767, in Whitehead, *Documents*, 9:583–85; Hasenclever, *Remarkable Case*, 5–11.

112. "An Account of Money Sent by Peter Hasenclever for the Use of Ring Wood and Long Pond Iron Works," 1 November 1767, CO 5/1074/48–50, TNA; *New York Journal; or the General Advertiser*, 21 May 1772, 628; *New York Gazette and Weekly Mercury*, 6 September 1773, 1; Wallace, *Regimental Chronicle*, 81; Hasenclever, *Remarkable Case*, 58–60.

CONCLUSION

1. Williams, "The Prevosts of the Royal Americans," 22–37; La Rochefoucauld-Liancourt, *Travels through the United States . . .*, 2:220–23.

2. Quotations ("traders, settlers, and migrants") from "Introduction," in Armitage and Braddick, *British Atlantic World*, 1; ("effective trust networks") from Nuala Zahedieh, "Economy," ibid., 66; and Chaplin, "Expansion and Exceptionalism," 1431–46.

3. Quotation from Col. John Stanwix to Israel Pemberton, 8 August 1757, Indian Committee Records, ca. 1745–1983, vol. 1, Haverford College Libraries, Haverford, Pa. I am grateful to Prof. Ian K. Steele for bringing my attention to this quotation from the Stanwix-Pemberton correspondence. Brumwell, *Redcoats*, 74–75, 318; A.G. Roeber, "'The Origin of Whatever Is Not English among Us': The Dutch-Speaking and German-Speaking Peoples of British North America," in Bailyn and Morgan, *Strangers within the Realm*, 220–44; Bailyn, *Peopling of British North America*, 59–64, 89–112.

4. McConnell, *Army and Empire*, 56–59; Brumwell, *Redcoats*, 79–96.

5. Col. Henry Bouquet to [?], 10 June 1759, in *Bouquet Papers*, 3:371–72; Carver, *Travels through North America*; Rogers, *Ponteach*; John E. Crowley, "A Visual Empire: Seeing the British Atlantic World from a Global British Perspective," in Mancke and Shammas, *Creation of the British Atlantic World*, 283–303; Anderson, *Crucible of War*, 421–50.

6. "Petition of German Non-Commissioned Officers and Private Men Held Prisoner in France," n.d., WO 34/99/182, TNA; *Pennsylvania Journal and Weekly Advertiser*, 14 October 1756, 3; *South Carolina Gazette Supplement*, 4 August 1757, 1; *Boston Post-Boy & Advertiser*, 11 May 1761, 1; Maj. Gen. Thomas Gage to Welbore Ellis, 10 March 1764, in *Gage Correspondence*, 2:224; Mante, *History of the Late War*, 114, 353, 406.

7. "Return of the Five Companies of the 1st Battalion 60th or Royal American Regiment of Foot," 26 December 1757, LO 6877, HEH; "Croghan Journal," 347 (entry of 3 September 1759); Capt. Gavin Cochrane to Col. Henry Bouquet, 6 May 1761, and Maj. Gen. Jeffery Amherst to Bouquet, 25 September 1763, in *Bouquet Papers*, 5:465 and 6:397; Maj. Gen. Thomas Gage to the Earl of Halifax, 10 August 1764, and Gage to Lord Barrington, 19 August 1768, in *Gage Correspondence*, 1:34 and 2:280.

8. Maj. Gen. Thomas Gage to Lord Barrington, 18 December 1765 and 13 July 1766, in *Gage Correspondence*, 2:319–20, 360.

9. Quotation from Bowen, *War and British Society*, 3; Butler and Hare, *Annals*, 1:1–319; Wallace, *Regimental Chronicle*, 1–14.

10. Quotation from Col. Henry Bouquet to John Bartram, 3 February 1762, in Berkley and Berkley, *Correspondence of John Bartram*, 547; Sir John St. Clair to Bouquet, 21 August 1761, in *Bouquet Papers*, 5:705.

11. Capt. Gavin Cochrane to Col. Henry Bouquet, 27 September 1761, and [?] to Bouquet, 10 February 1763, in *Bouquet Papers*, 5:783 and 6:160–63; Benjamin Franklin to Bouquet, 30 September 1764, in Labaree, *Papers of Benjamin Franklin*, 11:366–68; Pottle and Bennett, *Boswell's Journal*, 102 (entry of 31 August 1773); Norman, *Influence of Switzerland on Edward Gibbon*, 94; Ford, *British Officers Serving in America*, 79.

12. Quotation from Alison Games, "Migration," in Armitage and Braddick, *British Atlantic World*, 47.

Bibliography

MANUSCRIPTS AND ARCHIVAL SOURCES

British Library, London

Add. MSS 3,439: Egerton Manuscripts
Add. MSS 17,493–17,496: Calcraft Papers
Add. MSS 21,631–21,660: Bouquet Papers
Add. MSS 21,661–21,892: Haldimand Papers
Add. MSS 23,678: Narrative & Remarks Upon the Siege of Havana and Isle of Cuba by Admiral Sir Charles Knowles, Bart., in 1761 and 1762
Add. MSS 32,686–32,992: Newcastle Papers
Add. MSS 33,028–33,030: Newcastle Papers (American Affairs)
Add. MSS 33,046–33,048: Newcastle Papers (Papers Relating to the Army and Navy, 1600–1803)
Add. MSS 35,349–36,278: Hardwicke Papers
Add. MSS 73,546–73,769: Barrington Papers

College of Arms, London

MS Grants 13.125: James Prevost Mackay of Scowrey

Huguenot Society of London Library, University College, London

Henry Wagner Huguenot Pedigrees

The National Archives (formerly Public Record Office), Kew

Admiralty

ADM 1: In-Letters

Audit Office
AO 13: American Loyalist Claims

Colonial Office
CO 5: America and West Indies
CO 117: Havana
CO 217: Nova Scotia and Cape Breton
CO 323: Colonies General

State Papers
SP 78: State Papers, Foreign, France
SP 81: State Papers, Foreign, German States

Treasury Board
T 1: In-Letters

War Office
WO 1: In-Letters
WO 4: Out-Letters, Secretary at War
WO 12: Muster Books and Pay Lists
WO 25: General Registers
WO 34: Amherst Papers
WO 71: Courts-Martial, Proceedings

Gifts and Deposits
PRO 30/8: Chatham Papers

Maps
"A Chart of Lake Champlain Exhibiting at One View, the Claims of the French . . . and the Grants Made to the English Reduc'd Officers and Disbanded Soldiers . . ." N.d. CO 700, New York, no. 26.
Claude J. Sauthier. "A Chorographical Map of the Province of New York." 1779. CO 700, New York, no. 40.
"Map of the Country Showing Fort Presque Isle on Lake Erie . . . and Fort Cumberland in Maryland." Maps and Plans Extracted from War Office Records. No. 346.
"Plan of Part of Nova Scotia Referred to in Colonel McNutt's Memorial of 5 April 1766." N.d. CO 700, Nova Scotia, no. 43.

Royal Archives, Windsor Castle, Berkshire

Cumberland Papers

Centre for Kentish Studies, Maidstone

U1350: Amherst Family Papers

Bodelian Library, University of Oxford, Oxfordshire

North Papers

National Archives of Scotland, Edinburgh

Gifts and Deposits
GD 45: Dalhousie Muniments
GD 125: Rose of Kilravock Muniments

Alexander Turnbull Library, Wellington, New Zealand

Journal of Lieutenant John Grant, 42nd Foot, 1758–62

American Philosophical Society, Philadelphia

Burd-Shippen Collection
Fort Pitt Cash Book
Timothy Horsfield Papers
Miscellaneous Manuscripts on Indian Affairs, 1737–75
Shippen Family Papers

William L. Clements Library, Ann Arbor, Mich.

Thomas Gage Papers
William H. Lyttelton Papers
James Sterling Letterbook
Charles Townshend Papers

Fort Pitt Museum, Pittsburgh

FP2003.6.1: Enlistment Certificate of Johann Cristian Klepper, 14 August 1766

Haverford College Libraries, Haverford, Pa.

Indian Committee Records, ca. 1745–1983

Henry E. Huntington Library, San Marino, Calif.

Abercromby Papers
Loudoun Notebooks
Loudoun Papers
Orderly Book kept by Lieutenant Joseph Bull, First New York Regiment, 25 May–1 November 1759

Historical Society of Pennsylvania, Philadelphia

Ferdinand J. Dreer Autograph Collection
Frank M. Etting Collection, Autographs, American and British Army Officers
Simon Gratz Manuscripts
Penn Papers: Official Correspondence
Thomas Penn Letterbooks
Library Company Collection: Allen and Turner Letterbook

Maryland Historical Society, Baltimore

MS 2018: Colonial Collection, Manuscripts Division

Massachusetts Historical Society, Boston

Silas Brown Collection
St. John's River Society Records

Tracy W. McGregor Library, Charlottesville, Virginia

Headquarters Papers of Brigadier General John Forbes
Sir John St. Clair Letterbook

Newberry Library, Chicago, Illinois

Edward E. Ayer Manuscript Collection

New York Historical Society, New York

John Bremner's Diary and Memorandum Book, 1756–64

New York State Library, Albany

AO 272: Department of State Application for Land Grants

Library and Archives Canada (formerly National Archives of Canada), Ottawa

MG 18-L18: Henry Pringle Letterbook
MG 18-N46: "A Private Journal of the Siege of Quebec, 1759," by Edward Coats
MG 21-Add. MSS-28605: Journal of John Lees of Quebec, Merchant
MG 23-F1: DesBarres Papers
MG 24-A9: Select Papers Relating to Major General Augustine and Sir George Prevost and Family
RG 1-L3L: Lower Canada Land Papers

Maps

National Map Collection, 109811, H3/249/Louisbourg 1758: Plan of Louisbourg, The Harbour, Part of the Coast with the French Entrenchments along the Same and the Attack of the British Troops under the Command of Major General Amherst.

Bibliothèque Archives Nationales du Quebec, Montreal

Collections Notaries

CN401-73: Louis Pillard (1736–67)
CN601-362: Simon Sanguinet, pere (1748–71)
CN601-229: Pierre Lalanne (1765–92)

WORKS CITED

Books, Articles, and Dissertations

Abbot, William W., ed. *The Papers of George Washington: Colonial Series.* 10 vols. Charlottesville: University Press of Virginia, 1983–95.

Abler, Thomas S. "Scalping, Torture, Cannibalism, and Rape: An Ethnohistorical Analysis of Conflicting Cultural Values in War." *Anthropologica* 34 (1991): 3–20.

Adair, James. *The History of the American Indians: Particularly Those Nations Adjoining to the Missisippi, East and West Florida, Georgia, South and North Carolina, and Virginia.* London, 1775.

Alden, John R. *John Stuart and the Southern Colonial Frontier.* New York: Gordian Press, Inc., 1966.

Alexander, Ronald O., ed. "The Capture of Quebec: A Manuscript Journal Relating to the Operations before Quebec from 8th May, 1759 to 17th May, 1760. Kept by Colonel Malcolm Fraser." *Journal of the Society for Army Historical Research* 18 (1939): 135–68.

Allison, D. "Notes on 'A General Return of the Several Townships in the Province of Nova Scotia for the first day of January, 1767.'" Nova Scotia Historical Society, *Collections* 7 (1889–91): 45–71.

Alvord, Clarence W., and Clarence E. Carter, eds. "George Croghan's Journals, February 28, 1765–May 11, 1765." *Collections of the Illinois State Historical Library* 11 (1916): 1–19.

American National Biography. Edited by John A. Garraty and Mark C. Carnes. 25 vols. New York: Oxford University Press, 1999–.

Anderson, Fred. *Crucible of War: The Seven Years' War and the Fate of Empire in British North America, 1754–1766.* New York: Alfred A. Knopf, 2000.

———. *A People's Army: Massachusetts Soldiers and Society in the Seven Years' War.* Chapel Hill: University of North Carolina Press, 1984.

Anderson, Niles, and Edward G. Williams, eds. "The Venango Path as Thomas Hutchins Knew It." *Western Pennsylvania Historical Magazine* 49 (1966): 1–154.

Andrews, Stuart. *Eighteenth-Century Europe: The 1680s to 1815.* London: Longmans, 1965.

Antliff, W. Bruce, ed. *Loyalist Settlements, 1783–1789: New Evidence of Canadian Loyalist Claims.* Toronto: Ministry of Citizenship and Culture, 1985.

Appleton, Marguerite. "Richard Partridge: Colonial Agent." *New England Quarterly* 5 (1932): 293–309.
Armitage, David, and Michael J. Braddick, eds. *The British Atlantic World, 1500–1800*. London: Palgrave Macmillan, 2002.
Atkinson, Alan. "The Free-Born Englishman Transported: Convict Rights as a Measure of Eighteenth-Century Empire." *Past and Present* 144 (1994): 88–115.
Atwater, Caleb. *Remarks Made on a Tour to Prairie Du Chien; Thence to Washington City, in 1829*. Columbus, Ohio: Isaac Whiting, 1831.
Axtell, James. *The Invasion Within: The Contest of Cultures in Colonial North America*. New York: Oxford University Press, 1985.
Ayling, Stanley E. *George the Third*. New York: Alfred A. Knopf, 1972.
Bailyn, Bernard. *The Peopling of British North America: An Introduction*. New York: Alfred A. Knopf, 1986.
———. *Voyagers to the West: A Passage in the Peopling of America on the Eve of the Revolution*. New York: Alfred A. Knopf, 1986.
Bailyn, Bernard, and Philip D. Morgan, eds. *Strangers within the Realm: Cultural Margins of the First British Empire*. Chapel Hill: University of North Carolina Press, 1991.
Baker, Raymond F. *A Campaign of Amateurs: The Siege of Louisbourg, 1745*. Ottawa: Parks Canada, 1995.
Bancroft, George. *History of the United States from the Discovery of the American Continent*. 10 vols. Boston: Little, Brown, 1834–75.
Barrett, Amos, ed. *Journal and Letters of Rev. Henry True of Hampstead, New Hampshire, Who Was Chaplain in the New Hampshire Regiment of the Provincial Army in 1759 and 1762*. Marion, Ohio: Star Press, 1900.
Bartlett, Thomas, and Keith Jeffrey, eds. *A Military History of Ireland*. Cambridge: Cambridge University Press, 1996.
Beatson, Robert. *Naval and Military Memoirs of Great Britain, From 1727 to 1783*. 6 vols. London, 1804.
Beattie, Daniel J. "General Jeffery Amherst and the Conquest of Canada, 1758–1760." Ph.D. diss., Duke University, 1976.
Bell, Winthrop P. *The "Foreign Protestants" and the Settlement of Nova Scotia*. Toronto: University of Toronto Press, 1961.
Bellesiles, Michael A. *Revolutionary Outlaws: Ethan Allen and the Struggle for Independence on the Early American Frontier*. Charlottesville: University Press of Virginia, 1993.
Berkley, Edmund, and Dorothy S. Berkley, eds. *The Correspondence of John Bartram*. Gainesville: University Press of Florida, 1992.
Bethune, Joanna Graham, ed. *The Power of Faith, Exemplified in the Life and Writings of the Late Mrs. Isabella Graham*. New York: American Tract Society, 1843.
Billington, Ray A. *Land of Savagery/Land of Promise: The European Image of the American Frontier in the Nineteenth Century*. New York: W.W. Norton, 1981.
Black, Jeremy, *Britain as a Military Power, 1688–1815*. London: UCL Press, 1999.

———. *The British Abroad: The Grand Tour in the Eighteenth Century.* New York: St. Martin's Press, 1992.
Black, Jeremy. *Culloden and the '45.* New York: St. Martin's Press, 1990.
———. *Pitt the Elder.* Cambridge: Cambridge University Press, 1992.
———, ed. *European Warfare, 1453–1815.* London: Macmillan Press Ltd., 1999.
Bosher, John F. "The French Government's Motives in the *Affaire du Canada,* 1761–1763." *English Historical Review* 96 (1981): 59–78.
Bougainville, Louis Antoine de. *Adventure in the Wilderness: The American Journals of Louis Antoine de Bougainville, 1756–1760.* Edited by Edward P. Hamilton. Norman: University of Oklahoma Press, 1964.
Bourinot, Sir John George. *Historical and Descriptive Account of the Island of Cape Breton and of Its Memorials of the French Regime: With Bibliographical, Historical and Critical Notes.* Montreal: W. Foster Brown, 1892.
Bowen, Huw V. *Elites, Enterprise, and the Making of the British Overseas Empire, 1688–1775.* New York: St. Martin's Press, 1996.
———. *War and British Society, 1688–1815.* Cambridge: Cambridge University Press, 1998.
Brecher, Frank W. *Losing a Continent: France's North American Policy, 1753–1763.* Westport, Conn.: Greenwood Press, 1998.
Breen, Timothy H. "An Empire of Goods: The Anglicization of Colonial America, 1690–1776." *Journal of British Studies* 25 (1986): 467–99.
Brewer, John. *The Sinews of Power: War, Money, and the English State, 1688–1783.* New York: Alfred A. Knopf, 1989.
Bridenbaugh, Carl, ed. "Patrick M'Roberts Tour through Part of the North Provinces of America." *Pennsylvania Magazine of History and Biography* 59 (1935): 134–80.
Briggs, John, Christopher Harrison, Angus McInnes, and David Vincent, eds. *Crime and Punishment in England: An Introductory History.* London: UCL Press, 1996.
Brigham, Charles S., ed. *British Royal Proclamations Relating to America, 1603–1783.* Worcester, Mass.: American Antiquarian Society, 1911; reprint, New York: Burt Franklin, 1968.
Brock, Robert A., ed. *The Official Records of Robert Dinwiddie, Lieutenant-Governor of the Colony of Virginia, 1751–1758.* 2 vols. Richmond: Virginia Historical Society, 1883–84.
Brown, Jennifer S. H. *Strangers in Blood: Fur Trade Company Families in Indian Country.* Vancouver: University of British Columbia Press, 1980.
Browne, William H., et al., eds. *Archives of Maryland.* 72 vols. Baltimore: Maryland Historical Society, 1883–1972.
Bruce, Anthony P. *The Purchase System in the British Army.* London: Royal Historical Society, 1980.
Brumwell, Stephen. *Redcoats: The British Soldier and War in the Americas, 1755–1763.* Cambridge: Cambridge University Press, 2002.
Brymner, Douglas, ed. *Report on Canadian Archives, 1889.* Ottawa: Queen's Printer, 1890.
Buckner, Phillip A., and John G. Reid, eds. *The Atlantic Region to Confederation: A History.* Toronto: University of Toronto Press, 1994.

Bullion, John L. " 'The Ten Thousand in America': More Light on the Decision on the American Army, 1762–1763." *William and Mary Quarterly*, 3rd ser., 43 (1986): 646–57.

Bumsted, Jack M. *Land, Settlement, and Politics on Eighteenth-Century Prince Edward Island*. Montreal: McGill-Queen's University Press, 1987.

Bushman, Richard L. *The Refinement of America: Persons, Houses, Cities*. New York: Alfred A. Knopf, 1992.

Butler, Jon. *Becoming America: The Revolution before 1776*. Cambridge: Harvard University Press, 2000.

———. *The Huguenots in America: A Refugee People in New World Society*. Cambridge: Harvard University Press, 1983.

Butler, Lewis, and Sir Stewart Hare. *The Annals of the King's Royal Rifle Corps*. 6 vols. London: Smith Elder and Company, 1913–32.

Cahill, Barry. "A Man and His Lawyer: The Friendship of J.F.W. DesBarres and Richard Gibbons." Royal Nova Scotia Historical Society, *Collections* 43 (1991): 101–25.

Calhoun, Jeanne A., Martha A. Zierden, and Elizabeth A Paysinger. "The Geographic Spread of Charleston's Merchantile Community, 1732–1767." *South Carolina Historical Magazine* 86 (1985): 182–207.

Calloway, Colin G. "An Uncertain Destiny: Indian Captives on the Upper Connecticut River." *Journal of American Studies* 17 (1983): 189–210.

Cameron, Duncan., ed. *Explorations in Canadian Economic History: Essays in Honour of Irene M. Spry*. Ottawa: University of Ottawa Press, 1985.

Campbell, Alexander V. " 'To Stand in the Face of Danger for Us': The British Army and Maryland's Indentured Servants, 1755–1760." *Maryland Historical Magazine* 94 (1999): 419–39.

Campbell, John. *The Present State of Europe: Explaining the Interests, Connections, Political and Commercial Views of Its Several Powers*. 4th ed. London, 1753.

Campbell, R[ichard]. *The London Tradesman: Being a Compendious View of All the Trades, Professions, Arts, Both Liberal and Mechanic, now Practised in the Cities of London and Westminster*. London, 1747.

Canary, Robert H. *George Bancroft*. New York: Twayne Publishers, Inc., 1974.

Canny, Nicholas, ed. *Europeans on the Move: Studies on European Migration, 1500–1800*. Oxford: Clarendon Press, 1994.

Cardwell, Murray J. "Mismanagement: The 1758 British Expedition against Carillon." *Bulletin of the Fort Ticonderoga Museum* 15 (1992): 236–91.

Carter, Alice. *The Dutch Republic in Europe in the Seven Years War*. London: Macmillan, 1971.

Carter, Clarence E., ed. *The Correspondence of General Thomas Gage with the Secretaries of State and with the War Office and the Treasury, 1763–1775*. 2 vols. New Haven: Yale University Press, 1931–33.

Carver, Jonathan. *Travels through the Interior Parts of North America in the Years 1766, 1767, and 1768*. London, 1778.

Casgrain, Henri R., ed. *Collections des mansucrits du Maréchal de Lévis*. 12 vols. Montreal and Quebec: C.O. Beauchemin & Fils and Demers & Frère, 1889–95.

Casparis, John. "The Swiss Mercenary System: Labor Emigration from the Semiperiphery." *Review* 5 (1982): 593–642.

Cayton, Andrew R. L., and Fredrika J. Teute, eds. *Contact Points: American Frontiers from the Mohawk Valley to the Mississippi, 1750–1830*. Chapel Hill: University of North Carolina Press, 1998.

Chandler, David, and Ian Beckett, eds. *The Oxford Illustrated History of the British Army*. New York: Oxford University Press, 1994.

Chaplin, Joyce E. *An Anxious Pursuit: Agricultural Innovation and Modernity in the Lower South, 1730–1815*. Chapel Hill: University of North Carolina Press, 1993.

——. "Expansion and Exceptionalism in Early American History." *Journal of American History* 89 (2003): 1431–55.

Charbonneau, Andre, Yvon Desloges, and Mark Lafrance, eds. *Québec the Fortified City: From the 17th to the 19th Century*. Ottawa: Parks Canada, 1982.

Chet, Guy. *Conquering the American Wilderness: The Triumph of European Warfare in the Colonial Northeast*. Amherst: University of Massachusetts Press, 2003.

Childs, John C. *Armies and Warfare in Europe, 1648–1789*. Manchester: Manchester University Press, 1982.

——. *The Army, James II, and the Glorious Revolution*. New York: St. Martin's Press, 1980.

——. *The British Army of William III, 1689–1702*. Manchester: Manchester University Press, 1987.

Chipman, Willis. "The Life and Times of Major Samuel Holland, Surveyor-General, 1764–1801." *Papers and Records of the Ontario Historical Society* 21 (1924): 11–90.

Clark, Andrew H. *Three Centuries and the Island: A Historical Geography of Settlement and Agriculture in Prince Edward Island, Canada*. Toronto: University of Toronto Press, 1959.

Clayton, Roy T. "The Duke of Newcastle, the Earl of Halifax, and the American Origins of the Seven Years' War." *Historical Journal* 24 (1981): 571–603.

Cleaveland, John. "Journal of Rev. John Cleaveland, June 14, 1758–October 25, 1758." *Bulletin of the Fort Ticonderoga Museum* 10 (1959): 192–233.

Cobb, Samuel. "The Journal of Captain Samuel Cobb, May 21, 1758–October 29, 1758." *Bulletin of the Fort Ticonderoga Museum* 14 (1981): 12–31.

Cohen, Sheldon S., ed. "Triumph on the St. Lawrence: A New Historical Account." *Mid-America* 53 (1971): 245–63.

Coldham, Peter W., ed. *American Loyalist Claims*. Washington: National Genealogical Society, 1980.

——. *Emigrants in Chains: A Social History of Forced Emigration to the Americas, 1607–1776*. Stroud, Gloucestershire, U.K.: Alan Sutton, 1992.

Coleman, Kenneth, and Milton Ready, eds. *Colonial Records of the State of Georgia, Original Papers of Governors Reynolds, Ellis, Wright, and Others, 1757–1763*. Vol. 28, pt. 1. Athens: University of Georgia Press, 1976.

Colley, Linda. *Britons: Forging the Nation, 1707–1837*. New Haven: Yale University Press, 1992.

A Complete History of the Present War, from Its Commencement in 1756, to the End of the Campaign, 1760. London, 1761.
The Conduct of a Noble Commander in America, Impartially Reviewed. London, 1758.
Conrad, Margaret, ed. *They Planted Well: New England Planters in Maritime Canada.* Fredericton, N.B.: Acadiensis Press, 1988.
Conway, Stephen R. "From Fellow-Nationals to Foreigners: British Perceptions of the Americans, circa 1739–1783." *William and Mary Quarterly,* 3rd ser., 54 (2002): 65–100.
———. "The Recruitment of Criminals into the British Army, 1775–81." *Bulletin of the Institute of Historical Research* 58 (1985): 46–58.
Cooper, James Fenimore. *The Last of the Mohicans; A Narrative of 1757.* Edited by James A. Sappenfield and Elmer N. Feltskog. Albany: State University of New York, 1983.
Cort, Cyrus. *Colonel Henry Bouquet and His Campaigns.* Lancaster, Pa.: Steinman and Hensel, 1883.
Corvisier, André. *L'armée Française de la fin du XVIIe siècle au ministère de Choiseul Le Soldat.* 2 vols. Paris: Presses Universitaires de France, 1964.
Countryman, Edward. *A People in Revolution: The American Revolution and Political Society in New York, 1760–1790.* Baltimore: Johns Hopkins University Press. 1981.
Craig, Neville B., ed. *The Olden Time; A Monthly Publication, Devoted to the Preservation of Documents and Other Authentic Information in Relation to the Early Explorations, and the Settlement and Improvement of the Country around the Head of the Ohio.* Pittsburgh: Privately published, 1846.
Cress, Lawrence D. *Citizens in Arms: The Army and the Militia in American Society to the War of 1812.* Chapel Hill: University of North Carolina Press, 1982.
Crevecoeur, J. Hector St. John de. *Letters from an American Farmer and Sketches of Eighteenth-Century America.* Edited by Albert E. Stone. London: Penguin Books, Ltd., 1986.
Crowley, John E. " 'Taken on the Spot': The Visual Appropriation of New France for the Global British Landscape." *Canadian Historical Review* 86 (2005): 1–28.
Dann, Uriel. *Hanover and Great Britain, 1740–1760: Diplomacy and Survival.* Leicester, U.K.: Leicester University Press, 1991.
Darling, Anthony D. *Redcoat and Brown Bess.* Bloomfield, Ont.: Museum Restoration Service, 1970.
Darlington, Mary C., ed. *Fort Pitt and Letters from the Frontier.* Pittsburgh: J.R. Weldin and Company, 1892.
———. *History of Colonel Henry Bouquet and the Western Frontiers of Pennsylvania, 1747–1764.* Privately printed, 1920.
Darlington, William M., ed. *Christopher Gist's Journals with Historical, Geographical and Ethnological Notes.* Chicago: Argonaut Publishers, Inc., 1969.
Daudelin, Don. "Numbers and Tactics at Bushy Run." *Western Pennsylvania Historical Magazine* 68 (1985): 153–79.

Davis, Elvert M., Mrs., ed. "History of the Capture and Captivity of David Boyd from Cumberland County Pennsylvania, 1756." *Western Pennsylvania Historical Magazine* 14 (1931): 28–42.
Davis, N. Darnell. "British Newspaper Accounts of Braddock's Defeat." *Pennsylvania Magazine of History and Biography* 23 (1899): 310–28.
Dawes, Ephraim C., ed. *Journal of General Rufus Putnam Kept in Northern New York during Four Campaigns of the Old French and Indian War, 1757–1760.* Albany: J. Munsell, 1886.
Dederer, John M. *War in America to 1775: Before Yankee Doodle.* New York: New York University Press, 1990.
de Peyster, J. Watts, ed. *Commissary Wilson's Orderly Book: Expedition of the British and Provincial Army under Major General Jeffery Amherst, against Ticonderoga and Crown Point, 1759.* Albany: J. Munsell, 1857.
Derounian-Stodola, Kathryn A., and James A. Levernier. *The Indian Captivity Narrative, 1550–1900.* New York: Twayne Publishers, 1993.
DesBarres, Joseph F. W. *A Statement Submitted by Lieutenant Colonel DesBarres, for Consideration.* London, 1796.
Dickason, Olive P. *Louisbourg and the Indians: A Study in Imperial Race Relations, 1713–1760.* Ottawa: National Historic Parks and Sites Branch, 1976.
———. *The Myth of the Savage and the Beginnings of French Colonialism in the Americas.* Edmonton: University of Alberta Press, 1984.
Dictionary of Canadian Biography. Edited by George W. Brown, David Hayne, and Francess G. Halpenny. 15 vols. Toronto: University of Toronto Press, 1966–.
Dictionary of National Biography. Edited by Leslie Stephen and Sidney Lee. 22 vols. London: Oxford University Press, 1921–22.
Ditchfield, P. H. "The Family of Riou." *Proceedings of the Huguenot Society of London* 10 (1912–14): 236–64.
Dixon, David. *Never Come to Peace Again: Pontiac's Uprising and the Fate of the British Empire in North America.* Norman: University of Oklahoma Press, 2005.
Doughty, Arthur G., and G. W. Parmelee, eds. *The Siege of Quebec and the Battle of the Plains of Abraham.* 6 vols. Quebec: Dussault and Proulx, 1901.
Dowd, Gregory E. *War under Heaven: Pontiac, the Indian Nations, and the British Empire.* Baltimore: Johns Hopkins University Press, 2002.
Draper, Lyman C., ed. "Lieut. James Gorell's Journal." *Wisconsin Historical Society, Collections* 1 (1903): 24–48.
Duffy, Christopher. *The Army of Frederick the Great.* New York: Hippocrene Books, Inc., 1974.
———. *Fire and Stone: The Science of Fortress Warfare, 1660–1860.* London: David and Charles, 1975.
———. *The Fortress in the Age of Vauban and Frederick the Great, 1660–1789.* London: Routledge and Kegan Paul, 1985.
———. *Instrument of War: The Austrian Army in the Seven Years War.* Rosemont, Ill.: Emperor's Press, 2000.
———. *The Military Experience in the Age of Reason.* New York: Atheneum, 1988.

Duffy, Michael. *The Englishman and the Foreigner*. Cambridge: Chadwyck-Healey, 1986.
Dulany, Daniel. "Military and Political Affairs in the Middle Colonies in 1755." *Pennsylvania Magazine of History and Biography* 3 (1879): 11–31.
Dunbar, John R., ed. *The Paxton Papers*. The Hague: M. Nijhoff, 1957.
Duncan, Francis. *History of the Royal Regiment of Artillery*. 3rd ed. 2 vols. London: John Murray, 1879.
Dunn, Walter S., Jr. *Frontier Profit and Loss: The British Army and the Fur Traders, 1760–1764*. Westport, Conn.: Greenwood Press, 1998.
Dunnigan, Brian L. *The Necessity of Regularity in Quartering Soldiers: The Organization, Material Culture, and Quartering of the British Soldier on Michilimackinac*. Mackinac Island, Mich.: Mackinac State Historic Parks, 1999.
———. *Siege—1759: The Campaign against Niagara*. Youngstown, N.Y.: Old Fort Niagara Association, 1986.
Eccles, William J. *France in America*. New York: Harper and Row, 1972.
———. "The Fur Trade and Eighteenth-Century Imperialism." *William and Mary Quarterly*, 3rd ser., 40 (1983): 341–62.
———. "The History of New France According to Francis Parkman." *William and Mary Quarterly*, 3rd ser., 18 (1961): 163–75.
Eddis, William. *Letters from America*. Edited by Aubrey C. Land. Cambridge, Mass.: Harvard University Press, 1969.
Egnal, Marc. *New World Economies: The Growth of the Thirteen Colonies and Early Canada*. New York: Oxford University Press, 1998.
Eid, Leroy V. "'A Kind of Running Fight': Indian Battlefield Tactics in the Late Eighteenth Century." *Western Pennsylvania Historical Magazine* 71 (1988): 147–71.
———. "'National' War among Indians of Northeastern North America." *Canadian Review of American Studies* 16 (1985): 125–54.
Ekirch, A. Roger. *Bound for America: The Transportation of British Convicts to the Colonies, 1718–1775*. Oxford: Clarendon Press, 1987.
Ells, Margaret. "The Philadelphia Merchants and the Petitcodiac." *Nova Scotia Historical Review* 11 (1991): 102–11.
Ettinger, Amos A. *James Edward Oglethorpe, Imperial Idealist*. Oxford: Clarendon Press, 1936.
Evans, Geraint N. D. *Uncommon Obdurate: The Several Public Careers of J.F.W. DesBarres*. Toronto: University of Toronto Press, 1969.
Everest, Allan S. *Moses Hazen and the Canadian Refugees in the American Revolution*. Syracuse: Syracuse University Press, 1976.
Feest, Christian F., ed. *Indians and Europeans: An Interdisciplinary Collection of Essays*. Lincoln: University of Nebraska Press, 1999.
Fenn, Elizabeth A. *Pox Americana: The Great Smallpox Epidemic of 1775–82*. New York: Hill and Wang, 2001.
Fenske, Hans. "International Migration: Germany in the Eighteenth Century." *Central European History* 13 (1980): 332–47.

Ferguson, Adam. *An Essay on the History of Civil Society*. Edited by Fania Oz-Salzberger. Cambridge: Cambridge University Press, 1995.

Ferling, John E. *A Wilderness of Miseries: War and Warriors in Early America*. Westport, Conn.: Greenwood Press, 1980.

Fischer, David H. *Albion's Seed: Four British Folkways in America*. New York: Oxford University Press, 1989.

Fischer, Joseph R. *A Well-Executed Failure: The Sullivan Campaign against the Iroquois, July–September 1779*. Columbia: University of South Carolina Press, 1997.

Fisher, George H. "Brigadier-General Henry Bouquet." *Pennsylvania Magazine of History and Biography* 3 (1879): 121–43.

Fogleman, Aaron S. *Hopeful Journeys: German Immigration, Settlement, and Political Culture in Colonial America, 1715–1775*. Philadelphia: University of Pennsylvania Press, 1996.

Ford, Worthington C. *British Officers Serving in America, 1754–1774*. Boston: Privately printed, 1894.

———, ed. *General Orders of 1757 Issued by the Earl of Loudoun and Phineas Lyman in the Campaign against the French*. New York: Dodd Mead and Company, 1899.

Fraser, Alexander, ed. *Second Report of the Bureau of Archives for the Province of Ontario*. Toronto: King's Printer, 1905.

Fregault, Guy. *Canada: The War of the Conquest*. Translated by Margaret M. Cameron. Toronto: Oxford University Press, 1969.

Frey, Sylvia R. *The British Soldier in America: A Social History of Military Life in the Revolutionary Period*. Austin: University of Texas Press, 1981.

Fry, Bruce W. *"An Appearance of Strength": The Fortifications of Louisbourg*. 2 vols. Ottawa: Parks Canada, 1984.

Fuller, John F. C. *British Light Infantry in the Eighteenth Century*. London: Hutchinson and Company, 1925.

———. "The Revival and Training of Light Infantry in the British Army, 1757–1806." *Journal of the Royal United Service Institution* 57 (1913): 1187–1214.

Gale, Robert L. *Francis Parkman*. New York: Twayne Publishers, 1973.

Galenson, David W. *White Servitude in Colonial America: An Economic Analysis*. Cambridge: Cambridge University Press, 1981.

Galiffe, Jacques A. *Notices généalogiques sur les familles genevoises, depuis les premiers temps, jusqu'à nos jours*. 7 vols. Geneva: J.Barbezat, 1829–95.

Gallay, Alan, ed. *Colonial Wars of North America, 1512–1763: An Encyclopedia*. New York: Garland Publishing, Inc., 1996.

Gilbert, Arthur N. "The Regimental Courts-Martial in the Eighteenth Century." *Albion* 8 (1976): 51–66.

———. "Why Men Deserted from the Eighteenth-Century British Army." *Armed Forces and Society* 6 (1980): 553–67.

Gipson, Lawrence H. *The British Empire before the American Revolution*. 15 vols. New York: Alfred A. Knopf, 1936–70.

Glatfelter, Charles H. *Pastors and People: German Lutherans and Reformed Churches in the Pennsylvania Field, 1717–1792*. 2 vols. Breinigsville, Pa.: Pennsylvania German Society, 1980.
Godfrey, William G. *Pursuit of Profit and Preferment in Colonial North America: John Bradstreet's Quest*. Waterloo, Ont.: Wilfrid Laurier University Press, 1982.
Gordon, William A., ed. "Journal of the Siege of Louisbourg," *Royal United Services Institute Journal* 60 (1915): 117–52.
Gouin, Jacques, and Lucien Brault. *Les Panet de Québec: Histoire d'une lignée militaire*. Montreal: Bergeron, 1984.
Gould, Eliga H. *The Persistence of Empire: British Political Culture in the Age of the American Revolution*. Chapel Hill: University of North Carolina Press, 2000.
Grabowski, Jan. "French Criminal Justice and Indians in Montreal, 1670–1760." *Ethnohistory* 43 (1996): 405–29.
Grace, Henry. *The History of the Life and Sufferings of Henry Grace, of Basingstoke in the County of Southampton*. Basingstoke, 1764.
Graham, Dee L. R., Edna I. Rawlings, and Roberta K. Rigsby. *Loving to Survive: Sexual Terror, Men's Violence, and Women's Lives*. New York: New York University Press, 1994.
Graham, Dominick S. "British Intervention in Defence of the American Colonies, 1748–1756." Ph.D. diss., University of London, 1965.
Grant, Alexander, and Keith J. Stringer, eds. *Uniting the Kingdom: The Making of British History*. London: Routledge, 1995.
Grant, Anne. *Memoirs of an American Lady with Sketches of Manners and Scenery in America, as They Existed Previous to the Revolution*. New York: D. Appleton and Company, 1846.
Greene, Jack P. *Pursuits of Happiness: The Social Development of Early Modern British Colonies and the Formation of American Culture*. Chapel Hill: University of North Carolina Press, 1988.
———. "The South Carolina Quartering Dispute." *South Carolina Historical Magazine* 60 (1959): 193–204.
Greene, Jack P., and J. R. Pole, eds. *Colonial British America: Essays in the New History of the Early Modern Era*. Baltimore: Johns Hopkins University Press, 1984.
Greer, Allan. *The People of New France*. Toronto: University of Toronto Press, 1997.
Gregory, James, and Thomas Dunnings, eds. *The Horatio Gates Papers*. 20 reels. New York: Microfilming Corporation of America, 1979.
Gridley, Luke. *Luke Gridley's Diary of 1757 While in the Service in the French and Indian War*. Edited by F. M. Hartford: Hartford Press, 1907.
Griffin, Patrick. *The People with No Name: Ireland's Ulster Scots, America's Scots Irish, and the Creation of a British Atlantic World, 1689–1764*. Princeton: Princeton University Press, 2001.
Grotius, Hugo. *The Rights of War and Peace, Including the Law of Nature and of Nations*. Edited and translated by Archibald C. Campbell. Westport, Conn.: Hyperion Press, 1979.

Grubb, Farley. "Redemptioner Immigration to Pennsylvania: Evidence on Contract Choice and Profitability." *Journal of Economic History* 46 (1986): 407–18.

Guy, Alan J. *Oeconomy and Discipline: Officership and Administration in the British Army, 1714–1763*. Manchester: University of Manchester Press, 1985.

Gwyn, Julian. *The Enterprising Admiral: The Personal Fortune of Admiral Sir Peter Warren*. Montreal: McGill-Queen's University Press, 1974.

Hale, Richard W., Jr. *The Royal Americans*. Ann Arbor: William L. Clements Library, 1944.

Hamilton, Charles, ed. *Braddock's Defeat: The Journal of Captain Robert Cholmley's Batman, The Journal of a British Officer, Halkett's Orderly Book*. Norman: University of Oklahoma Press, 1959.

Hamilton, Milton W., ed. "The Diary of the Reverend John Ogilvie, 1750–59." *Bulletin of the Fort Ticonderoga Museum* 10 (1961): 331–81.

Hancock, David. *Citizens of the World: London Merchants and the Integration of the British Atlantic Community, 1735–1785*. Cambridge: Cambridge University Press, 1995.

Hanway, J[onas]. *An Account of the Society for the Encouragement of the British Troops in Germany and North America*. London, 1760.

Harding, Richard. *Amphibious Warfare in the Eighteenth Century: The British Expedition to the West Indies, 1740–1742*. Rochester, N.Y.: Boydell Press, 1991.

———. "The Growth of Anglo-American Alienation: The Case of the American Regiment, 1740–1742." *Journal of Imperial and Commonwealth History* 17 (1989): 161–79.

Harris, Richard C. *The Seigneurial System in Early Canada: A Geographical Study*. Montreal: McGill-Queen's University Press, 1984.

Hasenclever, Peter. *The Remarkable Case of Peter Hasenclever, Merchant*. London, 1773.

Hastings, Hugh, ed. *Orderly Book and Journal of Major John Hawks on the Ticonderoga–Crown Point Campaign, under General Jeffery Amherst, 1759–1760*. New York: Society of Colonial Wars in the State of New York, 1911.

Hay, Douglas, Peter Linebaugh, John G. Rule, E. P. Thompson, and Cal Winslow, eds. *Albion's Fatal Tree: Crime and Society in Eighteenth-Century England*. New York: Pantheon Books, 1975.

Hayter, Tony, ed. *An Eighteenth-Century Secretary at War: The Papers of William, Viscount Barrington*. London: The Bodley Head, 1988.

Hazard, Samuel, ed. *Minutes of the Provincial Council of Pennsylvania, from the Organization to the Termination of the Proprietary Government*. 16 vols. Harrisburg: State of Pennsylvania, 1851–53.

———, ed. *Pennsylvania Archives*. 12 vols. 1st ser. Philadelphia: Joseph Severns and Company, 1852–56.

Hening, William W., ed. *The Statutes at Large; Being a Collection of All the Laws of Virginia, from the First Session of the Legislature, in the Year 1619*. 13 vols. Richmond: Franklin Press, 1809–23.

Henry, Alexander. *Travels and Adventures in Canada and the Indian Territories; Between the Years 1760 and 1776.* Edited by James Bain. Toronto: George. N. Morang and Company Ltd., 1901.

Hervey, William. *Journals of the Hon. William Hervey, in North America and Europe, from 1755 to 1814: With Order Books at Montreal, 1760–1763, with Memoir and Notes.* Bury St. Edmond's: Suffolk Green Books, 1906.

Higginbotham, R. Don. "The Martial Spirit in the Antebellum South: Some Further Speculations in a National Context." *Journal of Southern History* 58 (1992): 3–26.

Hildeburn, Charles R. "Sir John St. Clair, Baronet, Quarter-Master General in America, 1755 to 1767." *Pennsylvania Magazine of History and Biography* 9 (1885): 1–14.

Hinderaker, Eric. *Elusive Empires: Constructing Colonialism in the Ohio Valley, 1673–1800.* Cambridge: Cambridge University Press, 1997.

Hinke, William J. *Ministers of the German Reformed Congregations in Pennsylvania and Other Colonies in the Eighteenth Century.* Edited by George W. Richards. Lancaster, Pa.: Historical Commission of the Evangelical and Reformed Church, 1951.

Historical Magazine, and Notes and Queries Concerning the Antiquities, History, and Biography of America. 10 vols. New York, 1857-66.

Hitsman, J. Mackay, and C. C. J. Bond. "The Assault Landing at Louisbourg, 1758." *Canadian Historical Review* 35 (1954): 314–30.

Home, James A., ed. *The Letters and Journals of Lady Mary Coke.* 4 vols. Edinburgh: David Douglas, 1889–96.

Hough, Franklin B., ed. *Diary of the Siege of Detroit in the War with Pontiac: Also a Narrative of the Principal Events of the Siege by Major Robert Rogers, a Plan for Conducting Indian Affairs by Colonel Bradstreet, and Other Authentick Documents Never Before Printed.* Albany: J. Munsell, 1860.

Houlding, John A. *Fit for Service: The Training of the British Army, 1715–1795.* Oxford: Clarendon Press, 1981.

Howard, Michael, George J. Andreopoulos, and Mark R. Shulman, eds. *The Laws of War: Constraints on Warfare in the Western World.* New Haven: Yale University Press, 1994.

Hughes, Basil P. *British Smooth-Bore Artillery: The Muzzle Loading Artillery of the 18th and 19th Centuries.* London: Arms and Armour Press, 1969.

———. *Firepower: Weapons Effectiveness on the Battlefield, 1630–1850.* London: Arms and Armour Press, 1974.

Hunter, William A. *Forts on the Pennsylvania Frontier, 1753–1758.* Harrisburg: Pennsylvania Historical and Museum Commission, 1960.

———, ed. "Thomas Barton and the Forbes Expedition." *Pennsylvania Magazine of History and Biography* 95 (1971): 431–83.

Hutchins, Thomas. *A Topographical Description of Virginia, Pennsylvania, Maryland, and North Carolina.* Edited by Frederick C. Hicks. Cleveland: Burrows Brothers Company, 1904.

Hutton, Sir Edward., *Colonel Henry Bouquet, 60th Royal Americans, 1756–1765: A Biographical Sketch.* Winchester, U.K.: Warren and Son, Ltd., 1911.

An Impartial History of the Late Glorious War. Manchester, 1764.
Ivers, Larry E. *British Drums on the Southern Frontier: The Military Colonization of Georgia, 1733–1749.* Chapel Hill: University of North Carolina Press, 1974.
Jacobs, Wilbur R. *Diplomacy and Indian Gifts: Anglo-French Rivalry along the Ohio and Northwest Frontier, 1748–1763.* Stanford: Stanford University Press, 1950.
Jaenen, Cornelius J. *Friend and Foe: Aspects of French-Amerindian Cultural Contact in the Sixteenth and Seventeenth Centuries.* Toronto: McClelland and Stewart, 1976.
James, Alfred P., ed. *Writings of General John Forbes Relating to His Service in North America.* Menasha, Wisc.: Collegiate Press, 1938.
James, Alfred P., and Charles M. Stotz. *Drums in the Forest.* Pittsburgh: Historical Society of Western Pennsylvania, 1958.
Jameson, J. F., J. Franklin, Douglas Brymner, Talcott Williams, Frederick J. Turner, and William P. Trent, eds. *Report of the Historical Manuscripts Commission of the American Historical Association; First, Second, and Third Reports.* Washington: Government Printing Office, 1897.
Jenks, Samuel. *Diary of Captain Samuel Jenks, during the French and Indian War. 1760.* Cambridge, Mass.: John Wilson and Son, 1890.
Jennings, Francis. *Empire of Fortune: Crowns, Colonies, and Tribes in the Seven Years War in America.* New York: W.W. Norton, 1988.
———. "Francis Parkman: A Brahmin among Untouchables." *William and Mary Quarterly,* 3rd ser., 42 (1985): 305–28.
Johnson, James M. *Militiamen, Rangers, and Redcoats: The Military in Georgia, 1754–1776.* Macon, Ga.: Mercer University Press, 1992.
Johnson, Richard R. *John Nelson, Merchant Adventurer: A Life between Empires.* New York: Oxford University Press, 1991.
Jones, Douglas L. *Village and Seaport: Migration in Eighteenth-Century Massachusetts.* Hanover, N.H.: University Press of New England, 1981.
Jordan, John W., ed. "Journal of James Kenny, 1761–1763." *Pennsylvania Magazine of History and Biography* 37 (1913): 1–47, 152–201, and 395–449.
Journal of the Commissioners for Trade and Plantations, 1704–1782. London: His Majesty's Stationery Office, 1920–38.
Kalm, Peter. *Peter Kalm's Travels in North America.* Edited by Adolph B. Benson. 2 vols. New York: Wilson-Erickson, Inc., 1937.
Kammen, Michael G. *A Rope of Sand: The Colonial Agents, British Politics, and the American Revolution.* Ithaca: Cornell University Press, 1968.
Kappler, Charles J., ed. *Indian Affairs: Laws and Treaties.* 5 vols. Washington: Government Printing Office, 1904–41.
Keith, Charles P., ed. *The Provincial Councilors of Pennsylvania Who Held Office Between 1733–1776.* Philadelphia: Privately printed, 1883.
Kernaghan, Lois K. "'A Most Eccentric Genius': The Private Life of J.F.W. DesBarres." *Nova Scotia Historical Review* 5 (1985): 41–59.
Kettner, James H. *The Development of American Citizenship, 1608–1870.* Chapel Hill: University of North Carolina Press, 1978.

Kierner, Cynthia A. *Traders and Gentlefolk: The Livingstons of New York, 1675–1790*. Ithaca: Cornell University Press, 1992.

Kim, Sung Bok. *Landlord and Tenant in Colonial New York: Manorial Society, 1664–1775*. Chapel Hill: University of North Carolina Press, 1978.

Kimball, Gertrude S., ed. *Correspondence of William Pitt When Secretary of State with Colonial Governors and Military and Naval Commissioners in America*. 2 vols. New York: Macmillan Company, 1906.

Kirk, Robert. *The Memoirs and Adventures of Robert Kirk, Late of the Royal Highland Regiment*. Limerick, 1770[?].

Klepp Susan E., and Billy G. Smith, eds. *The Infortunate: The Voyage and Adventures of William Moraley, an Indentured Servant*. University Park: Pennsylvania State University Press, 1992.

Klinck, Carl F., and James J. Talman, eds. *The Journal of Major John Norton, 1816*. Toronto: Champlain Society, 1970.

Klyza, Christopher M., and Stephen C. Trombulak. *The Story of Vermont: A Natural and Cultural History*. Hanover, N.H.: University Press of New England, 1999.

Knoblauch, Edward H. "Mobilizing Provincials for War: The Social Composition of New York Forces in 1760." *New York History* 78 (1997): 147–72.

Knox, John. *An Historical Journal of the Campaigns in North America for the Years 1757, 1758, 1759, and 1760*. Edited by Arthur G. Doughty. 3 vols. Toronto: Champlain Society, 1914.

Koehn, Nancy F. *The Power of Commerce: Economy and Governance in the First British Empire*. Ithaca: Cornell University Press, 1994.

Kopperman, Paul E. *Braddock at the Monongahela*. Pittsburgh: University of Pittsburgh Press, 1977.

———. "The British High Command and Soldiers' Wives in America, 1755–1783." *Journal of the Society for Army Historical Research* 60 (1982): 14–34.

———. "Religion and Religious Policy in the British Army, c. 1700–96." *Journal of Religious History* 15 (1987): 390–405.

———. "The Stoppages Mutiny of 1763." *Western Pennsylvania Historical Magazine* 69 (1986): 241–54.

Krause, Eric, Carol Corbin, and William O'Shea, eds. *Aspects of Louisbourg: Essays on the History of an Eighteenth-Century French Community in North America*. Sydney, N.S.: University College of Cape Breton Press, 1995.

La Rochefoucauld-Liancourt, Francios-Alexandre-Frederic, Duc de. *Travels through the United States of North America, the Country of the Iroquois, and Upper Canada in the Years 1795, 1796, and 1797, with an Authentic Account of Lower Canada*. Translated by Henri Neuman. 2 vols. London, 1799.

Labaree, Leonard W., ed. *The Papers of Benjamin Franklin*. 36 vols. (to date). New Haven: Yale University Press, 1959–.

Lafitau, Joseph-François. *Customs of the American Indians Compared with the Customs of Primitive Times*. Edited and translated by William N. Fenton and Elizabeth L. Moore. 2 vols. Toronto: Champlain Society, 1974–77.

Lamb, Roger. *Memoirs of His Own Life*. Dublin: 1811.
Lambert, Sheila, ed. *House of Commons Sessional Papers of the Eighteenth Century*. 147 vols. Wilmington, Del.: Scholarly Resources Inc., 1975–76.
Landsman, Ned C. *From Colonials to Provincials: American Thought and Culture, 1680–1760*. New York: Twayne Publishers, 1997.
Langford, Paul. *The First Rockingham Administration, 1765–1766*. Oxford: Oxford University Press, 1973.
———. *A Polite and Commercial People: England, 1727–1783*. Oxford: Clarendon Press, 1989.
———. *Public Life and the Propertied Englishman, 1689–1798*. Oxford: Clarendon Press, 1991.
Langworthy, Edward, ed. *Memoirs of the Life of the Late Charles Lee*. New York, 1792.
Lätt, Arnold. "Schweizer Offiziere als Indianerkreiger und Insturtoren der englischen leichten Infanterie." In *Neujahrsblatt der Feuerwerker-Gesellschaft (Artillerie-Kollegium) in Zurich auf Das Jahr 1933*. Zurich: Kommissionsverlag Beer, 1933, 3–45.
Leach, Douglas E. *Roots of Conflict: British Armed Forces and Colonial Americans, 1677–1763*. Chapel Hill: University of North Carolina Press, 1986.
Lehmann, William C. *Henry Home, Lord Kames, and the Scottish Enlightenment: A Study in National Character and in the History of Ideas*. The Hague: Martinus Nijhoff, 1971.
Lemon, James T. *The Best Poor Man's Country: A Geographical Study of Early Southeastern Pennsylvania*. Baltimore: Johns Hopkins University Press, 1972.
Lewis, Wilmarth S., Warren Hunting Smith, and George L. Lam, eds. *Yale Edition of Horace Walpole's Correspondence*. 48 vols. New Haven: Yale University Press, 1961–83.
Lincoln, Charles H., ed. *The Correspondence of William Shirley Governor of Massachusetts and Military Commander in America, 1731–1760*. 2 vols. New York: Macmillan Company, 1912.
Linn, John B., and William H. Egle, eds. *Pennsylvania Archives*. 2nd ser. 19 vols. Harrisburg: State of Pennsylvania, 1874–93.
Livingston, William, and William Smith. *A Review of the Military Operations in North America*. New York, 1770.
Loescher, Burt G. *The History of Rogers Rangers*. 3 vols. San Francisco: Privately printed, 1946–69.
Lonergan, Carroll V. *Ticonderoga: Historic Portage*. Ticonderoga, N.Y.: Fort Mount Hope Society Press, 1975.
Low, David. *Low's Political Parade with Colonel Blimp*. London: Cresset Press, 1936.
Lucas, Silas E., Jr. *Index to Deeds of the Province of South Carolina, 1719–1785, and Charleston District, 1785–1800*. Easley, S.C.: Southern Historical Press, 1977.
Lydenberg, Harry M., ed. *Archibald Robertson: His Diaries and Sketches in America, 1762–1780*. New York: New York Public Library, 1930.

Lydon, James G. *Pirates, Privateers, and Profits.* Upper Saddle River, N.J.: Gregg Press, Inc., 1970.

Lynn, John A. *Giant of the Grand Siècle: The French Army, 1610–1715.* Cambridge: Cambridge University Press, 1997.

Mackay, John. *Life of Lieut. General Hugh Mackay of Scoury.* Edinburgh: Laing and Forbes, 1836.

Mackay, Robert. *History of the House and Clan of Mackay.* Edinburgh: Andrew Jack and Company, 1829.

MacKillop, Andrew. *"More Fruitful Than the Soil": Army, Empire, and the Scottish Highlands, 1715–1815.* East Linton, Scotland: Tuckwell Press, 2000.

MacKinney, Gertrude, ed. *Pennsylvania Archives.* 8th ser. 8 vols. Harrisburg: State of Pennsylvania, 1931–35.

MacLeod, D. Peter. *The Canadian Iroquois and the Seven Years' War.* Toronto: Dundurn Press, 1996.

MacLeod, Malcolm. "Fight at the West Gate, 1760." *Ontario History* 58 (1966): 172–85.

Maguire, W. A., ed. *Kings in Conflict: The Revolutionary War in Ireland and Its Aftermath, 1689–1750.* Belfast: Blackstaff Press, 1990.

Mahon, Reginald H. *Life of General the Hon. James Murray, a Builder of Canada.* London: John Murray, 1921.

Malone, Patrick M. *The Skulking Way of War: Technology and Tactics among the New England Indians.* New York: Madison Books, 1991.

Mancall, Peter C. *Deadly Medicine: Indians and Alcohol in Early America.* Ithaca: Cornell University Press, 1995.

———. *Valley of Opportunity: Economic Culture along the Upper Susquehanna, 1700–1800.* Ithaca: Cornell University Press, 1991.

Mancke, Elizabeth, and Carole Shammas, eds. *The Creation of the British Atlantic World.* Baltimore: Johns Hopkins University Press, 2005.

Mante, Thomas. *The History of the Late War in North America and the Islands of the West Indies.* London, 1772.

Marsella, Anthony J., Matthew J. Friedman, Ellen T. Gerrity, and Raymond M. Scurfield, eds. *Ethnocultural Aspects of Posttraumatic Stress Disorder: Issues, Research, and Clinical Applications.* Washington: American Psychological Association, 1996.

Marshall, Peter J. *The Making and Unmaking of Empires: Britain, India, and America, c. 1750–1783.* Oxford: Oxford University Press, 2005.

Matson, Cathy. *Merchants and Empire: Trading in Colonial New York.* Baltimore: Johns Hopkins University Press, 1998.

May, George S., ed. *The Doctor's Secret Journal.* Mackinac Island, Mich.: Fort Mackinac Division Press, 1960.

Mayer, Holly A. *Belonging to the Army: Camp Followers and Community during the American Revolution.* Columbia: University of South Carolina Press, 1996.

———. "From Forts to Families: Following the Army into Western Pennsylvania, 1758–1766." *Pennsylvania Magazine of History and Biography* 130 (2006): 5–43.

McCardell, Lee. *Ill-Starred General: Braddock of the Coldstream Guards.* Pittsburgh: University of Pittsburgh Press, 1958.
McConnell, Michael N. *Army and Empire: British Soldiers on the American Frontier, 1758–1775.* Lincoln: University of Nebraska Press, 2004.
———. *A Country Between: The Upper Ohio Valley and Its Peoples, 1724–1774.* Lincoln: University of Nebraska Press, 1992.
McCusker, John J. *Money and Exchange in Europe and America, 1600–1775: A Handbook.* Chapel Hill: University of North Carolina Press, 1978.
McCusker, John J., and Russell R. Menard. *The Economy of British America.* Chapel Hill: University of North Carolina Press, 1985.
McDowell, William L., Jr., ed. *Documents Relating to Indian Affairs, 1750–1765.* 2 vols. Columbia: University of South Carolina Press, 1958–70.
McIlwaine, Henry R., ed. *Executive Journals of the Council of Colonial Virginia.* 6 vols. Richmond: Virginia State Library, 1925–66.
McLennan, J. S. *Louisbourg: From Its Foundation to Its Fall, 1713–1758.* London: Macmillan and Company Ltd., 1918.
McLynn, Frank J. *Crime and Punishment in Eighteenth-Century England.* New York: Routledge, 1989.
McNairn, Alan. *Behold the Hero: General Wolfe and the Arts in the Eighteenth Century.* Montreal: McGill-Queen's University Press, 1997.
McNeill, John R. *Atlantic Empires of France and Spain: Louisbourg and Havana, 1700–1763.* Chapel Hill: University of North Carolina Press, 1985.
Meek, Ronald L. *Social Science and the Ignoble Savage.* Cambridge: Cambridge University Press, 1976.
Merchant, Carolyn. *Ecological Revolutions: Nature, Gender, and Science in New England.* Chapel Hill: University of North Carolina Press, 1989.
Mereness, Newton D., ed. *Travels in the American Colonies.* New York: Macmillan, 1916.
Merrell, James H. *The Indians' New World: Catawbas and Their Neighbors from European Contact through the Era of Removal.* Chapel Hill: University of North Carolina Press, 1989.
———. *Into the American Woods: Negotiators on the Pennsylvania Frontier.* New York: W.W. Norton, 1999.
Merritt, Jane T. *At the Crossroads: Indians and Empires on a Mid-Atlantic Frontier, 1700–1763.* Chapel Hill: University of North Carolina Press, 2003.
Middleton, Richard. *The Bells of Victory: The Pitt-Newcastle Ministry and the Conduct of the Seven Years' War, 1757–1762.* Cambridge: Cambridge University Press, 1985.
Migliazzo, Arlin C. "A Tarnished Legacy Revisited: Jean Pierre Purry and the Settlement of the Southern Frontier." *South Carolina Historical Magazine* 92 (1991): 232–52.
Millan, J[ohn]. *A List of the General and Field-Officers, as They Rank in the Army. A List of the Officers in the Several Regiments of Horse, Dragoons and Foot, &c.* London: J. Millan, 1765.
———. *A List of the General and Field-Officers, as They Rank in the Army. A*

List of the Officers in the Several Regiments of Horse, Dragoons and Foot, &c. London: J. Millan, 1774.
Mingay, Gordon E. *English Landed Society in the Eighteenth Century.* London: Routledge and Kegan Paul, 1963.
Minutes of Conferences, Held at Easton, in October, 1758. Philadelphia, 1758.
Moens, William J., et al., eds. *Publications of the Huguenot Society of London.* 59 vols. (to date). London: The Society, 1887–.
Moneypenny, Alexander, Captain. "The Moneypenny Orderly Book." *Bulletin of the Fort Ticonderoga Museum* 12 (1969–70): 328–57, 434–61; 13 (1970–71): 89–116, 151–84.
Monro, Donald. *An Account of the Diseases Which Were Most Frequent in the British Military Hospitals in Germany.* London, 1764.
Morgan, Gwenda, and Peter Rushton. *Rogues, Thieves, and the Rule of Law: The Problem of Law Enforcement in North-East England, 1718–1800.* London: UCL Press, 1998.
Morris, Michael P. *The Bringing of Wonder: Trade and the Indians of the Southeast, 1700–1783.* Westport, Conn.: Greenwood Press, 1999.
Morris, Thomas, Captain. *Miscellanies in Prose and Verse.* London, 1791.
Morse, William I., ed. *The Canadian Collection at Harvard University: Harvard University Bulletin* 6 (1948–49).
Mowat, Farley. *The Regiment.* Toronto: McClelland and Stewart, 1955.
Multhauf, Robert P. *Neptune's Gift: A History of Common Salt.* Baltimore: Johns Hopkins University Press, 1978.
Murdoch, Tessa. *The Quiet Conquest: The Huguenots, 1685 to 1985.* London: Board of Governors of the Museum of London, 1985.
Murray, David. *Indian Giving: Economies of Power in Indian–White Exchanges.* Amherst: University of Massachusetts Press, 2000.
Murray, James. *Governor Murray's Journal of the Siege of Quebec from 18th September 1759 to 25th May, 1760.* Toronto: Rous and Mann Ltd., 1939.
Namier, Sir Lewis, and John Brooke. *Charles Townshend.* New York: St. Martin's Press, 1964.
——. *The House of Commons, 1754–1790.* 3 vols. London: Her Majesty's Stationery Office, 1964.
Nash, Gary B. *The Urban Crucible: Social Change, Political Consciousness, and the Origins of the American Revolution.* Cambridge: Harvard University Press, 1979.
Nelson, Paul D. *General James Grant: Scottish Soldier and Royal Governor of East Florida.* Gainesville: University Press of Florida, 1993.
Neu, Irene D. "The Iron Plantations of Colonial New York." *New York History* 33 (1952): 3–24.
Norman, Brian. *The Influence of Switzerland on the Life and Writings of Edward Gibbon.* Studies on Voltaire and the Eighteenth Century, no. 3. Oxford: Voltaire Foundation, 2002.
The Northcliffe Collection. Ottawa: King's Printer, 1926.
Norton, Thomas E. *The Fur Trade in Colonial New York, 1686–1776.* Madison: University of Wisconsin Press, 1974.

Nosworthy, Brent. *The Anatomy of Victory: Battle Tactics, 1689–1763.* New York: Hippocrene Books, Inc., 1990.
Nye, Russel B. *George Bancroft, Brahmin Rebel.* New York: Alfred A. Knopf, 1944.
O'Brien, Susan. "A Transatlantic Community of Saints: The Great Awakening and the First Evangelical Network, 1735–1755." *American Historical Review* 91 (1986): 811–32.
O'Callaghan, Edmund B., ed. *Calendar of New York Colonial Manuscripts: Indorsed Land Papers in the Office of the Secretary of State of New York, 1643–1803.* Albany: Weed, Parsons and Company, 1864.
———, ed. *The Documentary History of the State of New-York.* 4 vols. Albany: Weed, Parsons, and Company, 1849–51.
O'Callaghan, Edmund B., and Berthold Fernow, eds. *Documents Relative to the Colonial History of the State of New York.* 15 vols. Albany: Weed, Parsons, and Company, 1856–87.
Ochberg, Frank M., and David A. Soskis, eds. *Victims of Terrorism.* Boulder, Colo.: Westview Press, 1982.
Odintz, Mark F. "The British Officer Corps, 1754–1783." Ph.D. diss., University of Michigan, 1988.
Olson, Alison G. *Making the Empire Work: London and American Interest Groups, 1690–1790.* Cambridge: Harvard University Press, 1992.
Olwell, Robert, and Alan Tully, eds. *Cultures and Identities in Colonial British America.* Baltimore: Johns Hopkins University Press, 2006.
Padeni, Scott A. "Forgotten Soldiers: The Role of Blacks in New York's Northern Campaigns of the Seven Years War." *Bulletin of the Fort Ticonderoga Museum* 16 (1999): 152–69.
Palmer, Peter S. *History of Lake Champlain from Its First Exploration by the French in 1609 to the Close of the Year 1814.* Albany: J. Munsell, 1866.
Papineau, D. B. "Le général Francis Mackay (1700–1770) venu en Amérique en 1756, au Canada en 1760 Ses descendants." *Memoirs de la Sociéte Genealogique Canadienne-Française* 15 (1964): 100–119.
Pargellis, Stanley, M. *Lord Loudoun in North America.* New Haven: Yale University Press, 1933.
———, ed. *Military Affairs in North America, 1748–1765: Selected Documents from the Cumberland Papers in Windsor Castle.* New York: D. Appleton-Century Company, 1936.
Parker, Anthony W. *Scottish Highlanders in Colonial Georgia: The Recruitment, Emigration, and Settlement at Darien, 1735–1748.* Athens: University of Georgia Press, 1997.
Parker, Geoffrey. *The Military Revolution: Military Innovation and the Rise of the West, 1500–1800.* 2nd ed. Cambridge: Cambridge University Press, 1996.
———. *The Thirty Years' War.* London: Routledge and Kegan Paul, 1984.
Parkman, Francis. *The Conspiracy of Pontiac and the Indian War after the Conquest of Canada.* 6th ed. 2 vols. Boston: Little, Brown, 1902.
———. *Montcalm and Wolfe.* New Library ed. 2 vols. Boston: Little, Brown, 1898.

Peckham, Howard H. *Pontiac and the Indian Uprising*. Princeton: Princeton University Press, 1947.
——, ed. "Thomas Gist's Indian Captivity, 1758–1759." *Pennsylvania Magazine of History and Biography* 80 (1956): 285–311.
Pencak, William. *War, Politics, and Revolution in Provincial Massachusetts*. Boston: Northeastern University Press, 1981.
Pickering, Danby, ed. *The Statutes at Large from the Magna Carta, to the End of the Eleventh Parliament of Great Britain, Anno. 1761*. 46 vols. Cambridge: J.Benton, 1762–1807.
Piper, William S., ed. *Diary and Journal (1755–1807) of Seth Metcalf*. Boston: Historical Records Survey, 1939.
Plank, Geoffrey. *Rebellion and Savagery: The Jacobite Rising of 1745 and the British Empire*. Philadelphia: University of Pennsylvania Press, 2006.
——. *An Unsettled Conquest: The British Campaign against the Peoples of Acadia*. Philadelphia: University of Pennsylvania Press, 2001.
Pottle, Frederick A., and Charles H. Bennett, eds. *Boswell's Journal of a Tour to the Hebrides with Samuel Johnson*. Toronto: Macmillan Company of Canada, Ltd., 1936.
Pouchot, Pierre. *Memoirs on the Late War in North America between France and England*. Edited by Brian L. Dunnigan. Translated by Michael Cardy. Youngstown, N.Y.: Old Fort Niagara Association, 1994.
Prete, Roy A., and A. Hamish Ion, eds. *Armies of Occupation*. Waterloo, Ont.: Wilfrid Laurier University Press, 1984.
Priestly, E. B. "Army Life, 1757." *Journal of the Society for Army Historical Research* 52 (1974): 197–208.
Procter, Jonathan. "Diary Kept at Louisbourg, 1759–1760, by Jonathan Procter of Danvers." Essex Institute, *Historical Collections* 70 (1934): 31–57.
Punch, Terrence M. "Montbéliard: An Unknown Homeland." *Nova Scotia Historical Review* 5 (1985): 74–92.
Purceval, John, Earl of Egmont. *The Memorial of John Earl of Egmont . . . [for] a Grant of the Whole Island of Saint John's in the Gulph of Saint Laurence*. London, 1764.
Purvis, Thomas L. "The European Ancestry of the United States Population, 1790." *William and Mary Quarterly*, 3rd ser., 41 (1984): 85–101.
——. "Patterns of Ethnic Settlement in Late Eighteenth-Century Pennsylvania." *Western Pennsylvania Historical Magazine* 70 (1987): 107–22.
Quaife, Milo M., ed. *The Siege of Detroit in 1763*. Chicago: Lakeside Press, 1958.
Ranlet, Philip. "The British, the Indians, and Smallpox: What Actually Happened at Fort Pitt in 1763?" *Pennsylvania History* 67 (2000): 427–41.
Rawlyk, George A. *Nova Scotia's Massachusetts: A Study of Massachusetts–Nova Scotia Relations, 1630 to 1784*. Montreal: McGill-Queen's University Press, 1973.
Ray, F[abius] M[aximus], ed. "The Journal of Dr. Caleb Rea, Written during the Expedition against Ticonderoga in 1758." Essex Institute, *Historical Collections* 18 (1881): 81–120, 177–205.

Raymond, W[illiam] O., ed. "Brigadier General Monckton's Expedition to the River Saint John in September, 1758." New Brunswick Historical Society, *Collections* 8 (1909): 113–65.

———. "A Sketch of the Province of Nova Scotia, and Chiefly of Such Parts as Are Settled, 1783." New Brunswick Historical Society, *Collections* 5 (1904): 142–53.

———. "Papers Relating to the St. John's River Society." New Brunswick Historical Society, *Collections* 6 (1905): 302–57.

———. *The River St. John: Its Physical Features, Legends, and History from 1604 to 1784.* Sackville, N.B.: Tribune Press, 1943.

Redington, Joseph, and Richard A. Roberts, eds. *Calendar of Home Office Papers of the Reign of George III, 1760–1775.* 4 vols. London: Her Majesty's Stationery Office, 1878–99.

Reed, George E., ed. *Pennsylvania Archives.* 4th ser. 12 vols. Harrisburg: State of Pennsylvania, 1900–1902.

Reese, George, ed. *The Official Papers of Francis Fauquier, Lieutenant Governor of Virginia, 1758–1768.* 3 vols. Charlottesville: University Press of Virginia, 1980–83.

Reflections on the Most Proper Means of Reducing the Rebels, and What Ought to Be the Consequences of Our Success. London, 1776.

Reid, Brian H. *J. F. C. Fuller: Military Thinker.* London: Macmillan Press Ltd., 1987.

Reid, John P. *In Defiance of the Law: The Standing Army Controversy, the Two Constitutions, and the Coming of the American Revolution.* Chapel Hill: University of North Carolina Press, 1981.

Richards, Henry M. *The Pennsylvania-German in the French and Indian War: A Historical Sketch.* Lancaster, Pa.: Pennsylvania German Society, 1905.

Richter, Daniel K. *Looking East from Indian Country: A Native History of Early America.* Cambridge: Harvard University Press, 2001.

———. "War and Culture: The Iroquois Experience." *William and Mary Quarterly,* 3rd ser., 40 (1983): 528–59.

Riley, James C. *The Seven Years War and the Old Regime in France: The Economic and Financial Toll.* Princeton: Princeton University Press, 1986.

Robertson, John. *The Scottish Enlightenment and the Militia Issue.* Edinburgh: John Donald Publishers Ltd., 1985.

Rodger, N. A. M. *The Wooden World: An Anatomy of the Georgian Navy.* London: Collins, 1986.

Rogers, Alan. *Empire and Liberty: American Resistance to British Authority, 1755–1763.* Berkeley: University of California Press, 1974.

Rogers, Nicholas. *Whigs and Cities: Popular Politics in the Age of Walpole and Pitt.* Oxford: Clarendon Press, 1989.

Rogers, Robert. *A Concise Account of North America.* London, 1765.

———. *Journals of Major Robert Rogers: Containing an Account of the Several Excursions He Made under the Generals Who Commanded upon the Continent of North America, during the late War.* London, 1765.

———. *Ponteach, or the Savages of America, A Tragedy*. London: J. Millan, 1766.
Ross, Dorothy. "Historical Consciousness in Nineteenth-Century America." *American Historical Review* 89 (1984): 909–28.
Rowen, Herbert H. *The Princes of Orange: The Stadtholders in the Dutch Republic*. Cambridge: Cambridge University Press, 1988.
Russell, Peter E. "Redcoats in the Wilderness: British Officers and Irregular Warfare in Europe and America, 1740 to 1760." *William and Mary Quarterly*, 3rd ser., 35 (1978): 629–52.
Russell, William H. *The Great War with Russia*. London: George Routledge and Sons, Ltd., 1895.
Rutherfurd, Livingston. *Family Records and Events Compiled Principally from the Original Manuscripts in the Rutherfurd Collection*. New York: De Vinne Press, 1894.
Salinger, Sharon V. *"To Serve Well and Faithfully": Labor and Indentured Servants in Pennsylvania, 1682–1800*. Cambridge: Cambridge University Press, 1987.
Sargent, Winthrop, ed. *The History of an Expedition against Fort Du Quesne in 1755; under Major-General Edward Braddock*. Philadelphia: Historical Society of Pennsylvania, 1856.
Saunders, William L., ed. *The Colonial Records of North Carolina*. 10 vols. Raleigh: Joseph Daniels, 1886–90.
Savard, Pierre, ed. *Mélanges d'histoire du Canada Français offerts au professeur Marcel Trudel*. Ottawa: Éditions de l'Université d'Ottawa, 1978.
Savory, Reginald. *His Britannic Majesty's Army in Germany during the Seven Years War*. Oxford: Clarendon Press, 1966.
Schwartz, Sally. *"A Mixed Multitude": The Struggle for Toleration in Colonial Pennsylvania*. New York: New York University Press, 1987.
Schwoerer, Lois G. *"No Standing Armies": The Antimilitary Ideology in Seventeenth-Century England*. Baltimore: Johns Hopkins University Press, 1974.
Seaver, James E. *DEH-HE-WA-MIS, or A Narrative of the Life of Mary Jemison*. 3rd ed. Batavia, N.Y.: William Seaver and Son, 1844.
Selesky, Harold E. *War and Society in Colonial Connecticut*. New Haven: Yale University Press, 1990.
Selig, Robert A. "Emigration, Fraud, Humanitarianism, and the Founding of Londonderry, South Carolina, 1763–1765." *Eighteenth-Century Studies* 23 (1989): 1–23.
Shammas, Carole. *The Pre-Industrial Consumer in England and America*. Oxford: Clarendon Press, 1990.
Shannon, Timothy J. *Indians and Colonists at the Crossroads of Empire: The Albany Congress of 1754*. Ithaca: Cornell University Press, 2000.
Shea, William L. *The Virginia Militia in the Seventeenth Century*. Baton Rouge: Louisiana State University Press, 1983.
Shortt, Adam, and Arthur G. Doughty, eds. *Documents Relating to the Constitutional History of Canada, 1759–1791*. 2nd rev. ed. Ottawa: King's Printer, 1918.

Shy, John W. *A People Numerous and Armed: Reflections on the Military Struggle for Independence.* New York: Oxford University Press, 1976.
——. *Toward Lexington: The Role of the British Army in the Coming of the American Revolution.* Princeton: Princeton University Press, 1965.
Simler, Lucy. "Tenancy in Colonial Pennsylvania: The Case of Chester County." *William and Mary Quarterly*, 3rd ser., 43 (1986): 542–69.
Simmons, Richard C., and Peter D. G. Thomas, eds. *Proceedings and Debates of the British Parliaments Respecting North America, 1754–1783.* 6 vols. London: Kraus International Publications, 1982–87.
Skaggs, David C., and Larry L. Nelson, eds. *The Sixty Years' War for the Great Lakes, 1754–1814.* East Lansing: Michigan State University Press, 2001.
Sleeper-Smith, Susan. *Indian Women and French Men: Rethinking Cultural Encounter in the Western Great Lakes.* Amherst: University of Massachusetts Press, 2001.
Smelser, Marshall. *The Campaign for the Sugar Islands, 1759: A Study of Amphibious Warfare.* Chapel Hill: University of North Carolina Press, 1955.
Smith, Abbot E. *Colonists in Bondage: White Servitude and Convict Labor in America, 1607–1776.* Chapel Hill: University of North Carolina Press, 1947; reprint, Gloucester, Mass.: Peter Smith, 1965.
Smith, Billy G. *The "Lower Sort": Philadelphia's Laboring People, 1750–1800.* Ithaca: Cornell University Press, 1990.
Smith, George. *An Universal Military Dictionary, A Copious Explanation of the Technical Terms &c., Used in the Equipment, Machinery, Movements and Military Operations of an Army.* London, 1779.
Smith, James, Colonel. *An Account of the Remarkable Occurrences in the Life and Travels of Colonel James Smith, during His Captivity with the Indians, in the Years 1755, '56, '57, '58, & '59.* Edited by William M. Darlington. Cincinnati: Robert Clarke and Company, 1870.
Smith, Richard. *A Tour of the Hudson, the Mohawk, the Susquehanna, and the Delaware in 1769.* Edited by Francis W. Halsey. Fleischmanns, N.Y.: Purple Mountain Press, Ltd., 1989.
Smith, William. *A Brief State of the Province of Pennsylvania.* 2nd ed. London, 1755.
——. *An Historical Account of Bouquet's Expedition against the Ohio Indians in 1764: Under the Command of Henry Bouquet, Esq. Colonel of Foot, and Now Brigadier General in America.* Philadelphia, 1765.
Sosin, Jack M. *Whitehall and the Wilderness: The Middle West in British Colonial Policy, 1760–1775.* Lincoln: University of Nebraska Press, 1961.
Spieler, Gerhard. "Peter Hasenclever, Industrialist." *Proceedings of the New Jersey Historical Society* 59 (1941): 231–56.
Stacey, Charles P. *Quebec, 1759: The Siege and the Battle.* Toronto: Macmillan Company of Canada, 1959.
Stanley, George F. G. *Toil and Trouble: Military Expeditions to Red River.* Toronto: Dundurn Press, 1989.
Starbuck David R. *The Great Warpath: British Military Sites from Albany to Crown Point.* Hanover, N.H.: University Press of New England, 1999.

Starkey, Armstrong. *European and Native American Warfare, 1675–1815.* London: UCL Press, 1998.
Statt, Daniel. *Foreigners and Englishmen: The Controversy over Immigration and Population, 1660–1760.* Newark: University of Delaware Press, 1995.
Steele, Ian K. *Betrayals: Fort William Henry and the "Massacre."* New York: Oxford University Press, 1990.
———. *Warpaths: Invasions of North America.* New York: Oxford University Press, 1994.
Stephenson, R. Scott. "Pennsylvania Soldiers in the Seven Years' War." *Pennsylvania History* 62 (1995): 196–212.
Steppler, Glenn A. "British Military Law, Discipline, and the Conduct of Regimental Courts Martial in the later Eighteenth Century." *English Historical Review* 102 (1987): 859–81.
———. "The Common Soldier in the Reign of George III, 1760–1793." Ph.D. diss. University of Oxford, 1984.
Stevens, Sylvester K., and Donald H. Kent, eds. *Wilderness Chronicles of Northwestern Pennsylvania.* Harrisburg: Pennsylvania Historical Commission, 1941.
Stevens, Sylvester K., Donald H. Kent, and Autumn L. Leonard, eds. *The Papers of Henry Bouquet.* 6 vols. Harrisburg: Pennsylvania Historical and Museum Commission, 1951–94.
Stock, Leo F., ed. *Proceedings and Debates of the British Parliament Respecting North America.* 5 vols. Washington: Carnegie Institution of Washington, 1924–37.
Stotz, Charles M. *Outposts for the War for Empire: The French and English in Western Pennsylvania.* Pittsburgh: Historical Society of Western Pennsylvania, 1985.
Strachan, Hew. *European Armies and the Conduct of War.* London: Allen and Unwin, 1983.
———. *The Politics of the British Army.* Oxford: Clarendon Press, 1997.
Stumpf, Stuart O. "South Carolina Importers of General Merchandise, 1735–1765." *South Carolina Historical Magazine* 84 (1983): 1–10.
Sullivan, James, Andrew C. Flick, and Milton W. Hamilton, eds. *The Papers of Sir William Johnson.* 14 vols. Albany: University of the State of New York, 1921–65.
Sumner, Percy. "Standing Orders for the Army, 1755." *Journal for the Society of Army Historical Research* 5 (1926): 191–99; 6 (1927): 8–10.
Syrett, David, ed. *The Siege and Capture of Havana, 1762.* London: Navy Records Society, 1970.
Taylor, Alan. "The Great Change Begins: Settling the Forest of Central New York." *New York History* 76 (1995): 265–90.
———. *Liberty Men and Great Proprietors: The Revolutionary Settlement on the Maine Frontier, 1760–1820.* Chapel Hill: University of North Carolina Press, 1990.
———. *William Cooper's Town: Power and Persuasion on the Frontier of the Early American Republic.* New York: Alfred A. Knopf, 1996.

Taylor, Stephen, Richard Connors, and Clyve Jones, eds. *Hanoverian Britain and Empire: Essays in Memory of Philip Lawson*. Rochester, N.Y.: Boydell Press, 1998.
Taylor, William. *The Military Roads in Scotland*. Isle of Colonsay, Argyll, U.K.: House of Lochar, 1996.
Thayer, Theodore. "The Army Contractors for the Niagara Campaign, 1755–1756." *William and Mary Quarterly*, 3rd ser., 14 (1957): 31–46.
Thomson, Don W. *Men and Meridians: The History of Surveying and Mapping in Canada*. 3 vols. Ottawa: Queen's Printer, 1966–69.
Thoresen, Timothy H. H., ed. *Towards a Science of Man: Essays in the Science of Anthropology*. The Hague: Mouton, 1975.
Thwaites, Reuben G., ed. *Early Western Travels, 1748–1846*. 32 vols. New York: AMS Press, 1966.
Titus, James. *The Old Dominion at War: Society, Politics, and Warfare in Late Colonial Virginia*. Columbia: University of South Carolina Press, 1991.
Trigger, Bruce G. *Natives and Newcomers: Canada's "Heroic Age" Reconsidered*. Montreal: McGill-Queens University Press, 1986.
Trudel, Marcel. *La Régime militaire dans le Gouvernement des Trois-Rivières, 1760–1764*. Trois-Rivièrs: Editions du Bien Public, 1952.
Trythall, Anthony J. *"Boney" Fuller: Soldier, Strategist, and Writer, 1878–1966*. New Brunswick: Rutgers University Press, 1977.
Ultee, Maarten, ed. *Adapting to Conditions: War and Society in the Eighteenth Century*. University: University of Alabama Press, 1986.
Valentine, Alan. *Lord Stirling: Colonial Gentleman and General in Washington's Army*. New York: Oxford University Press, 1969.
Van Kirk, Sylvia. *Many Tender Ties: Women in Fur-Trade Society, 1670–1870*. Winnipeg: Watson and Dwyer Publishing Ltd., 1980.
Van Ruymbeke, Bertrand, and Randy J. Sparks, eds. *Memory and Identity: The Huguenots in France and the Atlantic Diaspora*. Charleston: University of South Carolina Press, 2003.
Vann, James A. *The Making of a State: Württemberg, 1593–1793*. Ithaca: Cornell University Press, 1984.
Varga, Nicholas. "Robert Charles: New York Agent, 1748–1770." *William and Mary Quarterly*, 3rd ser., 18 (1961): 211–35.
Vattel, Emmerich de. *The Law of Nations; or, Principles of the Law of Nature, Applied to the Conduct and Affairs of Nations and Sovereigns*. Philadelphia: P.H. Nicklin and T.Johnson, 1829.
Vaughan, Alden T. *Roots of American Racism: Essays on the Colonial Experience*. New York: Oxford University Press, 1995.
Vezon, Joseph Fournerie de. "Événements de la Guerre en Canada depuis le 13 septembre 1759 jusqu'au 14 juillet 1760." *Rapport de l'Archiviste de la province de Québec, pour 1938–1939*, 1–9. Quebec: R.Paradis, 1939.
Vickers, Daniel. *Farmers and Fishermen: Two Centuries of Work in Essex County, Massachusetts, 1630–1850*. Chapel Hill: University of North Carolina Press, 1994.
Virgil. *Aeneid*. Translated by John Dryden. The Harvard Classics, no. 13. New York: P.F. Collier and Son, 1909–14.

Volwiler, Albert T., ed. "William Trent's Journal at Fort Pitt, 1763." *Mississippi Valley Historical Review* 11 (1924): 390–413.
Waddell, Louis M., and Bruce D. Bomberger. *The French and Indian War in Pennsylvania, 1753–1763: Fortification and Struggle during the War for Empire.* Harrisburg: Pennsylvania Historical and Museum Commission, 1996.
Wade, Mason. *Francis Parkman, Heroic Historian.* New York: Viking Press, 1942.
Wainwright, Nicholas B., ed. "George Croghan's Journal." *Pennsylvania Magazine of History and Biography* 71 (1947): 305–444.
———. *George Croghan: Wilderness Diplomat.* Chapel Hill: University of North Carolina Press, 1959.
———, ed. "Turmoil at Pittsburgh: Diary of Augustine Prevost, 1774." *Pennsylvania Magazine of History and Biography* 85 (1961): 111–62.
Wallace, Nesbit W. *The Rebellion in the Red River Settlement, 1869–70: Its Causes and Suppression.* Barnstaple, U.K.: Henry T. Cook, 1872.
———. *A Regimental Chronicle and List of Officers of the 60th, or the King's Royal Rifle Corps, Formerly the 62nd, or the Royal American Regiment of Foot.* London: Harrison, 1879.
Wallace, R. F. H., ed. "Regimental Routine and Army Administration in North America in 1759: Extracts from Company Order Books of the 42nd Royal Highland Regiment." *Journal of the Society for Army Historical Research* 30 (1952): 8–19.
Ward, Harry M. *"Unite or Die": Intercolony Relations, 1690–1763.* Port Washington, N.Y.: Kennikat Press, 1971.
Ward, Matthew C. "An Army of Servants: The Pennsylvania Regiment During the Seven Years' War." *Pennsylvania Magazine of History and Biography* 119 (1995): 75–93.
———. *Breaking the Backcountry: The Seven Years' War in Virginia and Pennsylvania, 1754–1765.* Pittsburgh: University of Pittsburgh Press, 2003.
———. "Fighting the 'Old Women': Indian Strategy on the Virginia and Pennsylvania Frontier, 1754–1758." *Virginia Magazine of History and Biography* 103 (1995): 297–320.
———. "Redeeming the Captives: Pennsylvania Captives among the Ohio Indians, 1755–1765." *Pennsylvania Magazine of History and Biography* 125 (2001): 161–89.
Way, Peter. "Rebellion of the Regulars: Working Soldiers and the Mutiny of 1763–1764." *William and Mary Quarterly*, 3rd ser., 57 (2000): 761–92.
Webster, John C. *The Forts of Chignecto: A Study in the Eighteenth-Century Conflict between France and Great Britain in Acadia.* Shedica, N.B.: Privately printed, 1930.
———, ed. "Journal of Abijah Willard, 1755." New Brunswick Historical Society, *Collections* 13 (1930): 4–75.
———, ed. *The Journal of Jeffery Amherst: Recording the Military Career of General Amherst in America from 1758 to 1763.* Toronto: Ryerson Press, 1931.
———, ed. "Journal of John Montresor's Expedition to Detroit in 1763." *Transactions of the Royal Society of Canada*, 3rd ser., 22 (1928), sec. ii, 8–31.

———, ed. *Journal of William Amherst in America, 1758–1760*. London: Butler and Tanner, 1927.
Weslager, Clinton A. *The Log Cabin in America: From Pioneer Days to the Present*. New Brunswick, N.J.: Rutgers University Press, 1969.
West, Jenny. *Gunpowder, Government, and War in the Mid-Eighteenth Century*. Rochester, N.Y.: Boydell Press, 1991.
Western, John R. *The English Militia in the Eighteenth Century: The Story of a Political Issues, 1660–1802*. London: Routledge and Kegan Paul, 1965.
White, Philip L., ed. *The Beekman Mercantile Papers, 1746–1799*. 3 vols. New York: New York Historical Society, 1956.
White, Richard. *The Middle Ground: Indians, Empires, and Republics in the Great Lakes Region, 1650–1815*. Cambridge: Cambridge University Press, 1991.
Whitehead, William A., ed. *Documents Relating to the Colonial, Revolutionary, and Post-Revolutionary History of New Jersey*. 42 vols. Newark: New Jersey Historical Society, 1880–1949.
Whitworth, Rex. *Field Marshal Lord Ligonier: The Story of the British Army, 1702–1770*. Oxford: Clarendon Press, 1958.
———. *William Augustus, Duke of Cumberland: A Life*. London: Leo Cooper, 1992.
Williams, Edward G., "The Prevosts of the Royal Americans." *Western Pennsylvania Historical Magazine* 56 (1973): 1–38.
———, ed. *The Orderly Book of Colonel Henry Bouquet's Expedition against the Ohio Indians, 1764*. Pittsburgh: Privately printed, 1960.
Williams, Joseph, Colonel. Orderly Book. In "The Expedition to Fort Craven, Oneida Great Carrying Place, and Frontenac in 1758." *Colonial Wars* 1 (1914): 178–215.
Williams, Michael. *Americans and Their Forests: A Historical Geography*. Cambridge: Cambridge University Press, 1989.
Williams, Noel St. John. *Redcoats along the Hudson: The Struggle for North America, 1754–1763*. London: Brassey's, 1997.
Williamson, John. *A Treatise on Military Finance; Containing the Pay, Subsistence, Deductions, and Arrears of the Forces on the British and Irish Establishments; and All the Allowances in Camp, Garrisons, and Quarters, &c. &c.* London, 1782.
Williamson, Peter. *French and Indian Cruelty Exemplified in the Life and Various Vicissitudes of Fortune of Peter Williamson Who Was Carried Off from Aberdeen in His Infancy and Sold for a Slave in Pennsylvania*. Edinburgh, 1792.
Willson, Beckles. *The Life and Letters of James Wolfe*. London: William Heinemann, 1909.
Wilson, Kathleen. *The Sense of the People: Politics, Culture, and Imperialism in England, 1715–1785*. Cambridge: Cambridge University Press, 1995.
Wilson, Peter H. *German Armies: War and German Politics, 1648–1806*. London: UCL Press, 1998.

———. "The German 'Soldier Trade' of the Seventeenth and Eighteenth Centuries: A Reassessment." *International History Review* 18 (1996): 757–92.

Wokeck, Marianne S. *Trade in Strangers: The Beginnings of Mass Migration to North America.* University Park: Pennsylvania State University Press, 1999.

Wood, Betty. *Slavery in Colonial Georgia, 1730–1775.* Athens: University of Georgia Press, 1984.

Wright, Esther C. *The Petitcodiac: A Study of the New Brunswick River and of the People Who Settled along It.* Sackville, N.B.: Tribune Press, 1945.

Wright, John W. "Sieges and Customs of War at the Opening of the Eighteenth Century." *American Historical Review* 39 (1934): 629–44.

Wrong, George M. *A Canadian Manor and Its Seigneurs: The Story of a Hundred Years, 1761–1861.* Toronto: Macmillan Company of Canada, Ltd., 1926.

Zimmerman, John J. "Governor Denny and the Quartering Act of 1756." *Pennsylvania Magazine of History and Biography* 91 (1967): 266–81.

Military Manuals

Bland, Humphrey. *A Treatise of Military Discipline; in Which Is Laid Down and Explained the Duty of the Officer and Soldier, through the Several Branches of the Service.* 8th ed. London, 1759.

Cuthbertson, Bennett. *A System for the Complete Interior Management and Oeconomy of a Battalion of Infantry.* 2nd ed. London, 1779.

Frederick the Great. *Military Instructions, Written by the King of Prussia, for the Generals of His Army: Being His Majesty's Own Commentaries on His Former Campaigns, Together with Short Instructions for the Use of His Light Troops.* Translated by an Officer. London, 1762.

Hamilton, Robert. *The Duties of a Regimental Surgeon Considered.* 2 vols. London, 1787.

LeBlond, Guillaume. *A Treatise of Artillery.* London, 1746.

Simes, Thomas. *The Military Guide for Young Officers.* 2 vols. Philadelphia, 1776.

———. *The Military Medley, Containing the Most Necessary Rules and Directions for Attaining a Competent Knowledge of the Art.* Dublin, 1767.

Vauban, Sebastien LePrestre de. *A Manual of Siegecraft and Fortification.* Edited and translated by George A. Rothrock. Ann Arbor: University of Michigan Press, 1968.

Webb, Lieutenant [Thomas]. *A Military Treatise on the Appointments of the Army.* Philadelphia, 1759.

Wolfe, James. *General Wolfe's Instructions to Young Officers: Also His Orders for a Battalion and an Army.* London, 1780.

Newspapers and Periodicals

American Magazine, and Monthly Chronicle of the British Colonies
Annual Register

Boston Evening Post
Boston News-Letter
Boston Post-Boy & Advertiser
Boston Weekly Advertiser
Boston Weekly Newsletter
Georgia Gazette
Gentleman's Magazine
London Chronicle or Universal Evening Post
London Gazette
Maryland Gazette
New London Summary; or *The Weekly Advertiser*
New York Gazette and the Weekly Mercury
New York Gazette or the Weekly Post Boy
New York Journal; or the General Advertiser
New York Mercury
Pensylvanische Berichte
Pennsylvania Gazette
Pennsylvania Journal and Weekly Advertiser
Scots Magazine
South Carolina Gazette
Virginia Gazette
Virginia Gazette [Purdie and Dixon]
Virginia Gazette [Rind]

Papers of Historical Societies

New York Historical Society, Collections

1871: The Lee Papers, Volume One. New York, 1872.
1881: The Montresor Journals. New York, 1882.
1921: The Letters and Papers of Cadwallader Colden, Volume Five, 1755–1760. New York, 1923.
1928: The Letter Book of John Watts, Merchant and Councillor of New York, January 1, 1762–December 22, 1765. New York, 1928.

Nova Scotia Historical Society, Collections

1884: "Journal of Colonel John Winslow of the Provincial Troops, while Engaged in the Siege of Fort Beausejour in the Summer and Autumn of 1755." Halifax, 1885.

Sermons

Adams, Amos. *Songs of Victory Directed by Human Compassion, and Qualified with Christian Benevolence: In a Sermon Delivered at Roxbury, October 25th, 1759, on the General Thanksgiving for the Success of His Majesty's Arms.* Boston, 1759.
Eliot, Andrew. *A Sermon Preached October 25th, 1759: Being a Day of Public Thanksgiving Appointed by Authority for the Success of the British Arms This Year Especially in the Reduction of Quebec.* Boston, 1759.

Foxcroft, Thomas. *Grateful Reflexions on the Signal Appearances of Divine Providence for Great Britain and its Colonies in America.* Boston, 1760.

Woodward, Samuel. *A Sermon Preached October 9, 1760: Being a Day of Public Thanksgiving on Occasion of the Reduction of Montreal and the Entire Conquest of Canada by the Troops of His Britannic Majesty.* Boston, 1760.

Index

Abercromby, James, 11, 91, 100, 225; campaign of 1758, 34, 93–97; recalled to London, 104; regimental colonel-in-chief, 11, 225

Acadians: deserted farms, 195; security threat, 33, 92, 103–104; as tenants, 202

Admiralty Office: employs Lieutenant J. F. W. DesBarres, 195, 202; source of foreign Protestant recruits, 52, 70

Agriculture: frontiersmen enlist to protect farms, 59; garrison gardens, 131, 148–49, 164, 192; livestock, 128, 132, 192; Indians encouraged to adopt European practices, 172–73; veterans establish frontier farms, 192

Aix-la-Chapelle, Treaty of, 17, 18

Albany, N.Y., 28, 90, 205, 207, 209, 210, 216; army concentration point, 86, 145, 146, 147; supply and distribution hub, 123, 125, 127, 131, 132, 153

Alcohol: Indian demand for, 163, 166; pay supplement, 134, 152; sold to troops, 131, 145

Alsace, recruits from, 68

American Indians: diplomacy, 156–61, 183, 211; European alliances, 9, 19, 34, 65, 90, 97–99, 103, 106–108, 110, 132, 141, 145, 155–73, 222; grievances of, 165–67, 172, 177–78; as prisoners, 10, 107, 174, 178, 183–84, 193; relations with the army, 155–86; rum consumption, 163, 166; trade, 163–64, 166, 183, 207–211, 214, 221; warfare, 10, 19, 31, 44, 58–59, 81, 89, 91, 97–98, 103, 107–108, 110, 132–33, 141, 173–76, 179–82, 185; Western perceptions of, 171–74

Amherst, Sir Jeffery, 11; campaign of 1758, 33, 96, 99–102, 104; campaign of 1759, 37, 104, 109, 125; campaign of 1760, 39, 80, 112–13, 142, 208; commander of North American operations, 36, 39, 75, 113, 209; Indian diplomacy, 161; Pontiac's Rebellion, 44, 177; regimental colonel-in-chief, 11, 46, 225

Annapolis, Md., 56, 74, 146

Appalachian Mountains, 97, 128, 132, 165

Arouet, Francois Marie (Voltaire), 46, 223

345

Artillery, 145; battalion guns, 82; ceremonial salutes, 143, 159; deployed against the Paxton Boys, 167; at Fort Levis, 112; at Fort Ontario, 110, 117; at Fort Pitt, 180; at Fort Ticonderoga, 34, 94, 96; French artillery, 29, 91, 106; at Havana, 116; at Lake George, 19; at Louisbourg, 100–101, 122–23; at Martinique, 114–15; at Quebec 105, 107, 109; "swivels," 176

Atlantic history, 10–11, 14, 216–24

Austria, recruits from, 68, 69

Austrian Succession, War of, 16, 18, 29, 64, 81, 99

Badden-Württemberg, Germany, recruits from, 68, 69

Bancroft, George, 8

Barrington, William Wildman Shute, second viscount of, 23, 24, 25, 66, 83

Bartram, John, 149, 223

Bayern, recruits from, 68, 69

Bay of Fundy, 103, 197, 200, 202

Blacks, as recruits, 75, 217

Blandford (ship), 19

Board of Trade: American Indian policies, 171–73, 185; land grants, 198, 200, 203

Bosomworth, Abraham, 53, 158, 183; leads warriors in Forbes's expedition, 159

Boston, Mass., 122, 196, 197

Bouquet, Henry, 11, 25, 120, 212, 225; campaign of 1758, 97, 159; enlightened improver, 149–50, 223; foreign service, 22; frontier commander, 12, 81, 128, 132; in Pennsylvania, 86, 104; in South Carolina, 31, 64, 88–89, 157; Indian diplomacy of, 157, 159–61, 182–85; investments and land speculation, 32, 194, 198–99, 211; and Pontiac's Rebellion, 44, 80, 81, 175, 181–83, 207, 211; promotions, 41

Braddock, Edward, 18, 92; defeat of, 19, 20, 58, 98, 104, 175

Bradstreet, John, 53, 208

Brandenburg, recruits from, 68, 69

Brehm, Dietrich, 212

British army: adaptation to the New World, 7–8, 12, 36, 86, 92, 102, 104–105, 175–77, 182, 222; American Establishment, 43–44, 76, 116, 188; celebrations, 143–44, 153, 218; daily routine, 101–102, 120–54; demobilization, 43, 188–89, 220; desertion from, 52, 59, 62, 64, 71, 76, 89, 136–39, 147, 151, 164, 188; encampments, 129–45; enlistment of indentured servants, 54–57, 249n21; ethnic diversity of, 49, 52, 73, 75, 79, 139, 141, 217; grenadiers, 35, 94, 95, 100, 102, 104, 105, 108, 112, 114; funerals, 144; half pay, 20, 22, 44, 46, 194, 200, 204, 206, 207, 211, 214; Irish Establishment, 23, 52, 71, 78, 88, 260n24; light infantry, 92, 102, 103, 104, 108, 111, 115, 132, 176; military justice, 137–39; and prize money, 205; rangers, 92, 103, 76; rations, 123, 130–31, 137, 152–53, 163; recruiting, 50–52; relations with Indian allies, 145, 164–65; relations with provincial troops, 72–75, 139–41; religious observance, 142, 143, 144; training and tactics, 36, 81–83, 87–88, 133, 151, 175–77, 222; troop drafts, 71; troop numbers and distribution, 17–18, 151, 179; uniforms and equipment, 36, 50, 121–22, 136, 137, 143, 145, 152, 188, 222; veterans, 43, 188–215, 220; enlistees' wages, 50, 55, 57, 64, 68, 72, 78, 121, 134–35, 137, 145, 152; winter quarters, 145–46, 154

British army units (except the 60th Regiment): First Foot Guards, 20; 15th Foot, 107; 17th Foot, 97; 27th Foot, 94; 35th Foot, 28, 52, 103;

40th Foot, 54, 57; 42nd Foot (Oglethorpe's), 20–21; 42nd Foot (Royal Highland Regiment), 28, 52, 95, 114–15, 181; 43rd Foot, 87; 44th Foot, 36, 54, 57, 92, 196; 45th Foot, 54, 57; 47th Foot, 54, 57; 48th Foot, 54, 57; 50th Foot (Shirley's), 18, 28, 54, 57, 61, 71, 88, 189; 51st Foot (Pepperrell's), 18, 28, 54, 57, 61, 71, 88, 189; 77th Foot (Montgomery's), 34, 89, 97–98, 181; 78th Foot, 108; 80th Foot (Gage's Light Infantry), 92; Gooch's Regiment of Foot, 23–24, 53; independent companies, 57; Royal Artillery, 57
British identity, 5, 24, 41, 141–44, 153, 218–19
Bullen, Johnny (Catawba), 159
Bushy Run, battle at, 7, 44, 181–82, 184
Butler, Lewis, 7

Campbell, Donald (captain, first battalion), 163, 178, 185
Campbell, Donald (lieutenant, second battalion), 53
Campbell, John (fourth earl of Loudoun), 11, 29, 217; attitude toward provincial troops, 65, 74; campaign of 1757, 29, 87, 90; campaign of 1758, 92–93, 158; commander of North American operations, 57–58, 60–61, 86, 123, 147; friction with James Prevost, 29–30, 37; governor of Virginia, 63; recalled to London, 33, 92; regimental colonel-in-chief, 11, 24, 25, 52, 53, 66, 83, 203, 225
Canada: as British possession, 6, 13, 41, 43, 80, 117, 119, 169, 188, 220, 222; as British military objective, 18, 32, 39, 43, 93, 97, 109; as French colony, 31, 90
Cape Breton Island, 112, 222; campaign of 1757, 30, 87; campaign of 1758, 33, 99, 122
Caribbean: campaign of 1762, 43, 75, 113, 188, 220; disease and mortality, 116, 181
Carlisle, 31, 72, 89, 128, 157, 220
Cartagena, 23, 53, 54
Catawba Indians, 13, 158, 159
Charles Town (Charleston, S.C.), 64; mercenary investments in 31, 45, 199; Royal American garrison in, 88–89, 93, 157, 206
Cherokee Indians, 13, 65, 157, 158
Chesapeake Bay/region: recruiting in 55, 64, 78; winter quarters, 86, 146, 220
Claus, Daniel, 41, 53, 169, 185, 196
Cochrane, Gavin, 171–73, 185, 220
Colonel Prevost (ship), 35
Commerce, 16, 198; the "American Company," 212–13, 223; arms dealing, 30; brewing, 40; fur trade, 163, 166, 183, 207–11, 214; government contracts, 27–28, 70, 123, 211–12; privateering, 35, 47, 113; retail, 32, 131, 166, 190, 191, 196; rice and indigo production, 31–32, 45, 47; sugar production, 113; timber exports, 196, 204, 207–13
Crown Point (Fort St. Frédéric), 203; as British military objective 18, 19, 28, 37, 125; British post, 109, 112; veterans' settlements, 191
Cumberland, William Augustus, Duke of, 33, 101; political power and influence, 25–27, 38, 45; relationship with James Prevost, 15, 27, 29, 32, 40; deployment of the regiment, 52–53, 61, 83
Cumberland, Henry Frederick, Duke of, 46

Delaware Indians: French allies, 97; attend 1756 Easton conference, 156; attend 1758 conference at the Ohio Forks, 161; and Pontiac's Rebellion, 175, 178, 182–83
Denny, William, 146, 156
De Noyelles, John, 39–40

DesBarres, Joseph Frederick Wallet, 41, 195, 200–202, 205, 218
Dinwiddie, Robert, 63, 64
Disease, 89, 93, 108, 151; scurvy, 92, 110–11, 147–48, 192; smallpox, 10, 146–47, 180–81; tropical, 44, 115–16
Dunbar, Thomas, 61
Duncan, John, 208–10
Dusseaux, Joseph, 86, 117, 225
Dutch: mercenaries employed by, 17, 20, 29, 66; officers and NCOs, 22, 24, 39

Ecuyer, Simeon, 164, 180
Europa (ship), 70

Fesch, Andrew, 45, 199
Fesch family, 213
Fesch, John Rudolph, 67
Fesch, Rudolph, 45, 67, 200
"Filius Gallicae," 23
First battalion of the Royal American Regiment, 12–13, 40, 46, 74, 76, 80, 86, 207; campaign of 1757, 31, 87–89; campaign of 1758, 34, 35, 93–99; campaign of 1759, 104; casualties, 45, 95, 98–99, 133, 178; desertion from, 76, 89, 147; escort duty, 132–33; grenadiers, 99, 156; and Pontiac's Rebellion, 9–10, 44–45, 176–84; relations with American Indians, 9–10, 161–73, 220; relations with provincial troops, 72–75, 141; strength and distribution, 31, 34, 44, 45, 76, 86, 88, 93, 97, 104, 127, 128, 162, 179, 220; training, 86–89, 93, 99, 104, 118–19; winter quarters, 86–87, 88, 118, 146–47
Florida, 187, 189, 220, 222
Forbes, John, 11, 34, 128, 140, 141; campaign of 1758, 34, 97–99, 159
Forbes's Road, 128, 132, 133, 162, 180, 182
Foreign Protestants, 17, 77; employees of the American Company, 213; legal disadvantages, 22, 24, 35, 39–40; migration, 6, 21, 23, 47, 54–56, 58, 67–68, 70–71, 73, 77–78, 189, 197–200, 202, 213, 214, 223, 224; integration of, 23, 41; in Louis XV's service, 17, 29, 52; naturalization, 41, 218; political neutrality, 23; recruits in the Royal American Regiment, 28, 29, 46, 58, 59, 65–71, 77, 198, 217, 219–20, 222
Foreign regiments: Regiment *de Budé*, 17; Regiment *de Croye*, 22; Scots Brigade, 17; Swiss Guards, 22; Volontaires Etranger, 70
Fort Bedford, 44, 162, 179, 181
Fort construction and repair, 133–34, 151–52
Fort Detroit, 204; as British post, 128, 153, 162, 163, 169; as commercial center, 208, 209; and Pontiac's Rebellion, 44, 179, 182; as supply hub, 127
Fort Duquesne, 204; campaign of 1755, 18; campaign of 1758, 11, 34, 93, 97, 128, 140, 158, 159
Fort Edward, 35, 133; campaign of 1757, 90, 91, 118, 174; and veterans' settlements, 191; as supply hub, 36, 125, 132
Fort Edward Augustus (La Baye), 150, 155, 162, 212
Fort LeBoeuf, 162, 179
Fort Levis, 112
Fort Ligonier, 133, 162; campaign of 1758, 98; and civilian settlement, 206; and Pontiac's Rebellion, 44, 179, 181
Fort Miami, 162, 169, 179, 210
Fort Michilimackinac, 150, 162, 179
Fort Niagara: as British military objective, 18, 19; as British post, 44, 128, 162, 167, 169, 179, 187; as commercial and transportation hub, 127, 153, 208, 209, 211; garrison life, 150–51; and scurvy, 148; siege of, 37, 109–10, 118, 204
Fort Ontario: campaign of 1760, 39, 112; construction of, 109, 133;

defense of, 37, 110, 117; garrison life, 148–49; and scurvy, 148; as supply hub, 126
Fort Oswego, siege of, 28, 29, 60, 61, 65, 80
Fort Ouiatenon, 162, 179, 210
Fort Pitt (Pittsburgh), 212; construction, 7, 34, 99, 133; as diplomatic center, 161–62, 164, 168, 170, 171, 207; as first battalion headquarters, 104, 118, 128, 149, 162, 165, 171, 220; garrison life, 150; and Pontiac's Rebellion, 44, 179–82, 184
Fort Presque Isle, 162, 171, 220; construction, 128, 133; garrison life, 150; and Pontiac's Rebellion, 179, 182; as supply hub, 128
Fort Sandusky, 133, 162, 169, 179
Fort Schlosser, 127
Fort St. Joseph, 162, 179
Fort Ticonderoga (Carillon), 132; battle of, 34, 35, 93–96, 99, 117, 118, 148, 203; and campaign of 1759, 37; 109
Fort Venango, 110, 162, 179
Fort William Henry, 96, 118; siege of, 31, 90–91, 174
Fourth battalion of the Royal American Regiment, 25, 27, 33, 70, 203, 207; campaign of 1757, 30, 87; campaign of 1758, 34, 35, 93–97; campaign of 1759, 37, 104, 109–110; campaign of 1760, 39, 112–113; casualties, 95–96, 112; disbandment, 43, 44, 188, 205; grenadiers, 109, 118; light infantry; 109, 117–18; numbers and distribution, 30, 34, 37, 39, 86, 87, 93, 109, 112; and scurvy, 110, 147–48; training, 87–88, 117; winter quarters, 87
Fox Indians, 172
Frankfurt am Main, 28, 67
Franklin, Benjamin, 167, 223
French Canadians: brides, 203–204, 217; land claims, 193; and Pontiac's Rebellion, 204; troops, 97, 107, 108, 110, 141

Frontier diplomacy, 185; ceremony, 159–62; emissaries, 171–73; 185; humanitarian aid, 167–69, 185; intermarriage and kinship, 159, 169, 178, 185; and intervention, 165–67, 185; mediation, 165, 171; negotiations, 158–61, 182–83; and presents/gifts, 157–59, 161, 162, 163, 164, 177
Frontier garrisons, 31, 89, 133–34, 147–53; economic activity, 164, 166, 209, 210–12
Frontier settlement, 191–93, 214, 216, 224
Fuller, John Frederick Charles, 7–8

Gage, Thomas, 11; commander of the 80th Regiment of Foot, 92; and Paxton Boys, 167; as regimental colonel-in-chief of the Royal Americans, 225; veterans' activities, 190
Gasser, Johann, 53, 64, 65
George II, 6, 19, 20; assents to mercenary employment, 21, 25; elector in the Holy Roman Empire, 67; relationship to British soldiers, 142–43, 218; restricts sale of military commissions, 38
George III, 40, 195; favors to James Prevost, 45–46; receives treatise on American Indians, 173; relationship to British soldiers, 142–43, 194, 218
Georgia, 20, 31, 53, 61, 64
German (language/people): officers and NCOs, 22, 27, 39, 46, 142; immigrants, 23, 24, 58, 74, 198, 199, 212–13, 223; recruits, 28, 30, 52, 59, 68–69, 70, 73, 138, 141; troops hired to defend England in 1756, 66
Germany, 52, 141
Gibbons, Edward, 223
Glasier, Beamsley, 74, 196–97
Gmelin, George Adam, 70, 197–98
Gorrell, James 141, 185
Governors Island, N.Y., 28, 83

350 INDEX

Grant's Hill, Battle of, 34, 97–99, 118
Grass, Michael, 41
Great Britain, 8, 38, 47, 54, 67, 81, 116, 149, 220; governmental oversight of the army, 49; imperial economy, 204, 212; military recruitment in, 76–78, 81; at outbreak of war, 20, 22, 23, 25, 65; victories and identity 143, 195
Great Lakes, 126, 127, 172; British military objective, 19, 37, 109, 110, 169, 204, 222; commerce and natural resources, 207, 208, 210; Royal American activities around, 6, 9, 13, 47, 76, 119, 147–48, 162, 169, 212, 220, 223
Gugy, Conrad, 41, 204
Guinand family, 28, 31, 45, 70, 211; bankruptcy of, 45
Guinand, Henry (the elder), 20
Guinand, Peter, 32, 45

Haldimand, Frederick, 11, 25; defense of Fort Ontario, 37, 110; field commander of fourth battalion, 35, 39; foreign service, 22; investments and land speculation, 32, 196, 198–99, 204; in New York, 86, 212; promotions, 41, 44, 199, 204, 225; recruiting activities of, 52; wounded, 35
Half Moon, N.Y., 125, 145
Halifax, 196; advanced training at, 87–88, 117; British garrison at, 19, 103, 104, 202; winter quarters, 34
Hamburg, 28, 67, 77, 219
Handsome Fellow (Creek), 158
Harriot (ship), 28, 64
Hasenclever, Peter, 198–99, 212–13
Havana, 194; siege of, 43, 115–16, 143, 205
Haviland, William, 113, 114, 115, 226
Hay, Jehu, 169–70, 185
Hessen, recruits from, 68, 69
Ho-Chunk (Winnebago) Indians, 155, 172

Holland, Samuel, 41, 195, 196, 203
Holmes, Robert, 169, 210
Holy Roman Empire, recruiting in, 22, 27, 65–69, 76–77, 219
Hoowaunookaw (Ho-Chunk), 155
Hopewell Township, N.S., 198–99
Howe, George Augustus, viscount, 34, 93, 226
Hudson River, 123, 125, 126, 145, 191
Huguenots, 20, 31
Hunting and fishing, 149, 164, 192
Hutchins, Thomas, 170–71, 185
Huron (ship), 127

Indentured servants, 53–58, 63; redemptioners, 58
Indian conferences, 161; Easton (1756), 156, 157; Easton (1758), 159, 183; Keowee, S.C., (1758), 158; Lancaster (1757), 156–57; Ohio Forks (1758), 159–61; Tuscarawas (1764), 211
Indian Department, 164, 166, 169
Industry (ship), 70
Ireland, 52, 196, 218
Irish, 200; soldiers, 71, 73, 88, 139, 217
Iroquois Indians (Six Nations), 109, 156, 172, 183
Island of St. John (Prince Edward Island), 195, 204, 222; settlement of, 202–203

Jefferyes, Charles, 86, 226
Jenkins' Ear, War of, 23, 54
Jocelyn, Thomas, 133
Johnson, Samuel, 223
Johnson, William, 19, 169, 173, 193, 204, 207, 209

Kellelusstekey (Cherokee), 158
King George's War, 18, 54

Lake Champlain, 28, 34, 37, 90, 93, 109, 141; British settlements along, 190, 191, 193, 204; French land claims, 193

INDEX

Lake Erie, 127, 128, 162, 208
Lake George, 28, 143, 176; as British operational base, 96, 109, 123, 125, 132, 141, 145, 153; Royal American activities around, 31, 34–35, 90–91, 147
Lake Huron, 162
Lake Ontario, 123, 125, 126, 153, 208
Land grants ("the king's reward"), 13, 213, 216, 217, 220; acquisition, 191; distribution scale, 189–90, 194; as enlistment incentive, 43, 55, 59, 68, 77, 78; and plan of 1756, 188–89; and plan of 1763, 189; sale of bounties, 190, 194, 200, 213–14; settlement duties, 190
Land speculation, 195–203, 205, 214
Lawrence, Charles, 34; governor of Nova Scotia, 195, 217; third-battalion commander, 90, 91, 225
Ligonier, John, 20, 39
Lithuania, officers and NCOs from, 22
Logistical support, 86, 97, 122–28, 131–33, 211–12, 214
London, 35, 52, 92, 104, 121; government seat, 8, 18, 21, 22, 33, 53, 56, 75, 90, 99, 173, 185, 197–98, 202; James Prevost in 16, 27, 29, 31, 32, 37, 39, 45, 46, 67; merchants, 83, 121, 199
Long Sault Rapids, 113
Louisbourg: British military objective, 30, 87, 90, 93, 195; siege of 1745, 99, 117; siege of 1758, 33, 40, 70, 99–103, 122, 143, 219
Louis XV, 6, 9, 31, 80, 99, 109; employs foreign mercenaries, 17, 29, 52, 70; releases political detainees in 1755, 20
Lower South, 55, 61, 64
Lyttelton, William Henry, 19

Mackay, Francis, 203–204
Mackay, Samuel, 203–204
Mackay of Scowrey, Hugh, 17, 46

Maryland: recruiting in, 56, 57, 61, 76, 87; provincial troops, 74, 141; winter quarters, 118, 146, 220
Mary Musgrove (Creek), 158
Martinique, 43, 113, 220
Massachusetts Bay, 189, 196; provincial troops, 18, 139–40; winter quarters, 146
Menomonee Indians, 172
Michigan (ship), 127
Middle Colonies, 221; immigration, 73; recruiting in, 53, 55, 61, 74, 79; winter quarters, 118, 154, 220
Mi'kmaq Indians, 92, 103
Milne, James, 167
Mingo Indians, 175, 183
Mohawk (ship), 112
Mohawk River, 37, 123; staple production and export, 212; as transportation artery, 61, 88, 125, 140; veterans' tenancy along, 193–94
Mohican Indians, 156
Monckton, Robert, 217; and campaign of 1758, 103, 117; and campaign of 1762, 43, 114; as second-battalion commander, 103, 111, 117, 225
Monongahela River, 159; battle of, 19, 54
Montcalm, Louis-Joseph, Marquis de: at battle of Fort Ticonderoga, 93–96; defense of Quebec, 37, 105–109; and siege of Fort William Henry, 31, 90, 91, 174; and siege of Oswego, 28, 61, 86
Montmorency Falls, Battle of, 5, 105–106
Montreal, 109, 204; British garrison, 196, as British military objective, 37, 93, 97, 112–13, 142, 208; surrender of, 39, 44, 75, 80, 143, 196, 204, 208
Munster, Herbert von, 38, 67, 156
Murray, James, 108; and defense of Quebec, 111; as governor of Quebec, 204; land speculation, 203; as second-battalion commander, 76, 225

Muskingum Forks/Valley, 183, 184, 207

Naturalization Act (1740), 30, 39, 40
Naturalization Act (1762), 41, 42, 45
Netherlands. *See* United Provinces
New England, 6, 92, 99, 142, 196; recruiting in 53, 71–72; regular regiments from, 18, 54, 61, 71, 88; provincial troops, 19, 112, 140, 146, 153; winter quarters, 146, 154, 220
New France, 9, 28, 65, 71; as British military objective, 88, 90, 93, 104; British occupation of, 76; capture of, 75, 92, 155
New Hampshire, 189, 193
New Jersey, 205, 212, 213, 224; provincial troops, 72, 74, 140, 176; winter quarters, 86–87
New York, city of, 30, 34, 35, 39, 52, 67, 181, 188, 198, 212, 220; army headquarters at, 36, 204, 209; commerce, 47, 221; harbor, 28, 29, 54, 62, 63, 64, 65, 69, 70, 77, 88, 93, 122, 123, 219; winter quarters, 86–87, 117, 146
New York, colony of, 40, 43, 190, 196; as British operational theater, 31, 34, 37, 57, 61, 90, 92, 128, 132; land grants in, 13, 189, 193, 194, 205, 207, 214, 216; provincial agents, 22, 23; provincial troops, 74, 140; recruiting in, 53; Royal American officers from, 53; staple exports, 223
Niedersachsen, recruits from, 68, 69
Nordrhein-Westfalen, recruits from, 67, 68, 69
North American campaigns of the Seven Years' War: in 1755, 18–19; in 1756, 28–29, 61, 80, 86; in 1757, 29–31, 87–91; in 1758, 33–34, 74, 92–104; in 1759, 37, 105–10; in 1760, 39, 75, 80, 111–13; in 1762, 43, 113–16
North Carolina: recruiting in, 64; provincial troops, 65

Nottingham (ship), 28
Nova Scotia: as British operational theater, 30, 31, 57, 103; land grants and speculation in, 13, 189, 195–98, 202, 205, 214

Ogilvie, John, 53, 142, 196
Oglethorpe, James, 20
Ohio Country/Valley, 18, 204; campaign of 1758, 93; disputed control of, 17, 62; exploration of, 149; Pontiac's Rebellion, 44, 199, 211
Ohio Forks, 20, 93, 128, 158, 159
Ohio Indians, 170; attend 1758 conference at the Ohio Forks, 159, 161; attend 1758 Easton conference, 159; fed by the army, 168; land grievances of, 177; Pontiac's Rebellion, 182
Ojibwa Indians, 178
Onondaga (ship), 112
Oswegatchie, mission of, 110
Oswego River, 126
Ottawa Indians, 169, 178
Ouchterlony, David, 5

Parker, John, 74
Parkman, Francis, 9
Pauli, Christopher, 169
Paxton Boys, 166–67
Penn, Thomas, 59, 68, 88
Pennsylvania, 205; defense of, 88, 132; ethnic diversity in, 79; immigration to, 68; provincial agents, 22, 23; provincial troops, 58, 74, 141, 156, 184; recruiting in, 28, 53–54, 56–58, 76; winter quarters, 146
Pensacola, 116, 188, 220
Pepperrell, Sir William, 18, 61
Petitcodiac River, 198, 223
Peyton, Henry, 5
Pfister, Francis, 211–12
Philadelphia, 31, 171, 190, 196, 198, 211; army concentration point, 122; Indian affairs, 158, 161, 167; recruiting in, 56, 58, 61, 211; winter quarters, 86–89, 146

Pitt, William, 11, 24, 40, 90, 92
Plains of Abraham, battle on, 37, 108–109
Poland, officers, NCOs, and recruits from, 22, 69
Pomerania: officers and NCOs from, 22
Pontiac (Ottawa), 9, 44, 177
Pontiac's Rebellion, 44, 150, 171, 199, 204, 207, 220, 222; causes, 177–78; course of, 178–85; historiography of, 9–10, 155
Prevost, Augustine (the elder), 28, 39, 90; estate value, 205; foreign service, 22; investments and land speculation, 205; promotions, 41, 43, 46, 205, 225; recruiting activities, 53–60, 77; wounded, 106
Prevost, Augustine (the younger), 205, 207, 216
Prevost, James, 11, 15, 45, 47, 88, 217, 226; and campaign of 1757, 30–31; and campaign of 1758, 35–36; and campaign of 1760, 39; in England, 15, 19, 20, 31, 37–39, 40–46, 212; in Europe, 22, 28, 29, 46, 64, 65–69; family of, 16, 17, 46–47; formative years, 16–17; grant of arms, 46; investments and personal wealth of, 21, 27–28, 30, 36, 37, 35, 48; in North America, 29–36, 39–40, 86, 97; patronage of, 43, 47; promotions, 40, 41, 45, 46, 225; proposed regiment of foreign Protestants, 21–25; purchases ancestral estate, 45; quest for naturalization, 38–41; recruiting activities, 22, 27–28, 46, 58, 65–69, 198
Prevost, James Mark, 35, 39, 206
Prideaux, John, 37, 109, 208
Prisoners of war: in Canada, 28, 31, 91; in England, 52, 103; in France, 70; join Royal Americans, 52, 70–71, 78; scalped and mutilated, 107, 141
Privateers, 35, 47, 70, 103, 113, 206

Protestantism, 141–43, 172, 174, 203, 204, 218, 222
Provincial troops, 9, 18, 28, 34, 35, 36, 78, 93, 109, 122, 153, 170; interprovincial rivalries, 140; relations with regular troops, 72–75, 139–41. *See also under individual colonies*

Quebec, city of: British garrison, 46, 76, 111, 113, 219, 220; as British military objective, 29, 30, 87, 90, 103; and scurvy, 148; siege and capture of 1759, 37, 105, 143
Quebec, colony of, 40, 41, 189, 195, 204, 205, 211

Rheinland-Pfalz, recruits from, 68
Rhine River, 66, 67, 68, 197
Road construction, 131–32
Rogers, Robert, 92
Rotterdam, 30, 58, 66
Royal American Regiment, 29; chaplains in, 64, 65, 142; and cronyism, 209–10, 211, 213, 214; desertion from, 62, 64, 71; disbandment, 43, 44, 188, 205; discharges from, 74, 75; division into four battalions, 86; enlistment of backcountry settlers, 59; enlistment of convicts, 63, 78; enlistment of indentured servants, 54–58, 63, 78; enlistment of prisoners of war, 52, 70–71, 78; escort duty, 86; establishment of, 20–25; ethnic diversity in, 49, 52, 73, 75, 79, 217, 224; frontier garrisons, 147–53; life within ranks, 120–54; numbers and distribution, 61, 74, 75, 86; recruiting, 50–79, 218; recruits from Britain, 52, 76; recruits from the Carolinas, 64–65; recruits from Europe, 65–71; recruits from Maryland, 62, 74; recruits from New England, 71–72, 74, 76–77; recruits from Pennsylvania, 56–60, 74; recruits from Virginia, 62–64, 74; relations with

Royal American Regiment (*cont.*)
American Indians, 9, 13, 155–86, renumbered from 62nd to 60th, 28; training, 8, 83–90; troop drafts, 71; uniforms and equipment, 8, 83, 121–22; winter quarters, 33–34, 86–88, 118, 146–47
Royal Proclamation of 1763, 43, 189, 194, 195
Rutherfurd, John, 53, 54, 59
Rutherfurd, Walter, 207–10

Sachsen, recruits from, 68, 69
Sainte-Foy, Battle of, 108, 111
Salt production, 212, 214
Saratoga, N.Y., 29, 86, 125, 131
Sauk Indians, 172
Saur, Christopher, 56
Schlatter, Michael, 53, 65, 142
Schlosser, John, 59, 167
Scotch-Irish (Ulster Scots): frontiersmen, 58; immigrants, 199–200; recruits, 73
Scotland, 47; military roads, 131; recruits from, 52, 69, 218
Scott, George, 92, 104
Scottish: immigrants, 202; recruits, 52, 73, 139, 141; regiments, 20, 141, 181; soldiers, 17, 34, 97, 172, 203–204, 217, 223
Second battalion of the Royal American Regiment, 44, 70; in Battle of Sainte-Foy, 111; campaign of 1757, 30, 87; campaign of 1758, 33, 100–104; campaign of 1759, 37, 104–108; campaign of 1760, 111–12; casualties, 103, 106, 108, 111; grenadiers, 102, 108; light infantry, 103, 108; numbers and distribution, 30, 33, 37, 86, 87, 100, 103, 104, 112, 115, 116; survey team, 195; training, 86–87, 117; winter quarters, 34, 86
Seneca Indians, 169, 177, 209
Sentry duties, 121, 144, 154; aboard ships, 123; at a siege, 101–102; challenge and parole, 143; in encampment, 135–36, 153, 164; garrison settings, 151, 165, 166
Seven Nations of Canada, 169
Sharpe, Horatio, 61, 62
Shawnee Indians: at 1756 Easton Conference, 156; at Fort Duquesne, 97; and Pontiac's Rebellion, 175, 178, 182, 183, 184
Shirley, William, 18, 19, 61, 62, 189
Small arms, 97, 167, 176, 179; "Brown Bess," 82, 132; ceremonial salutes, 143–44, 159; coup de mousqueterie, 94, 96, 100; demonstrations, 158; French musketry, 95, 100, 106; Indian musketry, 180; refurbished arms sent to Royal Americans, 83
South Carolina, 141, 157, 220; foreign Protestant immigrants, 17; foreign Protestant investment, 45; recruiting in, 53, 64; Royal Americans in, 31, 88, 89, 93, 220; Royal American officers from, 53
Spanish Succession, War of, 54, 81
Stade, Germany, 28, 67, 69
Stanwix, John, 96, 217; and campaign of 1757, 31, 88–89; and campaign of 1758, 140; and campaign of 1759, 99, 118; concern for his troops' fitness for service, 88, 93, 96; as first-battalion commander, 74, 225; Indian diplomacy of, 157, 161, 171; in New York, 86; promotions, 34, 99; recruiting, 72–74
St. Clair, Arthur, 205
St. Clair, John, 53, 226; aids John Bartram, 149; denied promotion to first battalion, 46; in New Jersey, 86, 205
Sterling, James, 208–10
Stevenson, James, 169, 203
Stewart, Robert, 53, 141
St. John River, 24, 103, 117, 195, 198
St. John's River Society, 196–97, 200
St. Lawrence River, 33, 109, 191; as British military objective, 29, 39; and campaign of 1759, 104, 105,

108; and campaign of 1760, 111, 112, 113, 208
Susquehanna River, 59, 89, 146
Sweden, officers and NCOs from, 22
Swiss, 19, 27, 31; chaplains, 64, 142; in French service, 17, 52, 71; immigrants from, 19, 24, 64, 142, 216; officers and NCOs, 22, 39; recruits, 66
Switzerland, 22, 64; recruits from, 66–69

Teedyuscung (Delaware), 156
Tenancy, 193–94, 207, 214, 220
Third battalion of the Royal American Regiment, 70; in Battle of Sainte-Foy, 111; campaign of 1757, 31, 87, 90–91; campaign of 1758, 33, 100–103; campaign of 1759, 37, 104, 106–108; campaign of 1760, 111–12; campaign of 1762, 41, 113–16; campaign of 1763, 43; casualties, 31, 91, 103, 106, 111, 114, 115–16; disbandment, 43, 188; grenadiers, 90, 102, 114; light infantry, 102; numbers and distribution, 31, 33, 37, 43, 86, 90, 100, 104, 112, 113; training, 87, 90, 113, 118; and tropical disease, 115–16; winter quarters, 33, 87, 118
Thüringen, recruits from, 68, 69
Townshend, Charles, 24, 40
Transatlantic migration, 16, 21; British immigrants, 55–56, 73, 202, 223; business dimension of, 27, 47, 54–56, 66–67, 212–13; chain migration, 68–69, 212–13; dangers of, 67–68, 70; foreign Protestant immigrants, 6, 21, 23, 56, 58–59, 68, 70–71, 73–74, 76–78, 197–99, 212–13, 223; postwar dynamics, 189, 199–200; "pull" factors, 11–12, 22, 68–69; "push" factors, 68
Treaty of Paris, 6, 16, 112, 150, 169, 178, 195, 197, 221
Turnbull, George, 53, 185

United Kingdom, 20, 21, 187, 218; home defense, 66; imperial commerce, 152, 221; postwar recruiting efforts in, 76–77; troops' ethnic origins, 139; veterans return to, 188
United Provinces: mercenaries in, 17, 22, 27; recruiting in, 66

Venango Trail, 128
Virginia, 56, 57, 61, 62, 63, 171; provincial troops, 62, 63, 89, 98, 140, 141; Royal American officers from, 53
Von Stumple, Johann Henirich Christian, 198
Von Weissenfells, Frederick, 213

Wallace, Hugh, 198
Wallace, Nesbit Willoughby, 6
Walpole, Horace, 24
Walters, William, 185, 209
Warfare, European: amphibious expeditions and landings, 30, 33, 43, 87, 99–100, 106–107, 112, 113, 115, 123; conventional operations, 81–83, 87–88, 93–98, 100–102, 113–16, 175, 176, 181, 222; irregular operations, 81, 91–92, 97, 103–104, 107, 111, 132, 175, 176, 182, 184, 222
War Office, 139, 179, 188; need for troops, 21, 23, 65, 83; plans 1755 campaign, 18; plans 1759 campaign, 104; recruitment of mercenaries, 27, 66–67; Royal American accounts, 37, 75; solicitations for employment and leave, 25, 36, 39
Washington, George, 8, 17, 18
West Indies, 18, 24, 40, 78, 147, 206
Westminster, 19, 58, 157; authorization of servant enlistments, 56; foreign Protestant naturalization in 1762, 40–41; oversight of the army, 23, 83
Wharton, John, 204

Whitehall, 10, 37, 53, 78, 123; postwar retrenchments, 43; rejects monopoly at Niagara, 208–209; supports foreign Protestant regiment, 23, 25, 222
Williamsburg, 56, 63, 64
Wllyamoz, Samuel, 29
Wolfe, James, 5, 9, 36, 37, 100; and campaign against Quebec, 105–109
Women and children, 184; officers' dependents, 17, 19, 46, 148–49, 167, 169, 185, 203–207, 209, 217, 222; other ranks' dependents, 66, 69, 150, 204; winter wives, 169, 185
Work regimens, 86, 122–36, 151–53
Wriesberg, Daniel, 196, 213
Wyandot Indians, 169

Yorke, Charles, 38
Yorke, Joseph, 67
Young, John, 91